ALVAR AALTO

Göran Schildt

RIZZOLI
NEW YORK

Alvar Aalto

The Decisive Years

First published in the United States of America in 1986 by
RIZZOLI INTERNATIONAL PUBLICATIONS, INC.
597 Fifth Avenue, New York, NY 10017

Printed and bound by
Kustannusosakeyhtiö Otavan painolaitokset
Keuruu 1986, Finland

Library of Congress Cataloging in Publication Data

Schildt, Göran, 1917–
    Alvar Aalto, the decisive years.

Bibliography: p.
First published in Swedish under title: Moderna tider. 1. Aalto, Alvar,
1898–1976. 2. Architects–Finland–Biography. 3. Arhitecture,
Modern–20th century–Finland. I. Title.

NA1455.F53A237313 1986   720′.92′4 [B] 86-4874

ISBN 0-8478-0711-8

"A conscious regard in artistic creation for the problems of our own time implies a tremendous goal, the step by step transition of industrialism into what it is in any case destined to be some day – a harmonious factor of civilization."

Alvar Aalto, 1928

Contents

THE TECHNOCRATIC UTOPIA 9

BIOGRAPHY 1927–1939 19

The Turku years 19
First steps on the new road 19
Working with Erik Bryggman 29
Aalto's first modern furniture 33
The Turku office 39
Sven and Viola Markelius 46
Travelling in 1928 54
Encounter with CIAM 58
The Stockholm Exhibition 62
Autumn excursion to the Continent 65
Minimum Apartment Exhibition in 1930 68
Laszlo Moholy-Nagy – friend and inspirer 70
The wooden chair perfected 78
A politically coloured year 85
The decisive breakthrough 88
CIAM meeting in Athens 90
Move to Helsinki 102
Exhibition in London 1933 103
1934: Consolidation 106
Aalto through Japanese eyes 107
The Projektio film club 114
Another low point 117
Birth of the Artek company 121
On the way to the top 128
Aalto's own house 128
The Paris pavilion 130
Aalto as a glass designer 136
A fortunate friendship 139
The Sunila Mill and housing area 144
Villa Mairea and the New York competition 152
To the great land of the future 165
Second journey to America 172
The human side 180

AALTO AND THE RATIONALIST IDEOLOGY 187

I. An aesthetic dilemma 189
The artist's role in society 189
Independence Monument for Helsinki 191
The architect as social administrator 193
Art takes its revenge 196
Aalto's aesthetic games 201
Life's total harmony 202

II. Rationalism and the problem of form 205
Functionalism à la Markelius 205
Sources of Functionalist form 207
The theory of types 212
The machine as a model 216
Nature as a model 216
The precepts of Moholy-Nagy 219
The biological synthesis 221

III. Harmony and the cultural heritage 224

LIST OF WORKS 1928–1939 233

THE TECHNOCRATIC UTOPIA

The film *Modern Times* by Charlie Chaplin is just as modern today as it was fifty years ago. It deals with the status of 'the little man' in industrialized society. More immediately it concerns the collapse of the American Dream of a better world in the Wall Street crash and the depression of the early '30s. From the perspective of our time, it deals with the crisis of a whole technocratic civilization based on exploitation, a crisis that is increasingly urgent both in market economies and in State capitalism today. 'The little man' – who is in fact Everyman, since every individual is small in relation to the forces which control his fate – the little man so vividly evoked in Chaplin's vagabond figure is just as helpless to-day as he was then, in East and West alike. Chaplin's presentation of his trials, his capacity to preserve his human integrity even in the least auspicious circumstances, his innocent enrollment in political mass movements by merely happening to be going in the same direction as a group of demonstrators, his duel with the machine Goliath, which sends him sliding back and forth between its cogwheels, and finally his escape from doom with his heart's beloved to a better existence (at least so we hope): all this expresses an inspiring belief in human values, in the possibility of coming to terms with technocracy and of making the world a real home for individual people.

The present book, the second volume of my biography of Alvar Aalto, deals with Aalto's confrontation with technocratic civilization — a confrontation that was markedly similar to Chaplin's — leading one to believe that in the '30s Aalto was probably directly inspired by his great 'predecessor'. Aalto's behaviour was sometimes vividly reminiscent of the famous comedian's humour, and his pet idea of 'the little man' had an obvious connection with the Chaplinesque vagabond.

Ludwig Wittgenstein, who had personal experience of the architect's role, had good reasons for writing: "Architecture perpetuates and glorifies something. Therefore there can be no architecture where there is nothing to glorify." One might add that architecture has a reformative or utopian emphasis: it preaches a standard for people to live up to and points the way for social progress. Therefore, if Wittgenstein is right, an age which dares not believe in anything has no architecture of its own, or more precisely, it has bad architecture, since people can hardly be expected to stop erecting new buildings. Another conclusion to be drawn from Wittgenstein's thesis is that architecture which glorifies rejected or dubious values is doomed artistically. It is clear that we can reinterpret old buildings and discover features in them which our former prejudices or expectations had prevented us from seeing. Architectural works tend to stand long enough to incarnate many different expectations of the direction progress should take.

Aalto's work illustrates all these points. He was always a glorifying architect, an artist who believed in visions which he hoped to share with his fellow men, but practical architectural experience modified his ideas and gave rise to new visions. His ability to reassess his position constantly, his sceptical feeling for reality which saved him from being tied down by barren principles, and above all the almost somnambulist intuition which took him safely past all pitfalls made Aalto's artistic career almost a model for how to

deal with some of the key hopes and illusions of our age.

As I wrote in the first part of this biography, it all started with an ardent dream of reproducing in a northern setting the flourishing, anarchic lifestyle of the early Italian Renaissance, which was based on the unlimited freedom of the individual. Interest in Neo-Classical trends in the Scandinavian architecture of the '20s has revived recently in connection with criticism levelled at the international Rationalist movement which followed it. It was pointed out by Henrik C. Andersson in the exhibition catalogue *Nordic Classicism 1910—*

1. Perspective of Aalto's 'standard' cinema, drawn for an article in Kritisk Revy in 1928.

1930 (1982) that the playful disposition of colonnades, gables, domes and other well-known motifs from the Classical repertoire successfully smoothed the social, technical and economic conflicts between manual and industrial construction and between agrarian and urban economy which typefied the transition from a society of privilege to one of democratic equality. Neo-Classicism legitimated nouveau riche luxury housing by tasteful refinement, giving a civilized air even to speculative rented housing and a traditional dignity to the new administrative buildings and bank palaces in the industrial metropolises. In other words, it provided a veil to the all too bitter contrasts of the age and softened the conflicts, thereby relieving the violence of the upheaval. Many architects of the '20s took up Neo-Classicism as an aesthetic game, and excelled in fantastic and witty effects. The interesting thing about Aalto's Neo-Classicism was that he did not accept the prevailing social conditions or content himself with covering up the unattractive realities with decorative facades. Finland's newly won independence filled Aalto with dreams of a radical reform of the country's social and cultural climate. His romantic enthusiasm for Italy called forth visions of an imminent Finnish Renaissance in which Jyväskylä, his home town, would be a new Florence, its inhabitants fired by self-conscious local patriotism and an unbounded individualism, from which magnificent works of art and a refined feeling for culture would blossom together with a sense of social responsibility.

This utopia is bound to seem naive to the modern reader, although it is more attractive than mere blasé aestheticism. The important thing was that Aalto was possessed by the young man's need of an ethical goal to fight for. When his dream was confronted with the social realities and he acquired more practical experience in building, his attitude soon became more realistic. He realized that the happier and more meaningful future he wished to help build would be more likely to materialize with the help of modern technology and common sense than through an impossible return to the historical past.

Despite this, he never completely managed to break free from his dream of a Finnish Renaissance. He preserved its core intact throughout his life: a belief in the absolute value of the individual and the demand for environmental planning in harmony with nature's order. He always loved and continually revisited the historic cities of northern Italy, which were emotionally connected with his special brand of humanism. Thus to some extent his architectural standards remained unchanged. A recently rediscovered fragment of text, written by Aalto around 1926 as an introduction to a book he was planning but never got round to writing, remained completely valid for him in his old age:

The Church of Eremitani in the small town of Padua has some frescoes by Mantegna; in one of them the landscape predominates. This painting provides the ideal point of departure for the first chapter of the present book. In the first place, it contains something we might call a synthetic landscape. This is an architectural vision of the setting, a small hint to our present-day urban planners on how they should approach their task. Moreover, it is a brilliant analysis of the earth's crust. It was Mantegna's painting that made me analyse the topography of Finnish towns. We also have hills which are sometimes reminiscent of the holy land of Tuscany. In some places, where railways and the engineers' mania for levelling have not yet made everything ungainly, the houses mount the slopes in terraces and the twists and turns of the roads follow a higher law . . .

Rome was built on seven hills. But not only Rome, for many of the gems of urban planning can thank the hills on which their pavements are laid for their aesthetic value. Whoever has once been bewitched by the magic of small Italian towns, who has but once experienced that feeling of perfection –

aroused in me, at least, when memories of the hills of Cagnes, Bergamo, Fiesole emerge from the shadows of my mind – he will be left with a strange bacillus forever circulating in his veins, and the disease caused by it is incurable.

Beauty always causes pain. If you have but once been permitted to enjoy it, you will suffer forever from the ugliness which surrounds us every day. The deeper your perception of beauty, the more bitter your daily suffering. He who has never entered that world does not suffer.

For me "the rising town" has become a religion, a disease, a madness, call it what you will: the city of hills, that curving, living, unpredictable line which runs in dimensions unknown to mathematicians, is for me the incarnation of everything that forms a contrast in the modern world between brutal mechanicalness and religious beauty in life.

2. Townscape, detail from Mantegna's Christ in the Garden, 1459, Tours Museum.

It is a form which the modern age denies both on the everyday level and in its most splendid and refined art. It is a form which the predominant mentality today goes to great lengths to avoid.

We shall not go any further into the reasons which made people settle on these hills in ancient times. They are common knowledge and so natural that there is no need to repeat them here. But aesthetic value arose as a by-product, just like the beautiful lines which mark human civilization in Mantegna's frescoes.

The town on the hill . . . is the purest, most individual and most natural form in urban design. Above all, it has a natural beauty in that it reaches full stature when seen from the level of the human eye, that is, from ground level. A vision the senses receive whole and undisrupted, adapted to human size and sensory limitations.

After this paean to the past, the reader may well ask why Aalto suddenly turned his back on Neo-Classicism in 1927. To understand the inevitability of this step, we should consider a completely different feature of Aalto's personality, a trait which in fact predestined him to be a Functionalist.

The background was provided by his spiritual legacy, which was represented by a positivist attitude to science and progress and inherited from his inventor-grandfather and from his surveyor-father. This legacy is illustrated by the "Book of Inventions" inherited by Aalto from his grandfather, and described in the first volume of this biography. This remarkable book, published in the 1880s, presented several theses which were still considered new, even revolutionary, by some of the Rationalist architects of the 1920s. The "Book of Inventions" set technical feasibility, practical needs and especially the demands of hygiene above all pomp and aesthetics. It devoted a good deal of space to industrial architecture and workers' housing. Aalto's admiration of old Italian towns was thus tempered early on by a strong interest in new inventions and social reform.

As a little boy Aalto dreamed of being an engine driver, and the fact that he later drew a steamboat for the family's holiday use in connection with one of his first architectural assignments should surely be put down as the normal outgrowth of any ordinary boy's dreams; but throughout his life he continued to be fascinated by technological innovations. His first flight over Helsinki in his student years aroused, as we have seen, an all but Futuristic excitement in him. (Alvar Aalto: The Early Years, p. 134) *The sun is shining and the machine climbs straight up towards it. I have heard people call the sun beautiful. They should see it through a propellor, a wing engine revolving at dizzying speed – then it is really something. But one thousand and four revolutions per minute is also beauty of a high order. There is almost more art in that figure than in all of the watercolours and antique furniture in the world, to say nothing of porcelain painting.* His delight was in no way less when he and Aino started their honeymoon in a rather unusual way for the times, that is, by air. *We are flying in the brightest sunlight – the first Hellenic day of my life,* he wrote with a characteristic blend of Futurist and Classicist fervour.

Other inventions and 'modern' phenomena also appealed to the young Aalto. In 1925, when the newly founded Finnish Broadcasting Company was to transmit a test programme from Jyväskylä, he was quick to offer to make the ceremonial address. It was in this speech, reproduced in volume 1 of this biography, that he lectured to the town's academic society on Abbé Coignard and the spontaneous growth of old towns.

His enthusiasm for motor cars was equally characteristic. His father bought a car in 1923 in order to facilitate his surveying work. It was the first private car in Alajärvi, and was called 'The Blue Beauty' by the local people. Alvar was sometimes allowed to borrow it when he had architectural assignments at distant places such as Kauhajärvi. In 1927, when he received

the prize money for the Agricultural Cooperative Building in Turku, he was finally able to buy a car of his own: the final touch needed to confirm his success as a modern architect. In August of that year he was accepted as a member of the Finnish Automobile Association and for a few years remained an eager motorist. His weakness for speed resulted in two crashes – fortunately with no casualties save financial ones.

Other modern inventions also held an irresistible attraction for him. Even as a young boy he was an addict of the seventh art, which he enjoyed at Jyväskylä's one cinema, called *Opiksi ja huviksi* (Learning and Pleasure). When in 1926 he drafted his competition entry for the Defence Corps Building, he worked on the *Bio Majakka* (The Lighthouse Cinema) with particular care. Fully in character, too was his purchase of a film camera in 1929, a Pathé Baby, with which he began capturing scenes of family life on film – sometimes in a highly experimental style. Snapshots he wisely left to his wife Aino, who attained real mastery in this field. Aalto was also 'modern' in his radical views on women's equality, implanted in him in childhood by the three strong-willed women who brought him up.

In fact, Alvar and Aino's enthusiasm for the modern way of life showed itself in everything they did. They bought a gramophone in order to practise the fashionable foxtrot at home; they devoted themselves to the Continental sport of tennis – in Jyväskylä only on outdoor courts, but once they moved to Turku they could play all the year round. An incipient interest in the newly liberated clothing fashions and curiosity about the United States, the land of the future, complete this picture of the growing attraction that Modernism as a way of life had for them from the mid 1920s on.

It is surprising in some ways that this attitude did not begin to influence Aalto's architectural idiom sooner than 1927. A plausible explanation is that his isolation in Jyväskylä was the main

reason for adhering to the Neo-Classical forms implanted in him during his student years in Helsinki, but in fact his colleagues in Turku and Stockholm were not very far ahead of him at the time. Erik Bryggman in Finland and Gunnar Asplund and Sven Markelius in Sweden were still working in the old style in spring 1927. The great surge originating with Le Corbusier's Pavillon de l'Esprit Nouveau at the Art Déco exhibition in Paris 1925 and with his polemical writings had reached them, however, and debate on Functionalism ran high wherever architects met. Aalto's move to Turku drew him in the turbulence from the Continent and thus put him on the world map of architecture after a delay that first placed him in the position of a pupil in relation to his colleagues, but which he soon made up for by his Modernist attitude to life. Aalto was quite simply predestined to become a prophet of the Modernist awakening, but also to discover its limitations before its more simplistic adherents did. At the time of the triumph of Functionalism around 1930, no one could have foreseen that Aalto's greatest achievement would be to go straight past Functionalism into a Modernist traditionalism that was his ultimate solution to the problems of modern architecture.

What was the significance of the Rationalist awakening? What were the ideas which swept not only Aalto but also his friends among the younger Swedish generation of architects, as

3. After his first flight in 1920 Aalto drew these sketches for the satirical magazine Kerberos.

well as his most alert Finnish colleagues, off their feet?

One could try to describe this architectural trend by appealing to the old but basically rather vague idea that the form of a building should be dictated by its practical function. It might also be defined as an architectural idiom borrowed from contemporary Cubist painting and sculpture, radically divergent from both the flowing lines of Art Nouveau and from the well-known Classicist vocabulary of columns, gables and arches. But above all the movement must be described as a utopia of society which emerged from the special social conditions of the 1920s.

The background was provided by the First World War, which had been fought for manifestly senseless reasons. The Europeans of the '20s thought they had learned their lesson about where obsolete traditions, muddled emotions, and the obduracy of a corrupt older generation could lead humanity. Nothing like this should ever be allowed to happen again; now was the time to listen to the voice of reason and to shake off the weight of the past once and for all. The League of Nations was founded as a forum for international cooperation, many of the previously subjugated small nations of Europe won their independence, and countries were no longer ruled by a collusion of crowned heads, a conservative church and a privileged upper class, but by a Parliament chosen by the people. Above all, people imagined that industrialization would result in an irresistible rise in the standard of living, and for the first time in history welfare would be distributed to the great masses instead of merely to a small élite. This was the ground in which optimism, gratitude to science and industry, and a belief in objective problem-solving and rational solutions sprouted and took hold of so many of Europe's intellectuals.

Architects were particularly smitten by the new optimism: it offered them such a flattering role. Critics have quite rightly been astonished by the gullibility of the architects of the '20s and '30s in imagining that virtually all social problems could be solved by the new architecture. How could they imagine themselves in the role of social reformers, when in practice they had no power at all? The explanation lies in

4. 'The Blue Beauty', surveyor J.H. Aalto's car, bought in 1923.

their idea that they were pioneers of the rationalism which was bound to conquer by its own force. Their task was simply to make the visions concrete and to plan for the future which would inevitably arrive. Behind their self-confidence was the illusion that the only real conflicts in society were due to illogical patterns of thinking and prejudices held by some people, while other people clearly envisaged what was to come. Thus the struggle was not between various interest groups or classes, but between knowledge and blindness. All that was needed for all men to share in the common happiness was to spread the gospel of enlightenment and to fight irrationality.

Le Corbusier, who became the leading utopian architect of his age, expressed the idea in an effective slogan: *architecture or revolution*. Either the old social order would collapse, as it had done in Russia, and a new, rational order would be born through painful paroxysms like those suffered by the young Soviet state, or common sense would be allowed to establish itself painlessly through forward-looking environmental planning, which would also result in a healthy improvement of our way of life. Architects had the same ideal goal as the political left: a world of reason, social justice, and material welfare, free from the weight of tradition. In fact a clear connection between the two different kinds of utopians can be noted. Most of the champions of the new architecture openly declared their left-wing sympathies, and many went to the Soviet Union for a while to take part in building the new ideal society. To avoid being carried away by the general wave of enthusiasm, one had to have an unusually large dose of natural caution, a scepticism about slogans and simplifications, a rare ability to distinguish suspicious undertones, and a sensitivity to unpleasant facts.

The new utopian architecture started out with a handful of experimental works, such as Le Corbusier's pavilion at the Paris exhibition in 1925 and Gropius's Bauhaus in 1926. The signifi-

5. *Le Corbusier's* Pavillon de l'esprit nouveau *at the Paris Exhibition in 1925, exterior and interior.*

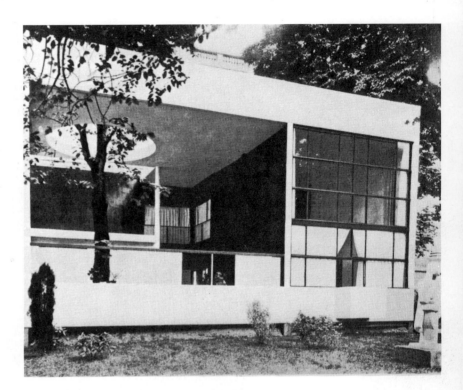

cance of these buildings was largely symbolic, since they were few and relatively modest in scale, but they embodied the visionary future. The response from other architects obsessed by the same unfulfilled dreams was not slow in coming: other Functionalist buildings started appearing throughout the Western world. What they appeared to have in common was everything that was lacking in the previous architectural environment: light and air, satisfactory hygienic standards, rational planning, industrial construction methods, and adaptation to the economic potential of the masses, while also being able to satisfy the aesthetic tastes of the more fastidious connoisseurs. Technology, which had celebrated such fearsome triumphs in the war, had been tamed and made man's friend, and it seemed to offer the cornucopia from which a better future would emerge.

The only problem was that the new alternative rested on wholly hypothetical assumptions concerning human inclinations, natural resources and the consequences of technological civilization. In short, architects had an all too ready belief in the spontaneity of progress. Just as old failings in the social system had been overcome only for new ones to appear unexpectedly around the corner, so architecture, too, was confronted with new problems. Communism gradually established itself in an increasing number of countries, but in so doing rigidified into a suffocating straitjacket. The International Style in architecture was victorious all round the world, but it resulted in quite unexpected drawbacks, such as unscrupulous exploitation of the natural environment, the dead weight of collectivism, alienation and rootlessness. One might ask why the architectural utopia continued to gain ground in spite of its gradual transformation into a nightmare. Why did the architects not protest? Why did the people who were the victims of this error which led architecture astray not demand a change of course?

The answer probably lies in the advantages Rationalist architecture gave to planning in connection with industrial exploitation, economic growth and centralized control. Moral idealism and visions of a happy society had soon faded in the construction business. It has not made things any better that even the mask — that well-known idiom of the utopian architecture no one believes in any more — has been discarded in later days in order to camouflage the bitter reality with the Post-Modernist recipe of superficial cosmetic tricks, meanwhile making the International Style the scapegoat for a still-continuing trend.

In this drama, which is increasingly beginning to look like a tragedy, Alvar Aalto appears as a strange hero, a Chaplin who first allows himself to be duped by great expectations and does his ambitious best to promote this seemingly promising trend. Even at the outset, however, he was the odd man out among the flock of obedient Utopians. He could never keep step with others; his incorrigible individuality always revealed itself, and he was too natural and spontaneous to stay in line. Instinctively he broke the given rules; inadvertently, the ivy started to creep up the white Le Corbusier facades in his work, living surfaces of wood appeared to hide the concrete, and leafy trees and meandering lakefronts pushed aside the strict geometry of machines as stylistic models. Instead of the geometrically planned *villes radieuses,* housing areas adapted to nature's spontaneous system of equilibrium took shape on his drawing-board.

In an understandable effort to exonerate Aalto from the shortsightedness of Rationalism, some modern historians of architecture have made him out to be its consistent opponent right from the start. This work attempts to show his career in a more complex, even ambivalent, light. It is clear to me that Aalto was strongly attracted by Functionalism and had few reservations on its account at first. He was deeply influenced by the ideas of Le Corbusier, Gropius, Moholy-Nagy and other representatives of the International Style. Some of the principles of Functionalism remained features of his creative work right to the end. Yet there is no denying that he half-consciously moved farther and farther away from Rationalism, driven by his artistic daemon and by his feeling for the human and natural. So, like Chaplin's tramp, he set off with undiminished hope in search of freer horizons.

THE TURKU YEARS

Aalto's move from Jyväskylä to Turku in June 1927 was dictated mainly by practical reasons. In the spring he had won the prestigious competition for the Southwestern Finland Agricultural Cooperative's multi-purpose building, to be built on a large plot on the corner of Humalistonkatu and Puutarhakatu in Turku. Since construction was to start as soon as possible, and frequent consultations with the client were necessary while the working drawings were under preparation, Aalto had to make himself available. He was living at his new office in Humalistonkatu 7. The main advantages Turku offered him were better international contacts and opportunities to travel afforded by the daily steamboat to Stockholm and, later, by international flights. The world opened up for him during his years in Turku. Without having to take the detour via Helsinki, he literally stepped straight out of the small-town world of Jyväskylä into what was the equivalent of the big world for Finnish architects in those days.

FIRST STEPS ON THE NEW ROAD

The interesting thing about Aalto's geographical move was that it coincid-

6. *Alvar Aalto's study in Turku from 1928 to 1933.*

ed exactly with his adoption of Rationalism. His first known plan from the Turku period was the competition entry for Kinkomaa Sanatorium, dated June 1927. The open wards in the plan bear the imprint of Le Corbusier, and the plan takes the differentiation of functions even further than the competition entries for Töölö and Viinikka Churches, which were completed a few weeks earlier. By autumn Aalto was collaborating with Erik Bryggman on a more or less fully-fledged Functionalist competition entry for an office block in Vaasa.

Meanwhile, we may note that in some of his projects he was carrying on with his old Neo-Classical programme. This is true at least of the competition entry for the Jyväskylä Rural Parish Church, submitted on July 1 (cf. Figs. 275 and 276 in Part I) and Viipuri City Library, for which the last date of entry was October 1. The latter plan was dominated by ideas reminiscent of Asplund's Stockholm City Library but also contained older references, including a Classical frieze running the length of the facade just above the plinth. In a later context I will tackle the reasons for Aalto's apparent vacillation at this time. In fact he had definite opinions about which assignments should be based on traditional models and which on modern solutions.

This attitude also explains why the sketches he began in spring 1928 for Perniö's relatively inauspicious rural history museum (not built in fact to Aalto's plans) were still pronouncedly Neo-Classical in their final form in 1929, and why the giant cinema Suomen Biografi (likewise never built) in Turku was done in the same vein as Asplund's Skandia Cinema. Aalto's cinema design consisted of a wedge-shaped building mass reaching a height of four storeys on the street side and seating a maximum of 820 spectators. The auditorium had rows of stalls on either side, each furnished with a small curtain which could be drawn, transforming the stall into a *chambre séparée* for two. This could perhaps be called a functional arrangement in that

20

it was doubtless convenient for the sexual mores of the times, but the plush upholstery was certainly anything but Functionalist.

On the other hand, the technical solution to the problems of lighting and acoustics in the auditorium was truly rational. The solution was introduced by Aalto in this design and carried out later in the Jyväskylä Defence Corps Building cinema. Aalto was so proud of his idea that he wrote an article on the subject in 1928 for Poul Henningsen's radical Danish magazine *Kritisk Revy*. The point was that the piano player, sitting in front of the screen in the long, narrow, silent film theatres of the day, was apt to produce inappropriate echo effects between the parallel walls; moreover, the magic darkness was spoiled by the fact that the side walls were indirectly lighted by the screen. These difficulties could of course be overcome architectonically by placing the side walls at an angle. Aalto, however, discovered a simpler solution: he broke up the wall surface at the front into small folds which effectively absorbed both echoes and light. Aalto considered that he had thereby solved the problem of the 'standard cinema'; that is, he had made it possible to convert virtually any interior space, regardless of its shape, into a cinema (F 1).

If at this time Aalto thought that libraries, churches, museums, theatres, and even cinemas were in principle based on old architectural discoveries, he was all the more eager to apply new ideas to modern building assignments. As we have seen, these included the competitions for Kinkomaa Sanatorium and an office block in Vaasa, but since both juries were made up of conservative members, Aalto's chances to carry out really radical innovations were minimal. It was easier to seek response among private builders interested in modern architecture, either by personal preference or for professional reasons. Aalto, who had a keen perception of client psychology,

7. *Kinkomaa Sanatorium, solarium wing. Exterior and view of wards.*

started looking for likely patrons as soon as he arrived in Turku. With his extroverted way of life, contagious optimism and persuasive charm, it did not take him long to find not just one but two forward-looking clients.

With the first of these he came into daily contact: Juho Tapani was the contractor handling the construction of the Agricultural Cooperative Building. Tapani owned a small industrial enterprise producing prefabricated concrete building units with ready-made ducts for ventilation and pipes. They had been used in Turku to some extent since 1917, but it was immediately apparent to Aalto that they were ideal for the kind of serial manufacture the new architecture was aiming at. He predicted a thundering triumph for the 'Tapani unit' to the astonished industrialist and set out to design an experimental model building (the Tapani Building, W 108), which was supposed to attract a widespread following. This was how Aalto came to design his much-discussed 'Functionalist Block of Flats' on Läntinen Pitkäkatu in Turku. The building still exists, but has lost most of its revolutionary aura. With its bearing lateral walls, between which facades and room arrangements can be freely varied, the Tapani Building

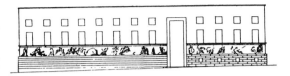

9. Viipuri Library, main elevation, competition entry 1927.

10. Standard block of flats in Turku, view from the courtyard.

8. Suomen Biografi cinema, interior.

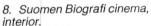

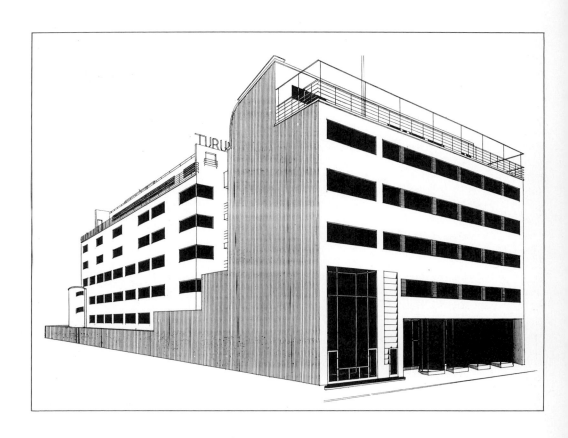

11. Perspective of Turun Sanomat newspaper offices, Turku.

provides evidence that Aalto had read about Le Corbusier's Maison Citrohan, Mies van der Rohe's Stuttgart apartment block with variable room disposition and other controversial creations by Continental architects (cf. F 277 in Part I). Unfortunately the promised success for the Tapani unit never materialized; instead, the contractor went bankrupt, though this can hardly be blamed on Aalto but rather on the unexpected economic depression.

The other private client whose interest Aalto succeeded in arousing was Arvo Ketonen, owner of *Turun Sanomat,* the town's leading newspaper. Ketonen was a youngish man with modern ideas stimulated by the paper's growing circulation and the economic boom that had been going on for some time in Finland. Until then the paper had used Gothic print, which was still common in Finnish books and newspapers in the '20s. Now Ketonen wished to give his newspaper a mod-

ern look by going over to Latin typography and by erecting an office building in the style of the future. When the two gentlemen first met sometime in the winter of 1927−28, Aalto had never yet seen a Functionalist building in real life, still less built one himself. Within weeks, however, he produced such convincing sketches for Ketonen that the latter decided on the spot to commission the plans for his new building from Aalto. The architect had in fact gone all the way in applying all of the *cinq points d'une architecture nouvelle* set forth by Le Corbusier in his pamphlets − that is, bearing columns, a free plan, a free-form facade, strip windows and a terrace garden. (Turun Sanomat Building, W 124). He combined these with a variation of the facade motif he and Bryggman had already used in their competition entry for the Vaasa office block, involving a raised entrance connected with the street level shops, and strip windows for the upper floors (cf. Part I, F 278).

12. *Turun Sanomat editorial office. Note the PH lamps and Aalto's 'hybrid' chairs, 1929.*

An extra treat that enchanted Ketonen was the idea of projecting the daily text of the newspaper in colossal format, page by page, on a display screen which would make the building look like a mirage of Manhattan in the dark. It was unimportant that owing to technical difficulties the idea could not be carried out; the suggestion had been made. Ketonen toured the newspaper offices of the Scandinavian capitals in 1928 to see if they had anything better or more modern, and discovered to his satisfaction that his own building would be by far the most advanced. The only changes he suggested on returning concerned minor details in the room disposition of the printing works and editorial offices. Ketonen was so pleased with Aalto that he immediately commissioned new drawings for a block of rented flats he intended to build in Uudenmaankatu in Turku. When the repercussions of the Great Depression reached Finland in 1929,

however, he was obliged to give up the project after Aalto had already completed the initial drawings. It was hard enough to cope with the cost of building the expensive newspaper offices.

From early in the summer of 1927, Aalto had thus staked all of his usual enthusiasm and inventiveness on applying the new architectural ideas that were spreading north from continental Europe. It should also be noted that at the outset he was equally inspired by aesthetic and constructive ideas deriving from Le Corbusier as by the social housing design practised by German architects. The Turun Sanomat Building and the standard flats stood for each of his continental models, respectively; together they formed a magnificent overture to Aalto's Rationalist output. The fact that these buildings were carried out at such an early stage gave Aalto an incontestable front-line position among radical Scandinavian architects. All the same, his buildings did not spring up overnight: the Tapani Building was completed in the summer of 1929, while the newspaper offices, begun in autumn 1928, were not completed until spring 1930.

It was not easy for the young would-be reformers to put up with the slow pace of construction, and they sought short cuts to disseminate their new doctrine. One of the paths open to them was journalistic propaganda. Le Corbusier's success in this field set an encouraging precedent. Far away in the North, fanfares to Rationalism rang out in architectural and cultural magazines and in the daily press. It went without saying that a man with Aalto's verbal talent could not remain dumb. I will return in a later context to some of the manifestos and debate articles he published in these years. Another opening was afforded by architectural competitions, in which the young radicals took part with zest, although as

the juries of the time were generally conservative they had little chance of a prize. It was enough for them to have their entries published and discussed, as this was bound to contribute to the dissemination of their ideas. This was particularly evident in the many church design competitions in which Aalto, together with most of the other young Rationalists, participated obstinately though with no illusions about the outcome.

A competition of great publicity value was announced in spring 1928 by the household magazine *Aitta*. The assignment called for designs for one large and one small freely reproducible holiday dwelling, i.e. a summer house and a weekend cottage respectively, both to be placed in an isolated spot in the usual Nordic way. The competition presented the young Finnish architects with a welcome opportunity to apply the new rational idiom as well as to propagate the informal, healthy way of

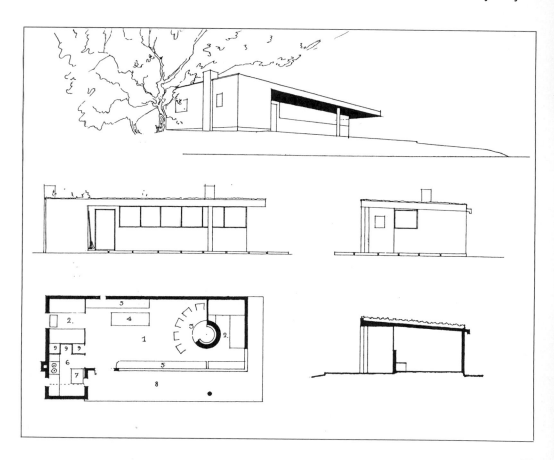

13. 'Konsoli', Aalto's winning entry in the Aitta weekend cottage competition, 1928.

living which was such an integral part of their vision of the future.

Eighty-two entries were received and examined by a jury composed – for once – of young, progressive architects. It was thus no surprise that two of the most radical proposals won in both categories. It turned out that both winning entries were by Aalto. The weekend cottage, 'Konsoli' (Console) contained a large living room with an open fireplace, two bedroom cubicles and a tiny cooking recess; the house, 'Merry-Go-Round', comprised a living room, a kitchen and a servant's room, two bedrooms and a sauna. If these room arrangements were rather conventional, corresponding exactly in the first case with Aalto's summer cottage in Alajärvi, the forms used were quite the opposite. The cubic building mass of 'Konsoli' was covered by a flat roof, and the balcony was embedded in the cube and roofed by a concrete slab. Seen from the outside, 'Merry-Go-Round' looked like a flat, round cheese with the rooms huddled in a circle around an open inner courtyard, while a strip window cut into the building mass like a horizontal section.

These new forms represented an expression of the modern lifestyle to Aalto, as appears from the comments he appended to the drawings. About 'Konsoli' he wrote: *The idea of making use of ethnographic or stilted forms borrowed from old rural architecture never once came into the author's head.* About the ground plan of 'Merry-Go-Round' he stated: *The entry of sunlight into the rooms, the view and protection from wind suggested the round form of the building. Other considerations included the need for concentration and the wish to spare the legs of the lady of the house for tango and jazz . . . If modern people who can read and count and speak three civilized languages spend the summer in this building, the exterior of the 'villa' is not intended to conceal these facts. The author was not looking for originality or unusual effects, but for a natural solution. Therefore the building may seem 'original' to some.*

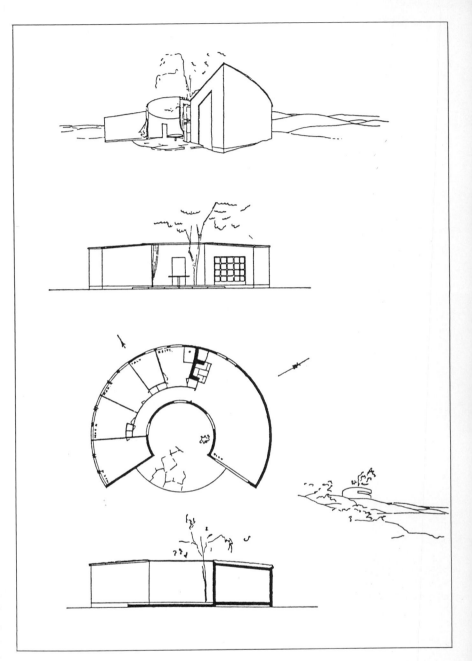

14. 'Merry-go-round', summer villa by Aalto, 1928.

What is interesting is that at such an early stage Aalto combined a 'Formalist' motif – the segment of a circle – with psychological variables like lighting, surroundings, and the blending of exterior and interior space, to which he would adapt his later buildings in less constricted ways.

Publicity in the press and success in competitions was complemented in

Aalto's case by an even more striking opportunity to spread the message of Rationalism by means of exhibitions. Le Corbusier had made a remarkable contribution to the dissemination of the new ideas with his *Pavillon de l'Esprit Nouveau* at the 1925 Art Déco exhibition in Paris. Another important event was the 1927 Weissenhof exhibition in Stuttgart, for which the entire radical guard of Continental architects produced experimental designs. The Stockholm exhibition of 1930 had an even greater impact in the Nordic countries, but Aalto and Bryggman had actually got off to a head start the year before, when they conjured up a similar though less pretentious manifestation in Turku, the pretext being the celebration of the town's fictitious 700th anniversary and the occasion of the third Finnish Fair. I shall describe this event, as well as Aalto's important 1930 exhibition of small dwellings in Helsinki, in greater detail in a later chapter. What I wish to emphasize here is the consistency with which Aalto adopted Rationalism for various purposes from his very first months in Turku.

It was another matter that the special conditions attached to the architectural profession obliged him to continue on his old course for quite a considerable time. Writers, painters and other artists who can implement their ideas on their own are privileged in that they need not look back unless they wish to do so. Architects, on the other hand, are fortunate if they see their plans carried out within a year or two: sometimes it may take decades. Aalto designed his Neo-Classical Muurame Church in 1926, the foundation stone was laid on June 30, 1928, and the church was consecrated in 1930. The Casa Laurén in Jyväskylä, designed in 1925, was not completed until 1929, and the Defence Corps Building in the same town, designed in 1926, was inaugurated on November 15, 1929. Naturally these projects were affected to some extent by Aalto's conversion to Rationalism. In Muurame the church interior received modern PH lamps, the vestry was furnished in semi-Functionalist fashion, and the campanile was equipped with a spiral staircase in the style of Le Corbusier. Aalto swept out all of the planned decoration of Classical reliefs and columns from those sections of the Defence Corps Building which were completed last, that is, the market hall and the cinema, substituting chrome rails and stainless steel surfaces as the main

15. Turku 700th anniversary exhibition, 1929. Perspective from main entrance towards Bryggman's circular restaurant.

accent for the market hall, and adapting the cinema to the previously described idea of standardization.

The changes Aalto made in two major competition plans, the Agricultural Cooperative Building in Turku and the Viipuri Library, are of particular interest. The building contract between the clients and the contractor, and the relevant drawings countersigned by Aalto on June 26, 1927, called for an even richer Neo-Classical ornamentation — with columns, coffers, friezes, statues, mouldings and gables — than the original competition entry. Fortunately these elements were to be added only after the main structures were completed, which enabled Aalto to delete most of them from the new drawings in January 1928. No colonnettes were placed in the facade window openings, the balconies on the yard side were given tubular iron railings in Le Corbusier style, and the theatre auditorium was stripped so bare that at the inauguration in 1928 the journalists wrote of "the first Functionalist theatre in the North".

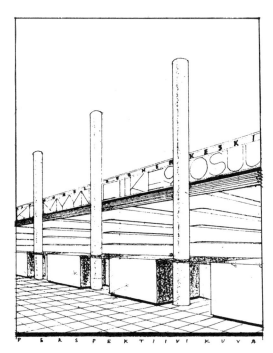

16. Market hall in the Jyväskylä Defence Corps Building, March 1929.

17. Auditorium of the Turku Finnish Theatre.

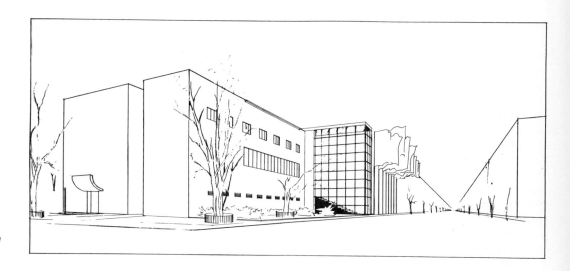

18. *Viipuri Library, second version, which still had the ground plan of the competition entry.*

Viipuri Library had to await construction much longer than the Agricultural Cooperative Building, and it underwent such drastic changes that we may speak of four different plans. The original Neo-Classical competition entry was transformed in the summer of 1928 into a Rationalist design with many features borrowed from Le Corbusier, including a free-form facade, a rooftop terrace garden and a volute-shaped concrete slab over the entrance at one end. The people of Viipuri were alarmed by so much new-fangledness, and a lively debate ensued in the local press. Aalto's antagonists went to the length of commissioning a model of another, irreproachably conventional, entry and displaying it in a bookshop window in an attempt to appeal to public opinion. The most influential person in Viipuri at the time was Consul Eugen Wolff, who had headed a delegation at the turn of the century which was to submit a great citizens' address to the Czar on the subject of infringements of Finland's civil rights. Wolff was nearly 80 years old in 1928, but his opposition to Aalto's library carried great weight in the city administration and business circles. In the resulting deadlock Aalto resolved, or so he told me, to seek out the lion in his den. Dressed in his best suit, Aalto was admitted to the old man's presence, and in his impeccable Swedish explained the background to the controversial plan. Wolff listened to him without interrupting for a long time, until at last he burst out: "My God, but you're a gentleman! That changes everything!"

According to Aalto, this formal social call altered the course of the library controversy, although construction was still far off. In 1929 a quarrel broke out about the building site, which was to be on Aleksanterinkatu according to the competition programme; but an increasing number of citizens wanted it moved next to the church in Torkkeli park. At last it was decided in 1933 that the library should be placed in the park, and Aalto was able to complete his final, completely Modernist version.

WORKING WITH ERIK BRYGGMAN

After our general examination of Aalto's work during his early years in Turku, it seems appropriate to take a look at the setting in which he worked, and particularly at the many new friends and colleagues with whom he came into contact. One of the most important of these was Erik Bryggman, who was seven years older than Aalto and had been working in Turku since 1923. He had received a number of housing assignments, which were characterized by a spare Neo-Classicism tending towards the pure forms of Rationalism. Bryggman had taken part in the competition for the Agricultural Cooperative Building, winning third prize after Aalto and Hilding Ekelund.

One must admire the architects of the period for their compliance with the norms that governed their rivalry. They loyally accepted the decisions of competition juries, though these decisions were often debatable and always had a momentous impact on their careers. How often in those years did Alvar Aalto, Hilding Ekelund and Erik Bryggman submit entries of more or less equal merit, of which only one could be carried out. The losers might have to wait for years for another chance, and for lack of building assignments Ekelund, 'the eternal runner-up', was finally obliged to seek a living as lecturer at the Institute of Technology. Fortunately he twice did win first prize ahead of Aalto: in 1930 in the competition for Töölö Church, subsequently built to his plans, and for the Finnish Embassy building in Moscow in 1935. Bryggman also defeated Aalto in an important competition in 1930, namely that for Vierumäki Sports Institute, later built to his plans.

According to many witnesses, Bryggman was an unusually sensitive and withdrawn person, quite without Aalto's pushiness. Thus the division of roles between him and his wife Agda was the reverse of that between the Aaltos, and this had a certain influence on the relationship between the two families. In his old age Aalto liked to tell amusing anecdotes about his friends the Bryggmans, usually centring on Agda's desperate efforts to prop up the meek Erik's position. Thus Agda tried to dissuade Alvar from moving to Turku in the first place: "Don't come to Turku, this is Erik's town!" she declared. Another incident Aalto would recall chucklingly: one morning he went to the Bryggmans' to pick up some drawing he'd left there. When he rang the doorbell, Agda opened the door an inch and whispered with her finger to her lips: "Shush, shush! Erik is composing!" According to Aalto, Erik

19. Erik Bryggman in the early 1930s.

had married Agda after he broke his leg and went to the hospital where she happened to be working as a nurse. "He quite simply couldn't escape from the bed!" This did not prevent the two families from being fast friends during Aalto's years in Turku.

Bryggman and Aalto became all but inseparable soon after Aalto's arrival in Turku. They designed the competition entry for the Vaasa tradesmen's building together (cf. F 278 in *The Early Years*) and in 1928–29 they arranged the 700th anniversary exhibition of Turku in such intimate collaboration that only now that Aalto's archives are accessible is it possible to determine how they divided the various tasks between them. In fact Bryggman was the only architect of equal stature with whom Aalto collaborated during his whole life. No doubt the explanation partly lies in Bryggman's tactfulness and his charmingly Bohemian attitude to life which appealed to Aalto. But there was more to it than that: in those days Bryggman, who was Aalto's senior and had more insight into continental architectural developments, was professionally more advanced than Aalto. In the very early days of his career Bryggman had made a much more comprehensive study tour of Italy than Aalto; later he had studied the most recent Viennese architecture and had actually seen real-life Functionalist buildings. Aalto had a Picasso-like ability to snap up what was in the air through contacts with friends, to learn from others what he needed to know for his own progress and almost immediately to produce something both bolder and more skilful than did those who had provided the incentive. This had happened in his encounters with Asplund in his youth, and the pattern was repeated in his relationship with Bryggman; it was to be even more marked in his contacts with Markelius, Gropius and Moholy-Nagy in the following years. Lesser colleagues and collaborators could also serve to mediate for him in the same way. Picasso's comment on this process of assimilation might have been Aalto's, too: ''I do not seek, I find!''

In designing the Turku exhibition in 1928, Aalto and Bryggman appeared as Finland's first wholly Functionalist architects. The fact that their exhibition took place a whole year before the Stockholm Exhibition does not, however, prove that they were ahead of their Swedish colleagues. In fact they had both borrowed their main architectural idea as well as several details from the Stockholm plans, thanks to Aalto's intimate contact with

the architects who were working on the more laborious Swedish event. Whatever the case, they succeeded in carrying out the same programme as Asplund and his colleagues had taken on, in much less time. This was important to Aalto, who was doing his best to catch up with − and, if possible, to surpass − the leaders in the architectural race of European Rationalism.

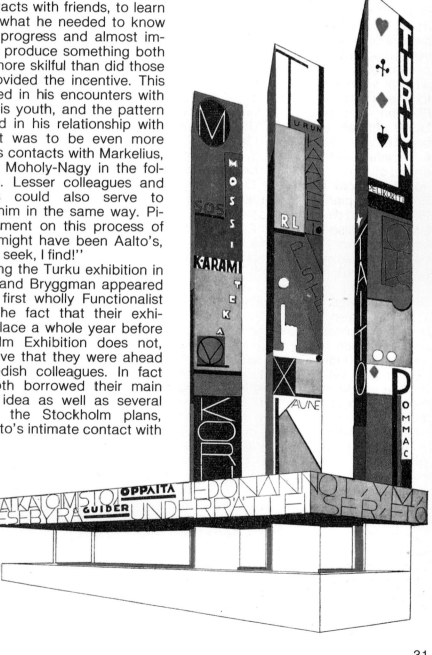

20. Turku exhibition 1929, information stand at the Railway Square.

The Turku exhibition consisted mostly of inexpensive board and plywood pavilions spread over Samppalinna hill, but it was highly radical in terms of form. The most demanding building architecturally, a two-storey circular restaurant with a flat roof, was designed by Bryggman by right of seniority, while Aalto was responsible for a bandstand with a design based on acoustic principles, differing sharply in form from the basic geometric solids that generally characterized early Functionalism. In fact it was a remarkable anticipation of the organic forms so typical of Aalto's later style. On the other hand, the high, square pylons which towered above the boxlike exhibition buildings were connected with contemporary Russian Constructivism, though the influence probably reached them through German architectural periodicals. What gave the event its real panache was the idea of making advertising – i.e., typography – one of the principal elements. Designing the Turun Sanomat Building had reactivated Aalto's experience as a journalist in Jyväskylä; he was now induced to transform the entire exhibition into a kind of gigantic newsspread. The grumbling firms whose goods filled the pavilions were obliged to revise their trademarks and slogans in accordance with Aalto's rigorous instructions, forming an elegant collage of letters.

In Bryggman's career the Turku exhibition represented the summit as well as a turning point as far as his Rationalist commitment was concerned. At the same time as he rose to the challenge of the exhibition facilities, he had a more 'serious' assignment in progress, a funeral chapel in Pargas. In this design he reverted to his earlier Classicism and admiration for the Swedish architect Sigurd Lewerentz. With its peaceful atmosphere and stark simplicity, this chapel anticipates Bryggman's best-known design, the Chapel of the Resurrection in Turku, built in 1940. It is true that many of Bryggman's later buildings can be labelled Functionalist in form, but they are of

the same idyllic, cautious kind of Functionalism that prevailed in Swedish architecture. For his part, Aalto had no intention of striking a retreat after the provocative Turku exhibition; he continued right beyond Functionalism into a new kind of architecture, which was to become his own.

21. Sketch for Turku exhibition choir platform.
The platform as it was built.

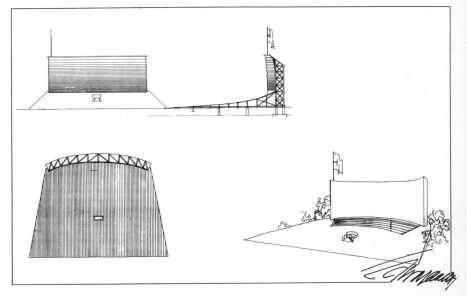

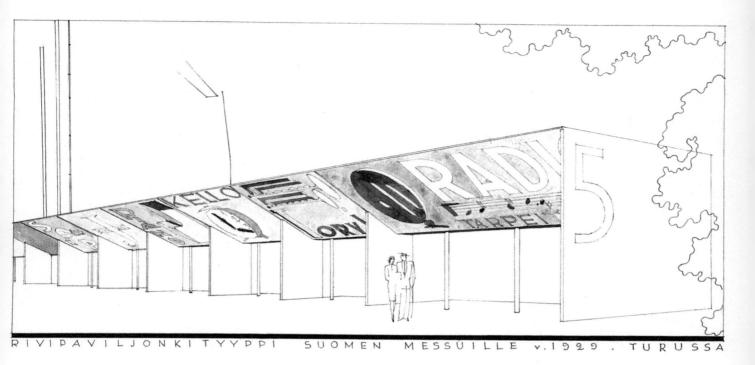

RIVIPAVILJONKITYYPPI SUOMEN MESSUILLE v. 1929 . TURUSSA

22. Pavilion for Turku exhibition, 1929.

AALTO'S FIRST MODERN FURNITURE

The story of Aalto's early Rationalist efforts would be incomplete without a look at the changes in his furniture design in those years.

As we saw in the first volume of this biography, Aalto put a great deal of time and effort into designing furniture for private clients and public spaces during his Jyväskylä years. These were unique designs, just as his buildings were unique creations for a specific client and site. His interest in serialized furniture, like his interest in serial architecture, was aroused by his Rationalist awakening in 1928. The standard flats built in Turku in 1928 naturally required standard furniture. Lacking his own, Aalto followed Le Corbusier's example: the latter had furnished his block of flats for the Stuttgart exhibition with Thonet's well-known 'Viennese' chairs. Aalto used the same chairs for furnishing a model flat in his standard apartment block.

His own furniture went through a rapid stylistic transformation under the influence of continental models during this period. The interior design for the vestry of Muurame Church and for various sections of the Agricultural Cooperative Building constitute an initial stage in this transformation. He was not content with designing merely the fixed seats for the theatre auditorium; he also drew the desks, tables, sofas and chairs for the bank section, all displaying a disconcerting quasi-Modernist monumentality reminiscent of the French *art déco* style (F 224). The chairs and tables for the Itämeri restaurant in the same building also bear witness to Rationalist ambitions for which he had as yet failed to discover a convincing form. The most interesting element was a bandstand with softly undulating forms derived from the shape of the top of a grand piano, foreshadowing Aalto's later design.

One of the many joinery firms which competed for the commission to make the furniture for the Agricultural Cooperative Building was the Huonekalu- ja Rakennustyötehdas (Furniture and Construction Factory) from Turku. This company failed to gain the assignment for the theatre seats and bank furniture, but was awarded the restaurant

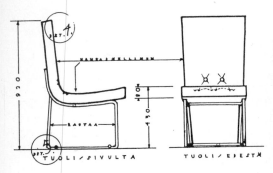

23. Upholstered chair for the
vestry of Muurame Church,
December 1928.

24. Model furniture for living
room in standard block of flats,
Turku 1929, photo Aino Aalto.

25. Bandstand for Itämeri
restaurant, May 1929.

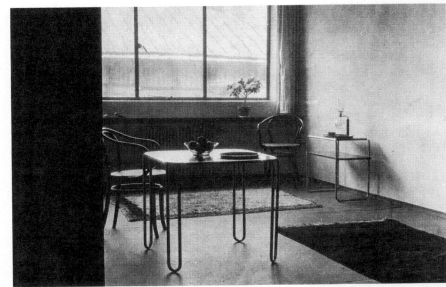

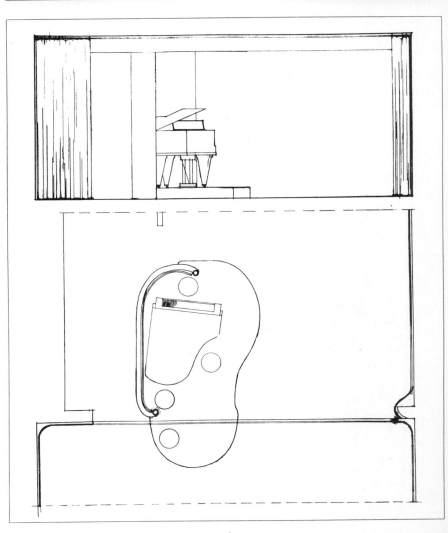

commission. This resulted in the first
meeting, which was to have momentous consequences, between
Aalto and Otto Korhonen, the technical manager of the company.

Huonekalutehdas was a well-established joinery firm which made high-
quality products and had produced
furniture for the Russian market as well
as for the well-known Helsinki company of Boman before the war. Otto
Korhonen was an experienced craftsman who had inherited a strong feeling
for technical efficiency and aesthetic
simplicity from his rural background.
He was also wisely aware of the new
demands made on a company like his
by industrialization, mass production
and modern marketing methods. The
problem was how to discard the old
handicraft philosophy while maintain-
ing quality requirements. He was
himself something of an inventor: he
had hit upon the idea of fastening the
legs of an ordinary chair to the sides of
the seats, thereby making the chair
stackable. Aalto, who was always on
the lookout for technical innovations,
was impressed by this, and he helped
Korhonen to improve the form of the
original stackable chair. This gave rise

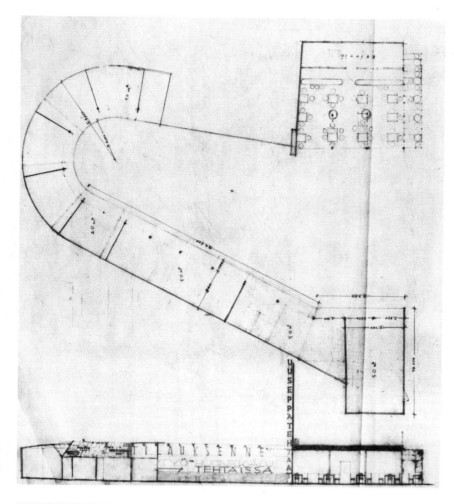

to their first joint creation, the stackable chair for which Korhonen acquired a Finnish patent (though it later turned out that three British inventors had hit upon the same idea earlier), although they were (and still are) sold under Aalto's name. This chair was completed just in time to be the *pièce de résistance* of the Jyväskylä Defence Corps Building assembly hall.

The connection between Aalto and Korhonen was soon to have even more interesting consequences. Huonekalutehdas had its own stand in the furniture pavilion designed by Aalto for the Turku exhibition in 1929, where the stackable chair and a number of other specimens of the collaboration between the joinery firm and the architect were displayed. Aalto was taking giant steps forward. The elegant stackable armchair with a touch of Art Nouveau, seen on the left in F 251, was stylistically archaic, but the other three chair models in the pavilion were full of budding future ideas. We shall look at them in the order in which they were probably completed.

To begin with there were a couple of strangely shaped chairs which formed part of a bedroom suite designed by Aalto in 1928 and comprising a double bed, two night tables, a clothes cupboard, a mirror and a large table, a dressing table and the two chairs, all in dark, polished wood with shining nickel fittings. Stylistically, the whole suite, apart from the chairs, bore traces of the Mondrianesque Constructivism we also find in the facade of the contemporary Turun Sanomat Building. This short-lived fad was soon discarded by Aalto; it is perhaps best described as an unwitting expression of solidarity with the European avant-garde. The chair form, however, was more genuine – and more complex. In purely general terms, it revealed Aalto's spontaneous attraction to organic forms, streng-

26. *Furniture factory pavilion at the Turku exhibition, 1929.*

27. *The Korhonen–Aalto stackable chair, 1929.*

28. Aalto's bedroom furniture,
exhibited in Turku, 1929.

29. Hugo Hamilkar Hackstedt's
repeater rifle had ergonomic
forms.

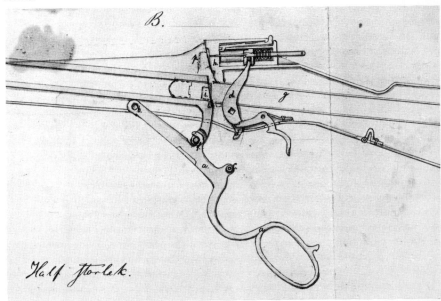

thened since his childhood by the influence of his admired grandfather Hugo
Hamilkar Hackstedt. Aalto kept a
framed drawing of one of his grandfather's inventions, an ingeniously con-
structed repeater rifle, on his wall
throughout his life (F 29). Note the
ungeometrical, contoured forms of this
strictly functional weapon.

Gunnar Asplund, whose manifold
influence on the young Aalto was emphasized in the first volume of this
biography, exhibited an armchair called 'Senna' at the art déco exhibition in
Paris in 1925 (F 30). This was an expensive piece of furniture assembled
from precious varieties of wood according to the oldest traditions of the
craft. It is not surprising that its exqui-

30. Gunnar Asplund's 'Senna' chair, 1925.

31. Aalto's 'Folk Senna', 1929.

site form, with seat and back forming one gently curving piece, made a dèep impression on Aalto. It is more surprising that in 1928 he combined the idea of the 'Senna' chair with his very first confrontation with the problems of industrial production, standardized furniture and social reform. Yet in that very year he set out to produce a kind of 'folk Senna' by modern methods.

The impulse that triggered this idea must have come from Otto Korhonen, who showed Aalto a way to produce a back and seat in one piece mechanically from plywood. Technically the method was well known in Finland; it was used in manufacturing plywood suitcases by a Jyväskylä factory. There is no reason to assume (as the American architecture historian P.D. Pearson does) that Korhonen and Aalto had an eye on the seats of

32. Joint between leg and seat of the 'Folk Senna'.

benches in public places, which were made from moulded plywood that had been produced by an Estonian factory called Luterma since the beginning of the century. The serial production of

37

furniture made of wood pressed in a form had been invented back in 1836 by the ingenious Austrian joiner Michael Thonet, and the technique was so common by the 1920s that the only challenge it presented to the imagination of furniture manufacturers was how to find new applications.

The *Uusi Aura* newspaper published a report on the Turku exhibition on June 15, 1929, probably on the basis of an interview with Aalto. The paper characterized "architects Aino and Alvar Aalto's bedroom furniture" as "a first effort in the direction of a new matter-of-factness". In making the furniture, "a completely new production method had been used, the technique being thoroughly tested for this particular purpose", and had resulted in "very far-reaching standardization potential". This description must refer to the chairs, since the other items of the suite had been made by conventional joinery methods. The seat and back of the chairs consisted of thin wooden veneers, which were heated and glued onto one another, then placed in form presses in which they hardened into an immutable shape. This process can be reproduced mechanically any number of times with identical result. The successful application of this manufacturing method for the bedroom chair justifies our considering it as the embryo from which all the ensuing variations and generations of Aalto's laminated wood furniture grew.

Aalto's 'folk Senna' was almost as perfect in form as the Asplund chair which served as its model, but it had two drawbacks. The first was its uncomfortableness: it was as hard as stone and as slippery as ice. The remedy Aalto hit upon was an upholstered cover which could be fastened with studs to the back and under the seat (see F 28). Worse still was the fact that the chair was still an exclusive − and expensive − handicraft article, since only the seat and back unit was a modern industrial product, while the legs, which had to be joined to the seat elegantly, still called for expensive individual work (see F 32). But Aalto was

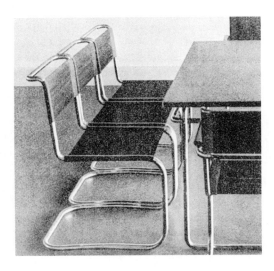

33. Breuer's cantilever chair, bought by Aalto in 1928.

already preparing to tackle this problem as well.

Help arrived from a rather unexpected direction. Aalto's 'conversion' to Functionalism in 1927 had naturally made him familiar with the tubular steel furniture made in continental Europe. In the autumn of 1928 he ordered from the richly illustrated catalogue of the *Thonet Mundus Konzern* in Berlin a series of these chairs and tables for the gallery level of the Itämeri restaurant (in the Agricultural Cooperative Building) as well as for his own home. The consignment, which arrived in Finland in December, comprised a number of Marcel Breuer's famous 'Wassily' armchairs (see F 6), a few dozen of the same designer's simpler tubular steel chairs with sprung legs (F 33), and some small tables known as 'Ablegetische' (F 24). It should be pointed out that in discussing these pieces in interviews and articles Aalto consistently referred to them as "Thonet standard furniture", not as Breuer furniture. It was their quality as industrial, mass-produced, inexpensive articles with a social function, rather than their aesthetic snob value, that interested him.

The arrival of the tubular steel furniture in Turku solved Aalto's urgent problem with the handcrafted wooden legs of the 'folk Senna'. By fastening tubular steel legs to the laminated wooden seat he was able to convert

34. 'Hybrid chair' with fixed
tubular steel base and round
smoking table, 1929.

35. 'Hybrid chair' with sprung
base, 1929.

the entire chair into a modern industrial
product. During the spring of 1929
Korhonen completed two applications
of this idea: one a chair with a fixed
tubular steel base, somewhat like the
'Wassily' chair (F 34); the other with a
spring base, also of tubular steel (F
35). The prototypes of these chairs –
which we will call 'hybrid chairs', since
they combine wooden parts with steel
– were displayed at the Turku exhibition. With his knack for the striking
phrase, Aalto called his springy hybrid
chair "the world's first soft wooden
chair". His pride was understandable.
He had made his first independent
contribution to modern design by combining the dynamic flexibility principle
of the Bauhaus school with Finnish
wood processing technology in a way
that both respected the demands of
industrial production and expressed
the artistic idea of organic growth. For
this he was praised by the English critic
P. Morton Shand, who said in a radio
lecture (printed in *The Listener* on
November 11, 1933: "Aalto has left
the gnawed bone of doctrinaire Functionalism far behind." This he had in
fact done back in 1929 when he created his hybrid chair.

THE TURKU OFFICE

Two Norwegian architects, Harald
Wildhagen and Erling Bjertnaes, are
inextricably linked with Aalto's Turku
years. Not only were they the most
accomplished assistants in his office;
they formed an important part of
Aalto's circle of friends. The reason
that two experienced Norwegian architects, one of whom was older than
Aalto, the other the same age, came to
Finland was that the construction
business was already very sluggish in
Norway before the economic crisis of
the '30s, whereas Finland enjoyed a
boom in construction which lasted up
to 1929. Wildhagen and Bjertnaes first
came into contact with Aalto through
Sigvart Fürst, another Norwegian
architect already working in Finland. At

the time Aalto had more than enough work on his hands, since during his first months in Turku his only permanent employee was his old 'slave' Takala.

In replying to the job applications of his Norwegian colleagues in the autumn of 1927, Aalto welcomed them warmly, promised them 25 marks per hour and assured them that they could easily live on 5,000 marks (about 850 dollars today) a month in Turku, since a rented room with a private entrance cost about 400 marks and "coffee with cognac was cheap because of Prohibition". The only condition was that they should take a close look at Asplund's library and Skandia cinema on their way in Stockholm, which they conscientiously did.

Bjertnaes started work at the beginning of December 1927, and described his first impressions in a letter to Wildhagen: *Aalto is a fine fellow, a little pushy in Bergen style, but a good chap right down to the baggy knees of his unironed trousers. He suggested we should get on first-name terms on the very first day. It was a little strange to say 'du'* to one's boss before even drawing a single line for him. There's a town planner Sutinen, a building*

*Informal address in Swedish (= 'thou').

36. *Office assistants Wildhagen and Bjertnaes celebrating Christmas at the Aalto home in Turku.*

inspector Ahonen and an architect Bryggman here. They're all young lads, good friends of Aalto's and decent, straightforward types. We have no office hours. We work as long as we feel like it, make a note of the hours, and then leave. You can come at 11 a.m. if you like, but then you can stay until 11 p.m. Bjertnaes winds up by telling his friend that he had been asked to spend Christmas with the Aaltos; the invitation was repeated every year for as long as the two Norwegians worked in Finland – Wildhagen left at the end of 1930, and Bjertnaes in the summer of 1931.

A large number of the office's most important drawings, beginning with those for the Agricultural Cooperative Building and the Jyväskylä Defence Corps Building and continuing right up to the competitions for Paimio Sanatorium, Zagreb Hospital, and several churches, are signed with the initials of one of the two Norwegians. When I discovered this while rooting in the Aalto archives in 1978, my curiosity was aroused. Were these two early assistants still alive? If so, was there something they could tell me about the years they spent in Finland in their youth? I found Bjertnaes's address in the Oslo telephone directory and wrote on the off-chance to ask if I could visit him. The reply arrived a fortnight later:

37. Alvar Aalto in the early 1930s.

Oslo, August 23, 1978
Dear Göran S.
May I be so familiar as to say 'Du' to Alvar's friend. His name awakens memories of some of the happiest years of my life. A few young Norwegians in a youthful, inspiring milieu in Turku. I am not a young man any more, with my 79 years. Memory fails, details are blurred, all that is left is a hazy picture like a beautiful watercolour dream. A happy, sorrow-free time. I am hardly a good interviewee. My thoughts advance as slowly and haltingly as my legs. Perhaps I can write a little better, since that puts time on my side.

There were 3 of us Norwegian architects in Turku: Harald Wildhagen and myself with Alvar, Sigvart Fürst with Erik Bryggman. Fürst has been gone for some years now and Wildhagen is in an old people's home. He is completely paralysed and can only get out individual words with the greatest difficulty. Because of my own failing health, I have not been able to visit him for more than a year.

Naturally you know Alvar the architect from plentiful global sources – I can tell you nothing new in that respect. Instead you will have to be content with a few small, insignificant flashes of the spectrum that makes up a great personality. Small glimpses of character: Alvar as boss, colleague and friend. But it is not easy; it was all so self-evident then. You never realized while you were right in the midst of it.

Hours, days, weeks and years flowed through the hourglass in a steady, satisfying, swift stream. You never had time to stop and cry out: "Ha, this is good, this is characteristic. I must remember this to be able to tell Göran Schildt half a century later what a unique person Alvar Aalto was." For that he truly was.

He certainly had his human weaknesses, but we did not see them. And this indeed was a small, but by no means trivial facet of his personality. Was our life in Finland then nothing but the fleeting flight of summer birds above a perpetual bed of roses? No. There was sunshine and rain; parties were followed by hard, hard work. It's true Alvar was the witty, party-going type, that was in his blood. But side by side with this intense enjoyment of life went an intense enjoyment of work — an energy which knew no bounds. And we got to feel it in our bones. After a cheerful get-together at home with Aino and Alvar — or at a tavern — it was all day at the office, where we took turns now and then to doze off for an hour or two on the floor or on some unencumbered desk. He was the leader by virtue of his overwhelming superiority. His ideas were like fireworks aimed at heaven. But afterwards the damned meteor had to be brought down to the ground and clothed in concrete, brick and wood. It was for us, the foot soldiers, to tackle the hard task of making the fireworks come true without losing too much of their brilliance. Alvar watched over us vigilantly, and helped us whenever our own capacity failed.

He was our friend. He was a part of us, just as naturally as we were a part — if an insignificant one — of his office. If he won a competition we were just as proud as if we had won it ourselves. And when he didn't win — such things happened — it was we who thought that the imbecile jury did not understand a whit about real architecture. Alvar himself took it with supreme indifference, praised a few undeniably successful features of the winning entry and made fun of the whole thing.

But occasionally, when he forgot that the door was open, we would see him standing deep in thought in front of his masterfully executed perspectives. It was not a loser's dejection, but the certainty of the invincible that there would be other trains to take.

During the 3–4 years we had the experience of working with Alvar, I cannot remember a single dissonance, not even the slightest false or forced note. Right at the start there wasn't always much money around. It could happen that we had to borrow from one another or from others, for a week, perhaps longer. But then Alvar would sail through the draughtsmen's office, pick up a drawing pin from the nearest desk, and pin a few thousand mark notes on the door to the sanctuary: "Here's money, boys." We had to share it as best we could. Sometimes there was enough, sometimes it was too little. But that didn't matter to us: we — the office — had not earned any more that time, but Alvar would see us through. That — and much, much more — was the kind of person, boss and friend Alvar Aalto was.

No, now I can't write any more, I'm getting too tired. You must forgive me my nostalgia. The panegyrics cannot be exaggerated. I had thought of writing a little about Harald Wildhagen's importance to the young Alvar Aalto, but that will have to wait until we meet. Remind me of this when you come to Oslo. Unfortunately we can't offer you a bed, but if you can make do with a bite of something and a few drinks, my wife (who is Norwegian, but we married in Finland) and I will be happy to have you here. You must just close your eyes to the defects of our tattered home.

My warmest regards,
E. Bjertnaes

With such a letter in my pocket it was a joy to travel to Oslo. I spent a pleasant day with the old couple, and the next day we went together to the old people's home, where the paralysed Wildhagen listened, eyes sparkling with joy, to what I had to tell of the last years of Aalto's life. He had great difficulty in speaking, but he made sure that I was given part of his extensive correspondence with Aalto and Bjertnaes during the Turku years. Let me begin by quoting a brief report on life at the office, as Bjertnaes described it in a letter to Wildhagen in November 1930:

Sjevski (= the chief) is drawing sleepsitliebedcouches of tubes, iron rods and steel wire every time he's at home in Turku changing trains on the way from Frankfurt to Brussels or vice versa. We had the roofraising of the Sanatorium (= Paimio) – without a roof. Ahti couldn't cast the roof slab because the thing overflowed with rain-water, so we'll have to wait for the

38. Aalto with his daughter Mossi (Hanna-Maija) at Alajärvi, photo Aino Aalto.

39. Aino Aalto at Alajärvi in the 1930s.

spring sun and dry weather before putting in the coke lining. It's a damned impressive height. We had a Force 7–8 south wind right against the wards before they had a full load – you know they haven't filled in between the columns yet. Thank God it wasn't all blown away, but Henriksson [Aalto's technical consultant] was still pale with nervousness the next day . . . [here the letter was interrupted and continued three weeks later.] *There was an exhibition* [the Minimum Apartment Exhibition in Helsinki] *– anyway we felt the heat at the office. Madam herself came over and worked for several hours a month . . . The result was an exhibition of toys with a rolling kitchen. That is, the kitchen is fixed, but practically all the equipment is on wheels.*

From the interview with Wildhagen (September 4, 1978) the following extracts are worth quoting:

It was Alvar who directed the work for the Turku 700th anniversary exhibition. Not that Bryggman had conflict-

ing opinions, he was just too accommodating and good-natured. Especially in the matter of the advertising texts, Alvar was dictatorial, though the companies were sour.

Alvar registered Aino as collaborator even when she was not involved in any way. They had a very strong family feeling and Alvar always discussed his assignments with Aino. Mrs Aalto was a real architect. Besides that she was both wife and mother to Alvar.

Alvar was often abroad – in Stockholm, Berlin, Zurich. The only Finnish I ever learned was to say "Hän on matkoilla" (He's abroad) when I had to answer the telephone.

From the interview with Bjertnaes on September 3, 1978:

To start with it was just us and Takala at the office; Bäckström, Totti Strömberg and Lasse Wiklund joined us later. Lasse was a wretched architect. "He's drawing the wrong windows as usual" was a standard joke at the office. But he was a good fellow. The whole office helped to draw the Columbus monument, night and day, for it was done at the last minute. But Alvar did the entry for Kälviä Sanatorium all on his own.

There was quite a lot of dancing in our set, at home and in restaurants. Aino was interested in fashion and textiles. She was more of a good critic than a good architect. She had no desk of her own at the office, she just came in now and then and 'considered' in front of the others' desks. Then of course she had little children to take care of. [Mossi, later called Hanni, was born on August 1, 1925 and Veikko, later known as Hamilkar, on January 8, 1928.] Aino was the family's 'Minister of Finance' and complemented Alvar in many ways. He was a complete Bohemian and drank like a fish, but that didn't stop him working. It was fantastic how hard he could work. Not that he had a drinking problem, he held his liquor well. But Aino would often say: "No, that's enough, Alvar" when we were out boozing. Aino had beautiful eyes, but she was too big all round. Alvar's non-

chalance about money was good for the artistic result; he never took a job on just for the money. In company he was always considerate and friendly. I find it impossible to believe what someone told me, that he had become a little tyrannical in his old age.

We all went to the Stockholm Exhibition [1930] together, but once we got there we went our several ways. Alvar associated with the 'big boys', both Swedish and foreign. He was particularly friendly with Markelius. The worst shock for us all was what we called 'NK Funkis' [from the fashionable Stockholm department store NK], impractical interiors and utility ware in quasi-modern style, false Functionalism throughout. Alvar and Markelius were genuine Functionalists. Not that Alvar was always so practical, his strength lay elsewhere. To my mind that wasn't important, for that part, the practical, dull bit, is for the assistants to take care of.

In his letter to me, Bjertnaes had asked me to remind him of a particular matter on his mind that he was too tired to write about: Wildhagen's importance to Aalto. What Bjertnaes stressed when we met was that Wildhagen, who was Aalto's senior, had much more extensive practical experience of building. He had graduated two years before Aalto, and after a few years of architectural practice in Germany he had worked as town planner in Drammen, where he had taken part in some large-scale building projects. Aalto often had daring new ideas which resulted in conflicts with the generally conservative technical consultants. Wildhagen understood and admired Aalto, but he also knew what was technically feasible and was able to restrain Aalto when the latter went too far.

Thus goes Bjertnaes's testimony. Wildhagen himself pointed out during our conversation that Aalto was greatly indebted to Emil Henriksson, a construction engineer who had studied in Germany and was the technical consultant for Aalto's main projects in Turku. A single technical detail is of

40. *The free-standing, asymmetrical columns in the* Turun Sanomat *printing works.*

special interest in this context – the asymmetrical, organically formed concrete columns in the Turun Sanomat printing works. They aroused the attention of architecture critics right from the start, no doubt because they differed so sharply from the mechanically geometric forms which characterized early Functionalism elsewhere. Together with the bandstand for the Turku exhibition, these columns anticipated the biological forms typical of Aalto's later architecture. The Swedish critic Gotthard Johansson associated the columns with those of the Gothic cathedral, while more sober commentators have sought other sources of influence to explain them. In her study on the breakthrough of Functionalism in Finland, the Finnish critic Raija-Liisa Heinonen argues that it was Emil Henriksson who had brought this form with him from Germany. The American critic David Pearson suggests in his book *Aalto and the International Style* that Aalto had copied them from

Markelius's Helsingborg Concert Hall (which is in fact quite different). Their true origin came to light by pure chance while I was leafing through Aalto's copies of the Swedish professional journal *Byggmästaren* in his library and discovered an article in no. 6/1927 with sketches by Aalto in the margin.

The article is headed *"Can concrete, particularly reinforced concrete, give rise to a new architecture?"* The writer is a Belgian architect called O. van Stapelmohr. His questions are: *How should we mould concrete in order to create a typical concrete architecture?*; and *How would the ancient Greeks have approached this question, and what would Viollet-le-Duc have done?* He believes the answer should be sought *on the basis of the same principles as form the foundation of all architecture, whether brick, stone or wood: from the physical characteristics of the material, from which theory and practice grow. It is therefore necessary for the engineer who carries out the architect's programme to provide a general outline, while the architect, with his greater sensitivity to harmony, should correct the drafts. Both the engineer and the architect are necessary for the creation and development of the new architecture.*

The author proceeds to illustrate this collaboration with a number of photographs of 'artistic' concrete structures in Belgium and France, none of which correspond to the asymmetrical columns in the Turun Sanomat printing works. The principle, however, is clearly expressed, and was evidently approved by Aalto. The result was Henriksson's, Wildhagen's and Aalto's joint achievement, and a fine demonstration of the fruitfulness of van Stapelmohr's method. The engineer and practitioner must first stake out the boundaries within which the artist's instincts have free play.

SVEN AND
VIOLA MARKELIUS

Markelius is a name that has cropped up time and again in this book. Our picture of Aalto's first years in Turku would be incomplete without more than just a few lines on this key figure in Aalto's development.

I pointed out in *The Early Years* (page 141) that it was probably during his Scandinavian journey in autumn 1926 that Aalto first met this 'kindred spirit' (as he called Markelius in a newspaper interview). It is possible that they did not meet again until Aalto moved to Turku nine months later and the prize money he had won in two major competitions enabled him to travel more frequently. In any case, they were in close contact from the summer of 1927 until the mid '30s, not merely through frequent visits but also by telephone. By a fortunate coincidence, Aalto's telephone bills for the trunk calls he made during these years have been preserved, and they show that out of all the calls he made, he

dialled Markelius's Stockholm number most often by far.

Sven Markelius was nine years older than Aalto. His original name was Jonsson, of which his younger colleague would frequently remind him with a certain irony (Aalto himself would never have dreamed of changing his relatively common surname into something finer). Markelius had worked as Östberg's assistant on the Stockholm City Hall plan during the First World War, had made an extensive study tour of Italy with Gunnar Asplund in 1920, and had later worked at the city planning office of the National Board of Building and Planning. In 1926 he won a competition for a new concert hall in Helsingborg, a breakthrough comparable to Aalto's competition victories in 1927.

Circumstances thus made Aalto and Markelius contemporaries in external success. They were also well-matched in terms of architectural ideology. In his competition entry for the concert hall, Markelius, like Aalto with his entries for the Agricultural Cooperative Building and the Viipuri Library, still spoke the Neo-Classical idiom; but the new winds from the Continent soon reached both architects. Comparing the architectural views of Markelius and Aalto in the summer of 1927, one can hardly say that those of the former were more advanced; in fact the Kinkomaa Sanatorium wards and the Vaasa tradesmen's building entry bear witness to Aalto's bolder modernism. Both architects had become familiar with Rationalist ideas through architectural publications and discussions with colleagues, the difference being that the discussions had been going on for a longer time and within a wider and more competent circle in Sweden than in provincial Finland.

The Swedish architects had in fact been debating Functionalism ever since Le Corbusier had published *Vers une architecture* in 1923 and exhibited his Pavillon de l'Esprit Nouveau in Paris in 1925. Uno Åhren's article "På väg mot en arkitektur" (On the way to an architecture), published in Byggmäs-

41. *Viola and Sven Markelius flanked by Alvar Aalto and an unidentified gentleman, photo Aino Aalto.*

taren in 1926, marked the final break-through of Le Corbusier's utopian ideas in Sweden. Since what was being introduced was not simply a new style or technical method, but expressly a new way to organize society and people's private ways of life, it was necessary – as is usual in matters of belief – to start by confirming one's own faith before setting out to convert others and form congregations. Like-minded people had endless dis-cussions, sermons were preached, and meetings held; the new doctrine was militantly announced to the world. Aalto sought and found all this in his contacts with Markelius and his other Swedish friends.

They had new matters to discuss after Markelius got back from his travels in the summer of 1927. He made an extensive tour of Europe in his own car in order to study airports in Denmark, the Netherlands, Belgium, France and Germany in preparation for the recently announced competition for Bromma airport in Stockholm. On the way Markelius made a point of

visiting the Weissenhof Exhibition in Stuttgart. In Dessau he visited two new buildings by Gropius: the newly open-ed Bauhaus school and the serially built housing in Siedlung Törten. The last-named project seems to have inte-rested him most, since after his return he published an article on it in *Byggmästaren* and gave a lecture on "A German example of organized housing construction". His contact with Gropius resulted in a lecture by the energetic Bauhaus director in Stockholm in March 1928.

A few weeks later it was Markelius's turn to act as missionary in Finland. On April 28, 1928 he gave a lecture at the annual meeting of the Finnish Associ-ation of Architects (SAFA) in Turku. In retrospect, Hilding Ekelund ironically commented that this event marked the official breakthrough of Functionalism in Finland, but he admitted that Markelius's speech had an overwhelm-ing impact on him personally. After the lecture, which was held at the assembly hall of the Academy, a ban-quet dinner was served in Bryggman's

42. The Seurahuone restaurant in Turku, architect Erik Bryggman.

brand-new Seurahuone restaurant, where the table was laid between stuccolustro walls beneath ultramodern PH lamps. According to a description in *Arkkitehti* magazine, this was "an event not soon to be forgotten in the history of SAFA", a feast overflowing with Dionysian enthusiasm and accompanied by solemn speeches and festive fanfares. Forty architects with their wives had arrived from Helsinki, Viipuri and Tampere, and the Turku guild was well-represented.

Markelius's lecture was entitled "Rationalization trends in modern housing design" and testified to the impact of the fresh impulses he had received from the socially oriented Gropius rather than the elegant flights of fancy and artistic emphasis of Le Corbusier. By a fortunate coincidence, the rather sketchy manuscript has been preserved at the Museum of Swedish Architecture, giving us the opportunity to take a closer look at the arguments which had such an inflammatory effect on Finnish architects at the time. I shall, however, postpone my discussion of Markelius's teachings and Aalto's views concerning them, and instead attempt to enlarge on their

friendship which had other dimensions besides the exchange of ideas.

It might seem an impossible task for an author to defy all-consuming oblivion and attempt to reconstruct episodes, relationships and feelings which took place more than half a century ago. Aino and Alvar Aalto are gone, and so is Sven Markelius. The participants in the debate on Functionalism in the '20s have dispersed; only a few newspaper articles, letters, pamphlets and a handful of photographs remain. Or so I thought until I heard that one key witness was still alive: Sven Markelius's wife Viola, whose lively, original contributions to Aalto's letter archives I had already scanned with interest. Her name is now Viola Wahlstedt-Guillemaut. Her vivacious appearance made it hard to believe that she was almost 80 when we met on January 14, 1979. Perhaps the only noticeable sign of age was the ironic distance with which she looked back on the adventures of her chequered career. During the excellent lunch of wine and shellfish that I had the honour to offer her, she was remarkably frank about her no longer controversial past. It turned out that not only Aalto but also

Sven Markelius occupied a relatively limited place in this past. "I have always had difficulties in keeping hold of anything", was her explanation for the fact that she had had a more eventful life than most. During our four-hour lunch I formed the following, probably incomplete, idea of her life:

Born the spoiled daughter of a solid Stockholm upper-class family, at an early age she married an Italian whose Catholic faith made their soon desired divorce impossible. In 1926 she and Sven Markelius therefore became pioneers of the later so common institution of cohabitation, and had several children together. Not only was Viola exceptionally beautiful (as can be seen from old photographs); she was also unusually independent. She wrote for the principal Stockholm newspapers, and was among the reporters who crossed over to Finland when the regular hydroplane service between Stockholm and Turku was started.

Her spiritual home was among the coterie of writers, artists, academicians and architects who sympathized with the *Clarté* movement, which was fairly widespread in Sweden at the time. This was a Socialist or Communist movement in the rather innocent fashion of the times, and also took an interest in the architectural utopianism that Le Corbusier and the Bauhaus were propagating. This circle included many of those who prepared and executed the 1930 Stockholm Exhibition, including Gregor Paulsson, Gotthard Johansson and Otto G. Carlsund, as well as such people as economists Gunnar and Alva Myrdal, novelist Vilhelm Moberg and poet Gunnar Ekelöf. For a while Viola was actually the editor of the group's radical cultural journal, *Spectrum* (for which Aalto also wrote articles).

Since Aalto and Markelius both had independent and intellectual wives, their friendship soon expanded into a foursome. Through the Markeliuses, the Aaltos soon became accepted members of Stockholm's radical set. The families visited each other so frequently that the guest room in the Markelius home came to be known as "Aino and Alvar's room". Viola passed through Turku on her way to the land of the future — the Soviet Union — in 1933 and tried to persuade Alvar to go with her. She stayed in Moscow for only a few weeks, but later returned for a longer spell, working at a malaria hospital in Baku and publishing a book on returning to Sweden with the title *Jag älskade Volodja* (I loved Volodya). This was literally true, and in the mid '30s her path diverged from Sven's for good. After this she lived for a few years with the Maya Indians in Yucatan, but returned to Sweden during the war. She then married a French artist who had come to Sweden as a refugee, and became a pioneer for biodynamic farming and the country life in a way that only became fashionable thirty years later. She went on to live in a barge off Norrmälarstrand in Stockholm, but after a few years was obliged to find a healthier place to live. At the time of our interview, however, life on dry land was beginning to bore her, and she dreamed of sailing across the Atlantic on her own before her 90th birthday. The only problem was to find a suitable boat . . .

"Have you had that gadget on all along?" she asked in horror when I changed the tape in my recorder during our conversation. "Oh well, never mind! I have nothing to hide, it was all great fun!" Here is a summary of the interview — that is, of the part that applied to Aalto:

When Alvar first appeared at our place he looked like a little country lad. His hat was too big and hung down over his ears and he was carrying a midwife's bag. But he started talking at once, and that made all the difference. Sven would always take ten minutes to consider before he opened his mouth, but Alvar just went straight at it. They complemented each other perfectly. Alvar helped Sven to soften down his architecture and taught him the value of wood. Deep inside they were both artists, however socially minded they tried to be.

Of course we danced when we met,

it was the Jazz Age. But mostly we just talked, sitting and gabbing for hours on end. What did we talk about? Everything, I suppose: philosophy, architecture, collective housing, the roles of the sexes. Yes, I had taken courses on Marxism and all that, but I never thought there was any difference between my political opinions and Alvar's, there was a kind of obvious affinity. But of course we were pretty naive and blind in many ways; the aesthetic side was more in our line.

Who else was in the gang? Well, there was Åhren and Carlsund and Gotthard [Johansson]; Gregor [Paulsson] wasn't a member of the inner circle − he took part in our quieter gatherings and discussions, but not in the drinking. The same goes for Asplund, too. He was a good friend of both Sven's and Alvar's, but his then wife was very religious, the revivalist type with her hair tied up in a bun. It was hard to get on with her. When Asplund married Wahlman's former wife Ingrid, things got easier; she's all right.

I can't remember much about the preparations for the Stockholm Exhibition. I had a baby just before the opening. But of course it was just one big party all summer. We had even more fun the next year when **acceptera** [the manifesto of the radical Swedish architects] was written at our place. Except that I had to stand in the kitchen and make sandwiches for the authors all night. Besides, their writing was pretty stiff. I had a terrible job getting Sven's officialese into modern Swedish.

Aino? Yes, I admired her and we got on very well. She spoke Swedish passably, German a little worse. Physically she was on the heavy side, or massive to be precise. The dark, Russian type. She took more of an interest in social issues than Alvar and − how should I say − her talent was deeper than his. Alvar was all sparkle and fireworks. Did he have a drinking problem in those days? No, we all drank, Aino too, but it wasn't a problem for any of us. And we always had fun. Aino wasn't a saint,

either. Sometimes we'd swop husbands, modern, liberated women that we were. And I must say that Alvar was a wonderful lover, my goodness! Such tenderness and softness isn't easy to come by. He had an incredible longing for tenderness. He was a ladies' man right down to the fingertips all right. He always tried with everybody. But his flirting was always so humorous and innocent that nobody could possibly be angry with him.

In 1931 we were all in Berlin, and we went to Ernst May's lecture on the Soviet Union and got all worked up. May and [Hans] Schmidt described the Soviet Union as an architects' paradise. When I went to Moscow later I lived with the Schmidts in a writers' building and had Pasternak as my neighbour. There were Germans and Frenchmen too. People came and went constantly, we talked endlessly. Of course the conditions were Spartan, but they had their charm. I had the impression that everyone had complete freedom. It wasn't till after Kirov's assassination that things got worse. There was a German friend I played tennis with in Baku. She had sacrificed everything for the Soviet Union, given everything she had to the Communist future, and all she got for it was a bullet in the neck.

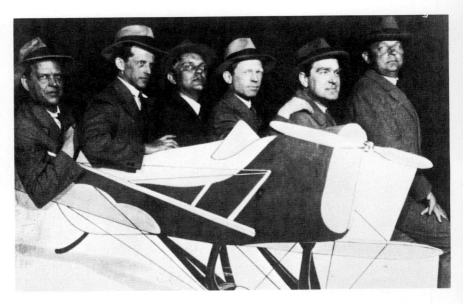

43. The men behind the Stockholm Exhibition and the pamphlet acceptera. Left to right: Sven Markelius, Uno Åhrén, Gunnar Asplund, Eskil Sundahl, Wolter Gahn and Gregor Paulsson.

44. *Nude in Aalto's sketchbook,
1930s.*

Gropius visited us in Stockholm several times, and during one of his visits Alvar also stayed with us. I spent a week at the Bauhaus and met Moholy [-Nagy]. He talked incessantly about art, was intense and emotional, but also shy and retiring. Actually he was very like Alvar – except in the matter of shyness, of course. As artists they also resembled one another: both had the same love of lines, the same aesthetic fixations. In Germany we naturally studied those famous 'Siedlungen', and I must say they were awful. There was a hidden class philosophy about them, they were horribly lower-class. Sven tried to raise the quality of similar housing in Sweden, but the problem still hasn't been solved.

This, then, was Viola's account of events which took place fifty years ago. She stands in this biography for the many women Aalto met during his long life, with whom he shared his zest for life and who retained a warm memory of him. This kind of contact was so natural to him that it was rarely misinterpreted either by the other party concerned or by his nearest and dearest, though Aino's patience failed more than once. Their relations with the Markeliuses, in any case, did not give rise to conflicts of any kind, and were obviously a source of delight to all those concerned.

How much Markelius learned from Aalto as an architect and a human being I leave to his biographers to determine. Instead I shall make an attempt to describe the surprising importance Markelius held for Aalto as a social model.

When Viola first met Aalto, he seemed "like a little country lad" to her. Bjertnaes, too, as we have seen, spoke of the "baggy knees of his un-ironed trousers". Two years later we see Aalto in a photograph of the nearly completed Agricultural Cooperative Building, dressed as elegantly as Markelius had been for many years: black tie, English trench coat, beret, razor-sharp trouser seams and well-polished shoes. Le Corbusier had taught his colleagues that this was

what an architect should look like: neither a Bohemian artist nor a gentleman of leisure, but more like an engineer. Aino also started taking an interest in fashion around this time and adopted the matter-of-fact elegance of the independent professional woman in contrast to the feminine and romantic emphasis that went with the traditional role of women. One might venture the guess that Viola Markelius had something to do with this process.

46. Aalto's Fiat, bought in 1927.

45. Alvar Aalto, a Turku dandy in 1929.

47. Markelius's Dodge, bought in 1928.

48. Aalto's Buick, bought in 1929.

For the small-town couple from Jyväskylä, confronting Stockholm's intellectual set was naturally a challenge. Their espousal of the continental architects' utopian belief in the future affected their daily life as well. It is also understandable that their 'best friends' Sven and Viola were models whom they set out to surpass if possible. Sven had bought a Fiat 509 in 1926 as an external symbol of his professional success and modern way of thinking. When Alvar drew the prize money for the Agricultural Cooperative Building, he immediately bought a car of the same make. In November 1928 Markelius changed to a Dodge, whereupon the Aaltos outdid him a year later by acquiring a Buick. It was not so easy to follow the Markeliuses' example when they built their own Functionalist house in Nockeby in 1931, but Aalto's rejoinder came in 1935 with the house in Munkkiniemi outside Helsinki, where both Aino and Alvar lived for the rest of their lives.

The fact that Aalto set off on a continental tour following the route Markelius had taken by car, but with an even more up-to-date means of transport − an aeroplane − does not surprise us any more than that, hard on his friend's heels, he entered the exclusive set of international architects who made up the CIAM, and soon became an even better friend of Gropius's than Markelius. Sven and Viola started studying English by the Linguaphone method in 1929; in this, too, Aino and Alvar followed their friends' example a few years later. Some have wondered whether Alvar really could have imagined in February 1930 that he had the slightest chance of getting the vacant professorship at the Institute of Technology in Helsinki against the formidable J.S. Sirén, architect of the Finnish Parliament House. Aalto was only 32 years old at the time, and all he had to show in the way of publications were "a few articles in Backwoods News" (as he himself once put it). His bravado in submitting his application all the same is easier to understand when we know that Markelius had applied for a similar professorship at Sweden's Royal Institute of Technology just six months before. Markelius was 40 and had published numerous serious articles on town planning in professional journals, but he was passed over all the same. For Aalto it was a triumph in itself that one of the experts, Sigurd Frosterus, actually declared him competent, though he, too, placed Sirén as his first candidate.

I have already mentioned (page 39) another apparently trivial idea Aalto picked up from Markelius. In September 1927 Markelius ordered five pieces of 'System Breuer' tubular steel furniture from Berlin, two of which were 'Wassily' armchairs. One year later Aalto put in a similar order, and this provided the initial impetus for his own modern furniture. Aalto's special ability to react to impulses received, immediately taking the borrowed idea one step further, set him apart from all of his Nordic colleagues and also enabled him to surpass Markelius. As a result, the contacts between them petered out in the mid '30s. For Aalto, Markelius had been a useful mediator of new ideas: through him Aalto had penetrated into the general philosophy of life inherent in Functionalism, and had assumed the external attributes of his professional role. As soon as he and Aino had caught up with or even surpassed their Swedish friends in this unspoken competition, the relationship lost its stimulation.

In terms of pure architectural creativity, Markelius was not really a source of inspiration for Aalto. In this respect Aalto was drawn more to his former idol and present friend Gunnar Asplund. The fact that Asplund superseded Markelius as Aalto's 'best friend' in Sweden must also have been partly due to the vivacious Viola's disappearance from the scene, whereas Asplund had his new, amiable wife Ingrid, as Viola mentioned in her interview. The basic reason for the shift in their relationship, however, was the special artistic affinity between Aalto and Asplund, which was not shared by Markelius. Asplund died in 1940, whereas Markelius lived almost as long as Aalto. After the war, however, they met only very occasionally. They were, quite simply, too different: Markelius was a serious person with a sincere belief in theories and ideologies, whereas Aalto was an incurable sceptic who never hesitated in following his artistic daemon towards new horizons.

TRAVELLING
IN 1928

In 1927 Aalto received a travel grant from the Kordelin Foundation, but his many commitments prevented him from making use of it immediately. He was harassed by lack of time and difficulty in getting away from work for the rest of his life. In the summer of 1928 he found an expedient which was to become typical: he made a lightning tour by aeroplane while the boys at the office completed the drawings he had assigned to them. After this he was frequently abroad, but he was never gone for long for fear of losing contact with his office.

A study trip to the Continent was an absolute must at this stage of his career. Its urgency was accentuated by the fact that his nearest colleagues were all travelling: Bryggman was preparing a trip to Germany the same summer, while Markelius, as we have seen, had toured the Continent in his own car. As the proud owner of a new automobile, Aalto certainly would have liked to follow his friend's example, but he could not afford the luxury of such a long holiday. Flying was not a bad alternative, however, since it was even more representative of the modern lifestyle. There has been some uncertainty about the exact timing and length of Alvar and Aino's study tour. We now know that they were in Paris on June 23, and thus did not take part in the congress on concrete architecture held there in May, as P.D. Pearson believes. In an interview published by the newspaper *Sisä-Suomi* on August 18, 1928, Aalto speaks with naive

49. The KLM Fokker with which Alvar and Aino flew to Paris in 1928.

pride about his extraordinary trip. The heading is *Early morning coffee in Paris, lunch in Amsterdam, afternoon coffee in Hamburg and dinner in Malmö*. According to the traveller, *flying is the only acceptable form of travel for modern civilized man,* since *trains and ferries are full of all sorts of folk, whereas in aeroplanes one only meets select people in whose company one need never feel embarrassed.* We also learn that the flight from Turku to Paris takes only twenty-three hours.

This did not, however, mean that Aino and Alvar went directly to France. In fact they started with Denmark, where Aalto made the acquaintance of Poul Henningsen. This extraordinary Dane was a true Renaissance character, who brought off such various feats during his eventful life as designing the famous PH lamp, writing witty music hall performances, and publishing a lavishly illustrated history of pornography in four volumes. He was also an important source of influence for Aalto. At the time, the PH lamp amounted to a symbol for progressive architecture, and Aalto immediately ordered a consignment of these lamps for all of his current projects, including Muurame

Church and the Turku Theatre. It thus provided the formal point of departure for his own Rationalist lamp design, which began with the Turun Sanomat offices in 1929 and with the Minimum Apartment Exhibition in Helsinki 1930.

The impulses Aalto received from Henningsen's radical cultural magazine *Kritisk Revy* may have had an even greater impact. This remarkably amusing, pugnacious, and versatile periodical fought for the total reform of both the built environment and society in general, but in a critical way that was not associated with any ideology. It attacked the biased dogma and political doctrine of salvation embraced by Functionalism, not with the purpose of sounding a reactionary retreat but with a view to improvement. A typical twist was, ''Traditionalism is our arch-enemy, Modernism our false friend.'' During its brief existence (1926–28), *Kritisk Revy* contributed to the Functionalist breakthrough in the Nordic countries, but it also lashed out against the sterile tendencies of the Bauhaus school and the unpleasant tactile and optical qualities of Breuer's tubular steel furniture. According to Henningsen, American rocking chairs and

50. Aalto's first Rationalist lamp designs for Turun Sanomat in 1929.

Thonet's Viennese chairs were much better standard products than metal chairs "which are so cold they give the modernly dressed woman a cramp in the thigh". This gave Aalto's innate scepticism about all authority a useful injection and provided quite concrete information about the weaknesses of modern tubular steel furniture. The very first result of his meeting with Poul Henningsen was an invitation to contribute to the critical review, which Aalto took up later that year.

The next stop on Alvar and Aino's journey was Amsterdam, where they "made the acquaintance of many Dutch architects and their works", as he mentioned in the interview quoted above. It seems probable that he met Duiker and saw his Zonnenstraal Sanatorium, and that this meeting had a certain impact on his plan for Paimio

Sanatorium, begun a few months later. There is, however, no reason to exaggerate this 'influence'. Aalto had already diverged from the orthogonal principle for the sake of sunlight in one of the house entries for the *Aitta* competition the spring before, while the division of the building mass on the basis of function into separate 'organs' appeared in both his early church entries and the Kinkomaa plan from the preceding year. The free-standing staff buildings at Paimio indicate, however, that he was more receptive to the architecture of Oud than to that of Duiker on his visit to the Netherlands.

The reason why Aalto went to Paris was that he wished to meet Le Corbusier, whose teachings he had so wholeheartedly applied to the Turun Sanomat Building, which was still under construction at the time. But Le Corbusier was in Moscow preparing the construction of the Centrosoyuz building commissioned from him by the Russian authorities.

At Le Corbusier's office, Aalto met instead the master's young Swiss assistant, Alfred Roth, who remained a lifelong friend. Aalto asked Roth to send him a selection of photographs of Le Corbusier's latest works, especially the house in Garches, completed the year before. The extent to which this house interested the Aaltos is shown by the many not particularly successful photos Aino took of it.

Of his other contacts in Paris, Aalto mentions in the interview that he had "made many pleasant acquaintances among a company of international realist-architects at a Saint-Germain café". The most important of these was undoubtedly André Lurçat (1892–1970), who was considered a worthy rival of Le Corbusier. According to the Swedish architect Sven Ivar Lind, who was well-versed in French events at the time, two competing Functionalist trends were being discussed: the 'Northern Protestant' headed by the 'Swiss watchmaker', i.e. Le Corbusier; and the 'Mediterranean Catholic' led by Lurçat. The friendship formed by Aalto with Lurçat in summer

51. *Aalto in 1928 in front of Le Corbusier's villa in Garches, completed in 1927, photo Aino Aalto.*

52. *Aalto and Lurçat in Paris 1928, photo Aino Aalto.*

1928 was certainly not based on Catholic leanings or even on political agreement. Lurçat was a professed Communist who worked in the Soviet Union for several years in the '30s, never failing to contact Aalto on his way there through Finland. More probably, temperamental factors and Aalto's attraction to Mediterranean culture accounted for the friendship. Lurçat was an extroverted and humorous person, in complete temperamental opposition to Le Corbusier.

Lurçat presumably told Aalto of the important architectural meeting to be held a few days later at the castle of La Sarraz in Switzerland. Lurçat was going there to sign the founding document of CIAM together with Le Corbusier, who was returning from Moscow for the occasion, and several other progressive colleagues. This organization, the *Congrès Internationaux d'Architecture Moderne,* was soon to be of the utmost importance to Aalto, too, but that summer he was still an unknown provincial whom nobody would have dreamed of inviting to this summit of celebrities.

In the absence of Le Corbusier, Aalto thus talked in his rather halting French with André Lurçat, was shown the latter's new houses in Paris, and was particularly impressed by a window in upside-down L shape designed by Lurçat for a hotel. This window was converted by Aalto a few months later into one of the main themes of his competition entry for Paimio Sanatorium.

Alvar and Aino managed a short detour through the south of France before returning to their work in Turku. The whole itinerary of their trip to Holland and France may seem surprisingly badly planned, considering the really exciting architectural experiences they missed in Germany. After all, Markelius had visited both the Weissenhof Exhibition in Stuttgart and the Bauhaus school building in Dessau the previous summer. Erik Bryggman visited the same places in the summer of 1928, and went on to Frankfurt, where Ernst May was busy building his epoch-

MOTTO:

53. Aalto's winning entry for the Paimio Sanatorium. The motto of the entry was Lurçat's window, originally to be used for the patients' rooms, but omitted at the construction stage.

making residential block for workers. Why did the Aaltos prefer the considerably less exciting western Europe? The answer is that they were more ambitious than Bryggman. They wanted to meet the Dutch pioneers and Le Corbusier first, and then make a study tour of Germany later that autumn. These plans, however, had to be postponed. Apart from their running assignments, a number of architectural competitions were announced, and Aalto plunged in with a will. First there was the highly controversial design competition for the Olympic Stadium in Helsinki, which was also to function as an independence monument (last date of entry, November 25), then the competition for Vallila Church (January 15, 1929), and finally the demanding competition for the Southwestern Finland Tuberculosis Sanatorium (January 31, 1929). Germany would have to wait; the impulses received in Holland and France would have to suffice.

And so they did. During the late autumn, Aalto designed the Paimio Sanatorium, today considered the classic example of European Rationalism together with Gropius's Bauhaus. This he accomplished without ever having seen the Bauhaus or met its chief exponents.

ENCOUNTER WITH CIAM

The international congress of modern architects, which I mentioned in connection with Aalto's visit to Lurçat

in Paris, owed its origin to fellow-feeling between the scattered representatives of Modern architecture, which found expression in the great exhibition of the Deutscher Werkbund in Stuttgart in 1927. The chief architect of the exhibition, Ludwig Mies van der Rohe, invited a number of radical architects from various European countries to design a residential block of their own as a model for future construction. So the first meeting between Modernist architects from various countries came about: Le Corbusier for French, Oud and Mart Stam for Dutch, and Josef Frank for Austrian Modernism; Gropius for the Bauhaus School; and independent German architects such as Mies himself, Peter Behrens, Hans Poelzig, Bruno Taut and Hans Scharun, took part in designing the famous Siedlung Weissenhof with its individual but coordinated buildings. The feeling these pioneering European architects had of belonging to a common cultural front was strengthened by the bitter controversy over the competition for the Palace of the League of Nations in Geneva, in which Le Corbusier's overwhelmingly superior entry was passed over for a building in the tired style of academic Classicism. The final decision was made in March 1928, and gave rise to a flood of protest from all progressive architects. Le Corbusier was still a Swiss citizen, and Professor Karl Moser, the Swiss representative on the jury, had fought hard on behalf of his compatriot.

The first CIAM meeting took place

58

54. La Sarraz, Hélène de Mandrot's castle, photo 1933.

on June 26–28 at the Château La Sarraz in Switzerland. The invitation had come from the owner of the castle, Hélène de Mandrot (1866–1948), a wealthy lady with cultural aspirations, who spent her time travelling back and forth between the great cultural centres and fashionable holiday resorts of Europe, and who liked to gather artists and authors around her. As chance would have it, Le Corbusier had been her guest in Paris, where she used to spend a few months every winter, and she had contracted a lively interest in Modern architecture and the attractive young men who were behind it. Professor Moser from Zurich helped her compile a list of the architects to be invited. There were nine Frenchmen, two Belgians, five Swiss, five Italians, one Spaniard, seven Germans, four Dutchmen, two Austrians, four Czechs, one Pole, and one Yugoslav on the list – a rather mixed lot that did, however, include the principal Modernists; above all, one of the 'men of the press' invited was Siegfried Giedion from Zurich, who became the energetic secretary and influential ideologue of CIAM, an organizing talent who gave the organization its direction.

Only twenty-four architects arrived for the first CIAM meeting, but its membership grew rapidly. No one could become a member on his own initiative; a formal invitation, extended only to persons with the right kind of attitude, was required. There was not a single Scandinavian among the founding members, though Sven Markelius, as we have seen, had visited the Bauhaus in 1927 and made the acquaintance of Gropius when the latter lectured in Stockholm in spring 1928. In February 1929 Markelius received a letter from Karl Moser, the president of CIAM, inviting him to become a member and asking him whether he could recommend any other suitable Nordic architects. Markelius suggested Alvar Aalto in Turku and Poul Henningsen in Copenhagen. Thus we see that the bridge by which Aalto reached the international arena was provided by Sweden and specifically by his

55. The participants of the first CIAM congress at La Sarraz in 1928. Madame de Mandrot in the centre, with the bespectacled Le Corbusier on her right.

friendship with Markelius. In autumn 1929 Aalto and Sven Markelius travelled together to the second CIAM meeting, held in Frankfurt on October 24—26, with the theme *Die Wohnung für das Existenzminimum,* or approximately, 'housing for low-income earners'.

Another member of the Stockholm set to which Markelius and Aalto belonged also went to Frankfurt. The art critic Gotthard Johansson became perhaps the most eloquent spokesman of Functionalism in Scandinavia. It is true that Aalto and Markelius also commented on their experiences in interviews and travel reports, but they confined themselves to the bare facts. Johansson's account of the emotions of the Nordic participants, published in 1940 in a retrospect entitled "The 1930s in memoriam", had a more personal ring:

I am one of those who crossed the threshold to the '30s with a new, liber- *ating feeling that the spirits had awakened and it was a joy to be alive. For the first time I felt I was living in an age which I could wholly accept as my own, and found myself almost to my own surprise in the midst of a battle of ideas in which I knew my place instinctively and had the great happiness of standing in a united front with people who saw and felt the same way as I did.*

An exciting expedition in my memory is a trip I made in late autumn 1929 to a Europe which I had never seen in a greyer season. The rain hung like a grey yoke over Berlin's endless landscape of tenements, the clay clumped up underfoot on the muddy construction sites of Cologne and Karlsruhe . . . But I have never seen Europe brighter than during that dark, wet autumn.

This light phenomenon was the vision of a city of the future conjured up by Frankfurt's leading town planner Ernst May in his model suburbs Römerstadt and Praunheim.

Did not I myself catch a glimpse of it [= the city of the future] *when I stood on a hilltop in Frankfurt am Main with the participants of an international congress of architects over which the spirit of Le Corbusier hovered, and like Moses gazed from the mountain of Nebo to the Promised Land – a dreamlike city of white building masses in the distance, rising like a fairytale castle amidst the green slopes? But I had also seen at close quarters that this dream city was not a mere deceptive illusion, not even a monumental architect's dream, but a town for ordinary people who had moved from the slum quarters of the big city out into light, air and verdure. The dream city was a modern housing development with small flats.*

For the three friends, May's 'Siedlungen' *were an almost symbolic expression of the will to solve the social problems of the new age with the aid of its own technology. Was it not symptomatic of Europe's recovery from the long post-war sufferings, and of the re-*turn of reason to the world in which so much more than just the buildings needed reconstruction?

At this CIAM meeting Aalto encountered for the first time the élite of the new architecture, headed by Le Corbusier, Gropius, Karl Moser, and Siegfried Giedion. We have a lively account in a letter Aalto sent home to Turku:

Dear Aino, Mossi and Veikko [the last two were Aalto's children, aged 4 and nearly 2 at the time]. *The congress has been in full swing since yesterday. It's very much more interesting than I expected. There are such extremely friendly and straightforward people here, about 100, some of them have come all the way from Japan and America. You should have come after all. You would have cut a magnificent figure beside the one or two skinny female architects here. Markelius and I are counted among the big animals, I was just elected to the international committee* [CIRPAC] *which is having its first session now. Stein Holz Eisen seems to be a world power – I didn't have to come here as a stray dog, but have been treated like a son right from the start. President Moser has asked about you and sends his best regards. And so do many others. Joseph Frank's wife is from Turku! J.F. also sends you regards. The Hungarians, too, have asked about you. At the official banquet offered by the City of Frankfurt, Gropius and his wife and Molnar* [Hungary] *sat at our table. Gropius's wife invited you to stay with them in Berlin. A tremendously relaxed and pleasant atmosphere here. The congress takes all my time – can barely make it to the barber's. The secretary of the meeting* [Giedion] *has invited Markelius, Hannes Meyer and me to lunch. Daddy here is thinking of Mummy and the poor dears all the time. Alvar.*

What Aalto says about the German architectural journal *Stein Holz Eisen* is significant. Its editor, Otto Völckers, had alertly asked Aalto to send photographs of the standard block of flats completed that spring in Turku and of

56. *View of Ernst May's Siedlung Römerstadt in Frankfurt, completed 1929.*

the Turun Sanomat building under construction. Völckers proceeded to publish the photos with favourable comments in the October issue of the magazine, giving Aalto the best introduction imaginable to the congress.

We see from the letter that Aalto had come into contact mainly with German-speaking CIAM members. He seems to have got on particularly well with Gropius, who was a full 15 years older and, with his many imposing buildings from the pre-war period as well as from the Bauhaus days, must have appeared as the leader of Modern architecture. Gropius had left his post as director of the Bauhaus in 1928 and moved from Dessau to Berlin, where he was occupied with extensive *Siedlung* projects. Aalto visited him in Berlin in 1930 and 1931, and they went to see various new buildings together. Their intellectual exchange became particularly lively when Gropius returned to Stockholm to give a lecture in 1931, and they both stayed at Markelius's new villa in Nockeby.

As far as the Bauhaus is concerned, the paradoxical fact is that, owing to his friendship with Gropius, Aalto never set foot in the famous building in which Gropius's successor Hannes Meyer was director from summer 1928 to spring 1930, when the post was assigned to Mies van der Rohe, who was not one of Aalto's friends either. Yet it is clear that the Bauhaus had a much more profound impact on Aalto than a mere passing visit to the school itself ever could have done. Gropius's personality and the Frankfurt 'minimum housing' exhibition were two obvious sources of this influence, but there was an even more important one to which I will return in a later chapter, namely, Laszlo Moholy-Nagy, thanks to whom the Bauhaus became very much a living reality to Aalto.

THE STOCKHOLM EXHIBITION

The social connections Aalto had formed in Frankfurt in 1929 were revived during the 1930 Stockholm Exhibition. In fact Aalto was not directly involved in this event, which was a purely Swedish effort, but he was almost as strongly committed to it emotionally as were Gunnar Asplund, Gregor Paulsson, Sven Markelius and Uno Åhren. He was naturally present at the opening ceremony, to which the continental friends of Modern architecture also flocked to forge optimistic plans for the future. Naturally enough, they all interpreted the exhibition in their own ways and sought to confirm their own beliefs. Aalto's anarchism did not desert him in Stockholm: it was the festive freedom of the event that interested him, whereas the dogmatists rejoiced at its more ideological aspects. Here is Aalto's comment on his return to Finland:

When I arrived at the official opening of the Stockholm Exhibition, I did not do so as a foreigner who hopes to see something new. I had followed the work of those responsible for the arrangements from the drawing of the very first guidelines to the final result. So I went around looking at things as 'a friend of the exhibition', not admiring at random, but as one whose relationship with the subject is on a deeper level.

The exhibition speaks out for joyful and spontaneous everyday life. It consistently propagates a healthy and unpretentious lifestyle based on economic realities. We may speak of surgery in the sense that what is being removed is the appendix which contains man's lust for luxury and affected superficiality.

I am very glad that Gunnar Asplund has hit the mark with this denial of architecture, pointing the way towards a philosophy which never brought architecture any laurels before . . . The deliberate social message which the Stockholm Exhibition is intended to convey is expressed in the architectural language of pure, spontaneous joy. There is a festive elegance, but also a childlike uninhibitedness about it all. Asplund's architecture breaks free of all limitations; the objective is a feast, and it is not predetermined whether it

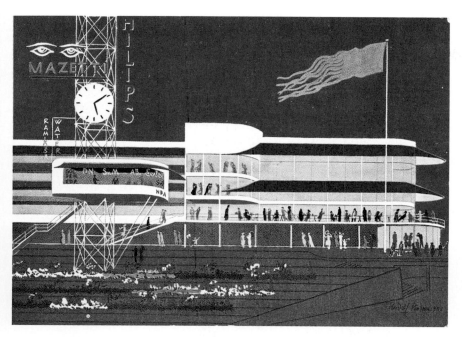

57. Stockholm exhibition 1930.
Postcard view of main
restaurant.

58. Stockholm exhibition 1930.
"A composition of houses, flags,
flowers and happy people".

will be reached architecturally or by any other means that might offer themselves. This is not a composition of stone, glass and iron, as a visitor who despises Functionalism might imagine; it is a composition of houses, flags, floodlights, flowers, fireworks, happy people and clean tablecloths . . . Whoever goes around criticizing architecture merely on the basis of road axes and facade angles – whether he arrives at a positive or negative conclusion in his little head – will never find the mentality which was the driving force of this enterprise.

Aalto sums up as follows: *Kritisk Revy* once published a picture of the Tivoli gardens: paper lanterns in the trelliswork above a café table. The caption was: eternal values. The Stockholm Exhibition has the same eternal value in its entire physiognomy. "As a concerted effect no other exhibition can compete with this", Siegfried Giedion told the author. "I think that Weissenhof [= the Stuttgart exhibition in 1927] *was historically more important, but Stockholm . . ."* I quite agree.

There is no mistaking the note of pride about his new friends among the CIAM élite. For Aalto the Stockholm Exhibition was a party at which he strengthened the social ties he had formed the year before and won many new friends among international architects and critics. His vital personality, flashing wit and harlequin social talent made him a noticed and popular figure everywhere he went. The bright summer nights of the North were an unforgettable experience for the visitors from central and southern Europe, and Aalto was the mischievous Pan of their late night revels.

In the British critic P. Morton Shand, Aalto discovered a kindred spirit with a taste for life and a feeling for quick repartee that rivalled his own. Morton Shand was one of the most influential architecture critics in Britain, and his enthusiastic articles in the reputable *Architectural Review* contributed significantly to the international fame of the Stockholm Exhibition. As it happened, he spoke and wrote German like a native. Much later Aalto concocted the story that Shand had been set down on the German coast during the First World War and had worked as a spy in the Kaiser's realm, but this was a typical Aalto myth in which the only shred of truth was the fact that Shand had an excellent knowledge of German. For Aalto, who spoke no English at all at the time, this was a most fortunate coincidence. Shand soon became a great admirer of Aalto's work, and played a significant role in his success in the international arena. The many long and highly entertaining letters by Shand in the Aalto archives testify to a growing friendship that culminated in Athens and London in 1933.

Giedion, whose duties as CIAM secretary had prevented him from seeking closer contact with Aalto the year before in Frankfurt, seems to have been drawn completely into the magic circle of Aalto's charm in Stockholm, and he remained a loyal friend through the years. The same goes for his wife Carola Giedion-Welcker, who was well acquainted with the leading artists of the European avant-garde, including James Joyce, Constantin Brancusi, Piet Mondrian and Max Ernst. Giedion's talent was not in the field of humour and imagination; he was a serious and methodical person who was probably mainly responsible for the increasingly narrow academicism that the CIAM movement developed over the years. Aalto, however, was immune to such influences, and he brought off the feat of retaining Giedion's regard although he was a very irregular participant at CIAM meetings, and when there he systematically sabotaged them with his whims. In the expanded edition of his famous book *Space, Time and Architecture,* published in 1949, Giedion staked all of his authority as chief ideologue of the Rationalist movement on presenting Aalto as a genius, even though Aalto's architecture did not fit very well into his pattern.

The opening ceremony of the Stockholm Exhibition ended for the Aaltos and many other Nordic guests with an eventful car journey through Sweden and the Norwegian fells to a Nordic architects' congress held in Trondheim. Both of Aalto's bosom friends, Asplund and Markelius, took part in the 'procession'. Alvar and Aino travelled in their own Buick, with their colleagues Hilding Ekelund and Aili Salli Ahde as passengers. They had more than their share of adversity: they crashed in Alvsjö, just out of Stockholm, then on a Norwegian mountain road they went into the ditch when Alvar instinctively steered as far away from the edge of the cliff as possible. Everyone took it all in good part, however, until on the return trip the group arrived in Oslo, where the jealous Aino threw out her female colleague and the trip continued in a less cheerful mood. We should remember that they were all young people in their early thirties, full of irrepressible vitality.

Trondheim had been selected as the venue for the meeting because the town's new Institute of Technology had a very lively architecture department. The culture columnist of the local newspaper *Nidaros* was also unusually familiar with the new architecture, and published such a detailed and comprehensive interview with Aalto on June 28 that there is reason to suspect that the two gentlemen wrote it together. In fact, this interview is the most exhaustive document preserved on a theme that Aalto discussed in lectures to the Swedish Association of Engineers and Architects (November 18, 1929) and the Finnish Association of Architects (annual meeting on February 16, 1932). Nothing but the title of these lectures remains: "Non-synthetic aspirations in architecture". In the summer of 1930 Aalto corresponded with Otto Völckers, the editor of *Stein Holz Eisen,* about publishing a book in Germany with the same title, *nicht synthetische bestrebungen in der architectur* (in accordance with Bauhaus principles, there were to be no capital letters in the book). The book was never published, and the manuscript has been lost. The *Nidaros* interview is thus important as a key to Aalto's early

59. Alvar and Aino Aalto on the way to the architects' congress in Trondheim, 1930.

Aalto was not the man to let the promising contacts formed with his Continental colleagues in Stockholm cool from too long a hiatus. In the autumn of 1930 he went to Berlin with Aino to meet Gropius and Moholy-Nagy. Gropius followed them to Frankfurt, where a number of CIAM delegates, including S. Giedion, K. Moser, G. Rietveld, H. Häring, E. May, R. Neutra, Mart Stam, and H. Schmidt, met at the Palmgarten on September 25. Aalto went on to Zurich with Moser and Giedion, and even managed to squeeze in a visit to Hans and Lilli Schmidt in Berne. They were preparing to emigrate to the Soviet Union; I will return later to their visit to Turku in 1932.

On this occasion Alvar also seems to have had the opportunity to charm Hélène de Mandrot, who soon became one of his most ardent admirers, judging by the countless letters in the Aalto archives from this key figure in the history of modern architecture. No doubt it called for great finesse, good humour and warm human understanding to hold an emotional balance with this eccentric, spoilt woman, who was reaching the threshold of old age: at one moment she expected her young protégés to treat her like Marlene Dietrich; the next, like the great lady she still was.

Aalto was never a spontaneous letter writer. Both his close friends and people who came into professional contact with him complained of his tendency to leave their letters unanswered or to reply inexcusably late. He must have had to do outright violence to himself in late autumn 1930 to force himself to concoct the necessary polite thank-you letters to the friends he had just visited. Since copies of outgoing letters are rare in the chaotic Aalto archives, these must have been considered especially important.

To Karl Moser, the 70-year-old president of CIAM, for whom Aalto had

uncritically Functionalist philosophy of architecture. I shall return to it in the more theoretical section of this book, and merely quote the opening lines here:

Trondheim was recently visited by an architect who is perhaps the most important Functionalist in northern Europe, a man who has worked along the new lines with the most interesting tools and the clearest results. He is the Finnish architect Alvar Aalto from Turku, one of the participants at the congress of Nordic architects.

This is the first time that Aalto was recognized as a leading force in Scandinavian architecture. The genuineness of his Norwegian colleagues' interest is shown by the invitation he received to lecture at the Architects' Association in Oslo, which he did on April 9, 1931.

great esteem for more reasons than one, he wrote:

Dear Papa Moser. After our return home our first thoughts turn to you. The generous hospitality and consideration you showed us in Frankfurt and Zurich make our thoughts fly to the only fixed spot on Earth where we know there are men who consecrate all their efforts to an international task.

Our thoughts linger in Zurich, but point to the future — we are thinking of our 'next trip'. This consoles us in our efforts to build houses for people whose brains will not comprehend the real meaning of the organic trend in the next 50 years. We hope to be able to return to Zurich next winter, and I am already rejoicing at the thought of seeing you there again. We liked your work very much. It taught us so much, and above all it gave us the courage to strive forward even more resolutely . . . Our warmest regards to your charming wife, your daughter and your son. Your ever grateful Alvar and Aino.

The tone of the letter to Gropius is a good deal more familiar:

Dear Gropius, We thank you for the pleasant days in Frankfurt and Berlin. We hope to be able to return soon in spite of the extra work we gave Mrs. Gropius in her capacity as Berlin's best hairdresser. The fact is that we are eagerly looking forward to our 'next time with the Gropiuses', while trying to make buildings for people into whose heads the 'organic line' will not fit for another 100 years. We know with astronomical certainty that the only fixed point of our collegial life is in international work. Our private statistics indicate that it isn't possible to find companions among the three million who surround us. Three million is too little . . . Our heartfelt thanks to you both.

Aalto wrote the longest and most intimate letter after receiving a reminder — to Giedion (owing to his dyslexia, he misspelled the name):

My dear Gideon. You call me a morose mute. Mute I may be, but not morose. Here we have been fabricating wonderful drafts for days and weeks in order to send you a truly intellectual letter. Being intellectual, however, is just as difficult as designing a minimum apartment — so we failed. We are so happy about the wonderful hospitality you showed us in Zurich that it really would have been difficult to find the right words to thank the Gideon family. If you could see a psychoanalytical diagnosis of the people we meet here, you might have an idea of the value we place on the days we had the good fortune of spending with you and our other friends in Zurich.

I now come to the realities, those damned realities which make up our work. They are in fair order, but too many at the moment. Some silly people fixed the opening date of an exhibition on 'rationalization of the small apartment', which was confided to me last spring, at the 29th of this month [November] *which means I am up to my ears in work and therefore unable to tell you whether I will have any chance of coming to Brussels* [where CIAM held its third meeting on November 22–27]. *Things looks rather dark, however* [In fact Aalto did not go to Brussels, but sent some imaginary town plan sketches of a Turku that never existed], *since the exhibition is very important though small. This is the first time we're out in the open. In fact we're on the way to achieving a functional combination of 'creative force and industry', but everything depends on the opening on the 29th. As for my iron window* [which Aalto had promised to send to the CIAM exhibition in Brussels], *I have done all I could. The factory's last word is: it will be sent on Friday. We have an economic crisis and demagogic politics here in Finland, which makes the firms cautious. I hope the window will make it to Brussels in time* [it did not]. *Pictures of my cinema* [in the Jyväskylä Defence Corps Building] *will arrive in a few days. Regards to your extremely charming wife. Madame Aino sends her love to you both. When we come back in the winter, we shall spend a longer time in Switzerland — after all, one must torment*

60. Paimio Sanatorium.
Perspective drawing of 'B'
building, east elevation.

one's friends. Cheerio!

The plans for going to Switzerland in the winter should hardly be taken seriously. As usual, Aalto was overloaded with work, from which he had stolen the time for his previous trips with great difficulty. Up to 1933 his main assignment was the enormous sanatorium project in Paimio, with everything that it involved in the way of special planning, interior design, service buildings, etc., but in 1930 he was also working on the Minimum Apartment Exhibition, as we have seen. Fur-

61. *Model of Toppila sulphite pulp mill in Oulu, 1930.*

thermore, he took part in competitions for the Mänttä headquarters of the big industrial company Serlachius (last date of entry February 12), for a water tower in Turku (February 28), for a sports institute in Vierumäki (March 31), for the siting of the Olympic Stadium in Helsinki (April 30), for Tehtaanpuisto Church in Helsinki (November 15) and for a large hospital complex in Zagreb (January 15, 1931). All this bears witness to his volcanic creativity during 1930, especially as we must add to these a number of minor assignments, including the interiors for the Itämeri restaurant and the stage design for Hagar Olsson's pacifist play *SOS,* both in Turku, and the major task of designing the many buildings for the Toppila sulphite pulp mill in Oulu.

It is amazing, under these conditions, that Aalto found time to get away from the drawing board at all.

MINIMUM APARTMENT EXHIBITION IN 1930

Among the many assignments described above, the Minimum Apart-ment Exhibition in Helsinki was a relatively minor event, but had perhaps the most far-reaching consequences in that it provided the impetus for Aalto's furniture design. The exhibition, of which Aalto was in charge, opened in late November at the Helsinki Art Hall. It included an apartment interior designed by Aalto down to the smallest detail, consisting of a kitchen, a living room and two bedrooms. The exhibition also contained a large living room interior designed by Erik Bryggman and a hotel room by Pauli and Märta Blomstedt. The theme was taken straight from the Frankfurt exhibition *Die Wohnung für das Existenz-minimum,* and the presentation – a stage set interior seen over a breast-height wall – was borrowed from an exhibition in Munich the year before.

The leading position held by Aalto from this date on in Finnish architecture was not least due to his close contacts with foreign colleagues and his knowledge of what was happening on the Continent. Naturally this gave rise to some distrust among his more provincial colleagues, as can be seen from the following comments by Hilding Ekelund in an article on the Minimum Apartment Exhibition in *Hufvudstadsbladet*:

With the same fiery enthusiasm as the academic architects of old copied Roman Baroque portals, Gothic finials, etc., Alvar Aalto sniffs out rational technical innovations from all four corners of Europe, and adroitly proceeds to utilize them by recasting. It is a pity that ingenuity and a certain super-mechanization occasionally dominate in his furnishing details.

Aalto's dependence on foreign ideas is incontestable, as is the fact that the problems he set out to solve were in many cases those formulated by his foreign colleagues, mainly the Bauhaus pioneers. The minimum apartment; standardization permitting maximum variety; the elastic, or gro-

wing, building; functionally designed serial furniture; the physiologically satisfactory lamp; these were examples of the goals Gropius and his associates had set down in their writings long before Aalto's time. What differentiated Aalto from the many epigones of Rationalism was that he was not content merely to produce variations on ideas borrowed from Continental colleagues, but created his own solutions, which were often better than those of his forerunners.

As far as the Exhibition was concerned, Aalto's ambition to make an independent contribution appeared, among other things, in the striking series of 'inventions' that were listed in the exhibition catalogue and reached such an advanced stage that the manufacturer's name was quoted for many of them. Aalto's kitchen contain-

62. Minimum Apartment Exhibition in Helsinki Art Hall, 1930. Aalto's living room in the background.

ed the following type products: a new kind of waste grinder, a special sink, an ingenious rubbish trolley, a complete set of kitchen cupboards, a practical spice rack, an inventive shelf for pots and pans, and an unprecedented carving board. Type objects in the living room included linked iron windows (so original that Aalto was asked to send a sample to the CIAM exhibition in Brussels that year), a dinner table, a sideboard on wheels, a serial bookshelf with a folding desktop, a pendant lamp, and a table lamp. The bedroom contained a window combining iron and wood parts, and at the technical stand Aalto displayed a rubber stepladder, a lockable doorknob, an original system of sheet metal mouldings, and a new compound material for wall surfaces, 'rubber linoleum'.

Aalto's inventions were thus not restricted to furniture, although that may be the most interesting feature of the exhibition as far as we are concerned. Photographs show that Aalto had further developed his hybrid chair of 1929 by giving the tubular steel leg a bend that made it stackable. Around the dinner table were the by now familiar stackable wooden chairs reminiscent of Art Nouveau. The real novelty was a couch made of metal tubes, which stood in the living room and could be easily converted into a spacious, comfortable bed (see F 251).

Aalto sent photos of the exhibition to Zurich to his newly recruited CIAM friend Siegfried Giedion, who had just founded the Wohnbedarf furniture firm and a wholesaling agency called Palag. Giedion was very excited about the stackable hybrid chair, which he called in a letter to Aalto "the egg of Columbus for tubular steel chairs in restaurants, bars and cafés". On his advice, Aalto applied for a patent for the bent leg. Giedion immediately acquired rights for Wohnbedarf to manufacture the hybrid chair and convertible couch. In early 1931 Aalto sent prototypes, which were modified slightly by Giedion before starting production (F 35). The plywood for the

hybrid chair was imported from Finland, and the chair was sold not only by Wohnbedarf but also by Thonet Mundus in Germany. Thus, three years after ordering Breuer chairs from Thonet, Aalto had himself become Breuer's rival within the same world-famous company.

LASZLO MOHOLY-NAGY, FRIEND AND INSPIRER

1931 was a rather quiet year for the Aalto office, with only one major competition, the Lallukka artists' home in Helsinki (last date of entry March 31). But it was an important, in fact decisive, year in Aalto's efforts to create a new kind of standard furniture. His travels and foreign contacts during 1931 played a significant role in his success.

Aalto had been elected at the Frankfurt meeting in 1929 to the innermost circle of CIAM, the Comité International pour la Résolution des Problèmes de l'Architecture Contemporaine (CIRPAC), the purpose of which was to prepare the meetings of CIAM. A CIRPAC meeting was called in Berlin on June 4–6, 1931, where two building exhibitions, the great Deutsche Bauausstellung and a protest event called Proletarische Bauausstellung, were opening simultaneously. Gropius, Mies van der Rohe and Marcel Breuer made outstanding contributions to the official building exhibition, at which Finland also had a small corner (though Aalto was not represented). The growing political tension in Germany was, however, beginning to cast a dark shadow over the architectural debate. The Nazis were infuriated by the direct protest made by the proletarian exhibition against the housing shortage, and proceeded to counterattack against the entire phalanx of progressive architects. The flat roof began to be considered a sign of Bolshevism.

Aalto travelled to Berlin both to see the exhibitions and to take part in the CIRPAC meeting. Although he spent some time with the Gropiuses and Mar-

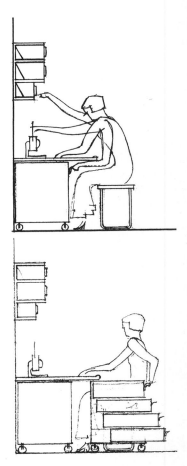

63. Housewife working, seated in front of sliding units in the minimum apartment kitchen.

cel Breuer, a new friend, Laszlo Moholy-Nagy, now claimed most of his attention.

The two men had already met at the CIAM congress in 1929, and they had renewed their acquaintance in Berlin in 1930. Aalto's stage design for Hagar Olsson's pacifist play *SOS* at the Turku Theatre in 1930 shows the influence of Moholy's famous sets for *The Tales of Hoffmann* at the Kroll Opera in Berlin in 1929. Aalto managed to incorporate a few of the effects with projected images later used by Moholy in his stage designs for Piscator from 1930 to 1933. The claim that Moholy might have imitated a trick of Aalto's that he had never had the opportunity of seeing is naturally indefensible. The explanation must be that Moholy had shared his ideas with Aalto, and the latter had got the chance to apply them first.

This, one is tempted to say, pedagogic tendency of Moholy's was typical of his relationships with other people. His versatile, generous personality, overflowing with ideas, had an impact on Aalto that has been given far too little attention up to now, so I think it is time to make a detour in my story of Aalto's development in order to draw the portrait of this extraordinary man.

Laszlo Moholy-Nagy (1895–1946) was only three years older than Aalto, but had managed to gather a far more extensive assortment of experiences and avant-garde cultural ideas than the stagnant Nordic idyll had offered to his friend. He fought in the First World War as an artillery officer, studied law in Budapest, then abjured his bourgeois background and became a painter. Like other left-wing intellectuals, he was involved in the Communist revolution of Bela Kun, and had to emigrate when the Conservative forces took over again in Hungary. From 1920 on, he lived in the midst of the lively cultural set of Berlin, exhibited his paintings at Herbert Walden's gallery, *Der Sturm,* and was closely involved in no less than three different progressive art movements. As an East European

64. *Sets for Hagar Olsson's* SOS *at the Turku Finnish Theatre by Alvar Aalto, 1930.*

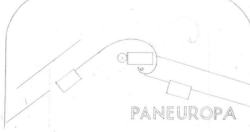

65. *Sets for* Hoffman's Tales *at the Kroll Opera in Berlin by Laszlo Moholy-Nagy, 1929.*

he was strongly attracted to Russian Constructivism, and tackled much the same problems as did Malevich and Lissitzky in their art; he was close to the Dadaists through his friendship with Schwitters, Arp and Picabia; and finally he allied himself with Theo van Doesburg, from whom he learned the formal composition principles of the De Stijl group.

All of this combined to give Moholy's art an anti-individualist character aiming at objectivity, while it also aroused his interest in rational experiments in form, modern technology and new media. With these qualities, he was exactly the man Gropius needed in 1923 to help him reform the Bauhaus School in conformity with the spirit of the age.

Gropius founded the Bauhaus in Weimar in 1919. Instruction was based on the *lernen durch tun* (learn by doing) principle, which meant that handicraft was taught through practical contact with materials and forms. This pedagogical method broke with the traditional academic study of given formal schemes, but the school's goals remained conservative; like Morris and the prophets of Art Nouveau, the Bauhaus aimed at a rebirth of handicraft, which was menaced by industry, and cherished the idea that art is an expression of the individual personality. In other words, the early Bauhaus had a Romantic, backward-looking character at a time when innovative artists in Russia, Holland and France were already discovering the idiom of the future industrial society. After a few years this discrepancy gave rise to criticism from outside and revolt from within. In 1923 Gropius realized that he must give the school a new direction. In this dilemma he turned to the 28-year-old Moholy-Nagy and invited him to take the school's basic course in hand and to coordinate the industrially oriented metals workshop.

The school's previous slogan, "Back to handicraft", was replaced by a new one: "Integration of art and industry." Instead of considering industry to be incompatible with art, the Bauhaus accepted it for what it is: a further development or rationalization of handicraft. The new goal was to make the pupils equally familiar with the potential of industrial materials and

66. *Gropius's Bauhaus School in Dessau, 1925–26.*

*67. Moholy-Nagy and Ellen
Frank in Finland, 1931.*

In 1933 the school was closed down by the Nazis, and several of its teachers were forced to emigrate from the country that called them "cultural Bolsheviks". It was a tragic end that, paradoxically, had fortunate consequences for other countries: the refugee intellectuals from the Weimar Republic disseminated German cultural impulses throughout the world, not least in the United States. The Bauhaus had been wiped out, but its ideas lived on.

A particular aspect of Moholy's wide-ranging impact on the Bauhaus from 1923 to 1928 should be emphasized. He seems to have been an inexhaustible source of inspiration to the people around him. He was a born teacher, and he strewed his ideas around him generously, never thinking of guarding them jealously for himself. His pupils and closest subordinates appear as creative geniuses, rather than Moholy himself. It may be difficult to determine the debt of gratitude his pupil Marcel Breuer owed him, but it is an incontestable fact that Breuer's famous Wassily chair, named after Kandinsky, who also taught at the Bauhaus, was created two years after Moholy became the director of the school's joinery workshop. Herbert Bayer has reaped all the honour for the revolution in typography and advertising connected with the Bauhaus, but it was his teacher Moholy who first defined this style and even designed the famous layout of the Bauhaus books. Even Josef Albers, who took experimentation with materials on the basic course furthest, and developed teaching methods that are used in schools of design around the world today, was Moholy's pupil for two years before becoming his colleague.

I wish to emphasize this pedagogical aspect of Moholy's personality before returning to his relationship with Aalto and the phase in their friendship heralded by Aalto's visit to Berlin in summer 1931. A little before that, Moholy (who in his younger days was quite as much of a lady-killer as Aalto) had left his first wife Lucia, a photogra-

manufacturing techniques as with clay and wood, the potter's wheel and the handsaw. Artistic control would then spring from technical proficiency. This new programme transformed the Bauhaus into the first school of modern design, imitated by innumerable industrial art schools around the world up to our day.

We need not dwell on the later fortunes of the Bauhaus. Suffice it to note that in 1925 the school was moved to Dessau, where Gropius erected his famous building, and that political tensions between the liberal Gropius and the orthodox Marxists had the result that Gropius – and Moholy-Nagy, Marcel Breuer and Herbert Bayer soon after him – left the school, leaving the directorship to Hannes Meyer. In spring 1930, however, Meyer was forced to seek refuge in Moscow with twelve of his students, and Mies van der Rohe attempted to steer the school back onto its old liberal course. But time was running out for the vision represented by the Bauhaus in Germany.

pher who had initiated him to the secrets of the art of photography, and was living with Ellen Frank, a well-known and charming actress. In Berlin, Aalto depicted the fascination of the northern summer and the beauty of Finland in such glowing colours that Moholy and Ellen were possessed by the desire to see this miracle with their own eyes. Why not go to Finland during their approaching summer holidays and spend some more time with their cheerful Finnish friend?

So it was that Laszlo and Ellen arrived in their own car in Turku on June 3, 1931, where they were welcomed by Alvar and Aino. They toured the interior together via Savonlinna in the east to Oulu in the northwest, where Moholy photographed Aalto's newly completed factory buildings for the Toppila Pulp Mill. In Oulu their ways parted: the Aaltos drove down to Alajärvi for a family holiday, while Laszlo and Ellen left their car in Finland and set out for Oslo and Stockholm via the North Cape and the Norwegian fjords. After a few days with their mutual friend Markelius, they were back in Finland, where they picked up their car in order to return to Germany. As souvenirs of his trip, Moholy brought back an experimental film, a quantity of photographs, and an unforgettable memory of the mediaeval church of Hattula. A few years later he had a daughter with another woman, Sibyl – whom he married shortly afterwards – and christened her Hattula. Behind him he left a blue shirt for Alvar, which was the latter's favourite piece of clothing for many years. Aino wrote to Ellen to thank her and Laszlo "for having given us the summer's greatest joy with your visit".

Their association continued in Berlin, at Madame de Mandrot's in La Sarraz (the lady had almost as great a weakness for Moholy as for Aalto); in Athens, where the two friends took part in the most famous of all CIAM meetings; in London, where Moholy emigrated (without Ellen) in 1934; and in the United States, where Moholy became the director of the New Bau-

68. Detail of Toppila Mill, photo Moholy-Nagy, 1931.

74

haus in Chicago. Moholy gave Aalto many of his own books and a lithograph from his *Kestner Mappe* from 1922. Aalto liked to tell about how Moholy and Ellen were thrown out of a boardinghouse outside Turku when the owner discovered that they were not married. He also spoke of his fruitless search for Ellen during a visit to the devastated Berlin in the 1940s. But he never said a word about his discussions with Moholy, what he learned from him about work at the Bauhaus and about avant-garde art and radical ideas in Europe between the wars. Yet it is evident that his friendship with a man who was in many ways so centrally placed and well-informed must have made a profound impression on him. I am not speaking now of formal influences and external loans, but of creative impulses that helped Aalto define his own problems and find his own independent path.

The impact of the Bauhaus on Modern architecture throughout the world can hardly be exaggerated. The amalgam of Cubist style and technical engineering introduced by the school gave rise to the international architecture which is universal today. Since this architecture has obvious shortcomings, our attitude to the Bauhaus has become critical. A reassessment of the ideas disseminated by the Bauhaus teachers is in fact necessary, but sophistication is needed if we are to find a way through the maze of difficulties. I believe that at this point it is useful to take a closer look at how Aalto reacted to the Bauhaus programme.

Like most of his Scandinavian contemporaries, Aalto was more attracted by Gropius's matter-of-fact argumentation and social realism than by Le Corbusier's high-flown utopianism and elegant formal solutions. Aalto borrowed many theoretical ideas from Gropius, as I shall attempt to demonstrate in detail in the ideological section of this book. Aalto's designs were often quite close to those of his German colleague, as is shown by the staff housing in Paimio and his own villa in Munkkiniemi, both of which have obvi-

ous connections with Gropius's 'masters' houses' in Dessau. An important sector of Aalto's work, comprising standard housing, industrial architecture and prefabricated building, is in fact more or less in the Bauhaus mould. This is a socially responsible and honourable kind of architecture, which was praised as progressive in its time, but does not differ very much from what innumerable other contemporary architects produced. Had Aalto left nothing but this behind, he would have been a forgotten architect today.

There was, however, a completely different Aalto: the artist, the lyricist and the humanist. He did not have two entirely separate personalities; on the contrary, he tried obstinately to reconcile both aspects of his character, but in some works we only meet one or the other. Since the period was dominated by the concept of a great redemptive social utopia, Aalto strove for many years to develop the social architect within himself. It is all but a miracle that Aalto's indomitable artistic will made itself felt in spite of everything, and that he succeeded in smuggling so much nature lyricism and humanist emotion into his works during those years of dry Rationalism and reactionary public architecture.

The question is: what saved Aalto from sober Bauhaus realism? How did his artistic intuition find an outlet? The answer may seem surprising: it was in fact the Bauhaus influence that liberated this side of his character. More precisely, it was Moholy-Nagy, whose inventiveness and profound knowledge of the most vital artistic trends of the time placed him on a level far beyond the reach of the school's engineer souls.

A little before his visit to Finland, Moholy had published a book called *von material zu architektur* (translated as *The New Vision,* 1930), which included the lectures he had given at the Bauhaus basic course in 1923–28. Straight after his return to Berlin, he sent a copy of the book to Aalto, who wrote a letter of thanks in which he called the book "grossartig, klar und

69. Workers' housing in Sunila, ROT type, built 1938.

70. Villa Mairea: the indoor staircase – Aalto's nature lyricism at its purest. Photo: Lars Hallén.

71. *Artek's neon sign in 1936.*

72. *Moholy and Aalto on the beach near Naantali, 1931.*

Among the superficial influences we may also cite Aalto's stage design for the Turku Finnish Theatre in 1930 and his work as chairman of the Projektio film club after he moved to Helsinki in 1933. Moholy had made some classic experimental films back in the '20s, and he undoubtedly opened Aalto's eyes to the problems of the new art form.

These influences are rather peripheral and insufficient to give Moholy a central position in Aalto's development. Much more important was a whole series of impulses which were probably decisive for Aalto's career. It should of course be remembered that external 'influences' do not make an artist; what counts is that the receiver is the active party who discovers, assimilates and converts the nourishment he needs. If Aalto had never met Moholy, he presumably would have found similar nourishment from another source. As things turned out, the young architect, who was at an explosive stage in his development, received a concentrated dose of the most creative ideas European culture had to offer within the space of a few summer weeks. It may have been a greater feat for Aalto to make such intelligent use of Moholy's knowledge so fast than for Moholy to accumulate this knowledge over the years.

In the section on ideas, I shall return to two important insights that Moholy helped Aalto to achieve and apply with increasing success to his work. The first was the realization that architecture must take biological nature as its model, and the second was a new concept of open space. In this context, I shall merely point out a less auspicious and more practical lesson that was quite as momentous in Aalto's development, which he learned during Moholy's summer visit. To begin with, it only affected Aalto's furniture design.

In his old age, Aalto himself described his idea of making experimental reliefs from wood by referring to the Finnish aestheticist Yrjö Hirn's theory of play, which was in fact a résumé of

schön, vielleicht dein bestes buch'' (magnificent, lucid and beautiful, perhaps your best book). We may assume that the topics dealt with in *von material zu architektur* were crucial to the discussions between the two friends that summer.

It is easy enough to point out Aalto's superficial borrowings from Moholy. There is the Bauhaus trick of using only small letters, of starting sentences and writing names (and German nouns) in lower case. All of the books edited by Moholy for the Bauhaus have this typography, which was also common practice in the letters written by the Bauhaus set to their friends. Aalto adopted this fashion in his letters for a while, and when he designed the logo for his new firm, *artek,* in 1935, he followed the convention, which had become an emblem of progressive modernity, as a matter of course.

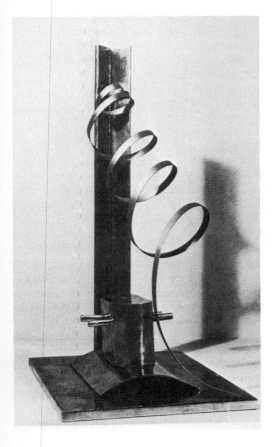

74. From Josef Albers's introductory course at the Bauhaus: corrugated board reliefs, c. 1928.

73. Moholy-Nagy: form experiment with nickle plate, 1921.

Schiller's ideas. According to this theory, play is one of the sources of art, and Aalto claimed that the learned professor's explanation had inspired him to 'play' with wood lamellae without preconceptions. In fact Aalto only became Hirn's friend in later years, and the reference sounds like a concealment of the debt he owed to the Bauhaus and Moholy, which was not very flattering to his self-esteem. It has already been pointed out that experiments with materials were pure routine for the basic courses taught by Moholy and Josef Albers, at which the students designed abstract works of art from the most variegated materials, from paper and steel thread to wood, steel plate and plexiglass. Both formally and theoretically the wooden reliefs Aalto started making with Korhonen in this very year, 1931, had a clear connection with the exercises with various materials performed at the Bauhaus. Naturally the realization that

Aalto learned a fruitful method from Moholy does not detract from his genius in any way. What is decisive, after all, is not the experiment or 'play' in itself, but the result of the experiment. Hundreds of Bauhaus students bent steel tubes into curious sculptures, but only Marcel Breuer had the idea of the Wassily chair. Let us take a look at what Aalto got from his experiments with wood.

THE WOODEN CHAIR PERFECTED

We may summarize the stage of development Aalto had reached in his furniture design at the time he became close with Moholy as follows: Otto Korhonen had made him familiar with the technical potential of moulded plywood, Marcel Breuer had impressed him with the elegance of his tubular steel furniture, the tactile inadequacy of which Poul Henningsen had, however, brought to his notice. He had therefore started experimenting with at least partly replacing the heat-conducting metal with wood, which in any case was a more interesting material for Finnish industry than steel. The hybrid chair provided a first tentative solution to these problems. Aalto attempted an alternative solution, doing away with steel tubes altogether, in the six entries he sent in autumn 1929 to the design competition arranged by the Berlin company Thonet Mundus in order to find new models to add to its prestigious collection.

Relations between Thonet and the new architecture were very close in those days. Le Corbusier was in the habit of furnishing his experimental exhibition buildings with ordinary 'Viennese' chairs, a solution imitated by Aalto when he exhibited a furnished model flat in his standard apartment block in Turku. Thonet's positive view of the Modern architects is shown by the fact that the jury for the 1929 furniture competition included Pierre Jeanneret (Le Corbusier's cousin), Josef Frank and Gerrit Rietveld.

Aalto's competition entry consisted of a simple chair, stackable according to Korhonen's patent, an armchair with two different sitting positions ('Arbeit-Ruhe'), a four-legged stool with the upper part in the same style as the hybrid chair (it had a similar removable padded cover to make it softer), and finally a solution which looked very attractive on paper to a problem Aalto had just set out to solve: making *a 'translation' of Breuer's cantilever tubular steel base into wood*. He linked three curved front legs together, the first merging smoothly into the seat and back (F 76). Aalto's entry included two more ideas that he later developed into viable models: the first was a small 'Ablegetisch' (a kind of serving table), which looked somewhat like a sledge with runners, and later turned into Aalto's famous 'tea trolley', and the second was a larger nest of tables, ten of which could be stacked with no more than 3.5 inches difference in height.

Aalto did not win a prize in the Thonet competition, and his drawings were returned. This was partly because there were over 4,000 entries, and it is unlikely that the jury had time to study them all in detail. But another reason was that Aalto was not familiar enough with the material, beech, whose strength and snakelike flexibility was the basic characteristic of Thonet furniture. The cheapest and most easily available furniture material in Finland, birch, is stiffer than beech and has other characteristics which only come into their own with a completely different treatment. Aalto's task was to invent the special type of furniture for which birch is appropriate. To do this, however, he first had to become familiar with the properties of his material. It was his friend Moholy who unwittingly gave him the liberating impulse.

Aalto had neither the time nor the inclination to follow the example of Moholy's Bauhaus pupils by starting to whittle and carve in order to discover the true nature of birch. As an architect, he was accustomed to having assistants to help him, and so he had Korhonen carry out his experiments with wood. It is uncertain whether the two partners started by making the abstract relief shown in F 77, and then produced a variation of the same form in the armchair version of the hybrid chair (F 78), or whether it happened the other way around. In any case, they advanced rapidly towards their goal of replacing steel tubes with Finnish wood.

Their first victory was the later famous Paimio chair and the small table that went with it. Aalto here applied the properties of moulded plywood to forming narrow frames of laminated and glued wood. To this rigid frame he fastened moulded slats of plywood: one bent, springy piece for the seat and back, two flat ones to make the table (see F 110). The constructive idea of the Paimio chair clearly went back to Breuer's Wassily chair.

Once it had proved feasible to make rigid moulded frames from laminated wood, the next step was to use the

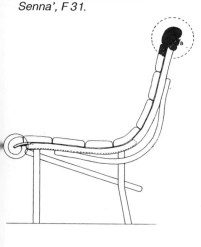

75. Thonet competition entry, 1929: variant of the 'Folk Senna', F 31.

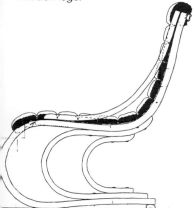

76. Thonet competition entry, 1929: plywood seat on springy wooden legs.

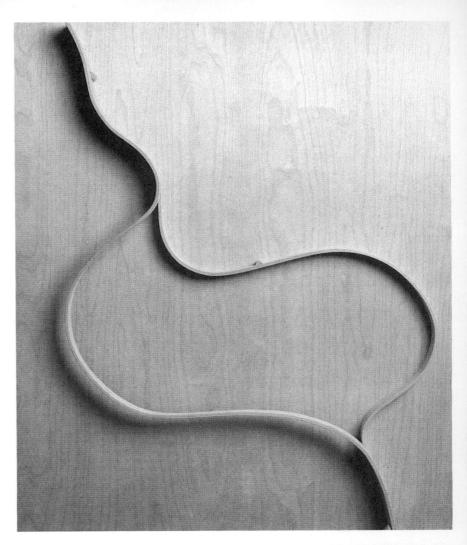

same material as a substitute for the springy steel leg of Breuer's chair. It is likely that Aalto and Korhonen made their first step forward in this direction with a form that minimized the technical problems. In 1930 Aalto had made a few hybrid chairs for his own children. A photograph from this year shows his daughter Hanna-Maija sitting on a children's chair with tubular steel legs. It was a natural idea to give this chair a springy frame of laminated wood – after all, the chair was not required to bear a heavy weight. A photograph from 1931 shows a springy all-wood children's chair and a table leg set at an angle from the board and laminated all the way to the floor.

Both ideas were soon developed further by Aalto. The children's chair acquired a full-grown sister, the technical properties of which, however, were only barely acceptable, since it had a tendency to become deformed in spite

78. The hybrid chair (F 35) converted into an easy chair connected with the wood relief in F 77.

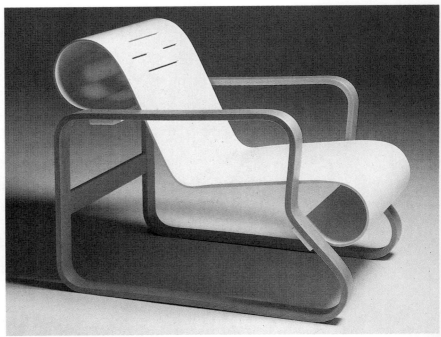

79. The 'Paimio chair', designed in 1931 for the sanatorium.

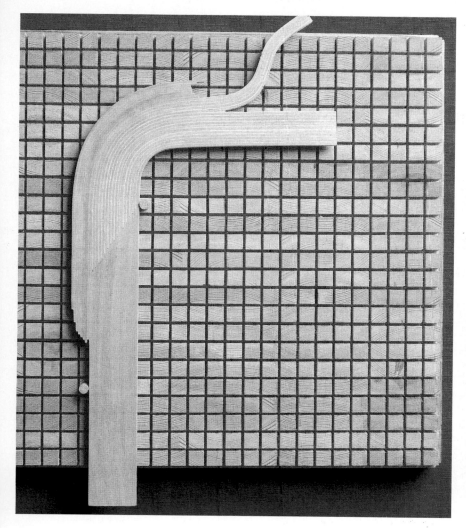

80. Experimental wood relief, c. 1937.

81. Aalto's daughter Hanna-Maija sitting in a children's variant of the hybrid chair (cf. F 35).

of efforts to reinforce the leg at the bend. Production was therefore discontinued after a few test specimens. Instead Aalto hit on the idea of raising the bend of the legs, thereby forming the armrests of a chair, while he fastened the seat lower down in order to anchor the bend into place. This is how Aalto's famous springy armchair came about, the first version having a combined seat and back similar to the Paimio chair (F 84). Over the years this chair, of which Aalto soon produced numerous variants, became Aalto's perhaps most admired contribution to modern furniture design.

Aalto himself, however, considered another of his inventions much more important. We might say that after the

82. Children's chair and table with laminated wood legs, 1931.

many applications of the principle of moulded plywood he and Korhonen had tried, he had become so familiar with the potential of both the material and the method of lamination that his own inventive genius could at last come into play. The idea was to saw the wood open only in the places where it had to be bent, but otherwise to let it keep its compactness and load-bearing quality. The chair leg, whose upper end bends 90° in a gradual curve and is fastened with screws straight to the bottom of the seat, was the first in the series of 'Classical orders', as Aalto humorously dubbed them. For if there is some reason to call the chair leg the little sister of the column, it is logical to follow the ancient Greeks in associating the form of the capital with the style it gives rise to. The simple bent chair leg was Aalto's 'Doric' order; in around

84. *The first version of the perfected wooden chair, 1932.*

83. *The cantilever chair with a wooden base was not entirely satisfactory.*

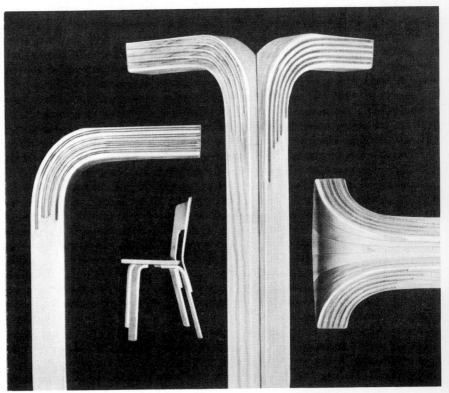

85. *Three versions of a furniture leg, the little sister of the column.*

1947 he created the *Y* leg, in which the laminated part veers in two directions, forming an angle, and finally in 1954 came the *X* leg, in which wedge-shaped lamellae spread out in the shape of a fan.

Aalto considered his invention of the leg with the *L* bend so important that he sought a patent for it, which he obtained in Scandinavia and Britain but not in Germany, where the authorities claimed that the idea was too close to previously granted patents. In practice it proved difficult to uphold patent rights in furniture design, and in the next few years such famous designers as Bruno Mattson in Sweden and Ernst Breuer in Britain came very close to imitating Aalto's inventions, while Aalto himself had legal problems with the Thonet company, which accused him of treading on its toes. In the end the difference between the various artists was in aesthetic design rather than in the technical manufacturing principle, and for a superb designer like Aalto this was no disadvantage. The furniture he designed in the '30s remains unsurpassed and is still mass-produced.

The Paimio sanatorium was inaugurated in summer 1933. The springy chair was fully-developed by then, and in principle it could have been included in the interiors. The interior planning and the deliveries to the huge sanatorium complex took such a long time, however, that the older type of Aalto furniture dominated in the end. The furniture for Paimio included some specially designed beds, armchairs and operating tables of tubular steel, the standard hybrid chair and some other conventional stackable chairs, the 'Paimio chair' with a small table that went with it, and finally a clothes cupboard bearing a certain rather unfortunate resemblance to a coffin. Of the new furniture generation of 1932, only a few test samples were included.

For the Viipuri Library, however, Aalto and Huonekalutehdas had plenty of time to investigate the potential of the 'Doric' leg for tables and stools as well as chairs. With this furniture, which

86. Aino Aalto in a chaise-longue designed specially for the Paimio Sanatorium.

87. Stools with and without backrest in the Viipuri Library auditorium.

is used today not only for exclusive interiors by designers sensitive to the requirements of settings, but also for countless ordinary homes, schools, cafés and offices, Aalto achieved the ambition of the reform movement of the '30s: to create rational, attractive and inexpensive serial furniture for everyday use. Otto Korhonen's son Paavo told me that when Aalto and his father made the first sample of the three-legged Aalto stool, they threw it around the workshop floor to test its durability. In his enthusiasm at the successful outcome, Aalto exclaimed: "This stool is going to be made by the thousands!" Not even with his notorious optimism could he dream that after fifty years there would be millions of Aalto stools.

Furniture design was an important chapter in Aalto's development, in that it solved his financial problems and paved the way for his international fame. Unlike buildings, furniture can be transported and displayed in the original at exhibitions. The Milan Triennales of 1933 and 1936, and the exhibitions in London in 1933, Zurich in 1934 and New York in 1938 established Aalto's international reputation as designer and architect.

Perhaps the most important consequence of his furniture design is yet to be discussed. Gustaf Strengell realized this as early as 1934, when he wrote in the *Helsingfors Journalen*: *Not only has Aalto discovered a new and original technique* [for making furniture], *but at the same time he has logically derived from it an equally new and original architectural idiom.* Two early examples can be mentioned: the horizontal slabs which form the solarium level of Paimio Sanatorium have rounded serpentine forms of the same type as the curve of the laminated wood in the Paimio chair, while the sculpturesque laminated wood ceiling of the Viipuri Library auditorium also derived from the experimental wood reliefs made in 1931 (F 87). This expansion of motifs from furniture design to full architectural scale recurs in many forms in Aalto's later buildings. The

88. *The ceiling of the Paimio Sanatorium solarium has the same forms as Aalto's laminated furniture.*

89. *The concrete arches bearing the roof of Riola Church remind one of the laminated wood base of the Paimio chair.*

90. The chancel of Wolfsburg Church has an affinity with the fan-shaped chair leg.

wavy, snakelike motif could take over a whole facade, as in the MIT dormitory in Boston. The bearing frame of his furniture could be 'translated' into concrete, as is shown by the roof-bearing beams in Riola Church. Similarly, the fan-shaped 'Corinthian' chair leg lent its shape to the vault of Vuoksenniska Church and the chancel of Wolfsburg Church. In later days, Aalto actually used his wood reliefs as such for auditorium and concert hall walls on acoustic pretexts: we see this in the Institute of International Education in New York as well as in the Finlandia Hall and the Essen Opera plan.

Thus the elasticity of wood fibre and the sensory qualities of wood showed the way for Aalto to break free from Rationalist formalism in the latter half of the 1930s and to create his own, 'natural' architecture.

A POLITICALLY COLOURED YEAR

As far as commissions and competitions went, 1932 was even more barren than the preceding year. The eco-

nomic depression paralysed the construction business and delayed the completion of both the Paimio Sanatorium and the Viipuri Library. Work at Paimio advanced slowly all year, but the office staff had to be reduced. Wildhagen had already returned to Norway at the end of 1930, and Bjertnaes had had to leave in the summer of 1931. Only Lasse Wiklund was left because Aalto did not have the heart to turn him out, as he would have been reduced to outright penury. Spirits were low in Turku, as can be seen from a New Year's letter Aino wrote to Wildhagen in January 1932: *It's a snowy winter, we go skiing with Brygge and Agda. The children also ski downhill. Life is quite different from what it was 2–3 years ago. Then we had too many parties and now we have none at all. Things are so quiet it takes getting used to . . .* There was no improvement that year, and in a brief Christmas letter to Wildhagen in December Aalto wrote: *A completely empty office and an unemployed chief send their greetings to the office manager of the days of the great rush.*

In fact, the earnings of the office that year only covered half of its expenses, with nothing left over to pay the taxes. Two days before Christmas Eve 1932, the bailiff came and glued distraint labels on the better pieces of furniture, with the maid as his official witness. The value of Aino's grand piano was estimated at 6,000 marks. With the help of a bank loan, however, Aalto weathered the storm and managed to find some minor assignments.

These included a club building for the Kemi Rural Parish Defence Corps and a private home in Tartu, Estonia, for the university professor August Tammekann. Aalto also participated in a couple of competitions in 1932 sponsored by two manufacturers of insulating board, The Insulite Co. of Finland and Enso-Gutzeit, with the purpose of stimulating the use of 'insulite' and 'ensonite' board respectively. Unfortunately, Aalto's entry only won a purchase for 500 marks. The most interesting feature in his entry was the small weekend cottage for Enso-Gutzeit. This was the very first occurrence of a motif that was so typical of his later work: the fan shape, motivated in this case by radiation from an oven placed at a corner of a triangle and by the entry of sunlight through the main window. Aalto also started work in 1932 on two other competition entries which were not sent out until the following year: the first competition for a church in Temppeliaukio square in Helsinki and the town plan for the renovation of the Nedre Norrmalm district in Stockholm. Aalto's church plan (which did not appeal to the jury) was based on a V form with the altar placed in the low, narrow tip of the interior.

It was, however, in furniture design that Aalto again made his principal contribution in 1932 by refining and perfecting his basic designs. It may even have been fortunate for him to be able to concentrate on this demanding effort. In early summer 1932 he introduced his most famous furniture invention, the springy armchair in which steel tubes had been replaced completely by laminated wood (F 84). This took place at a major Scandinavian event, the Nordic Building Congress in Helsinki on July 4–6, 1932, which included a whole series of exhibitions to be admired by the architects who took part in the congress. One of the big names was Gunnar Asplund from Stockholm, who managed a visit to Paimio Sanatorium with Aalto on the way; by then the structural parts of the Sanatorium had been completed. Asplund later said that seeing this magnificent work incited him to speak out much more boldly than he had originally planned in the lecture on "Architecture and the environment" that he had been invited to give at the congress.

The stormy debate on Functionalism that ensued after the Stockholm Exhibition was still at its height, and the conservative phalanx among Helsinki architects thought Asplund's speech highly provocative. The result was a curious incident in the history of the Finnish Association of Architects: Ber-

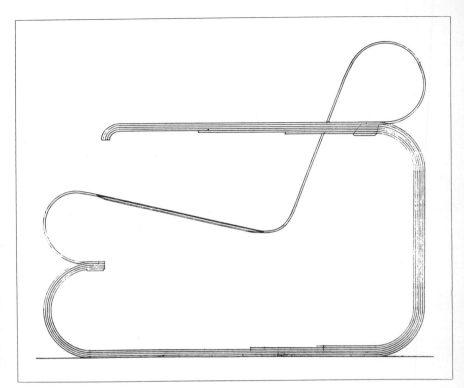

91. Plan for sprung version of the Paimio chair, 1932. The final solution to the problem was provided by the armchair seen in F 84.

92. Aalto on the Paimio Sanatorium solarium roof in the summer of 1932, photo Gunnar Asplund.

tel Jung went up to a restaurant table where Gunnar Asplund and Alvar Aalto were sitting and said: "So this is where the Bolshevik architects are!" Whereupon Aalto rose and gave Jung a box on the ear. There was a tremendous uproar. The Board of the Association set up a tribunal, which in turn delegated Carolus Lindberg to bring about a reconciliation; Lindberg finally succeeded in his task.

Jung's rudeness was unpleasant in view of the increasingly vociferous campaign against Modern art in Germany, but we may also note that 1932 was the high-water mark in Aalto's fluctuating feelings for the Soviet Union. We should bear in mind that many of his then friends, from Markelius and the Clarté group in Stockholm to the Bauhaus set in Germany and the Frenchmen Le Corbusier and André Lurçat, who were working in Moscow, regarded the Russian social experiment with lively sympathy and unlimited optimism. The Soviet Union was *'the land of the future'* for them — still a land of experimentation, progress and confusion, with much that was unsatisfactory, but where the new, better world had the greatest chance to come true in the shortest time. Aalto, who had taken part, weapon in hand, in warding off the Communist revolution in Finland, had since then lived under the constant influence of liberal left-wing ideas connected in various ways with his work as an architect.

The result was a cumulative process that culminated in 1932. During this year he attacked the speculative capitalist housing construction system in Finland, contrasting it with "The housing system in the USSR" in the Turku review *Granskaren,* and published an article commissioned by the well-known Socialists Cay Sundström and Mauri Ryömä on "Good housing" in *Soihtu,* the journal of the Academic Socialist Association. In the latter article he called down anathema on all forms of individualism in architecture and claimed that good housing can only be built in countries with a planned economy. This was also the year during which Aalto attended receptions arranged by the Russian embassy in Helsinki, and CIAM prepared to hold its next congress in Moscow. The members of the preparatory congress, Giedion, van Eesteren, Ernst May, Mies van der Rohe and Hans Schmidt, sent Aalto a postcard from Moscow, regretting that Aalto had not found the time to take part. It was taken for granted that he would attend the main event in the summer of 1933.

We may consider the visit paid by Hans and Lilli Schmidt to the Aaltos in Turku in October 1932 as a preparation for the Moscow congress. Hans Schmidt (1883–1972) was one of the Continental architects who had gone to the Soviet Union to take part in building the land of the future. For the first few years he and his wife lived in an artists' collective right in the heart of Moscow. When Viola Markelius went to

93. Hans Schmidt in the 1940s.

the Soviet Union in 1933 to report on conditions, she lived with the Schmidts (see page 50). When Walter Custer, the first of the young Swiss trainee architects at Aalto's office, visited Moscow in 1934, he also stayed with his compatriots, and wrote an enthusiastic letter to Aalto from Moscow, warmly recommending that he come to "the most interesting country on the face of the earth today". He particularly praised Moscow for the fact that "nowhere can one come and go as freely as here. No police, no 'undesirable' elements' to threaten one's security. One gets the impression that the people are better here than in the West."

Hans and Lilli Schmidt liked their new homeland well enough, but they wanted to spend a holiday in a more 'normal' setting from time to time, so they wrote to Aalto in the autumn of 1932 to ask if they could spend a week in Turku. The result was highly satisfactory for both parties, since Lilli and Aino got on just as well together as did Hans and Alvar. In their letter of thanks, the guests said that they "had never had such pleasant holidays as in Finland", where they had enjoyed the "parties, discussions and flirtation in all forms". They admired the Finns, "who really know how to live". Schmidt left Aalto a long, handwritten description of conditions in Russia, from which Aalto compiled an interview for the Turku newspaper *Åbo Underrättelser* and an article for *Arkkitehti* magazine. The description is interesting because in it Schmidt defends or explains the reaction against Modern architecture that arose in the Soviet Union around 1933 and was the reason why the Russian hosts cancelled the CIAM meeting in Moscow at the last minute.

The gist of Schmidt's argument was that radical Continental architecture and theoretical social ideas could not be applied to Russia, with its undeveloped industry, primitive conditions and uneducated population. One had to be content with what could be done in the long run to create an infrastructure and prepare the ground for future improve-ments. *Classicism, which is raising its head again, is just as passing and ephemeral a phase as was the thoughtless imitation of Le Corbusier. The worker or the specialist who comes from western Europe to the Soviet Union should not think that he is coming to a ready-built paradise, but to a clamorous battlefield, where energy and patience are called for. True, it is all directed dictatorially from above, but initiative, community spirit and control are also needed below.* Aalto underlined the last sentence in Schmidt's manuscript and wrote in the margin: *Is it permitted?*

Aalto was one of the CIAM members who started having doubts about developments in the Soviet Union after the Moscow meeting was called off. He was one of the few members of the circle who never went there – until he was invited by the Soviet Academy of Architecture in 1962 as a token of the policy of détente between Finland and her great neighbour. Nothing, however, could shake Schmidt's Communist convictions. In 1935 he went over to the Classicist style in obedience to the requirements of 'social realism', and took the style back with him when he was forced to return to Switzerland in 1937. After the war he moved to East Germany, where he became an Academy professor. But when in 1960 he applied to the Russian authorities for permission to visit the industrial city of Orsk on the Ural River, planned by him thirty years earlier, it was denied to him on the grounds that the city was not open to foreigners.

THE DECISIVE BREAKTHROUGH

1933 was an important year for Aalto. It brought his definitive breakthrough as a leading architect – somewhat doubtfully in Finland, but all the more convincingly abroad. In this year the Paimio Sanatorium was finally inaugurated after five years of construction, and the fourth (and final) version of the Viipuri Library was drawn. On the other hand, the architectural com-

94. Perspective of the final
version of the Viipuri Library,
1933.

95. Paimio Sanatorium in 1933.
The patients' wing is to the right,
with the lift shaft visible outside.

petitions in which Aalto took part in
1933 – the second phase of the
Helsinki Olympic Stadium, Tampere
Railway Station and the renovation of
the Stockholm district of Norrmalm –
did not yield anything.

The Sanatorium's daring conception had aroused interest even before
the vast complex was completed, and
one of the Swedish participants at the
1932 Nordic Building Congress, Efraim
Lundmark, had gone so far as to write:
*What has been seen so far of Aalto's
sanatorium complex must be considered unique in Scandinavia, and I
have no qualms about writing that the
history of Finnish architecture has entered a new phase with Aalto.* At the
Pörssiklubi ('Stock Exchange Club'),
where the Helsinki architects sat downing their grogs, sneering remarks were
made about the young upstart from
Turku in the style of "When will that
bubble burst?" until one of those present, the authoritative architect and
critic Sigurd Frosterus, asked: "Have
any of you gentlemen seen the Paimio

Sanatorium? No, I see you haven't, but I have. And my judgement is: hats off!" (It was Aalto himself who recounted this episode to me, so its veracity cannot be guaranteed. In any case it is certain that Frosterus gave Aalto much-needed support at this moment of breakthrough, and the latter never forgot this.)

Another influential Helsinki architect, Gustaf Strengell, also had a high opinion of Aalto's work. The witty Strengell has already made an appearance in the first part of this biography. In summer 1932 he published a long article in *Hufvudstadsbladet* entitled "Alvar Aalto, Finland's first Functionalist" and written in a half ironical, half appreciative tone. But when Strengell saw the completed Paimio Sanatorium he capitulated, as we can see from another long article published in the same paper on June 11, 1933. In it he asserted that the sanatorium was the most important building to be designed in Finland since the days of National Romanticism thirty years earlier. "The deep, tenacious will to achieve clarity and purity without any regard to incidental considerations" could only arouse one emotion in him: sincere admiration.

This did not prevent the majority of Aalto's Finnish colleagues from remaining cool towards their dynamic rival. Aalto was nominated for a place on the Board of the Finnish Association of Architects, but only gained nine votes from the fifty-odd members present.

Attitudes towards Aalto were much more generous abroad. Right at the beginning of the year, his London friend Morton Shand filled three consecutive issues of *The Architectural Review* with enthusiastic articles on the Paimio Sanatorium, and declared Aalto a leading figure in the new architecture. When Aalto's bentwood furniture was exhibited abroad for the first time at the Milan Triennale in June 1933, Giedion wrote enthusiastically that it was "one of the few bright spots at the whole exhibition". Back in Finland, *Arkkitehti* magazine complained

that the organizers had drawn too much attention to Aalto and had actually gone so far as to allow Sirén's Parliament House (which was presented by photographs at the Finnish stand) to be called "Czarist architecture".

CIAM MEETING
IN ATHENS

It was fortunate for Aalto that the fame of his phenomenal bentwood furniture and the bold sanatorium design had become well established among his foreign colleagues when they assembled in August 1933 for the most famous of all CIAM meetings: the romantic cruise from Marseilles to Athens and the plenary session in Athens on the theme "The functional city". The Russians had cancelled the Moscow meeting only late that spring, so one must admire Giedion and the other organizers for managing to arrange a more than adequate substitute at such short notice.

Giedion wrote to Aalto on July 16: *Athens is expecting a lecture from you. Kindly bring not only your genius but also suitable slides. We shall meet in Marseilles on the 27th.* As usual, Aalto was tangled up in a web of unfulfilled commitments and was unable to leave on the agreed date. Instead, he sent Nils-Gustav Hahl (1904–1941) as his outrider. This young man was not an architect at all, but with his magic power over people Aalto had succeeded in persuading him to give up a promising career as a museum official for the adventure without a permanent position offered by the cause of Modern architecture. Hahl was a Swedish-speaking Finn who was more fluent in French, English and German than in Finnish; he was endowed with a sensitive intellect, a wide-ranging knowledge of art history and a conscientious attitude to work, the value of which Aalto realized immediately. In a letter to Giedion, Aalto said that Hahl had the makings of "a provincial Giedion here in Finland" and asked Giedion to take him under his "broad eagle's wings".

96. *Nils Gustav Hahl, Aalto's selfless right-hand man.*

Fortunately, Giedion was willing to do this when it turned out in Marseilles on July 29 that Hahl, who was completely unknown to the members of CIAM, would represent Finland alone on the cruise. That very day Hahl was able to send a report to Aalto, who later joined them in Athens:

Received your letter on board before the congress actually opened. Was called to the meeting as your deputy and so penetrated straight into the 'inner circle'. Am writing this in case you should not come to Athens. Which would be a great pity, for though I've blended in very well, you're needed here as the true 'representative'.

On the way I called van Eesteren [president of CIAM] in Amsterdam, who sent me to Duiker – an excellent fellow who unfortunately isn't on board. Saw his Zonnestraal Sanatorium near Hilversum plus a lovely school built of glass in Amsterdam and various other buildings by him in Scheveningen. Oud, Brinckman and van der Vlught are not on board either. In Paris I made the acquaintance of a certain Goldfinger, *unknown until now, a Hungarian 2 metres tall, a fine fellow, 'type épatant'. Max Ernst and Tagore junior were with him. We set out with Goldfinger plus photographer's model and Fernand Léger from Dôme, picked up the Englishmen at the Gare de Lyon. Morton Shand is my friend and a fine chap, sends his regards and deplores again and again that you may not be coming. Fantastic journey in third class.*

As soon as we arrived in the harbour, I started looking out for you – at the office in Paris I had discovered that we two were still alone on the list [Aalto and Hahl had unsuccessfully attempted to persuade other Finnish architects to take part]. *My position without a ticket was just about to become critical when Giedion turned up and saved everything. There's also a horde of tourists on board, but we congressists couldn't care less. The foredeck is full of yelling Greeks of all sexes and sizes who sleep under the open sky, an inferno. Underneath we've been quartered into lead cabins for 4–8 men, but Shand and a red-bearded Englishman and I prefer to sleep in deck chairs on the third-class deck. We eat and drink copiously and well. The heat is unabated and we're all half-naked. Oh that you were here!*

The opening ceremony was an uncommonly dull affair with nonsense in halting French and equally halting German by van Eesteren. Then Le Corbusier sprang up and gave an oration which at least made more formal sense. His antagonist Lurçat did not come because of intrigues unknown to me. Moholy N is here, but I haven't got hold of him yet. No Swedes. Two Norwegians, one of them Munthe-Kaas. A pity that the congregation has shrunk somewhat. People are asking about you, van Eesteren named you in his opening address.

Hahl also presented a more official report on the congress in a light article in *Hufvudstadsbladet*, from which I quote the following extract:

Early in the morning of July 29, a bus draws up alongside a steamer in

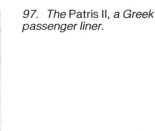

97. The Patris II, *a Greek passenger liner.*

the port of Marseilles. A dozen people crawl out and enter negotiations to get their luggage off the roof. They speak French with many different accents and degrees of perfection, since they are a mixed international bag. There are Frenchmen, Englishmen, Hungarians, Swiss – and one Finn.

Finally up on deck, they melt into an even greater confusion of nationalities: one can hear all of Europe's known languages and some of the unknown. Moreover, the officers and crew are yelling in Greek. But the new arrivals soon distinguish shouts of welcome, as if there were a band of Freemasons in the crowd who recognize one another by some secret sign. Actually this is an appointed meeting: the Fourth International Congress of Modern Architecture is gathering on the Greek tourist steamer Patris II. *It is an amusing paradox that this particular congress is meeting on this particular steamer. For if every vessel is a piece of national territory with its specific national character, there are few vessels with so much specific national character as* Patris II. *All you have to do is try to push through the bustling crowd on the foredeck or examine the characters in luxury class, as eccentric and refined as orchids, or have an ouzo in the bar and enjoy a substantial meal in the dining room of Edwardian elegance – and you begin to realize that the ship con-*

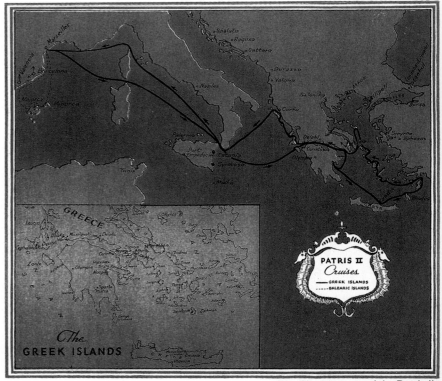

98. *The itinerary of the* Patris II *according to the shipping company's prospectus.*

tains a concentration of specifically Levantine life. As soon as the French coast has disappeared beyond the wake of the ship, you are deep in the midst of a nation's typical milieu. Whereas the congress is completely the opposite: a conscious, active international organization.

This time the object of the participants' interest is the functional city. This is the theme to be discussed while Patris II ploughs the Mediterranean on its way to Athens. On board are maps, photos and descriptions of thirty cities, from Stockholm and Athens to Warsaw and Los Angeles. The maps are spread out over a space partitioned off from the promenade deck, the chairs are arranged in rows: an auditorium. You can throw your cigarette straight into the Mediterranean, which surges bright blue and foam white below and tries to drown out the voices of the speakers. One lecturer follows another, new illustrative material is brought out, the listeners refresh themselves with ice-cold sherbet. And they have every reason to do so: the wind is slight and the heat is rising.

Their senses are not refreshed by what they are shown. Everywhere the same threatening traffic stagnation, the same disproportion between overcrowded housing and sparse settlement, the same senseless placing of housing and jobs at great distances from one another, the same shortsightedness in the face of changes which did not begin yesterday. The speakers appeal to their material in their brief, mordant accusations against private and municipal building speculators. In fact the programme should have been headed "the unfunctional city". It is easy enough to see that the functional, up-to-date city exists only in a handful of scattered examples here and there – and only on paper.

What is it really? In Athens its characteristics are defined in a lecture by Le Corbusier, the renowned father and prophet of Functionalism. He speaks in the courtyard of the Institute of Technology; two enormous loudspeakers convey his words to a few

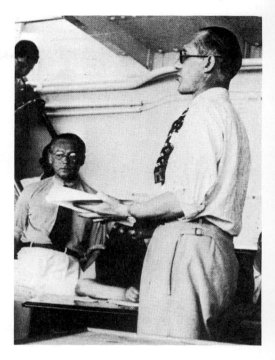

99. Le Corbusier expounding a text during the congress on the Patris II, Sigfried Giedion listening.

hundred listeners in this open-air auditorium surrounded by palm trees. He varies on his favourite theme "air, son, lumière", air, sound and light; the problem summarized in a formula. To simplify matters, what this means is: light and air for all the inhabitants, and protection from the growing noise of the great cities. A logical follow-up is the 'open' town plan which spreads buildings apart and places parks and streets in separate systems between them. The street shaft is not an invention of our time, however much literary great-city romantics may cherish it. It is a rudiment which has descended to us following the law of inertia from the compressed fortified towns of the Middle Ages.

It goes without saying that Le Corbusier is one of the foremost figures at the congress. He is on a plane of his own. One or two other pioneers of the movement who might lay claim to an *equal position are absent for some reason or another. A famous German architect, for instance, is missing [Hahl is thinking of Gropius]. This only goes to increase Le Corbusier's domination. He takes the floor whenever he wishes to make an unprogrammed speech, a speech carried by that French lyricism which envelops the argument in incense and silences any criticism from the audience. He is known as a Classic of Functionalism, but in his speeches he is its most passionate Romantic. His figure is thin and bony, behind the large goggles his eyes have the confidence of the unshakeable fanatic.*

A man who does not feature on the official programme but is nonetheless one of the central personalities of the congress is the Hungarian Moholy-Nagy. He is appreciated among us by only a small circle, though he spent several months in Finland two years ago. This is not the place to present him; I shall merely point out that he has had a greater impact than anyone else on the breakthrough of the modern feeling for form, e.g. in film and typography, and that his contribution to modern photography cannot be overestimated. On the Patris II *he and his perfect little film camera are ubiquitous; he finds subjects everywhere, whether group portraits or perspectives. At the break of dawn, sleeping in our folding chairs on top deck – few of us sleep in our cabins – we are sometimes awakened by a faint whirring: a few feet of film have turned in Moholy's camera. He gives a sly wink and tiptoes up to the next chair: the camera whirs and the facial movements of the sleeping Alvar Aalto are immortalized. One evening Moholy-Nagy's travel film is shown on the quarter deck: a realistic report which expands into a fantastic picture poem on life aboard ship. When it is completed it may attain the same quality as his famous film* Marseilles. *It makes one feel ashamed not to have oneself discovered these same cuttings from one's daily surroundings. Afterwards one looks at the ship – and at some of one's fellow-passengers – with new eyes.*

Greece. A few all too short days between our arrival in Piraeus and embarkment. One impression, the first, dominates all others: the Acropolis. These passengers are better equipped than most to enjoy the architectural qualities of the lovely temple hill in Athens.

During the voyage, a clique of twelve similarly-minded people has crystallized: together we tour the Peloponnese by car. For all of us, it is a journey which reaches far beyond the boundaries of our everyday life. The Homeric cities are stages on our journey in American cars through the high heroic idyll of the Greek landscape. The last evening, we tarry in the mountains above Sparta. We stand there under the stars, small and crestfallen at the thought of our impending separation from the great Hellas. Everyone experiences this farewell in a different way. For us Northerners it is something that cannot be expressed in words. The Frenchmen murmur: "Like a new mistress . . ." – "That's it, you don't know whether you can bear to be away from her . . ."

And then it's all aboard again. The committees write out their resolutions, the working method is duly criticized, the past work is summarized and future work is prepared for a book on the theme of the congress, "The functional city".

One night Le Corbusier and his cousin Pierre Jeanneret set up their gramophone on the promenade deck. They play Greek folk melodies and liturgical songs. The mild wind comes sighing over the flaming crater of Stromboli, a spell is cast, and the night runs out without our realizing it. One of the Italians gestures towards the sea and the musical group under a globe lamp on deck. "There you have it," says he, "air, son, lumière."

Hahl gives some interesting additional information on the congress in the *Tulenkantajat* review. Concerning the discussions at the meeting in Athens, he mentions that *the Frenchman Fernand Léger gave a lecture on the significance of colours in architec-*

100. The columns of the
Parthenon, photographed by
Aalto in 1933.

ture. This gave rise to an interesting debate, in which Le Corbusier and Alvar Aalto took part enthusiastically. In discussing the suitability of various colours, both of them typically considered only the physiological effect colours have on people, and almost wholly disregarded their aesthetic qualities. Aalto is highly esteemed everywhere, as the participants of the congress assured me. Many foreign architects have already visited his newly-completed sanatorium in Paimio, and their comments have been uniformly laudatory.

In contrast to the overall picture of the congress provided by Hahl, let us now take a look at Aalto's own experience of it as he described it in a few hasty letters to the folks back home. He did finally get to Athens on the Polish airline LOT's inexpensive flight via Warsaw and Budapest, where he took time off to see some colleagues. The last stage of the journey was accomplished in a third-class day carriage. Here is his (undated) letter from the Hotel Grande Bretagne in Athens:

Dear young 'uns and Aino, I hope you have sun and good weather back home there. Down here we have almost too much, though I don't suffer from the heat as the wind makes conditions bearable.

What a city this is. Yesterday and today I spent all morning on the Acropolis. It seems the taxi drivers can't find it. If you say Acropolis, you wind up at the Acropolis Hotel.

The Greek CIAM architects have arranged an incredibly friendly welcome, with dinner by the seashore last night and a whole lot of other highlights. Today I was invited to lunch with the big boss of the group. The others are just coming back from the islands [a cruise Aalto missed by arriving too late]. *I'm going to the beach now after being on the Acropolis since 8 a.m. (some 30 photographs). The car is waiting – perhaps I'll write some more in the evening.*

But it was not until the last day, when the congress (including Aalto this time) embarked on the *Patris II* for the return journey, that he found the time to write home again:

Dear little little Aino, The time has gone by at such a giddying pace, and me with so little of it to lose and so much to see. Sitting on the shady side of temple ruins has proved quite sympathetic after all compared to meetings and museums. I've taken a lot of photographs, we'll see whether anything comes of them. I had a little private chat with Moholy at a deserted café after the official banquet. Moholy is expecting a child any day, not with Ellen but with a lady who is living with them. Ellen took the lady's husband for a while, but is living alone now. That's the news from here. In half an hour's time, the boat is leaving Piraeus, so it's time to start packing. Alvar.

The next letter is dated Marseilles, August 4, 1933, and runs:

Dear little 'uns and Aino, Just got your letter at the Hotel Moderne, which made me very happy. I'm staying here for just one afternoon and morning. The heat and damp on the boat has somehow made me apathetic, I'm a little tired all the time and so haven't had the energy to take as good a look at this city as it might deserve. The whole lot of us did go out for a while last night, but we were all sleepy: on board we slept on deck in camp beds, with numb limbs and shirts dripping with sweat although the mistral blew — so the sleep we got wasn't very sound.

Moholy and I are going to Zurich through the French villages in Giedion's car. I'll probably come straight home from there, France is such an expensive country. Finnish currency isn't worth much here. There's some confusion about getting back half of my fare, as my ticket was given to someone else who went to Greece with it and on top of everything my ticket was paid twice. I'm going to see the captain at the ship's office today.

The Englishmen have been the bright spot of the congress, and quite exceedingly friendly to me. I've been very thrifty, but there are always unforeseen expenses — the ship had

pretty high 'official tips' etc. If I get just some of the fare back, I won't need any more.

Vaccination was obligatory on the ship but Giedion and I were vaccinated only on paper, a Swiss doctor took care of it.

The Straits of Messina were extraordinary — the first time in his life that Daddy saw volcanos. First Etna, then

101. Aalto drew caricatures of his colleagues at the CIAM discussions. Le Corbusier.

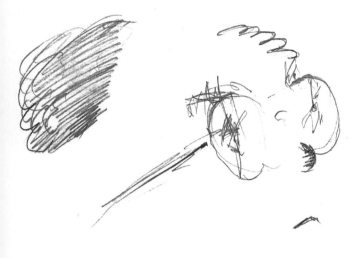

Stromboli at night – with a magnificent red flame rising up from time to time. Lots of kisses to all three of you. Daddy.

The impressions from the CIAM meeting and its epilogue in Marseilles and Provence were not so easily digested, however, and Aalto returned to them in a letter he wrote to Aino in Zurich on August 20. It is one of the few letters of any length which he wrote to his wife during the pre-war years. Here he gives us a lively glimpse of the closeness of their relationship:

Dear dear little Aino. I am writing to you in the evening calm. Am staying with the Giedions and it has been

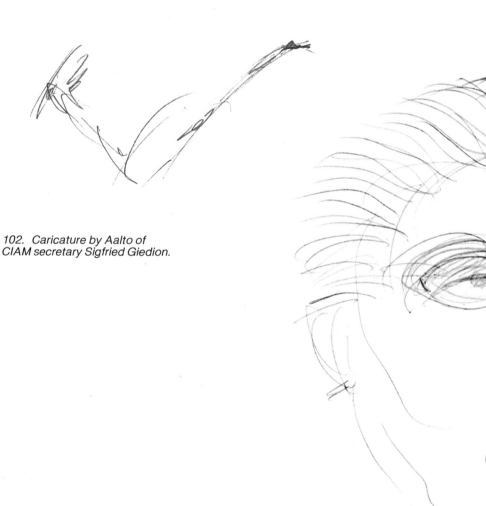

102. *Caricature by Aalto of CIAM secretary Sigfried Giedion.*

103. *Caricature by Aalto of CIAM chairman Cornelius van Eesteren.*

pretty hard to find a quiet moment for letter writing. I'd like to write an especially long and peaceful one, now that the impressions of the journey are beginning to clear up. It was so good to get your letter in Marseilles, such a kind, sweet letter. The car journey through France was an experience I won't soon forget. We spent the nights in small hotels in the forest and took our time (3 days). Moholy stayed as 'hostage' in La Sarraz with Madame Mandrot, though there were already 15 'young' gentlemen there, a mixed and awful lot. We were the aristocrats of the house, dined with 'Madame', whereas 'die Bande' ate 'là-bas'. Here in Zurich I've had so much to do at Wohnbedarf that there's no time to spare, especially as you're tied down anyway if you stay with a family.

You mustn't be upset about what happened in Marseilles. It was certainly the most awful and perverse city I've seen so far, but when we went to see the 'old harbour', I didn't go alone – I took a 'lifeboat' with me, a young lady from the congress, so that Marseilles wouldn't catch me. [Aalto still talked about this 'lifeboat' in his old age: apparently she was an American millionaire's daughter who had serious mental problems owing to a strictly puritanical upbringing – though Aalto claimed to have cured her.] Naturally it led to a 'liebesgeschichte', though without any danger to either body or soul. Tell you all about it when I get back.

The main danger in Marseilles is not the usual danger of cities – it's dangerous even in the daytime. I got a bucketful of dirty water down my neck on my way to photograph the Pont Transbordeur (which is right in the slums) and twice the streetwalkers took my hat, which I could only get back by resorting to my fists. A stinking hole. On the above-mentioned 'lifeboat excursion' we went to the 'Kino Port Said', which must have been a record of its kind [this porn theatre, or 'cinéma bleu', as he called it, was another unforgettable memory of this journey]. I just can't understand how it is possible that next to such a filthy though

after all amusing hole there can be countryside with such cool beauty as Provence.

I had thought of leaving today, but now I must stay to give a lecture. Giedion has arranged an oh so exclusive gathering at a South American millionaire's to which 40 of Zurich's wire-pullers have been invited. That's tomorrow night. The very next morning I'm taking a flight (which will be paid for me) to get to Stockholm on Wednesday, where I hope to find you, denn ich bin derartig verliebt, ganz toll verliebt in Aino, and kiss her in all the smooth places. Moholy is delighted with the nude photo of you (your back) and calls it "plastique Maillol". I think so too – my Marseilles lifeboat only

104. Caricature by Aalto of Richard Neutra. (The boat underneath is a later addition by Aalto's five-year-old son.)

106. *Caricature by Aalto of José Luis Sert.*

105. *Caricature by Aalto of Pierre Jeanneret.*

served to open my eyes to "plastique Maillol". I lie in bed, when I have the time, and think of seeing you again. *Mir kommt vor dass wir noch unglaublich viel von einander zu bekommen haben. So verstehe ich die Liebe.* [It appears to me that we still have unbelievably much to receive from each other. That's how I understand love.]

We sat together in Marseilles, Le Corbusier and I, every morning. He has been incredibly friendly to me. And so have others. In Athens I was treated "like Charlie Chaplin" according to Giedion. A trip like this gives a boost to one's self-confidence, but only when we're together can an unexaggerated balance and the right attitude be found — *obschon ich jetzt nur erotisch an dich denken kann* [although at the moments I have only erotic thoughts about you]. *Little little little Aino. Your Alvar.*

107. *Portrait from the 1930s of an unknown lady with a Classical profile.*

Why Aalto called the rather huge Aino 'little' in his tender moments shall remain their secret. What is moving about the letter is Aalto's appeal to his wife to subdue the hubris that success threatened to bring, to help him keep hold of his self-criticism and his sense of reality. The demand for genuineness, one of Aalto's strongest instincts, had to do battle all through his life with the desire to shine. It was surely to a great extent Aino's doing that he was able to avoid ridiculous pretentiousness and empty posing –

though nobody could cure him of his boastfulnes.

One exploit Aalto might have boasted of, but which he never even mentioned in the letters to Aino, was the applause he gained for a speech he made at one of the unofficial, presumably nocturnal, debates at the congress. The theme was 'the encounter with Classical Greece'. Aalto started by saying that like many others he had always associated white plaster and petrified limbs with Antiquity, and was in no way surprised when on the night train from Thessaloniki to Athens he found himself facing a beautiful girl with one leg enveloped in a white plaster cast. It turned out that she was on the way home from hospital, where she had been treated for a broken leg. "Naturally I was enthusiastic about meeting the Greece of my dreams in such authentic form", Aalto explained, going on to describe the difficulties and ultimate success he had in his efforts to reach the living creature under the plaster.

The finesse in this speech was that it could be taken purely as a joke that need not offend anyone, but that at the same time Aalto was clearly repudiating all forms of academicism. Not many, perhaps not even Aalto, realized at this point that the CIAM movement was well on its way towards embracing academicism, but he defended himself instinctively from the spirit of the dis-

cussions. His anarchistic imagination instead conjured up a counterbalance to the congress in the story of the girl who was not to be daunted by the rigidity of plaster. Carola Giedion has told me of the jubilation with which the speech was greeted. No doubt it appealed to instincts the serious debaters and rationalist simplifiers otherwise suppressed. The living Greece they had met outside the walls of the conference room remained as a bitter-sweet memory of something they had brushed against but had been unable to grasp. In a letter from Carola Giedion to Aalto in 1940, while war was raging in Europe, she asked: *Do you ever think of beautiful Greece and the girl in the plaster package who travelled with you through Macedonia while the mild summer night lay over Athens? I imagine that even the Kore girls in the Acropolis museum have*

108. Sketch from 1959 of the town centre of Seinäjoki. The church and parish centre is on the left, the library and town hall in the middle and the theatre on the right; all of these were built.

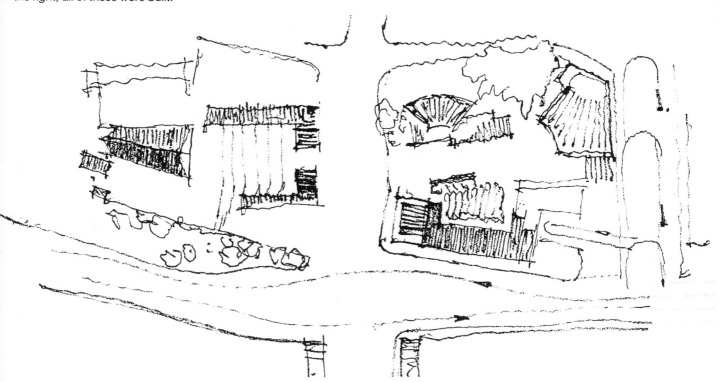

now been wrapped away in protective covers to wait out the headlong rush of events.

If we examine the CIAM meeting in Athens and its final document, the *Charte d'Athènes,* with the wisdom of hindsight, we find that the rules for the development of the modern city laid down there, and followed to an unfortunate extent in post-war reconstruction, placed the living urban organism in a stifling straitjacket. By splitting up the functions of the city according to the scheme Housing, Recreation, Work, Transport System and Historic Buildings, the unity of the city was shattered and such a crucial part of the body as its heart, the city centre, was entirely forgotten.

There are no grounds for the claim that Aalto understood the problem any better than his colleagues in 1933. His plan for the renovation of the Norrmalm district in Stockholm from this year shows that he shared Le Corbusier's and Gropius's excessive confidence in the blessings of the multistorey lamellar block and differentiated traffic arrangements. But his confrontation with the unrealistic utopianism and barren theories of the participants of the Athens congress aroused his instinctive opposition. Instead of taking part in the debates, he sat in the shadow of the Parthenon. There his old love revived for the monumental city centres of Italy, those piazzas which are both the architectural symbol of the city and the main setting of its social life. The ambition to design sterile, differentiated cities in the manner of the Athens Charter vanished and was replaced by the wish to create modern city centres with the same monumental dignity and practical functionality as the Acropolis of Athens once had.

Aalto made his first serious effort to realize this ambition in his town plan for the centre of Avesta in 1944. During the post-war years, a whole series of similar plans followed, and several of them were carried out in Finland. Aalto's work thus became the most

eloquent protest against the Athens Charter ever made by any of the architects who took part in formulating it.

MOVE TO HELSINKI

When Alvar and Aino returned to Finland from Stockholm in August 1933, it was to Helsinki that they went. After the inauguration of Paimio Sanatorium, they no longer had any work to keep them in Turku, while Aalto's growing international and national fame gave them hopes of better opportunities in the capital. They rented a flat in Mechelininkatu 20, where they had their home and office side by side as usual.

The past six years in Turku had been rewarding in many ways, but Aalto's finances were in an even worse state than when he opened his first office in Jyväskylä ten years before. The architect's fees for many of his plans had never been paid on account of the hard times. Juho Tapani, his client for the standard flats in Turku, went bankrupt. Professor Tammekann was never able to pay anything for the drawings for the house in Tartu, and part of Aalto's bill for the Turun Sanomat offices was never paid. No wonder that Aalto left 31,600 marks of rent unpaid in Turku, which led to another visit from the bailiff and a repetition of the previous year's distraint spectacle. He had no new sources of income in view, and as far as furniture was concerned, the Korhonen factory had been able to produce practically nothing more than the most indispensable exhibition specimens (apart from the major commission for Paimio). The trip to Athens and Marseilles had cost him 14,000 marks, while his royalties for the furniture made by Wohnbedarf in Switzerland amounted to 2,575 marks. This was a crisis that called for all of Aalto's financial irresponsibility to ward off discouragement. Something would have to turn up.

EXHIBITION
IN LONDON 1933

Unexpectedly, something did indeed turn up, not in Helsinki but in London. Aalto's career was dotted with exhibitions that marked important stages in his development, but from the present-day perspective the furniture exhibition which opened in London on November 13, 1933 appears to have been the most important of them all. It was actually far less the result of a combination of fortunate circumstances than one might think. The career Aalto made for himself was in fact largely based on his skill in marketing himself and in finding the right assistants. The building up of the Aalto myth went hand in hand with a unique life's work.

The man who made the London exhibition possible was Philip Morton Shand (1888–1960). We have already mentioned Aalto's first encounter with this 'kindred spirit' at the Stockholm exhibition in 1930, their correspondence, which was facilitated by Shand's excellent knowledge of German, and Shand's enthusiastic appraisals of Aalto's Turun Sanomat

building, Toppila Pulp Mill and Paimio Sanatorium in the two periodicals *Architectural Review* and *Architects' Journal,* of which Shand was the chief critic. Shand had been brought up as a gentleman of leisure, and architectural criticism was his hobby; he had spent much of his life on culinary voyages of discovery on the Continent and above all was a snob and an epicurean. In 1931 he suddenly lost his whole fortune in the economic crisis, and was faced with the tremendous challenge of moving into a two-room flat with wife, two children, two cats and a maidservant, and of making a living by his work. In this he succeeded barely thanks to contacts in the right places, among them Hubert de Cronin Hastings, the wealthy owner of both architectural journals.

But it was not enough for Shand just to write about architecture; he also felt the need to enter the business world. In December 1932 Aalto sent Shand photos of his new springy chair and the Aalto stool. Shand was immediately excited and promised to "make a real splash with them" in his journals. The idea of exhibiting them in London to get sales going was simple enough to occur even to such a green businessman as Shand. He proposed this to Aalto, who had another ingenious idea: by calling the Aalto exhibition suggested by Shand "an exhibition of Finnish industrial art" and simultaneously arranging a British trade fair in Helsinki, they could provide an attractive framework for the event and might also persuade the authorities to pay for the whole show. The two friends completed their plan of action when they met in Athens in the summer of 1933, and soon arrived at concrete results.

One of Aalto's most striking characteristics was his adaptability and his sensitivity to the psychological climate of his surroundings. During his holidays in Alajärvi he was the 'village son', and entertained the farmers with juicy stories in dialect. At the meetings of the Architects' Association he appeared as the urbane representative of the young Finnish-speaking intelli-

109. Philip Morton Shand.

gentsia. He spoke Swedish with a genuine Swedish-speaking Finn's accent when he was in Finland, in Sweden he immediately adopted the intonations of standard Swedish, and his Swedish started approaching Danish as soon as he crossed the Öresund. He similarly adapted his opinions to his company and rarely engaged in serious argument; he preferred to make irreverent fun of things. That is why the professed Communist Hans Schmidt could think he had found a fellow traveller in Aalto, while the liberal Socialists Markelius, Gropius and Giedion also always found him to be on their own wavelength. Later in life, he got on equally well with industrialists like Ville Lehtinen and Göran Ehrnrooth, with Communist party leaders like Matti Janhunen, and with church potentates like Cardinal Lercaro of Bologna, all of whom were his clients.

It should therefore come as no surprise to the reader that the contact with Morton Shand immediately transformed Aalto into the perfect English snob. Unfortunately only Shand's letters have been preserved, whereas Aalto's were destroyed during the Blitz. It seems in any case that Aalto proposed "a very restricted, but exclusively presented exhibition aimed at the right, influential circles in England", which was immediately accepted by Shand. He gave one of his friends, "Mr. Betjeman, who associates almost exclusively with the aristocracy", the task of investigating the practical chances of success, which led to negotiations with Fortnum & Mason. In a letter to Aalto, Shand wrote that the company "is in Piccadilly, 150 years old, the real snob shop for the upper class and the royal house plus American millionaires. They sell delicatessen, wine, fashion and nowadays also art. The company enjoys royal patronage and displays innumerable royal coats of arms." Shand concludes his eloquent description with the question: "Genügt das Ihnen, alter snob?" (Is that enough for you, old snob?)

Aalto rose to the occasion with his plans for 'English Week' in Helsinki: he suggested that it should be accompanied by a visit by the British Navy and opened with Scottish regimental music and a speech by a Sir Nigel Playfair (what is more, his suggestions were actually carried out).

Both Aalto and Moholy-Nagy had started studying English by the Linguaphone method after the Athens congress, giving rise to a playful exchange of letters between them in parodic beginner's English. Thus Aalto was able to manage somehow when he went to London. He immediately set about arranging the exhibition according to his own ideas with 'laboratory pieces of wood', i.e., the experimental wood reliefs we have discussed, as piquant and illuminating accents among the furniture. The exhibition was placed under the official protection of the *Architectural Review,* which was a good reason for both the Review and its sister, the *Architectural Journal,* to beat the drum with enthusiastic, well-illustrated commentaries. Morton Shand and his aristocratic friends turned out to have enough influence to bring not only the small band of radical Modernists but also the conservative circles to the exhibition. It was also symptomatic that C.F.A. Woysey, the grand old man of British architecture, paid a visit to the exhibition and exchanged words of mutual esteem with Aalto.

Above all, it turned out that economically Aalto furniture was sailing with a wind which blew stronger every day. This was opportune, particularly for the ruined Shand. Together with a rich friend, Mr. Boumphrey, he started up the FINMAR company and acquired sole rights for it to import and sell Aalto furniture. Demand rose rapidly not only in Britain, but everywhere where British architectural journals were read, including Canada, the U.S.A. and Australia. We will return to the difficulties that the rise in demand occasioned in the small Turku factory and in Aalto's administratively ineffectual office – let alone the master's own scandalous lack of business sense. In early 1934 it was the positive consequences of the

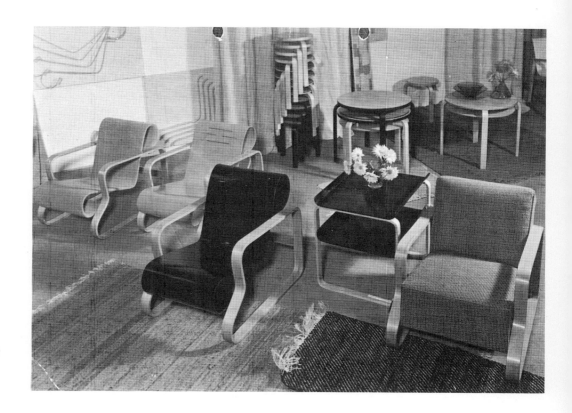

110. View of Aalto's London exhibition in 1933, showing the Paimio chair and table, the three-legged stool and experimental wood reliefs.

London exhibition that predominated. Finmar and Korhonen's factory flourished, Shand and Aalto saw the worst of their financial worries disappearing, and on the artistic plane both men had every reason to be satisfied as well. Shand wrote to Aalto in January 1934 and complained that life had again become "so dull compared to the liveliness your visit brought with it. It will be long before you are forgotten here in England. Everyone is talking about the change (in architectural ideas) your exhibition brought about."

What was it about Aalto's furniture that appealed so strongly to the British? Let us listen to what the two Englishmen most closely involved, H. de C. Hastings (owner of the journals) and Morton Shand, had to say in interviews with the Finnish press. The former declared:

I knew that Aalto was a great architect, but I had seen a good deal of modern furniture designed by 'great' architects, and it was always the same: expensive because modern, modern because snobbish, and snobbish because expensive. I went to the Aalto exhibition at Fortnum & Mason's prepared to find the usual lavish, refined rubbish.

It wasn't there. Instead I found the kind of furniture one dreams of. Wood used in a new − or ancient − way, without mannerism and with such exquisite economy, wood which made chrome and steel furniture vieux jeu. And the prices were as extraordinary as the forms. They were the same as for the cheapest English furniture. For many responsible people here in England, both architects and furniture manufacturers, it is evident that Alvar Aalto is the most interesting figure in the whole international field of design.

As usual, Shand was more wordy and more extravagant. I quote from one of his statements:

What has particularly made an impression on the British public is the steady high quality of the material, construction and execution of this furniture. However light it may be, one realizes immediately that it will also stand up to the criterion of enduring rough treatment, which is so important to us. There is nothing 'American' about it, a word which in Britain is synonymous with rushed production, clumsy finish, poor design and minimum durability.

The other thing that strikes us about the form of this furniture — however new and unusual and therefore alarming it may be — is that after all there is nothing 'functional' in the aggressive sense about it. It is what we would call 'reasonable', a word we prefer instinctively to 'rational'. And once we have accepted these forms as reasonable, made for people instead of arbitrarily dictated to them, we realize that the actual construction is also reasonable. The plastic wood reliefs at the exhibition play an important part, through them the public understands what it's all about and does not take them for affected humbug.

Aalto's resounding success in England gave rise to astonishment and some second thoughts among his German and Swiss friends, of whom Moholy and Gropius happened to be in London during the exhibition. Wohnbedarf, Giedion's company, wrote to Morton Shand the following year to ask him to act as agent for their Swiss furniture. They imagine that what a Finn has achieved in London must be possible for a Swiss, too. That's where they're mistaken, as Shand wrote to Aalto. In fact the London exhibition marked the moment when Aalto, with his usual competitive spirit, surpassed his CIAM colleagues, as he had previously surpassed his Nordic colleagues. Internal development within CIAM together with the Nazis' persecution of Modern architecture combined to move the focus in architectural reform away from continental Europe. Gropius, Breuer, Moholy, Mendelsohn and many other radical designers attempted at about this time to gain a foothold in Britain, later moving on to the United States. Without being banished from his own country like the German architects, Aalto established a strong bridgehead in 1933 in that part of the world which would later emerge victorious from the approaching World War. For anyone aspiring to play a leading cultural role, such a bridgehead was to prove indispensable twelve years later.

1934:
CONSOLIDATION

After the bustle of the London exhibition, 1934 was a relatively uneventful year for Aalto, marked by economic consolidation and the effort to achieve artistic integration of his new insights. He took part in several competitions, without success: the last date of entry for the Tampere Railway Station competition was January 10, then came the Helsinki Fair Hall on February 20, the Helsinki Main Post Office on October 1, and finally an ideas competition for Malmi graveyard on December 15. He did best in the Fair Hall competition, winning third prize and the appraisal "architecturally the entry is commendable"; in the other competitions he did not even earn a purchase, only criticism for the lack of prominence of the entrance to the station building and for the post office plan the comment "the disposition of the building masses gives a fragmented impression". As far as his work was concerned, the best that happened in 1934 was that construction of the Viipuri Library finally got under way and went on at full speed for the rest of the year.

In the spring he received a flattering and stimulating assignment to furnish the restaurant of the renovated Corso Theatre in Zurich together with Max Ernst. He found use for practically all of his existing furniture models in the restaurant; the room itself took on a modern character of unlimited space. During his visit to Zurich he also took the opportunity to arrange an exhibition of furniture and wood reliefs at Wohnbedarf — largely a repetition of the previous autumn's exhibition in London.

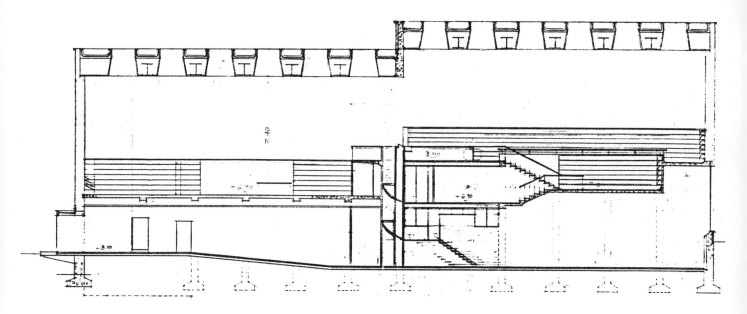

111. Section of Viipuri Library, showing the round skylights and to the right the lending office with the sunken floor section (cf. F 126).

112. Herbert Bayer made the catalogue for Wohnbedarf's Aalto exhibition in 1934.

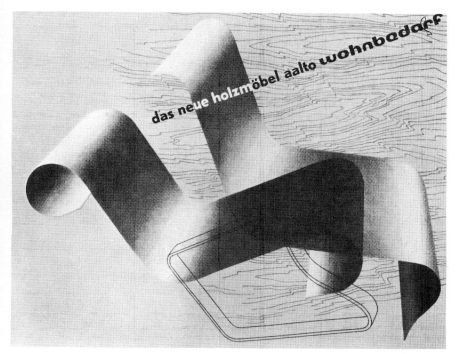

das neue holzmöbel aalto wohnbedarf

AALTO THROUGH JAPANESE EYES

Aalto and his family lived at Mechelininkatu 20 from September 1933 to autumn 1935, then at Turuntie 26, until in autumn 1936 they moved to their new home at Riihitie 20 in Munkkiniemi. There is little information regarding their first two residences in Helsinki or about conditions at the office and the family's everyday life. It therefore came as a pleasant surprise when a Japanese lady living in Finland, Miss Keiko Yoshizaki, supplied me with a completely unexpected but very lively description of the Aalto home, which was also of considerable interest to my quest for the sources of Aalto's architecture. Her information dates from 1934 or 1935, so now is a suitable moment to discuss it; the more so as this provides us with the opportunity to visit the Aalto home at Mechelininkatu. Our guides are Hakotaro Ichikawa, Japan's first ambassador to Finland, and his wife Kayoko Ichikawa.

The couple stayed in Finland from March 1933 to July 1937. Three years after they left their post in Finland they published a book entitled *Finland Zakki* (Essays on Finland), with contributions by both. Ambassador Ichikawa writes:

Of all the people I met in Finland, I particularly remember Alvar Aalto as a highly gifted man. He told me that he had read Marco Polo's memoirs in his youth and had conceived a liking for Japan. Later he had collected many books on our architecture, especially on tearooms. In his hospitals, libraries, dwellings and restaurants he used pure wood, even bamboo, with an unerring feeling for style.

His wife Kayoko goes into much more detail. Her description seems to provide a synthesis of impressions from a period of several years: the furniture firm mentioned is probably the Artek shop, which was opened in 1936, whereas Alvar and Aino went to Paris together in 1935 and Heikki was 6½ and Hanna-Maija 10 years old in 1934. Here is Mrs. Kayoko's account:

We made the acquaintance of architect and Mrs. Aalto through Dr. Ramstedt.* They are considered the leading Finnish architects together with Saarinen. Dr. Ramstedt took us into a furniture shop which displayed furniture designed by Mr. Aalto and glassware and textiles by Mrs. Aalto. Mr. Aalto has already designed a number of buildings, including a hospital, generally designing everything, including the furniture, for the interiors. Mrs. Aalto takes care of the remaining interior design.

The furniture developed by Mr. Aalto is most original, consisting of paper-thin laths of wood which are shaped into furniture in bent forms that remind one of Japanese rattan chairs. They are not, however, hard to sit on like rattan, but springy. I have been told that the laths do not come loose because they are held together by a special glue. Mr. Aalto proudly informed us that extraordinary curved shapes can be achieved by gluing these thin laths together. There was a photograph on the wall of a bent sample with a curious form reminiscent of the calligrapher's art. This picture alone was enough to prove Mr. Aalto's genius.

When I touched the back of one of the chairs with my fingers as cautiously as one handles precious gems, Mrs. Aalto asked me: "Do you value them so highly?" The objects on display were neither expensive nor luxurious, but simple and charming ware for everyday use. They deserve to be called genuinely aristocratic. A people who use and love such things in everyday life are truly aristocratic.

From that day on we met the Aaltos frequently, and during our stay in Finland we became quite well acquainted with them. Mr. Aalto was teaching at the time at the Swedish university** and Mrs. Aalto often went to Paris or Berlin for new furnishing ideas. This is why they usually invited us during holidays. The Finns take intense pleasure in their summer nights, and it happened more than once that our long conversations with the Aaltos lasted until the midnight light awakened the sparrows in the aspen tops.

Mr. Aalto has a lucid, penetrating mind and a sure instinct. Among all my acquaintances, he has the greatest gift for humour. After a serious, profound discussion he would make a joke to clear the air. When we had been discussing Oscar Wilde's Ballad of Reading Gaol, *he declared that England was an extraordinary country to have produced both a man like Wilde and the founder of the Salvation Army. Everyone laughed, but he did not bat an eyelid. In the same way he was able to change the subject with a joke whenever the conversation became too sharp or heated.*

Mrs. Aalto always speaks very calmly; her whole behaviour is well-balanced. She has very deep insight, and her gentle eyes observe everything quietly. As an interior designer she has a sensitive feeling for colour and material, yet her face never betrays the slightest disquiet. She dresses simply but freshly. She is always obliging, and almost seems like a young girl.

I have heard that the Aaltos now live in the attractive suburb of Munkkiniemi near the sea, where they were then planning to build the ideal private villa.

*G.J. Ramstedt (1873–1950), Finnish linguist and explorer, made extensive journeys through Mongolia and East Turkestan in the early years of this century. He was fluent in Japanese, and was Finland's first ambassador to Japan from 1919 to 1930.

**A mistake probably due to the fact that Aalto spent some time in Stockholm in autumn 1934 as an expert member of the jury which selected the professor of building engineering for the local Institute of Technology.

113. Table at Aalto's London Exhibition in 1933, with a revolving top and the 'Riihimäki flower' glass vase series in the middle.

114. Chair upholstered with the Belgian zebra-pattern fabric frequently used by Aino Aalto in the 1930s.

But when we were in Finland they were living in a flat, where we often visited them.

One afternoon in early summer our telephone rang. It was Mr. Aalto: "We got home from Paris yesterday. Can you come and have tea with us to-night?" That is how he invited us. We went to their place. Their well-lit, comfortable flat combined the advantages of American and German homes. The south wall of the living room was one huge window. The leaves of a green climbing plant sifted the daylight and gave the window glass a blue, sea-bottom colour. This bluish light was reflected from the floor of the large living room, on which there was a charming carpet newly bought in Paris. This Morocco rug had black figures on a red, damask background. On the white window shelf was a damask tablecloth with a few cactus pots placed on it. The tablecloth was woven of linen and its colour was pale orange. An armchair upholstered with a pale blue fabric stood in the middle of the guestroom. A loose cloth with a woven pattern was nonchalantly thrown across its back. This cloth was also from Paris. Mrs. Aalto sat relaxed in the chair. She was wearing a dress made of hand-woven Finnish fabric. I cannot remember the colours, but what impressed me was how beautifully the dress and the zebra-pattern cloth over the back of the chair matched.*

On Mrs. Aalto's invitation, we moved into an adjoining room, where tea was laid. In the centre of the smallish dining room, which had two windows, stood a round birch table designed by Mr. Aalto. In the middle was a two-level stand with round trays which could be rotated by hand. The table was laid with Swiss table mats and Russian teacups with saucers. Various courses were placed attractively on the trays in the middle. There was cucumber, red pepper, tinned salmon imported from Japan and crab on oblong white dishes. There was also tongue prepared at home and many other Finnish specialties. On the top tray were cheese, butter, spices, milk and sugar in simple glass bowls and vegetable dishes designed by Mrs. Aalto.

Mrs. Aalto poured the China tea herself. The servant girl served freshly-baked bread and then brought in a tray with apricot marmalade prepared by Mrs. Aalto herself and another kind of sweet, yellow jam. I was told that these yellow berries are called lakka and grow in marshlands. They have smooth leaves and flowers like apple blossom with five petals. Many species of wild berries grow in the Finnish forests and fields throughout the summer and long into the autumn.

Next to the dining room was Mr. Aalto's study, to which we moved after tea. Drawings were spread over Mr. Aalto's large table, and next to it was a smaller desk for Mrs. Aalto. On the latter were photographs of Mr. Aalto's buildings, furniture and other design.

Everything was in good order and carefully filed. I think Mr. Aalto is very happy that his wife has personally arranged everything so well. However efficient this lady may be at filing, she does not look at all like a clerk; she smiles almost girlishly as she shyly shows me the many things her filing cabinet contains. Mr. Aalto seems pleased to be able to devote himself fully to his creative work.

There can be but few married couples in the world who are able to

115. Aino Aalto's 'Bölgeblick' glass series.

* Aino Aalto used a Belgian zebra-pattern yellow and black damask fabric for many of her armchairs in the pre-war years (See F 268).

116. Aalto started in the mid '30s to use various wooden screens with a distinctly Japanese character, witness these in the Savoy restaurant, Helsinki.

work like this in complete harmony for a common interest. A typical example, of course, is provided by the radium scientists, Mr. and Mrs. Curie. Mrs. Aalto is surely a happy woman to have not only her architect husband and her healthy, gifted children but also her own feminine furniture and textile work.

The Aaltos have a ten-year-old daughter and a six-year-old son. We were shown the children's room, which was next to the study, was painted white and had a healthy look about it. The white room had a large window through which daylight streamed in. Such rooms are common in modern Finnish blocks of flats. The children's beds and tables were next to the wall, but there were none of the boxes of toys or even dolls or toy animals of the kind children of that age are usually so fond of and which are so common in children's rooms.

Finnish children are very shy. When these clean-scrubbed and artless children meet foreigners, their white, soft cheeks blush like a flower growing deep in the forest when the sun meets it, and they lower their eyes. Mr. Aalto's children also came up shyly to greet us. They both seemed engrossed in something. Wood shavings had caught onto the boy's trousers, and he seemed to be carving something. We were enchanted to find that it was a hoop net. During the long summer holidays fishing is one of the games the children of the North play. They carefully cast their nets in the shadow of a cliff, deep in the seaweed-coloured water, over which the gulls fly even at midnight. The stillness of the bright night entices the slippery-backed fish to swim leisurely into the net. Early in the morning, when the surface of the water begins to glitter, the Finnish boys get out of bed, run to the shore, and cautiously examine their nets. This is what the boys of the North dream of.

While we were admiring the boy Heikki's net, the girl Hanna-Maija stood restlessly at the window. There was a reason for her impatience: we had approached her own little secret world. Sweet little Maija was weaving. A tiny loom about a foot wide stood at the window, and in it we saw a beautiful weave with a striped pattern in the primary colours. Maija smiled shyly with sweet eyes. Through the large window a forest of conifers and birch stretched as far as the eye could see, and here and there between the trees there was a flicker of blue water. Helsinki is full of such sights.

Heikki, the little fisherman, soon got used to us and came to the living room to show us his little exercise book. In this important book he had drawn a jumble of letters and pictures with a pencil. He had not started school yet, but his older sister was teaching him to

118. The Villa Mairea sauna has a pronounced Japanese character.

write. There was a remarkable picture on the first page. According to Mr. Aalto, it represented the globe and the surrounding heavenly bodies as created by Heikki. There was more land than ocean on the globe, and the poles each had their own sun. Besides these, there were many moons and stars. It seems as if children in their pre-school years have the same unbridled imagination in all countries on earth.

The northern summer evening was turning into pale night, and the magic light fell in over the net and the small loom. I felt myself breathing the mysterious atmosphere of the sagas of the Kalevala or of Topelius. Children are like poetry. Only they can bring dreams and fantasies alive.

Before finishing my account of the Aalto couple, there is one other thing I should like to mention. One day Mrs.

119. The wintergarden of the Villa Mairea, with bamboo furniture, rice lampshade, stone floor and lattice, is a deliberate Japanese pastiche.

Aalto sent a particularly thoughtful gift to our residence, a glass vase of her own design [no doubt belonging to Aino Aalto's "Bölgeblick" series, manufactured by Karhula Iittala since 1932] , *with carmine flowers arranged to represent the unity of earth, heaven and man. I had sent Mrs. Aalto books on the art of Japanese flower arrangements, and she had clearly arranged the flowers according to the rules in these books.*

As the only Japanese woman in this remote country, I was touched and appreciated the gesture very much. It is one of my unforgettable memories.

The book on Japanese flower arrangements is still in the Aalto library, but I have been unable to corroborate Minister Ichikawa's claim that Aalto already had books on Japanese architecture at the time. The ambassador himself gave Aalto a nine-volume series of illustrated books on Japanese culture, published in 1935 and 1936 by the Japanese Board of Tourist Industry. Their subject matter ranges from Shinto religion and No theatre to tea ceremonies, cherry trees and woodcut, but also Japanese architecture and landscape gardening. In 1937 someone else gave Aalto Bruno Taut's expert book on Japanese architecture. Though the illustrative material in these books is relatively meagre by present-day standards, there is no reason to doubt that Aalto was well versed in the Japanese building traditions by the early 1930s.

There is also written evidence of his interest in Japanese culture. In a speech at the Swedish Society of Industrial Design in May 1935, he confessed to his admiration for *Japanese culture, which with its limited range of raw materials and forms has implanted in the people virtuosity in creating variation and new combinations almost daily. Their great love of flowers, plants and naturalia is exemplary. Contact with nature and enjoyment of its constant variation is a way of life that cannot be reconciled with overly formalistic ideas.*

In 1941 he wrote in a letter to the

then Japanese ambassador to Helsinki: *There is a very special affinity between us modern architects and the well-balanced architecture of your country. I believe that it is a deeper understanding of the language of materials which unites us.* The following year, writing to his old friend Otto Völckers in Munich, he says: *I am sending you a collection of photographs of our old Finnish buildings. The houses in the old Karelian area are especially close to my heart. They represent an almost extra-European architecture comparable with that of Japan.*

The idea that Japanese architecture helped Aalto break free from Rationalism, enabling him to formulate his own architectural idiom, nature-bound and characterized by a sensual feeling for material, does not seem too far-fetched. It was suggested as far back as 1935 by the leading Finnish architectural critic Gustaf Strengell. In an article on the newly inaugurated Viipuri Library, he wrote: *

The interiors of the building display Japanese characteristics in many places. Observe the pale, light colouring, which gives the rooms not just their charming airy quality but actually a scent. Quite particularly the Japanese streak appears in the choice of pale wood only – birch, pine, beech – for the panelling and furnishings, and it is even more striking in the treatment of smooth surfaces: in true Japanese manner, they are not treated at all, but left 'in their natural state', which is both attractive to the eye and pleasing to the touch, though perhaps not so well-considered from the practical point of view.

The affinity with the Japanese use of wood is not so easy for us to see today, now that Aalto's treatment of wood has been accepted so fully by his successors and has become such a general feature of Nordic architecture that no one would think it worth commenting on, but in the period 1933–35 it created a sensation.

* *Hufvudstadsbladet,* November 13, 1935.

We detect more obvious Japanese features in some of the forms used by Aalto: in wood panelling, screens and trelliswork both indoors and out. The overall effect is sometimes also very Japanese, as in the Villa Mairea winter garden, for which he actually used bamboo, and sauna, with its stylized lake-like swimming pool, and in the pergola at the back of the Säynätsalo Town Hall courtyard, which can be seen as a subtle paraphrase of a Buddhist temple. Compared to such obvious indications of Aalto's interest in Japan, the Japanese kimono received by Aalto from Ambassador Ichikawa and used by him as a practical dressing gown is of rather minor value as evidence.

THE PROJEKTIO FILM CLUB

Before we leave the year 1934 in Aalto's life, we should perhaps mention an initiative which had no connection with his architecture but all the more with some of his friends and the general Finnish cultural scene at the time. I am thinking of his activities as founder and chairman of the radical film club *Projektio*.

According to a letter from Hahl to Aalto (June 10, 1935), during the Athens congress the CIAM president van Eesteren gave Hahl the idea for this organization, which had counterparts in Paris and Amsterdam. As for Aalto, we already know that he was a film enthusiast and had had a movie camera of his own since 1929. His friendship with Moholy-Nagy, one of the great pioneers of experimental cinema, had naturally encouraged his interest in 'the new art of the people'.

Starting up a film club in Finland called for something besides a visionary chairman and an energetic secretary, and that was money. Hahl found an elegant solution to the problem. His good friend Maire Gullichsen's mother, Lilli Ahlström, was persuaded as a charitable gesture to subscribe to fifty paid seats to all of the club's showings (which she never attended). In November 1934 the club gave a free showing of René Clair's *Entr'acte* to recruit members, and on March 7, 1935, the club got properly under way in the presence of no less a person than the Minister of Education. Aalto spoke on this occasion of the importance of experimental photography in Moholy-Nagy's film *schwarz weiss grau,* which was then shown, followed by René Clair's *A nous la liberté.*

120. Scenes from Moholy-Nagy's film schwarz weiss grau *from 1930.*

The Projektio board included the influential professor of literature Gunnar Castrén and the future 'national sculptor' Wäinö Aaltonen. Neither they nor Aalto were involved in the practical work, which was handled by Hahl and a journalist named Hans Kutter. They were greatly helped by the Swedish film critic Gösta Werner, who managed a similar club in Sweden and was happy to send his programmes on to his Finnish friends. Aalto, however, was invaluable as a propagandist and as the witty arbiter of the debates that often followed showings. In 1982, Kutter still remembered word for word a slogan flung out by Aalto on one such occasion: *Good-looking, elegant young people must stream in from every door, talking about the cinema as though it was their mother tongue.*

The club soon numbered nearly 300 members, initially recruited mainly from among the upper classes, with foreign embassy representatives as a conspicuous element, but the proportion of working-class and left-wing forces soon grew, not least through the efforts of Nyrki Tapiovaara, later known as a film director. The showings took place five or six times per season at the Joukola cinema on Kapteeninkatu before the cinema's ordinary showings.

I was a newly matriculated student at the time, and met Alvar Aalto for the first time when I joined the club – more precisely, I saw him appear on select occasions. The films I particularly remember are Eisenstein's and Pudovkin's famous propaganda films, Bunuel's horrific *Andalusian Dog* and Sternberg's *Blue Angel* with the sinful Marlene Dietrich in the title role. In fact Projektio showed most of the films with artistic merit which were either so anti-commercial that they never reached the ordinary cinemas or were forbidden by the censors as politically or morally offensive. This ultimately led to the fall of the club. There was no place for a phenomenon like Projektio in the reactionary cultural climate brought about by the rise of Nazism in Germany and agitation by the Patriotic

People's Movement (IKL) in Finland. As the club had influential protectors, it was not actually banned, but it was strangled administratively by being forced to pay an arbitrary duty levied on the films it showed. The last showing took place in May 1936. During the war years, fear of all forms of left-wing activism rose to such a pitch that Kutter destroyed the club's archives to prevent the police from finding any concrete evidence in the event of a search.

However sad this turn of events was, there is no denying that Projektio's founders were politically rather naive. The letter sent by Hahl to Maire Gullichsen in England on April 1, 1936 included a report of the latest showing – possibly the one that sealed the club's fate:

Today we had Penal Colony *by Raizman, a pretty much unknown Russian silent film, which is not even mentioned in the books, but is tremen-* *dous. A prison in Siberia with criminals and a few political prisoners. A new director is appointed, brutal and degenerate, an extremely sharp portrayal. The political prisoners go on hunger strike, and the whole business looks like ending in catastrophe and despair. Then the revolutionaries come rushing at breakneck speed through the leafless Siberian birch forests. Realistically staged, attentive to detail, but so marvellously controlled that one's attention never wanders from the people, who are so perfectly characterized that just a shot of their boots is enough to show what sort of men they are. How can these Russians be such artists – I am amazed that such isolated people (as we see them) have been able to make such fresh, magnificent, refreshing works of art. But all they have to do is to play themselves.*

So strong was faith in the new Russia within liberal circles that it was not necessary for Hahl even to say

121. Scene from Raizman's Penal Colony *(Katorga).*

which regime was responsible for the mistreatment of prisoners and which represented freedom. None of us who watched Projektio's films with wide-eyed admiration ever dreamed that tens of thousands of political prisoners had recently been worked to death building the Stalin Canal from the White Sea to Lake Ladoga just off the Finnish border, and that millions of other political prisoners would have been glad to go on hunger strike if they had just got enough food to do so while they waited in vain in "the leaf-less Siberian birch forests" for the liberators who never came.

ANOTHER
LOW POINT

The year 1935 started badly for Aalto. In December he had contracted bronchitis, which soon developed into a dangerous case of pneumonia. Obviously his work suffered; thus he was unable to complete the small standard dwelling made of Enso board which he had agreed to present at the *Ideal Home Exhibition* at the Olympia in a contract drawn up in connection with the 1933 exhibition in London. Construction of the Viipuri Library was nearing its end, and Aino and the office assistant supervised the finishing touches.

On his sickbed Aalto spent most of his time designing his new home and office on Riihitie in Munkkiniemi. He had just acquired the plot, paying for it partly in town planning work for the owner, the Stenius company, which also owned much of Munkkiniemi's other unbuilt land. Construction got under way in summer 1935 and continued for a good year. Financially the venture was risky, and Aalto had to take out a substantial bank loan for it, but his income from the Viipuri Library and furniture sales did provide something of a realistic foundation for the investment.

The financial pressures on Aalto and the loss of strength due to his illness led to a "nervous crisis", as his

friends called it in some letters. Actually all this amounted to was that his basically hypersensitive and unstable temperament took over to such an extent that he was no longer able to put on the carefree front and 'top dog' attitude he had spoiled his friends with up to then. His friends often overlooked the fact that Aalto's profound artistic and psychological sensitivity was based on his unusually receptive nature, and that he was anything but robust. It could happen in later years, especially during the darkest months of the year, that he was paralysed and bedridden by depression. His assistant Marja Pöyry confirmed that the office was obliged to manage for weeks on end without its chief for the above reason on several occasions in the '30s; this naturally made great demands on his closest subordinates.

In spring 1935 Aino received a government grant of 8,000 marks for "studying industrial design of furniture, glass and textile production in continental Europe", enabling her to offer Alvar a much-needed holiday. In early June the couple left for Amsterdam, where a meeting of the CIAM executive committee and a Dutch architects' congress were in progress. Together with Siegfried Giedion, they went on to Brussels, where the great World's Fair had just opened its doors. Thanks to Wohnbedarf, the entire Swiss pavilion was filled with Aalto's bentwood furniture, whereas Finland preferred to present a more conservative image of her industrial art in a pavilion supervised by Nils-Gustav Hahl, Aalto's armour-bearer in Athens.

The industrial art section of the exhibition was naturally examined with particular interest by Aino, who was, after all, on a serious study tour. In an interview she gave to a Turku newspaper on her return,* she called attention to colonial interior design products, especially textiles, to which various plant fibres from bast to palm leaf gave a living quality. In general she thought

Uusi Aura, July 10, 1935.

European industrial art showed a revived interest in both the Far East and Africa. Rugs from Morocco, bamboo from Congo, and rush blinds from Sumatra appeared in many Continental furnishing shops (including Wohnbedarf in Zurich, she could have added). With his usual quickness, Alvar seems to have noticed the use of tree trunks with the bark left intact as pillars in primitive huts, the use of rattan switches to bind cross struts together, forming colonnades roofed with palm leaves, and other artistic ideas in the building traditions of native peoples. Only a year later he produced astonishing variations on these ideas in the Finnish pavilion at the World's Fair in Paris.

The Aaltos spent most of their month abroad in Switzerland, first in Lugano for a complete rest, then in Zurich for the relaxed company of their Swiss friends. One may guess that Aalto was thinking mainly of these summer days when writing Giedion's obituary thirty years later: *In Giedion's Doldertal* [the Zurich district in which Giedion's villa was located], *many critical trains of thought and impulses have seen the day beneath the green crown of the great plane tree, but so have cordial, encouraging thoughts directed to his architect friends, giving them strength and courage to go on with their task during a difficult but at the same time exceptionally creative period.* (*Arkkitehti*, 1968)

Discussions with friends about artistic and social problems were always important in Aalto's life. The opportunity to talk to people like Sigfried Giedion during these decisive formative years was a gift he grasped eagerly. What strikes one most when reading the writings of Giedion, Gropius, and other CIAM theoreticians of the period is that they were all basically aware of the limitations of Rationalism and pointed out the need for a biologically more satisfying, natural, individual variable — for architecture with more imagination and artistic vision than had been produced up to then. Giedion had contact with some of the leaders of irrational modern art, includ-

122. Aalto furniture in the Swiss pavilion at the 1935 World's Fair in Brussels, photo Aino Aalto.

123. Detail reminiscent of exotic native huts in Aalto's pavilion at the World's Fair in Paris.

ing Max Ernst, Mondrian and Brancusi, and in older days he became something of a Romantic in his books on the mysteries of prehistoric cave art. Yet none of this ever appeared in practice in the architecture he defended. The difference between him and Aalto was that Aalto was able to give concrete artistic shape to much of what was no more than pious, vague aspiration in his friend's declarations of principle.

When Aalto returned to Finland in July 1935, he brought with him a gen-

124. Alvar Aalto and Sigfried Giedion in Zurich in the 1950s.

eral demand for the humanization of Rationalism as well as practical knowledge about the kind of social housing his closest friends among the Swiss architects had developed as an alternative to the plain 'Siedlung' construction in Germany during the heyday of Bauhaus. A recent example of the humanized, though still very industrially oriented, Swiss housing production was the suburb of Neubühl just outside Zurich. The area contained 200 apartments in lamellar houses of two or three storeys, with a small garden for each family, and the result was

so exemplary that the area functioned as a temporary housing exhibition after it was completed in 1931. The complex was of moderate size, quite attractive and geared to middle-class requirements for comfort rather than to minimum proletarian standards. In fact Neubühl was the closest thing to a model for the social housing construction Aalto undertook to design in 1936 for Finnish industry (as Aalto himself points out in an interview with *Suomen Sosialidemokraatti* on July 14, 1935).

Aino and Alvar were back in Helsinki on July 9, 1935: this was probably the homecoming Mrs. Ichikawa described in the Japanese essay reprinted above. Alvar returned completely recovered and full of his customary optimism.

He immediately centred his efforts on a competition for the Finnish embassy building in Moscow, announced in June, with the last date of entry only July 27. That summer he had his office in an old house on the waterside promenade of Terijoki in Karelia, owned by one of his assistant's parents. From there he was able to supervise the finishing touches to the Viipuri Library, which was completed in the autumn.

The embassy competition was a disappointment for Aalto, since the jury thought he had placed the building badly on the site in raising the banquet suite on piers, which was "indefensible from both the financial and the practical point of view", in addition to which "the various rooms of the banquet suite were not attractively designed". Later that autumn Aalto took part in another competition for the factory and central warehouse of the State alcohol monopoly in Helsinki. He did no better in this competition, and earned reproof for impractical planning of spaces and communications, and for his brainwave in giving the floor level a continuous pitch of 1 : 70 to make it easier to move barrels and vats about within the complex. We can see that the myth Aalto cherished in his later years, according to which he had won or at least received a prize in most of the competitions he ever took part in,

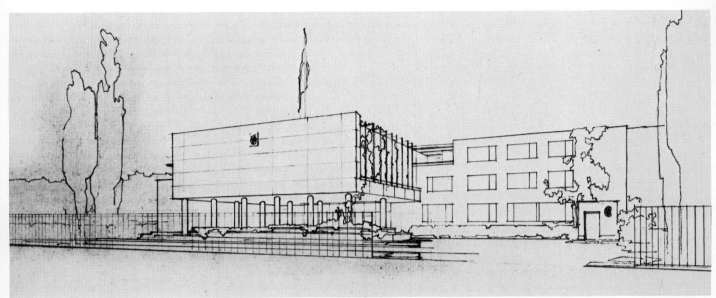

125. *Aalto's competition entry for the embassy building in Moscow, 1935.*

had no foundation in reality. In fact we find that he had remarkably little success in competitions during the '30s, and only his victories in the Viipuri Library and Paimio Sanatorium competitions back in 1927 and 1929 kept him going. From 1929 to his victorious Paris pavilion in 1936, he took part unsuccessfully in 22 competitions altogether, as is shown by the list of works at the end of this book. In the church competitions and the Mänttä offices his lack of success was partly due to the jury's preference for a more traditional kind of architecture, but in most of the other cases the winning plans were in the same Rationalist style as Aalto's. The decisive factors tended to be deficiencies in the planning of practical functions as well as overly bold, sometimes untested technical ideas that were also found quite frequently in his later work.

Incomparably the most important event for Aalto during 1935 was that the Viipuri Library was finally completed. It was a new masterpiece even more prestigious than the Paimio Sanatorium, which summed up the Functionalist commitment of his youth while anticipating his mature, more individual architecture.

126. *Lending office of the Viipuri Library (Cf. F 111).*

BIRTH OF THE ARTEK COMPANY

Another event in 1935 that proved significant in the long run was the founding of Artek, an interior design and furniture sales company. As usual, the key to success was Aalto's knack of finding dedicated, self-sacrificing and skilful assistants.

We already know the background: the extraordinary upswing in sales of Aalto's bentwood furniture following the London exhibition in 1933. It was soon clear that FINMAR, the agency set up to sell Aalto furniture in the English-speaking world, was unable to obtain sufficiently large deliveries from Finland. Morton Shand and FINMAR head Faulkner wrote letters to Huonekalutehdas in Turku, which were

left unanswered because nobody there understood English. They wrote and cabled Aalto, who did not reply because he had other worries. Finally FINMAR's wealthy sponsor G.M. Boumphrey wrote a letter from his magnificent country estate, Stirrups, where Aalto had spent a genuine English weekend in 1933, and threatened Aalto with financial reprisals. The letter was extremely polite in form, but gave an icy glimpse of the hunger for profit that can lie behind the English gentleman's mask. Boumphrey took it for granted that the main objective of Aalto's furniture design was financial profit, and that business is a game on which the players must bestow their entire attention. Something of the same petty shrewdness and propensity to cheat the unversed artist appeared in the letters Aalto received at approximately the same time from Giedion's Swiss company Wohnbedarf. It is not difficult to see that Aalto's nonchalance in money matters not only annoyed his correspondents, but actually offended their fundamental beliefs. They quite simply could not understand how anyone could behave so irresponsibly in something as serious as business.

In fact, English and Swiss businessmen were not the only people to be shocked by Aalto's incorrigible levity in money matters; his closest subordinates were also worried. It often resulted in painful situations for Aalto himself, as when he was obviously duped by canny adversaries or when distraint officers paid a visit. Basically, however, it was a defence mechanism that kept his work from being soiled by all the compromises the thought of financial profit would have necessitated, and allowed him to concentrate all his attention and energy on artistic creation and the important things in life. Aalto refused to become a mercenary soul and to adapt his work to Mr. Boumphrey's interest in profit. He ignored FINMAR's and Wohnbedarf's threats to break off all relations and continued unconcernedly on his own path.

The businessmen were not too fool- ish to find a rational solution. They left Aalto in peace and appointed a man- ageable go-between instead. As we already know, Morton Shand and Nils- Gustav Hahl had made friends during the Athens trip in 1933. By the summer of 1935, when furniture deliveries had got utterly out of hand, Shand could think of no other remedy than to travel to Finland himself to try and sort out the mess. During his trip he hit upon the bright idea of having FINMAR, Aalto and the furniture factory employ Hahl as their joint secretary.

This gave Hahl an even more bril- liant idea. He had often discussed the possibility of starting an avant-garde art gallery in Helsinki with his good friend Maire Gullichsen in order to give a boost to the international art they both admired so much. Maire Gul- lichsen was the daughter of Walter Ahlström, director and chief owner of the powerful industrial group A. Ahlström. At the time (autumn 1935) she was not yet personally acquainted with Aalto. Thus Hahl had two unplay- ed trump cards in his hand: Maire Gul- lichsen, who wished to open an art gal- lery but would not be able to manage it personally, and Alvar Aalto, who had created furniture but was incapable of organizing its sales. Hahl took Maire Gullichsen to see Aalto at his new home on Turuntie. "I was awfully ner- vous, for I had never been in an archi- tect's home before", Maire Gullichsen told me. "Nils-Gustav presented our proposition to start up a firm which would arrange art exhibitions and sell modern interior design, mainly Aalto furniture. Alvar looked at my legs, which were pretty in those days, and said: Why not? That was the beginning of Artek."

One is tempted to say that this in- terpretation is romanticized, but it is basically correct, though somewhat simplistic. The decision to found a company of the kind had matured over a much longer period. On June 19, when Hahl was in Brussels as acting superintendent of the Finnish pavilion at the World's Fair, he wrote Aalto a

127. Maire Gullichsen in Switzerland in the 1940s, photo Alvar Aalto.

letter (all in lower-case letters, of course): *am very glad of your* [Alvar and Aino's] *visit and have naturally thought about our last conversation. and of earlier conversations we have had on the same problems. consider- ing the much-regretted "lack of in- tellectual opposition" in helsinki – and finland in general – i still tend towards the view that a locale, a shop, an exhi- bition room, a palag branch office* [PALAG was Giedion's industrial art wholesaling company in Zurich], *something like that, would provide the ideal basis for action.*

On September 16, 1935, Hahl sent a letter from Helsinki to Maire Gul- lichsen in Noormarkku. This letter seems to be the key document on Ar- tek's birth, since it wound up in Aalto's archives after their negotiations. Here it is:

Dear Maire, I am sorry to have missed you on Saturday, when I tried to call you a couple of times to wish you a good journey. So I'm taking the opportunity to send you a few lines, especially as there seems to be a particular reason for doing so. You will have guessed that it concerns the plans we talked about a bit when we last met here in Helsinki. "A million" and all that. My ideas have developed in a definite direction over the last few days, they are in fact beginning to take concrete shape. These ideas are not particularly new, either. I have often turned these problems over in my mind and discussed them with Aalto. And now it suddenly seems as if everything is converging almost to force them to come true. So sit up and take note.

I mentioned to you that Finmar Ltd. in London and especially friend Shand half forced me into a sort of secretary job in order to save the rapidly growing exports to England, which have been mismanaged here. After many negotiations and a great deal of correspondence I have realized that Finmar must have an office to handle its business here and that Aalto and his factory need the same to be able to keep pace with the expansion of their enterprise.

This has been the point of departure for further discussions. I have repeatedly told Aalto that the moment has come to set up this office in the most intimate connection with a 'gallery' (or a place for exhibitions and sales), which would act as his main agent and wholesaler for the domestic market, take over – in return for shares – his licences and thereby take a percentage of all exports of his wares (= part of his royalties), start as a joint-stock company with the major holding here in Finland in private hands, with lesser holdings divided between various others (including some foreign companies which do business with us). In other words we would combine a secure income from managing his continually growing affairs with the riskier venture of running an art gallery and an "interior design office" on new, carefully planned lines.

Naturally Aalto is enthusiastic. Since all of his new inventions would be implemented by the new company in the form of direct orders from the factories, the company would play an international role as an agent for his models, which are in far greater demand abroad than here. And it would certainly thrive on this alone. It would start with the exceptional advantage of working with firms in Zurich, Paris, London and Stockholm, which have already been buying the same goods we would be supplying in great quantities for two years. We could also immediately count on importing goods so far unknown to us from companies in Zurich and Paris. Why start up merely as an agent, since sales and exhibition facilities are merely a problem of finding the premises? Why renounce this unexpectedly offered platform for the cultural propaganda which is so necessary? And why pass up the chance to publicly and purposefully explain to Finns the trends in our own industrial art which have only been fully appreciated abroad so far? I assume from experience that other countries are far more conscious of what is worth developing in Finland: we have a reputation as a land of modern industrial art and architecture, but we have no conspicuous centre to correspond to this reputation of which we are hardly even aware at home. In this I do not merely wish to further Aalto's interests, but also to the highest degree those of young people who wish to follow similar paths and would otherwise never find any response to their efforts. You may think this sounds arrogant or overambitious, but I assure you that someone must do it, and at the same time ask why we shouldn't be the ones to do it . . .

I venture to make the proposition not only because we recently discussed it but also because you asked me several times last winter about "when we would start up an art gallery". To get one going, someone will have to make a largish investment, so that there are not too many people making decisions and that someone should be a private person with an interest in the subject. That means you.

The letter also contains a fairly detailed plan for financial and practical arrangements for the venture, with sensible arguments which seem to have convinced Maire's husband and advisor Harry as well. Nils-Gustav and Maire really went to see Alvar only to confirm their plans. Before Artek – the name was a happy thought of Aalto's – could start operations, some practical problems had to be solved. The most important thing was to come to a binding agreement with the principal purchaser of Aalto furniture, that is, FINMAR in London, and Aalto was prevailed upon to go to England for negotiations in October. FINMAR had already sold two million marks' worth of furniture in 1934, but had only managed to increase its sales by 20 % in 1935 on account of the factory's hopeless lack of capacity. Aalto was now promised future orders amounting to at least five million per year if he could guarantee delivery. Together they sent an ultimatum to Korhonen's Turku factory: either the factory should be immediately enlarged or Aalto would go over to another manufacturer. In fact he had already entered negotiations with Oy Kolho, a member of the Serlachius industrial group in Mänttä. A few years later Aalto seriously considered having Artek set up a furniture factory of its own. The fact that Korhonen's Huonekalutehdas managed to maintain its position was probably due to confusion about the moral rather than the legal copyright to Aalto furniture, which was, after all, the fruit of the joint efforts of Aalto and Otto Korhonen, to the extent that the latter owned the patent to the first stackable Aalto chair.

Aalto's journey to London in autumn 1935 was made particularly pleasant by the fact that he met his old friends Gropius, Moholy-Nagy and Marcel Breuer there. By then they had left Nazi Germany for good and were stopping over in England before going on to the United States. He had less pleasure in meeting the friend to whom he owed his improved prospects. The unfortunate Shand had sunk even

deeper into financial misery, and was soon compelled to sell his share in the flourishing FINMAR to the shark Boumphrey. Aalto's harsh comments on Shand in a letter to Aino chill the heart: *A curious nervous old fool – everything's wrong with Shand – himself most of all. There's no use for someone like Shand in these matters any more.* In another letter he complains that he spends more than half his time in London in the tube. *A strange city. Had dinner with our attaché yesterday. Must eat without art conversation sometime, can't stand it*

128. Millions of Aalto stools from 1933 have been sold in the past fifty years.

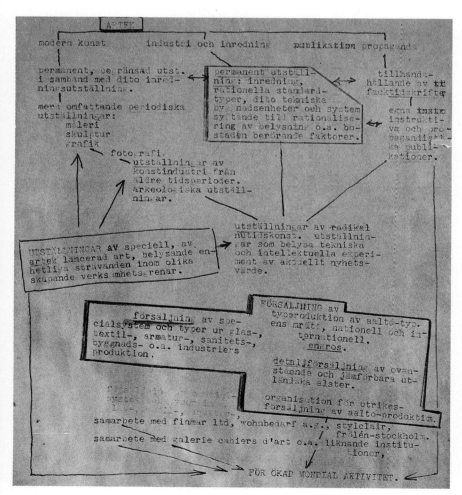

129. Artek's programme declaration as drafted by the founders.

otherwise. When he came home he felt he had done enough for Artek and left the remaining arrangements to Hahl.

The original holdings in the new company were as follows: Maire Gullichsen subscribed for 150 shares at 1,000 marks apiece, Nils-Gustav Hahl for eighty and his father, professor Carl Hahl for ten. Alvar Aalto received 190 shares in return for royalty rights, Aino Aalto twenty and Huonekalutehdas thirty. The remaining twenty shares were subscribed for by other private persons. In 1936, fifteen of Aalto's shares were transferred to Wohnbedarf in Zurich and twenty to Svenska Artek (Artek Sweden), owned by architect Sture Frölén of Stockholm. These transactions were probably dictated by the state of Aalto's finances following the construction of his house at Riihitie.

It soon proved that Hahl's financial calculations had not been unrealistic. FINMAR increased its purchases to eight million marks in 1936, Svenska Artek bought half a million marks' worth, and large quantities continued to be sold through Wohnbedarf of Zurich, Sidam of Brussels, Styleclaire of Paris, Herr & Co. of Johannesburg and Gatepak of Barcelona. From then on annual dividends from Artek made up for the decrease in Aalto's royalties, besides which the company paid Aino a salary.

Before starting operations, Hahl worked out a programme declaration defining the company's spheres of operation. Let us take a closer look at its principles, with which Aalto certainly agreed, though he left their implementation to Hahl and concentrated on his creative work.

The gallery, which was so important to Maire Gullichsen, was to concentrate on both Finnish and foreign new art (painting, sculpture, graphics and photography). This modern art was to be presented by means of exhibitions, while a permanent collection should also be built up and displayed in connection with interior design exhibitions. Work for the benefit of "radical modern art" would be supplemented with exhibitions of "artefacts from earlier times" and even with "archaeological exhibitions" as well as "exhibitions which would cast light on technological and scientific achievements of topical interest and national and international value". In addition to this wide range of exhibitions, Artek would maintain a reading room in which the public would have access to cultural periodicals. Furthermore, the company would publish art criticism, biographies and books of general interest.

The emphasis in operations, however, was to be on industrial and interior design. There was to be a permanent exhibition of all the standard products, technical building supplies and furnishing systems that make rationalization of homes possible. This would involve not only ordinary furnishing elements such as glass, textile and lighting details, but also fixtures for kitchens, water, heating and waste systems and windows, doors, wall and floor surfaces; in short, a complete building technology department.

As for the 'Aalto types', i.e., furniture and other inventions, they were basically only details in the overall rationalization scheme, in which foreign types were accepted on a basis of equality with Finnish ones. Aalto furniture was, however, to be considered Artek's own specialty, and to be sold by the company wholesale and retail, both in Finland and abroad.

It goes without saying that in practice such a comprehensive and demanding scheme was out of the question. Artek started out in December 1935 as an unpretentious agency. It acquired its first shop and office facilities in the new building of the Nordic Union Bank at Fabianinkatu 31 at the beginning of the following year. On April 1, 1936, Hahl proudly reported to Maire Gullichsen, who was in London at the time: *By the way, Artek is flourishing. We have such an awful lot of work that I've had to give up everything else I wanted to do apart from Artek. We should already double our staff. I don't know whether the bourgeoisie is really so delighted – perhaps just curious. Anyway I hope their idea that Aalto furniture is villa furniture will give us a good spring season. Artek cer-*

130. View of Artek's first shop in Fabianinkatu 31, Helsinki, with standard pieces of furniture which are still in production.

131. Today the fifty-year-old Artek is a flourishing enterprise thanks to worldwide exports of Aalto furniture.

tainly looks attractive, almost unique in its kind in the world, I should think. The impressively lighted windows are beleaguered by crowds of people in the evenings.

Artek also arranged successful exhibitions, some built around the theme of furniture, glass and textiles, others displaying controversial radical art, culminating in a double exhibition of Fernand Léger's paintings and Alexander Calder's sculptures in 1938, an event that was made possible by Aalto's friendship with both artists.

Artek never became the combined museum of design and modern art, institute of rationalization, and publisher of radical art literature that Finland undoubtedly needed at the time. This was too visionary a goal for the novices who conceived it and for their limited financial resources. Instead Artek became an internationally oriented art gallery and a small but excellent furniture company, which relied financially on exports of Aalto furniture and in-

terior design projects for public surroundings in Finland. Aalto himself contributed to Artek's work only occasionally, in later days not at all, but the company provided Aino with a convenient niche and gave her independent spirit more scope, while she continued to collaborate with Alvar.

It is obvious that Aalto furniture never would have attained the perfection it is renowned for if skilful interior designers at Artek had not constantly improved the models, created variants and supplemented them with other furniture, such as sofas, tables and cupboards. Part of Aalto's genius was in his ability to transmit his own enthusiasm to disinterested assistants, and he made particularly good use of this ability at Artek, where everyone worked 'in the Aalto spirit', to the extent that today it is often impossible to distinguish Aalto's own designs from what Aino and other collaborators, such as Maija Heikinheimo, designed.

It was particularly important that

maximization of profit never became the company's guiding principle. The temptation to go over to the kind of furniture in demand, to follow the caprices of fashion, in general to compromise in order to sell more, was always overcome by love of the special Aalto line or spirit. It was enough if the accounts balanced and work could go on. This was of course primarily Aalto's own attitude: with his civil service family background, he looked down on the least hint of greed and in general was critical of out-and-out capitalism. His collaborators were glad to follow his lead. Hahl was a true humanist who preferred culture to lucre, while Maire Gullichsen was rich enough to be able to concentrate fully on positive human contacts. The world Aalto and Hahl opened up to her gave her life meaning and satisfaction. In time she became one of the leading promoters of Finnish arts.

Päewaleht

nr. 59　　　　　　　　Pühapäewal, 28. weebruaril 1937

Uue Kunstimuuseumi projekte

132. *The Estonian newspaper* Päewaleht *published the Tallinn Art Museum competition entries of the two winning Estonian architects and of Alvar Aalto on February 28, 1937.*

ON THE WAY TO THE TOP

In many ways 1936 was another year of consolidation for Aalto. During the year Artek grew from modest beginnings into an effective tool and a recognized centre for the propagation of Aalto's ideas. The company, represented by Aino Aalto and Hahl, presented a selection of Aalto furniture which created quite a stir at the Milan Triennale in May. Aalto's reputation at home was also growing. He had finally been elected to the Board of the Finnish Association of Architects in autumn 1935, embarking on a career that brought him the post of vice-chairman in 1939 and the chairmanship in 1943. Opposition to Aalto among older colleagues and jealous rivals was as strong as ever, but his international success gradually led to a change in the wind.

An indication of the increasing confidence enjoyed by Aalto was the fact that he was selected as a member of the jury for two competitions that year, one for renovation of the centre of Tampere and the other for a church in Temppeliaukio square in Helsinki. An even more important honour was his selection by the Association as the Finnish representative in an invited competition for an art museum in Tallinn. The other participants were Ragnar Östberg from Sweden and a number of Estonian architects. Aalto's plan constituted an important stage of development in his chief concern of defining a new concept of interior space. It must have been a painful blow for him not to win – though neither did Östberg, for that matter. His plan was an epoch-making architectural feat, yet it could have been carried out with simple means; the Estonians, however, were determined that one of their own architects should have the assignment, though they also wanted to gain international prestige for their competition.

AALTO'S OWN HOME

Aalto's private life also became more stable in August 1936, when he was able to move into his new home at Riihitie 20. It was a combined home and studio on a charming, forested, but relatively small plot in the newly planned and exclusive suburb of Munkkiniemi. The feeling for texture and 'natural' materials evident in the Viipuri Library interiors appeared here in the exterior as well, partly square surfaces of vertical weatherboarding providing a collage-like contrast to whitewashed brick surfaces. In Viipuri Aalto had still kept to smooth white stucco walls in Le Corbusier style; here he brought out the brick structure under the thin layer of lime in a way which would be typical of his work from then on. In the plan itself, the exterior and interior space intermingle, and nature is allowed to invade the building with clinging vines such as one might see in an old ruin. The natural stone steps in front of the entrance and on the garden terraces accentuate the impression of harmony with nature on nature's own terms.

Aalto's home was long considered a Functionalist manifesto by shortsighted commentators. He himself held a completely different view, as appears clearly from a tragic anecdote he often told. His unhappy old colleague Gustaf

133. Aalto's house in the 1960s seen from the garden side, with the aging master in the foreground.

Strengell, whose book on 'the city as a work of art' had given Aalto fruitful impulses in his early years, and who had later lent him his critical support during the militant years of Functionalism, decided in 1937 that he had nothing more to live for. One summer afternoon he came to Aalto's house and asked if he could come in. "I have just been to Seurasaari [Helsinki's open-air museum with old buildings] to see the Niemelä farm. Now I should like to see the modern Niemelä farm once more." He sat for a while in the living room, then rose and took a taxi to the Pörssiklubi, where he shot himself.

For Aalto, Strengell's comment was the finest criticism he ever received of his home. Niemelä Farm, from the village of Konginkangas in central Finland, consists of a group of unpainted timber structures from the 18th and 19th centuries, set around a yard according to the principle of one building, one function. In its grey but elegant simplicity, this group of buildings shows the affinity with nature of the building idiom that the forest-dwelling Finns had applied with such mastery since the Iron Age.

THE PARIS
PAVILION

Many of the themes Aalto had experimented with in his own home, combined with bold new ideas, converged in the key work from 1936 that we shall discuss next. The competition for the Finnish pavilion at the impending World's Fair in Paris had been announced that spring, and no less than thirty-one architects sent in entries. The jury consisted of three modern-minded architects: Erik Bryggman, Martti Välikangas and Yrjö Lindegren. The two highest-placed entries were marked "Le bois est en marche" and "Tsit Tsit Pum", and both proved to be by Alvar Aalto together with his main assistants, Aarne Ervi and Viljo Revell. The exhibition committee consequently assigned Aalto to carry out the

first-named plan, which took shape in -Paris in 1937, and was Aalto's first building project abroad (apart from the botched villa project in Tartu).

The Paris pavilion was the first work in which the mature Aalto finally emerged in full stature. Everything that we can point to with the wisdom of hindsight as signs and omens in his earlier work burst into full bloom here. However splendid his previous masterpieces – the Paimio Sanatorium and the Viipuri Library – may have been, the Paris pavilion was the first specimen of an architecture that was genuinely Aalto's own.

Two particularly favourable circumstances made this breakthrough possible; in fact provoked it. The first was the unusual amount of freedom exhibition buildings offer. Here experimentation and boldness are not merely permissible but desirable; considerations of everyday use and durability do not count, since the buildings are intended as temporary. The other fortunate circumstance was the site in the wooded, irregularly sloping park adjacent to the Trocadéro in Paris. It was generally complained that Finland had received a poor site, not easy to master compared to the open, horizontal building sites designated to many other nations. The prohibition to cut down a single tree made the task almost hopeless in many architects' eyes. For Aalto, who instinctively loved differences in height, and increasingly consciously wished to break with the schematization of the technological world of geometrical abstractions in order to build in harmony with the principles of living nature, the site provided exactly the challenge he needed.

Of his two entries, "Tsit Tsit Pum" was by far the bolder, but since it was not carried out, it is difficult to determine whether it would have been as successful as "Le bois est en marche". The main idea in the former was a large pavilion of irregular shape on the treeless part of the site, with a uniform flat roof over its entire breadth (with five skylight openings at the top end), but with recesses for the existing trees,

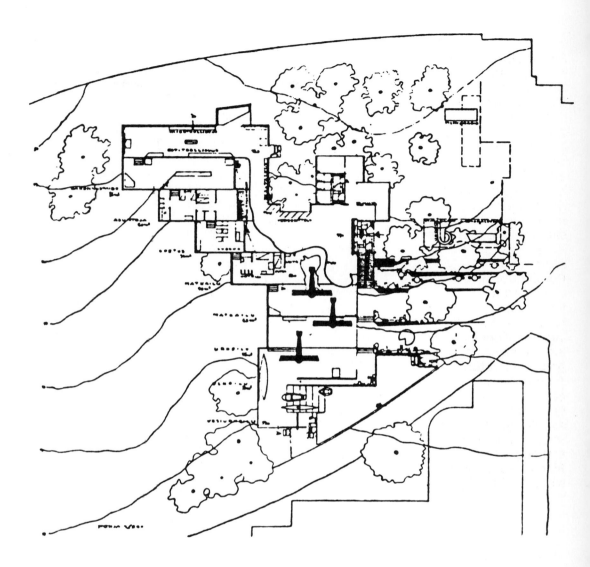

134. The 'Tsit tsit pum' entry, showing the great central exhibition hall with aeroplanes hung up to suggest the horizontal level, while the floor surface slopes downward stepwise.

and a floor forming a series of terraces giving the building something of the character of a stair hall with a very high ceiling at the lower end. At the upper end of the hall there was a kind of balcony with an irregularly curving front. This motif had already appeared in one of the sketches for Viipuri Library from 1934, in which Aalto was playing with the idea of rendering the apse-shaped protuberance of the reading room in free form. He took up the motif for the third time in his design for the New York pavilion in 1939, when he was finally able to carry it out (see pages 161–165).

The overall form of the exhibition hall in the "Tsit Tsit Pum" plan was opaque but organically balanced, and provided Aalto's first answer to Moholy-Nagy's question: "What is space in modern architecture?" It was not the 'flowing space' of Mies van der Rohe and the De Stijl architects, composed of geometrically placed screens, nor was it Le Corbusier's space, which often looked like a hall of sculptures. The point of the space created by Aalto in the "Tsit Tsit Pum" entry was that it was not based on a given Euclidic volume, nor was it intended to form a fixed, uniform whole; instead, like Cézanne's paintings, it consisted of suggested and partial figures balanced against one another in the formlessness that is our basic reality. Aalto's pavilion was literally a *forest space*, related to the spatial ex-

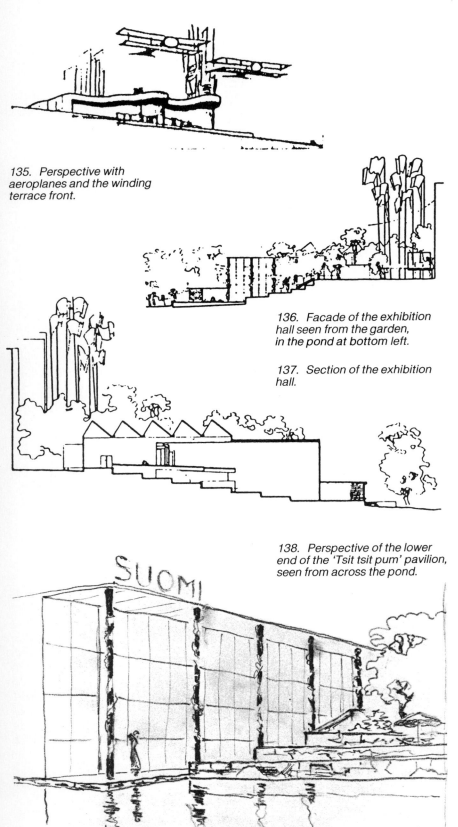

135. Perspective with aeroplanes and the winding terrace front.

136. Facade of the exhibition hall seen from the garden, in the pond at bottom left.

137. Section of the exhibition hall.

138. Perspective of the lower end of the 'Tsit tsit pum' pavilion, seen from across the pond.

perience of wandering among tree trunks, rocks and bushes in the broken terrain of a Nordic forest. The atmosphere differs from that of continental forests and English parks, but the principle, in the pure spatial experience offered by the glades in the park of the Trocadéro, has the same encircled openness. The "Tsit Tsit Pum" pavilion would have appeared to be a part of the wooded site; all the more so owing to the glass wall at the point where the room was highest. Eight high flagpoles were to stand in front of the pavilion in free formation as a man-made parallel to the freely-growing trees.

"Le bois est en marche" did not contain such an exciting interior with freely varied wall and floor plans, merely a more disciplined variant of the open interior space of which the Viipuri Library reading room was an early example, i.e., a square room with a sunken section in the middle and several rows of round skylights. And yet the inspiration for this entry was also closely derived from the forest. True, the motto principally alluded to the importance of Finland's forests as the country's industrial and economic resource. But the forest also appeared in more than one architectural theme. In the first place, there was the free, serpentine form that Aalto had clearly borrowed from Finnish lakeland scenery. Aalto placed giant aerial photographs depicting the curving lines of lakes and forests on the facades. The motif was reiterated by a pond with a shoreline in free form, placed by Aalto below the main pavilion. Another architectural reflection of forest scenery was provided by the external cladding of the main pavilion, consisting of vertical boarding, a further development of the facing used for his new home in Munkkiniemi. If the boards created the optical illusion of tightly packed tree trunks, the pavilion also had free-standing trees in many variations, from flagpoles to supports for climbing plants. Even more frequent, however, were tree trunks used as columns, either as conventional roof supports or grouped into sparse

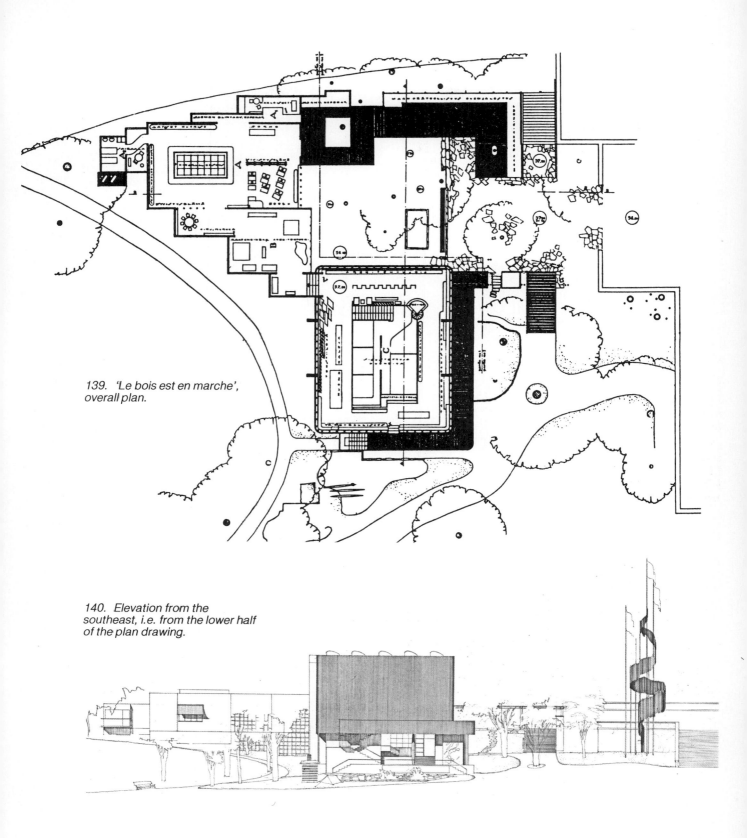

139. 'Le bois est en marche',
overall plan.

140. Elevation from the
southeast, i.e. from the lower half
of the plan drawing.

screens. In some instances, especially in the loggia supports lashed together with rattan bands (F 123), the influence of the exotic huts at the Brussels World's Fair could be clearly detected. In other cases Aalto 'translated' the foreign idiom into his mother tongue — I am thinking of the unstripped birch and pine trunks Aalto used as bearing columns in various designs.

The 'forest space' motif was also present, of course, although in a more discreet form than in "Tsit Tsit Pum". Wandering through the secondary pavilions, the visitor truly felt he was walking in the woods, with their ever-changing perspectives and spatial forms, while the wooded terrace garden in the middle could be compared to a Japanese garden with its elegantly irregular 'open closedness'.

Aalto went to Paris three times in 1936, first in May before he designed his competition entry, then in July, after the jury decision, to complete the working drawings for the French entrepreneur responsible for the rough construction. In March the following year, fifteen Finnish carpenters were sent to Paris to do the demanding woodwork. Aalto himself shuttled back and forth during the spring, taking part between journeys in assembling the exhibition material in Finland. For him the pavilion was merely the shell for his conception of a non-propagandist presentation of the Finnish people, nature, culture and industry, with the relationship with the forest as its pervading motif.

His presentation relied heavily on photography. For the Turku exhibition eight years earlier, Aalto had built everything around a basic typographic idea by disposing the material in the form of a gigantic newsspread. In Paris he wished to give the young art of photography the principal role, seeing it as a modern continuation of Akseli Gallen-Kallela's frescoes in the famous Finnish pavilion at the Paris Exhibition in 1900. Together with photographers Eino Mäkinen, Fred Runeberg, Heikki Aho and Heinrich Iffland, he assembled as representative a collec-

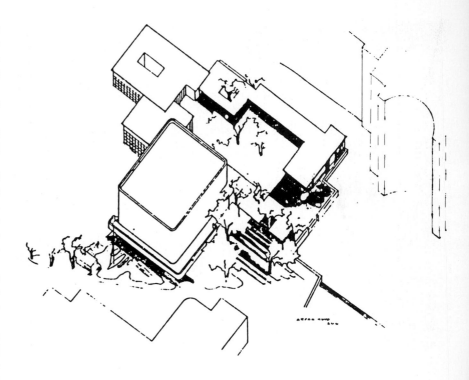

tion as possible of their work, with giant blow-ups of aerial views and life-size silhouettes of folk characters pasted onto boards as salient features. Aalto's fine overall plan for the exhibition unfortunately conflicted with the ambitions of the sponsors and the supervisors delegated by them, all of whom wished to make their contribution as conspicuous as possible. The art craftsmen insisted with particular tenacity on their right to hang their *ryijy* rugs and place their decorative vases in rows as at any trade fair, thereby sabotaging Aalto's whole idea. Unexpected extra expenses forced cuts in some arrangements that were particularly important to Aalto. The main items so ignominiously struck out were two 'lakes', one of them with wooden boats from the eastern province of Savo, which were to contribute to the fresh, summery overall impression. Disagreement between the architect and supervisors became so serious that Aalto did not attend the ceremonial inauguration on June 16, where the chief supervisor Eero Snell-

141. A bird's-eye view of the Paris pavilion.

142. Photographs and wooden poles which articulate space were two predominant elements in Aalto's Paris pavilion.

143. Alvar Aalto portrayed by Sandy Calder in Paris 1937.

man and Minister of Trade Voionmaa delivered eloquent orations on the ancient cultural contacts between Finland and France, but said not a word about who had designed the pavilion. Presenting the exhibition in *Arkkitehti* magazine, Aalto complained bitterly about the sabotage of his plans, and got his friends Le Corbusier and Fernand Léger to rebuke those responsible for it. It is easy to understand Aalto's disappointment and admit that in principle he was right, but the charm and ingenuity of the pavilion had such a compelling effect in spite of everything that most visitors never even noticed the minor blemishes. Scandinavian reporters generously admitted that the modest Finnish pavilion hidden away in a corner was the most successful Nordic contribution, but Aalto received his greatest praise from the top names in international architecture. Le Corbusier wrote: *In the Finnish pavilion the visitor is delighted by its deep-rooted authenticity. It has been a point of honour for the authorities to choose the right architect,* (reprinted in *Arkkitehti* no. 9, 1937). In Paris the watchful talent scouts of New York's newly-opened Museum of Modern Art also discovered Aalto, and invited him to appear at the museum the following year with a 'one man show'.

From a longer perspective, it is clear that in the Paris pavilion Aalto gave the myth of the Finns as a people deeply rooted in their environment, yet forward-looking and oriented to the present, its first convincing expression. This myth was taken up in the post-war years by a whole phalanx of Finnish architects and designers who succeeded in gaining a place among the leaders of international design in Aalto's wake. While Finnish painters and sculptors remained provincially backward-looking for many years to come, by 1938 Aalto had already discovered the synthesis of local traditions and international avant-gardism that was to prove so successful later on.

Aalto's longish stay in Paris in the early summer of 1937 was not exclusively devoted to hard work. As

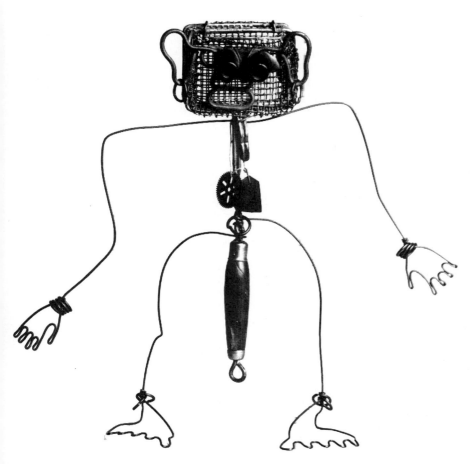

usual, he found time to do the social rounds in style. He renewed his friendship with Fernand Léger (whom he first met in Athens in 1933) and formed an even closer new friendship with Alexander Calder. He was introduced by Christian Zervos (a friend of Giedion's) to many of the avant-garde artists in Paris, including Constantin Brancusi, with whom he kept in contact for the rest of Brancusi's life.

We owe a whiff of the living reality of those days to Maire Gullichsen, who told me in an interview taped in 1977:

I was also in Paris, for it was Artek's first exhibition. Alvar was terribly disappointed with Harri Röneholm of Ornamo (the Finnish Association of Designers), who forced us to make dreadful compromises in the matter of art handicraft. No end of ryijy rugs we had no use for. Anyway that Paris Fair was wonderful. I was just a country lass, you know, and all Alvar said was "Now we'll go and see the Zervoses", and Madame Zervos was an utterly wonderful person. They had started publishing Cahiers d'Art, *and Alvar and I met Picasso at their place. Then we started going around with the whole*

gang, such fun it was. I must have looked a bit exotic to them. I wore a fine grey flannel suit and a shocking pink hat, and people said: "Who is this girl Alvar Aalto is going around with?" I was terribly proud. We sat at various bars and Alvar told me about his mother, how lovely she was. She had had such and such embroidered knickers, and it was from them – Mama's underwear – that Alvar had got the inspiration for his vases and lamps. Of course we worked hard at the pavilion, but somehow we always ended up at some bar or dance floor and had a marvellous time. Moholy was also in Paris. He was a rather charming fellow and I liked to promenade with him. In the Spanish pavilion he said: "Here's Calder's fountain and this is Picasso's Guernica". Yes, it really was wonderful, that quicksilver fountain . . .

AALTO AS A GLASS DESIGNER

Besides spurring Finnish architects to compete for the honour of designing a representative pavilion, the Paris

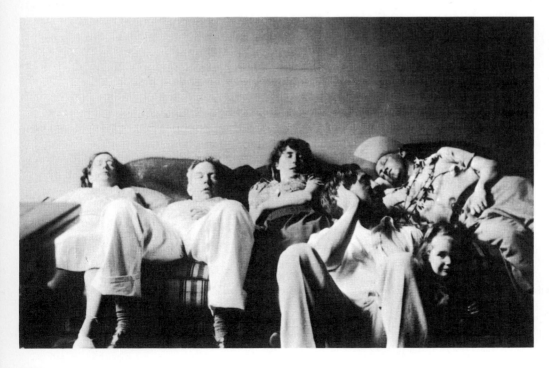

144. Siesta at Calder's near Paris in 1937. Aalto at the far right, Calder second from the left.

145. Calder between Picasso's Guernica and his own quicksilver fountain in the Spanish pavilion at the Paris World's Fair in 1937.

World's Fair also gave rise to a number of competitions to produce suitable design objects for display. Aalto took part in a competition announced by the Karhula Iittala glassworks in the autumn of 1936, with January 4 as the last date of entry. This was not his first

appearance as a glass designer: in the early '30s he had devoted considerable effort to the art. Since the details of Aalto's glass design have been analysed in detail by Timo Keinänen in an article published in *Arkkitehti* (no. 8, 1980), I shall restrict myself to a brief summary of the two competitions Aalto took part in before his glass design for Paris.

The first glass design competition Aalto took part in was in 1932, when Karhula Iittala invited designers to send in suggestions for new glassware and art glass. Alvar and Aino collaborated so closely in architecture that we are rarely able to distinguish between their respective contributions, but in industrial art it is obvious that Aino had personal ambition and took it as a sport in which she could compete with her husband. They both sent in entries to the Karhula Iittala competition. Aino won second prize in the category of pressed glass with her entry "Bölgeblick" (see F 115), while Alvar did not win a prize for his entry "karhiit", which consisted of nine different glasses and two carafes. The technical idea of the Bölgeblick series consisted of pressing the glass surface into concentric, wave-like rings, giving the objects strength and concealing the unremarkable quality of the material. The Bölgeblick series of carafes, bowls, jugs and drinking glasses was manufactured and sold with success throughout the '30s in Finland, and has recently come into production again. As for Aalto's entry, it formed part of his comprehensive design for the Paimio Sanatorium, where lamps, door locks, spittoons, washbasins and beds as well as drinking glasses were specially designed by the architect (though one wonders how Aalto came to include schnapps, beer, whisky and punch glasses in the sanatorium set). These glasses were stackable in a very ingenious way typical of Aalto's inventive spirit, but they were so complicated to make that the competition jury disqualified his entry.

At the beginning of the following year, 1933, the Riihimäki glassworks invited Aalto and nine other designers to take part in a competition for glassware and art glass to be sent to that year's Milan Triennale. This time Aalto won second prize in the glassware category with an entry called "Riihimäki flower" (see F 113), which was exhibited under the same name in Milan. It consisted of five simple articles: one large and two smaller bowls, a vase and a drinking glass, which could all be placed one within another to form a flower-like whole. The series was made in various shades of colour and in three different sizes, allowing for a variety of combinations. The "Riihimäki flower" was also displayed at his London exhibition in 1933 along with his wood furniture.

It was thus quite natural for Karhula-Iittala to invite Alvar and Aino to take part in the competition arranged by the company in 1936 for new glass design for the Paris exhibition. On this occasion, the majority of the jury were Aalto's sworn friends, headed by Gregor Paulsson from Sweden and Maire Gullichsen. Perhaps they suspected that the five carelessly but superbly drawn designs for vases with serpentine, wavy sides, bearing the motto "Eskimåerindens skinnbuxa" (The Eskimo girl's leather breech) came from Aalto's hand? Be this as it may, they awarded the entry first prize even though the technical aspect was problematical. Aalto suggested that a thin steel plate should be forced with steel pins into a closed serpentine shape on a rigid base, after which the glass could be blown into the mould. There was an obvious connection with his experimental wood reliefs. Aalto himself took part in the tests for making the moulds at the glassworks. The sharpest bends had to be modified, and in the end the moulds were blocks of wood instead of steel plates,

146. One of Aalto's sketches for the Karhula-Iittala glass design competition in 1936, motto "The Eskimo girl's leather breech".

147. Aalto's competition entry for stackable glasses, motto 'karhiit'.

148. Aalto's 'Savoy vase' from 1936 is made today in several sizes, but still blown into wooden moulds.

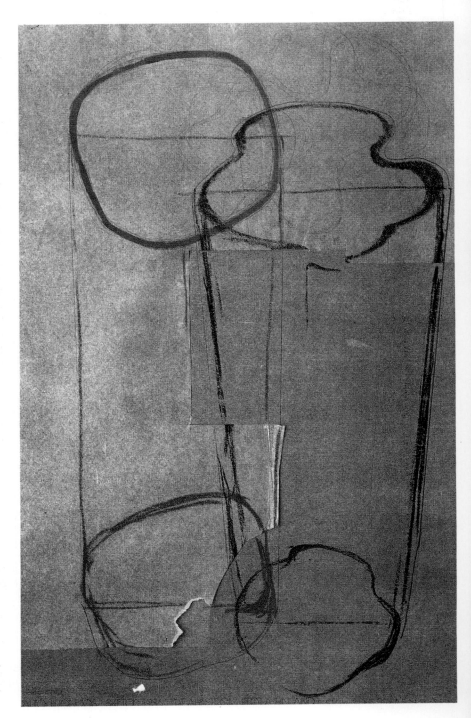

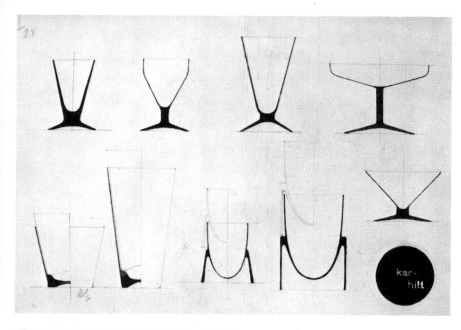

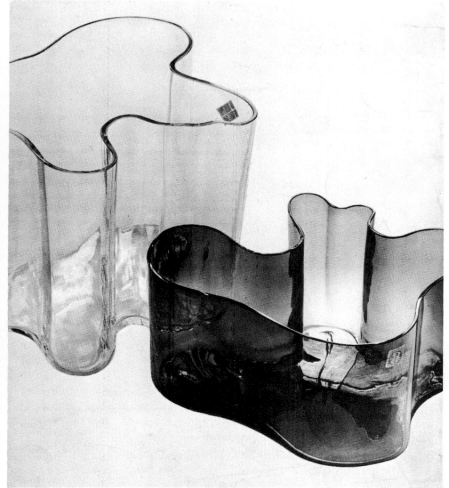

but at last the first sample of what was later known as the 'Savoy vase' was completed. Together with its sister vases, it deservedly created a stir when displayed in Aalto's Paris pavilion in the summer of 1937.

Aino also took part in the Karhula-Iittala competition of 1936, but did not win a prize for her studied, geometrically formed bowls, combinable hors d'oeuvre plates, glass boxes and serial candlesticks, all in a puritanical Rationalist style. On the other hand, Alvar went on to evolve new variants of his free-form vases and bowls, producing a new four-part 'flower' for the New York World's Fair in 1939.

Manufacture and sales of Aalto's glassware fell off after the war, and at the time of his death only the Savoy vase could be found in shops. The renewal of interest that has raised Aalto's reputation to unprecedented heights, however, has recently prompted Iittala to reintroduce Aalto's glass design on a large scale. The Savoy vase, in particular, has become something of a national symbol for the vitality and love of nature of modern Finland. The only remuneration by the glassworks for the copyright to these articles was the prize sum of 6,000 marks, which corresponds to something less than a thousand modern dollars – another piece of evidence of Aalto's nonchalance in money matters and the way profiteers exploited him.

A FORTUNATE FRIENDSHIP

1936 was an important year in Aalto's life, not just because he was able to move into his own house and take a decisive step forward with his winning entry for the exhibition pavilion in Paris. The friendship that grew between him and Maire Gullichsen's husband Harry during this year was of the greatest significance to his later work.

Maire Gullichsen's radical social ideas can be easily ascribed to a youthful need to break free from conservative parental authority and to the influence of the artistic and intellectual set she entered after she had left school at an early age. It may seem surprising that her views were shared by the man she married in 1928, who was appointed managing director of the great family company of Ahlström in 1932, since these views were apt to provoke conflicts with the company's old-style capitalist owners. If we seek a biographical explanation for Harry Gullichsen's ideas, we find that he was the son of an immigrant Norwegian who had advanced to the post of director of the large wood-processing company Enso-Gutzeit, and his mother was the daughter of a ship's pilot; his background may have given him a touch of the commoner. Other causes may, however, have been at the root of the Gullichsens' social radicalism. They should be sought in the social utopia whose architectural aspects are already familiar to us, in the dream of a world of reason, progress and human welfare that I discussed at the very beginning of this book. In this dream, as we know, technology and industry held pride of place as the motive force of progress. For young, dynamic, intelligent industrialists, this vision was just as stirring as for young architects. Harry and Maire Gullichsen were not such unusual representatives of their class as people were disposed to believe in backward Finland. As early as 1926, had not Le Corbusier found in Henri Frugès an industrialist who was responsive to his ideas on serially built Everyman's housing and sponsored the working-class housing area in Pessac? Did not the most forward-looking American millionaires sympathize with the programme of social reform instituted by the New Deal? There was a basic ideological affinity between the impecunious architect and the wealthy couple, which explains why in their sudden mutual infatuation they started calling each other "childhood friends" quite without justification. In an interview from 1984, Maire Gullichsen communicated her idea of this affinity to the author. To my question on whether the four friends

149. Harry and Maire Gullichsen, around 1939.

had a common belief in changing the world, she replied:

Of course we were eager to reform society and improve workers' conditions. My father Walter Ahlström had showed the way in building housing designed by architects for the company's workers and employees in Varkaus and elsewhere. He was deeply involved in this reform until his untimely death at the age of 52.

After his death, Harry was given charge of the company, and he wished to continue father's work. I was also very much aware of my responsibility, and we both set about to improve housing and working conditions. When we met Aino and Alvar, we felt they were a gift from heaven, with ideas similar to ours and healthy, rational suggestions. Together we started setting up and furnishing playparks and nurseries, redecorating workers' canteens and establishing clubs − whatever was needed in the various factories. It may have been on a small scale to start with, especially compared to conditions today. But it was a start, and the spirit was different. We knew everybody who worked in the factories, and we were young and enthusiastic.

Göran Schildt: *Did you get any support from the other shareholders?*

Maire Gullichsen: *It may be hard to judge afterwards like this, but we were often disappointed when we met with opposition and incomprehension. I might mention just one decision, typical of the times, which went right against our intentions. At a Board meeting at the Savoy restaurant, Harry*

150. *Alvar Aalto and Harry Gullichsen, around 1938.*

presented the plans for a new housing area in Savonmäki, Varkaus. The company had recently started up a wooden house factory there, giving Alvar the assignment of planning the area and designing new type houses. Alvar did not want his hands tied with stereotyped models; he wanted to make an experimental area of Savonmäki, with standardized building units which could be combined into various individual plans depending on the location and orientation of the site, and on the size of the family. It was to provide a sampling of the house factory's potential. But the plans fell through ignominiously because the company would have been obliged to have the area connected to the water mains − which would have cost a few million marks.

One of my aunts, who lived in Sweden, was particularly set against the plan. She sent the Board a letter which was read out at the meeting. In it she said that Maire and Harry had allowed themselves to be cajoled by the architects they went around with, which was why they dared suggest something as unheard-of as water pipes and toilets in workers' homes. She claimed that in Sweden workers had outhouses and their dung was used on the fields, which was how it should be. She added that Antti and Eva Ahlström [the founders of the company] would turn in their graves if they knew what Maire and Harry had suggested. "One just doesn't throw money away like that." All the other shareholders shared my aunt's views, and the proposal was buried. Harry and I felt as if we'd been put in the dock for having dared to express such radical ideas as running water in workers' housing. And this was in the thirties! Naturally the company had to put in the pipes anyway a few years later − and at many times the original cost.

The friendship between a humanist like Harry and a universal genius like Alvar did much for the fight against the front of short-sighted ultraconservatives. For my part, Aino's warm, humane approach to the problems of the times changed and broadened my ideas of the world around me. Reforms were certainly needed in that world. What would Finland look like today if we had not had such a strong, progressive social democracy? If the bourgeoisie had always held the reins? Would we have a Finland at all today?

It was not the first time that Aalto came into contact with Finnish big industry when Harry Gullichsen invited the young architect to work for Ahlström. He had already built employees' housing for the Schauman plywood mills in Joensuu and drawn up renovation plans for the Kangas paper mill offices in Jyväskylä. In 1930, the industrialist Gösta Serlachius (whose acquaintance Aalto had made as a young apprentice in Mänttä back in 1917) had given him a much more important assignment, which consisted of designing all the buildings for the new Toppila pulp mill in Oulu. This was the year of the Stockholm exhibition, when the young Finnish architects' idealization of machines and utility architecture reached its peak; the assignment was a real feather in Aalto's cap. That same year he was invited by Serlachius to compete with four older architects in designing a new head office for the company in Mänttä. Evidently the old tycoon appreciated Aalto more as a well-bred young man than as a pioneer of Modernist architecture, and the assignment went to Bertel Jung, a proven designer of elegant commercial palaces. In 1933 Aalto tried to arouse Enso-Gutzeit's interest in Le Corbusier's Domino system by designing two residential buildings in which a horizontal plane resting on concrete piers was to be complemented by freely variable insulating wall units made of 'ensolite' board, but the idea was far too radical for Finland at the time.

We may conclude that Aalto's tenacious efforts to arouse the interest of big industry were, on the whole, unsuccessful until he met Harry Gullichsen. The latter's unlimited confidence in Aalto changed the situation magically in 1936. There was a shower of definite commissions, large-scale planning assignments and far-reaching projects for him, not only from Ahlström, for other big companies followed suit. Aalto's office received so many assignments that he had to hire a great number of new assistants. For his later career, these industrial assignments provided a much-needed economic foundation for artistic freedom; on the other hand, it is astounding how his enthusiasm, inventiveness and ability to change survived the strain of the routine work thus forced on him. There was never any rift between commercial activity and ideology in Aalto's architecture.

The first assignment Aalto received from Harry Gullichsen was a new town plan for Varkaus. Ahlström's directors had realized long before that something must be done about workers' housing conditions in this town, which was the company's main site of operations. An investigative committee reported that 46 per cent of the workers' dwellings were run-down single rooms with wood stoves, but without water or plumbing, while 41 per cent were two-room homes of approximately the same standard. The first improvement undertaken by the company was to set aside a district called Luttila for single-family dwellings, where workers could buy a plot and build a small house of their own; for this they were offered a loan with easy terms. The new town plan drafted by Aalto in 1936 envisaged a gradual replacement of the entire building stock, and renovation of the company's various plants.

On September 19, 1936, an event called "the Warkaus housing and construction days" was arranged in the town.* The Artek and Asko-Avonius furniture companies each set up an exhibition of their own for visitors to study what a modern working-class home should look like, while the Ahlström company distributed prospectuses on house building and loans. Besides Harry and Maire Gul-

*Source: *Warkauden Lehti,* September 19 and 22, 1936.

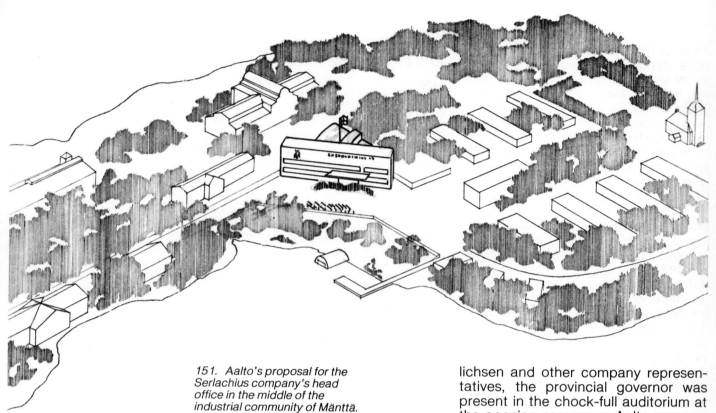

151. Aalto's proposal for the Serlachius company's head office in the middle of the industrial community of Mänttä.

152. Model of Aalto's first type house for Varkaus, 1937.

lichsen and other company representatives, the provincial governor was present in the chock-full auditorium at the opening ceremony. Aalto was one of the main speakers. He started by explaining the principles of the new methods of housing construction: by planning larger groups of buildings, in which traffic, sanitary and heating facilities were coordinated, costs could be brought down, while access to schools, shops and meeting places could be more easily provided for. As was his habit, he quickly went on to the actual plans, and showed drawings of the one-family houses he had designed for the Pitkälänniemi housing area and the two-storey lamellar buildings to be built along Savontie.

The exhibition attracted lively interest in Varkaus: 50 per cent of the population came to see it. The meeting decided to set up an association for housing reform, following the example of Helsinki, where back in the 1920s a similar organization had succeeded in carrying out the construction of the exemplary working-class district of Puu-Käpylä (Wood Käpylä). The Board elected for the new association included the mayor of Varkaus, the local Ahlström manager and Alvar Aalto.

During the next few years Aalto designed numerous buildings in Varkaus. Most important were the type houses he worked on together with the Ahlström factory: the windows, doors and other building components were serially produced, but full-scale prefabrication of larger building units was not yet adopted. The aim was flexible standardization, leaving scope for individual variation. Flat sizes were 40, 50 or 60 m², within which the rooms could be arranged in many different ways. Unfortunately it turned out that this kind of architecture, rational, social, and tasteful as it was, did not appeal to those whom it was intended to make happy – that is, the workers. Since they paid for the houses and to some extent built them as well, most of them rejected Aalto's puritanical and unusual forms. Only in a handful of buildings in the district were Aalto's plans followed to the letter, while romantic cottages and gentlefolks' homes in miniature were the rule. The genuine Aalto buildings in Varkaus are mainly those built by the company, such as a weekend cabin for office staff, a sauna and a caretaker's dwelling.

Aalto had no better luck in trying to implement a unified district of single-family homes in Karhula, the town plan for which was commissioned from him in 1936 on Harry Gullichsen's initiative. In 1938 he drew plans for the Otsola district consisting of a whole series of house variants with 60 m² of floor space under an asymmetrical saddleback roof, but again the individualism and conventional tastes of the owners carried the day. His work in Karhula did, however, lead incidentally to a commission for a local office of the Nordic Union Bank (today the Union Bank of Finland), and later for a three-storey prefabricated brick building for Ahlström employees.

THE SUNILA MILL AND HOUSING AREA

A much more satisfying assignment than Varkaus and Karhula involved the planning of the Sunila sulphate pulp mill and the connected housing area on a previously unbuilt site near the town of Kotka on the south coast. Ahlström was only one of the five big companies to join in the investment, but Harry Gullichsen was chairman of the coordination committee and he made sure that his friend got the job.

Aalto first visited the site on June 23, 1936, and by September he had the drawings for the extensive first stage of the housing area ready (the manager's house, the engineers' housing, foremen's housing, and a heating plant), while the drawings for the factory were completed in January 1937. The whole complex was actually built in just over a year.

Just as with the Toppila mill in 1930, the architect's role in planning the factory was restricted to cosmetic touches rather than actual design.* The disposition of functions between the buildings, their position in relation to one another, their size and even largely their form were determined by engi-

153. Club for company staff in Kinkamo, Varkaus, 1938.

*My main source of information for Sunila is an interview with Aulis Kairamo taped on August 23, 1983.

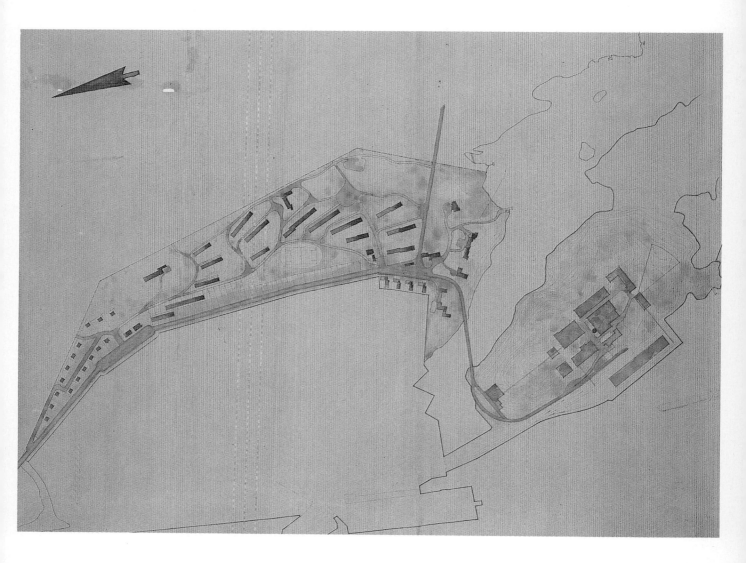

154. *Master plan from 1936 for the new Sunila. The mill is on an island, the housing area on the mainland.*

neer Aulis Kairamo, who was an expert on modern pulp-making methods, and later advanced to the position of technical manager at Sunila. Aalto's principal contribution was in designing the proportions, placing the windows, and choosing the materials. In some details, however, he was allowed to give free rein to his imagination, as in the interesting laminated wood roof construction for the sulphate storehouse down by the wharf, in which he converted the principle of his bentwood furniture into an architectural motif. In designing the office building, too, he had greater freedom than with the facilities more closely related to the manufacturing process.

In the matter of style, Aalto's model was Gutzeit's Kaukopää Mill, designed by Väinö Vähäkallio and completed one year earlier, but the terrain in Sunila lent the cubic red brick architecture a much more dramatic effect. Aalto often recalled that the engineers had wanted to blow up the whole cliff so as to place the buildings on level ground. He asked them whether pulp production did not follow the same process as downhill skiing: once you got as far as the highest point (the top of the conveyor belt), all you had to do was descend in suitable stages. The argument went home. The pulp at Sunila goes downhill all the way to the wharf and the ship's hold. The slope

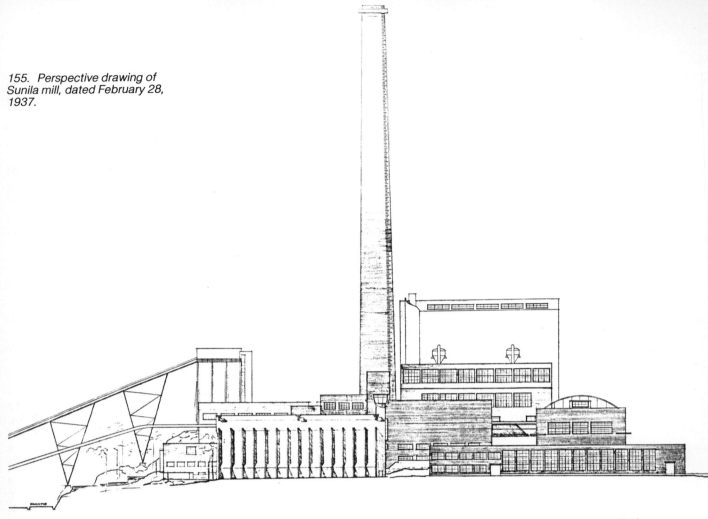

155. Perspective drawing of Sunila mill, dated February 28, 1937.

156. Sunila mill after enlargement in the 1950s.

provides the few workers who supervise the automated process in shifts with the rare opportunity of looking out on a wide expanse of attractive scenery. In terms of form, the factory complex actually resembles those Italian mountain towns with which Aalto had fallen in love on his trips to the South during his youth.

This aesthetic aspect, however, is marred today by the various rebuildings and annexes required over the years by enlargement and changes in the production process. In addition to this, our general attitude to industrial installations has changed since the days Sunila was built. Aalto saw the plant as a positive cultural factor, the symbol of a rising standard of living and the brave new world it was still possible to believe in then. He took a provocative satisfaction in furnishing a factory with an aesthetic dignity which previously had been given only to monumental buildings and to utility buildings camouflaged with decorations. In us this smoke-spewing monster, together with the whole industrial surroundings of Kotka's large harbour, arouses unpleasant feelings because of the contrast between man's rapacity and the remains of a violated natural environment. In other words, it is very difficult to look at the Sunila Mill with the same eyes today as in the '30s.

Similar difficulties are in store for us when we approach the housing area, which was the key part of the Sunila project as far as Aalto was concerned, and gave his ideas of reform greatest scope. What we find is a number of rather dreary lamellar and row houses spread out amid the remains of a forest in a way which reminds one of the most ordinary suburbs in modern big cities. We must summon up all our historical imagination and consider the laborious stages through which social progress has passed over the last fifty years in order to understand how Aalto and his contemporaries regarded the Sunila housing area when it was built (see F 69).

When Aalto spoke of Sunila in the '30s, it sounded almost as though he was making a vision come true – a vision Tony Garnier had had to be content to express on paper. This amounted to creating a complete, modern *Cité Industrielle* with work areas, housing and community buildings carefully balanced. In fact Sunila is a suburb of Kotka, which is why there was never any question of having even simple neighbourhood shops there, let alone schools, health care establishments, etc. As for community buildings, a handful of large wooden houses built at the turn of the century stood on the fringes of the area, and Aalto's task was to convert them for use as club rooms, a theatre and leisure facilities. He solved the problem of restoration and new building in the same way as he always did in similar situations: he never resorted to pastiche of old styles, but added modern elements – for example, a Rationalist porch to a Classicist facade – to produce a sensitive contrast. He considered that every period should make its own contribution to the community.

So Sunila never became Garnier's *Cité Industrielle*, merely a new factory with a housing area of its own. All the same, it must be considered one of Aalto's most important works because of the exceptional leeway he managed to obtain from the client. This was made possible partly by the good luck that had brought together several unusual decision-makers, but also to Aalto's extraordinary ability to convince clients of the excellence of his ideas. With his unfailing intuition, he found the right way to handle each of them, and always went exactly as far as was possible in each assignment.

In the summer of 1936, when he went to Karhula in preparation for drawing up the new master plan for the

157. Old house renovated by Aalto into a club building for the Sunila mill staff.

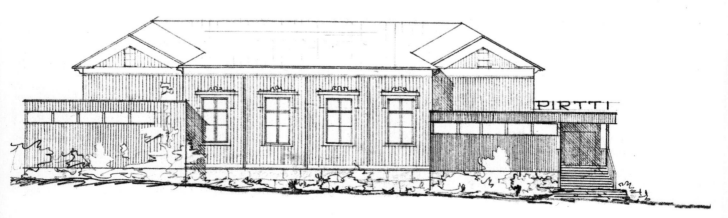

PIRTTI

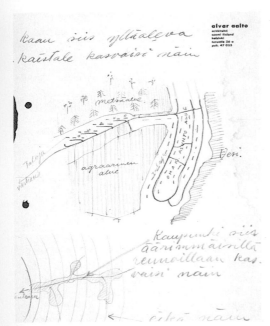

158. Idea sketch from a letter to Harry Gullichsen about how Varkaus should grow: in harmony with the terrain, not like rings on water.

with the terrain. He kept this wisdom to himself, however, since neither Kramer nor the gentlemen from Ahlström would have understood it.

In Sunila, too, one of his guiding principles was to blend the buildings with the natural surroundings, but here the client's receptivity made it possible for Aalto to make another theme, namely social reform, his main goal. We have already discussed the opinions shared by Aalto and Gul-

159. Overall plan of the area surrounding the engineers' housing (the 'B' house) in Sunila.

town, he met Ahlström's local manager Anders Kramer. It is amusing to read (in a letter to Harry Gullichsen) that he found Kramer to be "like one of Napoleon's generals", whereupon Aalto unconsciously expressed himself in battle terms in their discussions: *The buildings must be placed strategically on hills, with the front running along the edge of the forest.* When he wanted to persuade the economically minded members of Ahlström's board to accept the principles of the town plan for Varkaus, he wrote: *It is hardly either advantageous, attractive or right to have housing areas spreading out from the centre like ripples on water, until they cover everything. Instead, the various parts of the land should be used as God intended them − good forest should remain good forest and the same goes for good farmland. The housing should be placed in the areas between.* In fact both arguments meant that Aalto wished to plan the area in the greatest possible harmony

160. *Engineers' terrace house, Sunila. Photo Kidder Smith.*

lichsen about the classless society of the future. In the Sunila project there was actually yet another influential figure who agreed with them: Lauri Kanto, who had been appointed the first manager of the new factory. His humble background was in itself unusual for an industrial manager (his father was a village tailor), in addition to which he appeared openly as 'a man of the people'. Characteristically, once the Sunila Mill was in operation, he procured a bus to take the workers' children to school. As the company management would never have agreed to

this, the bus was hidden in the woods whenever gentlemen from higher up came to inspect the factory. Kanto's refusal to accept the honorary title of *vuorineuvos* (counsellor) later on in his highly successful career was also a unique occurrence in the unwritten history of Finnish vanity.

The outrage thus perpetrated by Aalto on the established hierarchical order of industrial towns in Sunila was thus the result of a conspiracy of three men, and it succeeded beyond all expectation. Aalto did not even try to repeat the feat in Inkeroinen, where he received assignments of similar magnitude from Tampella in the following years, for that company's decision-making counsellors were men of much tougher fibre.

The social principle expressed in Sunila was the same as that which prevails on the ferries that run between Finland and Sweden today: there is only one class, and equal access to facilities for all, but there are differences in the size and comfort of the cabins, depending on how much the passenger is willing or able to pay. In Sunila the only relic of feudal times was the imposing managerial residence standing near the shore in solitary splendour. Today — almost fifty years after it was built — it would seem inappropriate, and accordingly it has been turned into a clubhouse, since the manager prefers to live in a rented flat in town. The remaining residential buildings of Sunila are terrace houses or three-storey lamellar buildings with no visible class distinctions. These buildings appear quite normal when compared to the level of housing attained in Finland after the war, but they should be seen in the context of the miserable housing standards that were the subject of the Varkaus housing exhibition in 1936.

In form, the Sunila housing area was closely related to the type housing developed by Aalto's Swiss colleagues in areas such as Neubühl; in other words, they were middle-class versions of the ascetic German *Siedlungen*. With his usual inventiveness, however, Aalto aspired to create even more rational and individualized types of housing than those he had seen in Switzerland. He described Sunila as a laboratory; the experiments conducted there would gradually lead to improvements and new inventions. The houses and flats were given type numbers, which became increasingly complicated as Aalto invented new variants.

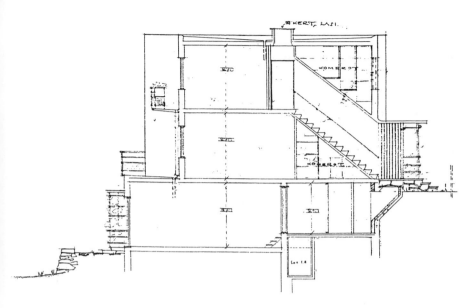

Anjala paper mill, which was under construction at the time. In 1938 he designed the Inkeroinen elementary school, in which he skilfully used and emphasized the sloping terrain, but otherwise seemed to be looking back towards orthodox Functionalism instead of attempting to apply the ideas of the Paris pavilion and the Villa Mairea. He continued to work for Tampella after the war both in Inkeroinen and in Tampere, but produced no major work for the company.

One of the prerequisites for good architecture is a good client. In this respect Harry and Maire Gullichsen were unsurpassable.

161. The three-storey residential house, type name ROT, stands on sloping ground, permitting direct access from ground level to the two lower flats, while the top flat is reached by a low staircase. Cf. F 69.

163. One of the three engineers' villas in Inkeroinen.

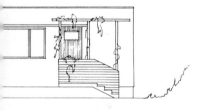

162. The type terrace house built in Kauttua has a ground-level entrance to all four floor levels and open balconies affording an unobstructed view.

One of the ideas that arose in Sunila was the three-storey prefabricated house in sloping terrain (type ROT), with an entrance from outside to the two lower storeys and a small staircase to the top storey. This idea, combined with the wish to increase the privacy of the dwellings, finally led to the terrace house proper, introduced by Aalto in Kauttua in 1938 and intended as a reproducible type building. He also experimented with ways of separating the flats laterally. One method consisted of extending the party wall over the balcony as a screen, another of making the flats open up on the surroundings like fans, a third of an indented front slicing up the ground rather like a cake. These methods could naturally be combined, as Aalto himself did in a masterful but little-known late work, a complex of terrace houses in Pietarsaari.

Aalto started working on the Inkeroinen-Anjala project for the Tampella company in 1937. This assignment was evidently a result of contacts formed with the company management when Tampella took part in the Sunila project. The assignment initially comprised plans for eight houses for high company officials and the renovation of some older buildings. Aalto was also asked to design the exterior of the

164. The WAC café in Inkeroinen, photo 1978.

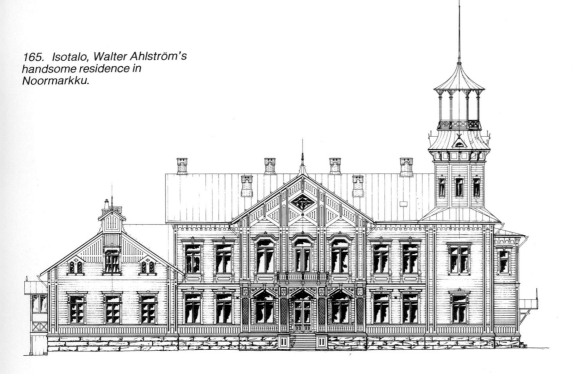

VILLA MAIREA
AND THE NEW YORK
COMPETITION

It may seem surprising in view of the Gullichsens' and the Aaltos' social commitment that in 1937 they engaged in what would appear to be a most dubious enterprise in relation to their social vision: building Finland's most exclusive millionaire's villa in Noormarkku. This had nothing to do with cynicism or double morality, however: paradoxically enough, the idea actually stemmed from their vision of a social utopia.

We have already pointed out that Harry and Maire Gullichsen considered that they belonged to the vanguard in the fight for the better world that reason and progress could not fail to make true. What could be more natural than their desire to give concrete architectural form to this world, to create a sample of the future in order to dazzle and convince their fellow beings? There was also the family tradition to consider. Maire's grandfather Antti Ahlström, the founder of the company, had built a magnificent wooden

palace, known as Isotalo, as the family residence in Noormarkku in 1877. At the turn of the century her father, Walter Ahlström, had given expression to the tastes of his generation by building a splendid new residence not far from the old house. These buildings bear witness to two phases in the development of bourgeois capitalism. The older building is still semi-feudal, outwardly reflecting the ruler's power and adapted to ceremonial needs inside. In contrast to this, the Art Nouveau house underlines the domestic happiness afforded by solid riches, with comfortable rooms, cosy furniture and luxurious, well-tended garden grounds. Maire and Harry rose to the challenge. For them it was a question of demonstrating the new generation's idea of the good life that the rising standard of living would soon bring to everyone. In the classless society they dreamed of, industrial managers and high civil servants would naturally have at their disposal the reception rooms their professional functions called for, as well as the facilities for a well-balanced family life.

The presentation of the building

written by Aalto for *Arkkitehti* in 1939 shows his approach to the social aspects of the assignment:

It is probably generally believed that there is a distinct opposition between small-scale mass-produced housing on the one hand and a residence designed solely for the needs of an individual on the other. Thus the special individual house has fallen somewhat outside the trend which has made the production of small dwellings the main social issue. All the same, a case from architectural practice in which an individual lifestyle and conception of culture form the foundation for the assignment can have far-reaching, even social significance in the long run. It points the way to a new individualism; what with the continuing development of production machinery and improved forms of organization, this will make a more flexible consideration for the individual possible, even in places where the only semi-developed machinery of our primitive mass production leaves its mark on housing today. The individual case can be used as an experimental laboratory where things can be done which would be impossible with present-day mass production, and

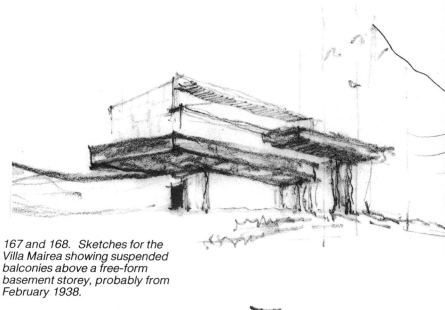

167 and 168. *Sketches for the Villa Mairea showing suspended balconies above a free-form basement storey, probably from February 1938.*

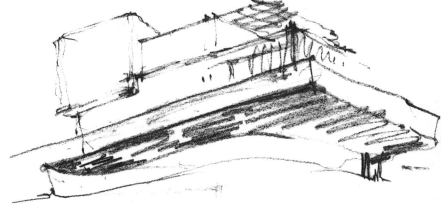

166. *Frank Lloyd Wright's Fallingwater House, Bear Run, Pennsylvania.*

169. *Sketch for the Mairea: hall perspective showing free-form studio wall.*

170. *Aalto's first free-form wall was the curtain dividing the reading room from the lending office in the Viipuri Library – a result of the asymmetrical placing of the staircase.*

these experiments can spread further and become available to one and all as production methods advance.

The intrepid experimentalist naturally had no idea of what results his 'experimental laboratory' would produce when he embarked on the assignment. Characteristically, the preliminary sketches for the Villa Mairea show a wealth of mutually incompatible ideas. The initial impetus seems to have come from Frank Lloyd Wright's Fallingwater, which had just achieved world fame in January 1938 through simultaneous publicity in *Architectural Forum, Life* and *Time Magazine,* and an exhibition at the New York Museum of Modern Art. According to Maire Gullichsen, Aalto tried to persuade her and Harry to build their home in the middle of a stream on Ahlström's land a few miles out of Noormarkku. They went to see the site together. There is no denying that it would have made an admirable location for a house intended to surpass Wright's masterpiece, but Harry insisted that the house should be within walking distance from his office, and Aalto had to settle for the present site. The 'eagle's nest' he designed for this

site did, however, retain Fallingwater's projecting balconies, but the stream was replaced by another 'natural element', a basement imitating the free form of a cliff face (F 167 and 168).

Wright's influence receded in the later sketches, while another idea caught Aalto's interest: he envisaged an interior hall one and a half storeys high with the serpentine wall of the studio above sunk by half a storey to form a decorative front, under which a more intimate section of the hall would be placed, with space for sitting around an open fire (F 169, 181 and 305). The theme appeared for the first time in 1933 in a discarded variant of the Viipuri Library reading room (F 170), and was a leitmotiv of the unbuilt 'Tsit tsit pum' entry for the Paris pavilion (F 135). It must have been frustrating to have to abandon the idea again in the Mairea, but the complicated stair system necessitated by the up-and-down pitch of the floor induced Aalto to omit the raised hall with the free-form interior facade from the version clean-drawn on April 14, 1938.

This plan, which we will call the Proto-Mairea, has an upper storey with a level floor, from which the raised studio with round corners soars, forming the dominant element when viewed from the outside. Wright's balconies are still there, accentuated with soapstone facing, but not as dominating as at the outset. Even the free-form basement has rigidified into a virtually normal wall. In this plan, as in the earlier one, the building has a marked L shape, closing in a half-open courtyard and providing a gradual transition from interior to exterior space. The sauna and swimming pool – the latter a provocatively 'American' element in Finland in those days – mark the next step in the progression from man's limited world to free nature. The narrow, elongated arm of the L is occupied by the dining room and extensive service facilities, comprising a serving room, a kitchen, and a suite of bedrooms and a common room for the servants. The individual rooms for the owners are also formulated in a satis-

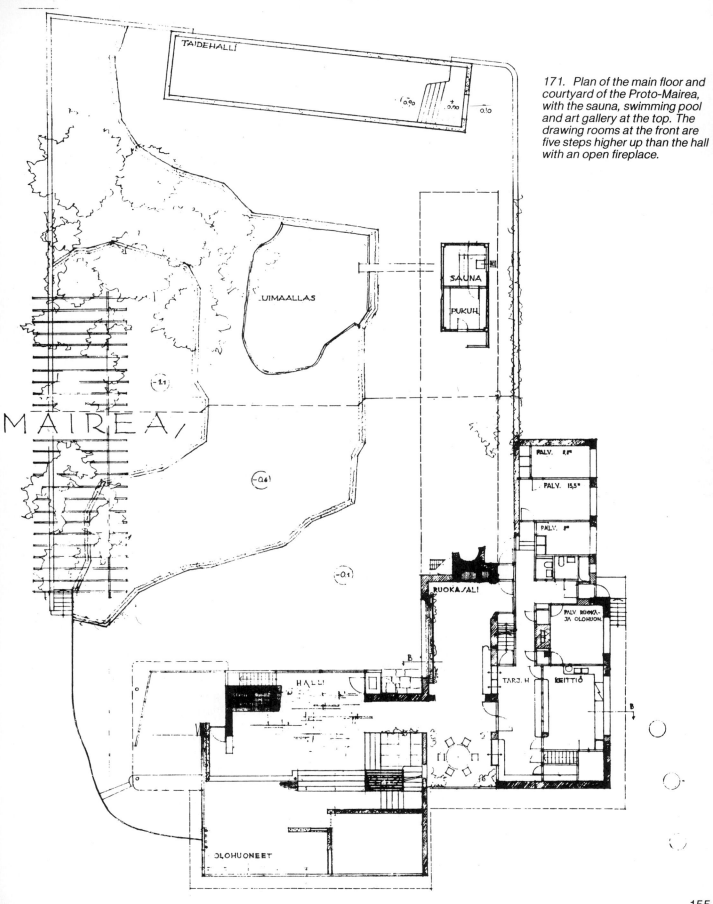

TAIDEHALLI

UIMAALLAS

SAUNA

PUKUH.

M A I R E A

RUOKASALI

PALV. 8,5ᵐ

PALV. 13,5ᵐ

PALV. 8ᵐ

PALV RUOKA-
JA OLOHUON.

HALLI

TARJ. H

KEITTIÖ

OLOHUONEET

171. Plan of the main floor and courtyard of the Proto-Mairea, with the sauna, swimming pool and art gallery at the top. The drawing rooms at the front are five steps higher up than the hall with an open fireplace.

factory way. Maire Gullichsen, who had studied painting in her youth in Paris, has a proper artist's studio, while their three (later, four) children each have a room of their own and a common playing room and gymnasium. All this, together with the parents' two bedrooms and a number of guestrooms are in the upper storey placed above the entire L level.

It seems to have been much more difficult for Aalto to find the right distribution for the formal rooms of the house. What should the family's assembly room and reception rooms look like? An analysis of the various functions this section of the house was to serve led to the following list of desirable rooms: entrance, hall with open fireplace, living room, gentlemen's room, ladies' room, library, music room, winter garden, ping-pong room, art gallery . . . Aalto placed the last of these in a separate building beyond the sauna and swimming pool, a lengthy room lighted by a series of diagonal openings in the ceiling. He grouped all the rest in the main building on various levels beneath the bedroom storey, held together by a still rather complicated stair system.

The 'Proto-Mairea' was approved by the clients in early spring 1938, and was adopted as the basis for construction, which began with excavation of the foundations. How it was that the Mairea came to look completely different in the end is a story that illustrates both Aalto's artistic temperament and the adaptability of his model clients. We shall follow the dramatic chain of events as seen by an assistant at Aalto's office, the young Swiss student of architecture Lisbeth Sachs. Nowadays she lives in Zurich, a senior architect with an established reputation. She is a lively lady with an excellent memory, and likes to talk about her youth in Aalto's office. The following excerpts from an interview taped in 1983 provide an interesting insight into the history of the Villa Mairea as well as more general glimpses of what life was like in Aalto's home and office at Riihitie 20, Munkkiniemi:

It was Bernoulli [a Swiss graduate architect who was working at Aalto's office at the time] *who tipped me off about writing to Aalto to ask whether he needed a trainee assistant. He answered my letter immediately and told me to come as soon as I could – they had lots of work at the office. I took a third class train ticket to*

172. East elevation of the Proto-Mairea, with vaulted ceiling over the 'children's hall' in the top storey. The art gallery is at the far right.

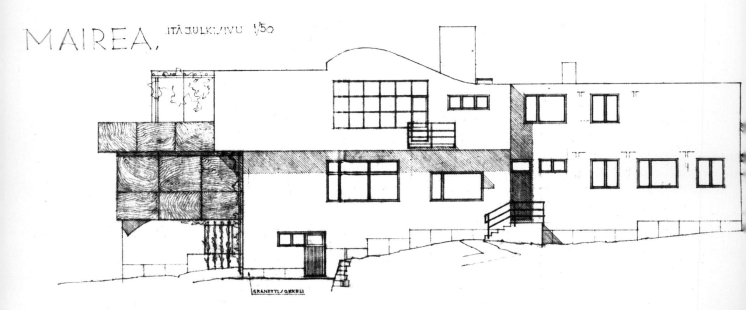

MAIREA, ITÄ JULKISIVU 1/50

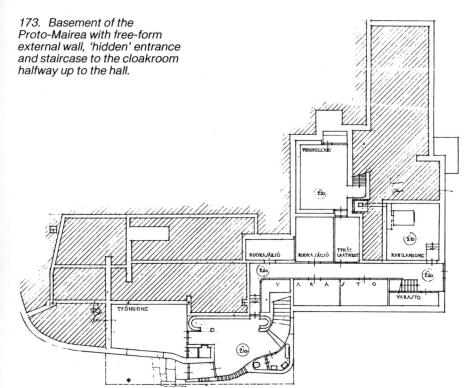

173. *Basement of the Proto-Mairea with free-form external wall, 'hidden' entrance and staircase to the cloakroom halfway up to the hall.*

Stockholm, but flew from there so I could see what Finland looked like from the air. It was a clear day in spring. I couldn't believe my eyes when I saw all those islands floating in the sea. When we passed over Turku, I could see the Paimio Sanatorium from the air. That same day I reported at the office. "I expect perfect penstrokes from you," Aalto said to make me feel suitably unsure of myself. "You will be the first woman in my office . . . after Aino, of course." A little later another woman architect joined us, Marja Paatela. There were ten of us at the office in those days: Alvar and Aino; Sarnivaara, the secretary; Otto Murtomaa, the building technician; architects Jarl Jaatinen, Elis Urpola, Olof Stenius, Paul Bernoulli and myself. My first job was to clean-draw Aalto's competition entry for the Helsinki University Library, with all the details, which had to be drawn in ink with very thin lines.

On the desk next to mine was a model of the Mairea in 1 : 100 scale, and every time Aalto walked past he cast a dissatisfied glance at it. He scolded it as if it was a dog: "It's no good, no, no good." And he explained: "Those people don't need so many rooms . . ." Obviously he had problems with his rich clients and their room programme. I thought the model was beautiful, but a little complicated. There were several building masses placed against one another at various levels in an interesting way.

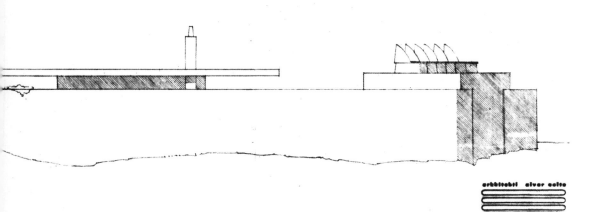

This model slept, as it were, while work at Noormarkku was in full swing. The foundations had been excavated, Murtomaa had calculated the steel reinforcement needed for the foundations and the shuttering was being made. One Monday when I came to the office, the others told me they'd been working almost without a break since Sunday morning. Aalto had phoned them (but not me, because my main work was clean-drawing), and told them he had a new idea for the Mairea. Now we had to get the new drawings done quickly so that work could continue. Instead of many small reception rooms, the new idea was to have just one of 14 x 14 m², with tubular steel columns to support the top floor. We were all enthusiastic and worked late every night that week. But we were also worried about what the client would say. He was a businessman after all, and required punctuality and order. He and his wife had to be pacified and persuaded. Aalto adopted a clever strategy. To the wife he said: ''What will you do when the children have grown up and you might

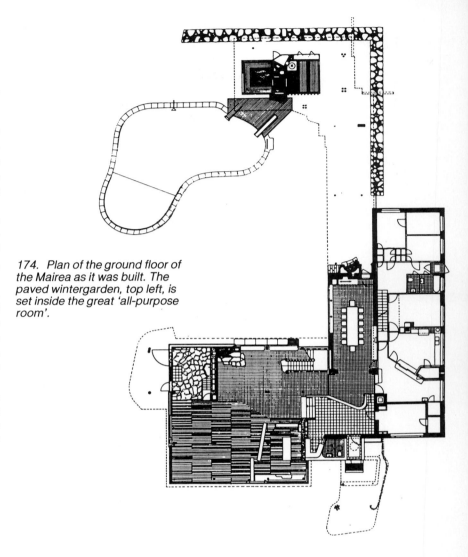

174. Plan of the ground floor of the Mairea as it was built. The paved wintergarden, top left, is set inside the great 'all-purpose room'.

175. Sketch of the south elevation of the Mairea, June 1938.

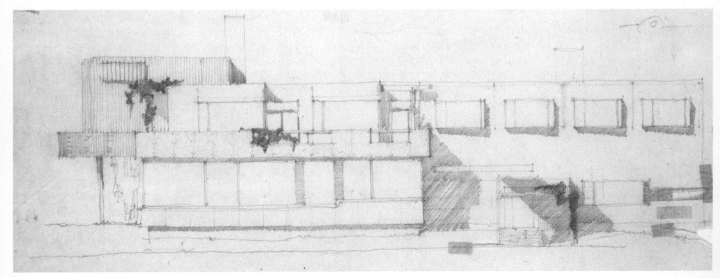

want to arrange art exhibitions in the house? If we make a big room we won't have to worry about a separate art gallery; you can live with your paintings." Maire was immediately struck by his reasoning, which proved quite correct later on, by the way. To persuade Harry, Aalto had me make a model with furniture, carpets and other furnishing details in proportion so that he could try out and 'play' with various furnishing alternatives. Harry was particularly pleased because the basement had disappeared, the main floor could be entered directly from ground level, and the house had become lower. The only problem was that he still wanted a separate library, an intimate room where he could have confidential business talks. This clashed with the idea of a single large room for everything, but Aalto found a good compromise. The library would be part of the room, only screened off with shelves which did not reach up to the ceiling. The shelves had wood panelling on the outside so that they resembled movable pieces of furniture, though there were rows of books inside. These sliding props would also contain compartments into which paintings could be set, taking up an idea suggested by Le Corbusier [in Vers une architecture], according to which paintings, like books, should be taken out only when one wants their company. The library was built according to Aalto's wishes, but Harry Gullichsen couldn't have confidential discussions there, since anybody could stand outside and listen, so in the end a transparent screen reaching from the shelves up to the ceiling had to be made. Besides, the panelling did not prove suitable for hanging paintings from, so it got a linen covering. So in the end the library wasn't mobile after all, but the fact that the continuous ceiling is visible still makes the Mairea living room 'a single room'.

When construction got going a little later that summer, Aalto set up a satellite office in Noormarkku, and sent Bernoulli and myself to work there. That way the detailed drawings did not have

176. Lisbeth Sachs on the Mairea building site in summer 1938.

to be sent back and forth between Pori and Helsinki. And I got some responsibility, especially when Bernoulli was gone for several days to confer with Aalto.

Thus said Lisbeth Sachs. The reader may ask at this point why it was so important for Aalto to eliminate the many social rooms in the Mairea. He himself writes in his presentation of the villa:

The salient feature of the plan solution is a single large living room of c. 250 m². Since there is no question of merely collecting art in the schematic sense, but of a deeper, more personal relationship with painting, the idea of having a separate art gallery was abandoned and the large, continuous room with partitions which can be grouped freely was designed to form an architectural whole, in which painting and everyday life can evolve in a more direct manner . . . The goal was to avoid an artificial architectural rhythm without giving up 'form' in itself . . . *In this building I have tried to apply a special concept of form which has connections with modern painting . . . Modern painting may be on the way to developing into a set of forms which have the capacity to evoke personal experiences in connection with architecture.* (*Arkkitehti,* no. 9, 1939).

In the first place, this declaration gives expression to Aalto's wish to apply the new conception of space we are already familiar with from the "Tsit Tsit Pum" plan for the Paris pavilion. The Mairea's "single living room" is open not only throughout its inner dimensions, but also outward through the glass wall which faces the inner garden and can be pushed aside behind the fireplace (though in practice this has been done only a very few times). This type of 'forest space', which is not dependent on any stereometric scheme, became Aalto's principal architectural theme from the Mairea on. What he says about the role of painting is interesting. In the first part of this biography, I dwelt on Cézanne's influence on Aalto's conception of space, and I find it noteworthy that in describing the Mairea, Aalto himself pointed out the connection with modern painting.

Aalto also hints that the large 'all-purpose room' of the Mairea has a connection with the practical needs of everyday life. In an article entitled "Our dwelling as a problem", published in *Domus* in 1930, he wrote:

The Finnish farmer's tupa [a combined dining room, living room and kitchen] . . . *is a combination of various functions and was never comparable with the concept of 'a room' until its decadence. No family can live in one room, not even in two if it has children. But any family can live in an area of the same size, if that area is distributed with an eye to the life and interests of the members of the family.*

The Mairea's flexible living room was an experimental return to the rural *tupa,* which could serve many different functions at the same time. Thus he

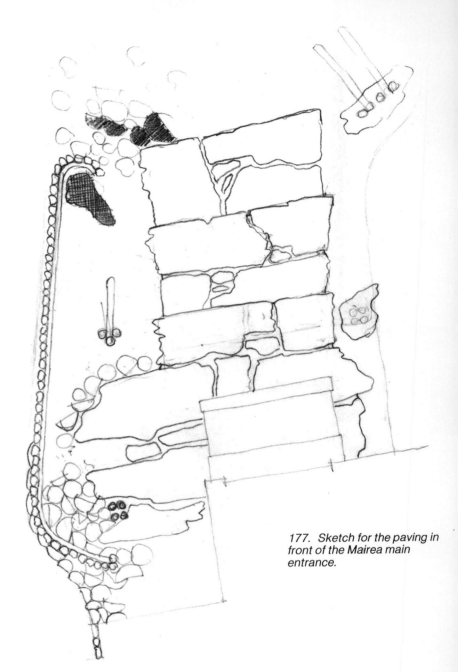

177. Sketch for the paving in front of the Mairea main entrance.

swept away the ceremonial architecture of a class society, creating the setting for the 'natural' life, liberated from social conventions, that the social utopians saw looming ahead. To accentuate the return to the farmhouse world, Aalto placed an open fireplace reminiscent of the monumental white-washed fireplaces of old in the Mairea living room.

This is not the only folkloristic accent in the Mairea. In fact we find several other 'quotations' from the idiom of vernacular architecture, from the sod roof of the sauna and the pergola to the stone fence and rustic wooden gate at the back of the inner courtyard, from the primitive open fireplace under the pergola to the slate slabs of the main entrance and garden paths. It seems that the task of bringing Finland alive to the international public in Paris had set Aalto's latent nationalism free, though he was not afraid to combine it with international impulses. The Mairea was a melting-pot in which Aalto combined apparently conflicting elements to produce an amazingly well ordered and richly orchestrated whole. In it the vernacular tradition, the organic overall conception of Art Nouveau, Neo-Classical humanism, rational Functionalism, Japanese feeling for texture and Aalto's personal susceptibility to the complex interaction of natural forces came together.

The Mairea assignment thus enabled Aalto to experiment with open, 'formless' space and folkloristic themes, both of which he was later able to apply in his more socially oriented architecture. The Mairea also involved numerous other experiments, from unconventional combinations of material to effects with purely aesthetic motivation. Another important step was the adoption of air conditioning — a fairly recent innovation in Finland at the time. The living room ceiling, made of pine boards, contains 52,000 tiny vents made with a manual drill — a rather laborious way of distributing heated or cooled air evenly throughout the room.

May 1938 was not just the month in which the final version of the Villa Mairea was born. Another plan that was equally important for Aalto's artistic reputation dates from the same time. Lisbeth Sachs, who started at Aalto's office around April 20, had some extremely interesting information to give about what went on in Aalto's office that spring:

My first job for Aalto was to clean-draw his plan for the University Library annex. This was a replay between Aalto and his former assistant Aarne Ervi [who took part in drawing the Paris pavilion in 1937], who had won the first competition. Aalto put all he had into it and was sure he would win, but again the jury preferred Ervi's entry. Both Aalto and the whole office were terribly disappointed and our spirits sank to rock bottom. Then one day Aalto came back from lunch in town and said: "We're going to do New York after all." The competition for the Finnish pavilion at the World's Fair had three more days to go, and Aalto had not been interested until then because all it amounted to was furnishing a given module in a long exhibition building which the Americans placed at the disposal of several indigent nations. He tore out two sheets from his pocket calendar, about 2 inches wide and 3 long, on which he had very clearly drawn two completely different proposals for the exhibition interior. "Here's the solution, all you have to do is clean-draw it," he said, and we were all happy. It didn't bother anyone that we had just three days and nights left, we thought it was fun and quite normal to work like that.

One of his sketches showed the pavilion the way it was finally done, with the serpentine 'Northern lights wall'. The idea pleased him very much, and the whole office set out to tackle it. My job was to clean-draw the other entry. The idea was to hang up a kind of gondola or submarine in the box we had been given as a pavilion, to surround it with balconies and have a small bridge by which it could be entered. "The Americans like sensational effects," he explained. In fact the gondola contained the small cinema which formed part of the competition programme.

So we did two entries, but the general enthusiasm was so contagious that Aino suddenly quite calmly declared that she also intended to take part with an entry of her own. She had her own working room on the other side one flight of stairs away from the main office and she set to work there. While we were all working like this, Aalto walked back and forth in the garden in a trance, but came in every now and then to correct our drawings or explain his new ideas. He also went in to Aino's room, and we heard lively discussions in Finnish from there. He certainly contributed to Aino's plan, too, but the basic idea of having lots of intersecting balconies was very ingenious and all her own.

Spirits were high all the while, and we whistled and shouted encouragement to each other. A meal was served just after midnight. The old cook with a ruff over her head and a falsetto voice brought in various tidbits. Aalto sat at the head of the table telling funny stories in his inimitable fashion, and made solemn jokes about the fact that the entries had to be submitted within a few hours. Wine was served, too, but in moderate quantities, since we would soon have to concentrate again. The real wine that raised us to heights of euphoria was Aalto's personality. I had never known that it was possible to work with such concentration, to immerse oneself in an assignment so completely, and then to be suddenly so completely relaxed and full of fun as at that supper. Generally, during the pauses we did not talk about architecture, but about everything else under the sun. We read a lot of books. Aalto had a fantastic library with all kinds of exciting, unconventional books in various languages, modern books about love life, psychology, social issues. I often borrowed books from him and took them home to read late at night. They were a unique source of intellectual stimulation for me. It was always fascinating to watch Aalto, who could fling out architectural ideas as a volcano spews lava, until they formed a mountain – and between times he would talk, completely relaxed, about a flower in the garden or something else. Never before had I seen anything like this, and it made an extraordinary impression on me. Part of the secret of his genius must have been this ability to alternate between extremes.

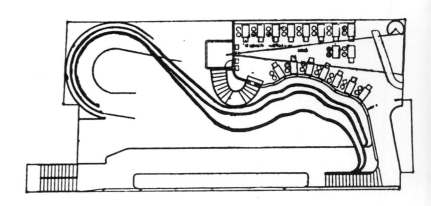

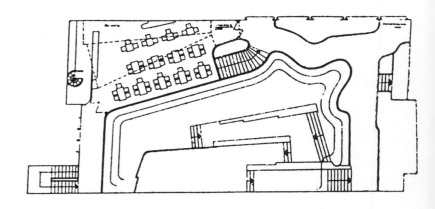

178. Aalto's winning entry for the Finnish pavilion at the New York World's Fair. Two alternatives for the 'Northern Lights' wall and the film projection room.

162

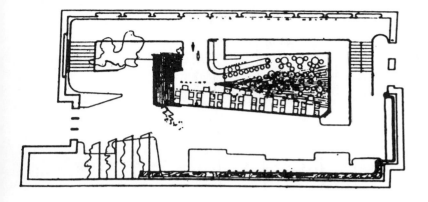

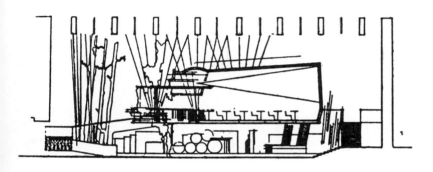

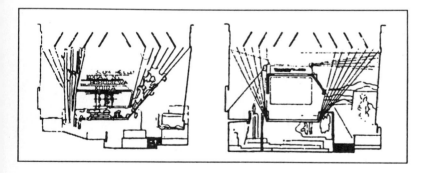

179. Aalto's entry which won second prize. The gondola-like suspended cinema can be seen at the top of the plan drawing and in the longitudinal and cross sections of the pavilion.

We worked nonstop for three days on the New York entries, and were all very pleased with the feat we had brought off when we sent them in. I can't remember how long the jury took to make its decision, but when the results came it turned out that we had won first, second and third prize.

Then it was party time. First a big dinner for Helsinki's crème de la crème. No one was invited from the office except the two foreigners, Bernoulli and myself. I was working up in the gallery above the office, and to my surprise saw the drawing board moved to make place for a long dining table which reached right across the house. Aalto shouted something about my being responsible for the 'décoration de table', which I understood as an order to make the flower arrangements, but Bernoulli explained that I must dress up in my best. So I rushed home and put on a black velvet gown which I had sewn myself and a matching oblong shawl that I could wrap around myself rather like a shroud. The end stuck out like a little tail. I was terribly young and slim in those days, and I think I didn't look so bad. All the guests wore dark clothes, and it was all very solemn. Harry and Maire Gullichsen were there – I didn't know the others. But they were probably mostly official people and a few artists, about forty all told. It was a pretty stiff occasion to start with and the pauses between courses were long. While we waited, we smoked and drank – schnapps all the time. I thought these pauses were customary, but perhaps they were due to the capacity of the kitchen. Aino wasn't to be seen until towards the end, she helped out in the kitchen. Nobody made speeches, but Aalto was talkative and entertaining all the time; he had a word for everybody. The liquor helped to break the ice, and soon spirits were very high indeed. Since I didn't understand much of the table talk, I may have had a little too much to drink. Towards half past twelve, two Italian musicians arrived, a pianist and a fiddler, and started to play. The table in the office was moved

180. *Perspective drawing of the New York pavilion as built.*

to the side to make way for the piano. It was like a small stage, and the idea was that we should dance. I got so carried away by the wonderful music that I took a few dance steps, and one of the gentlemen came forward and led me to the dance floor. To my surprise, he let go of me there and I suddenly found myself performing solo. I'd never done anything of the kind back home in Switzerland, but as I said I was a little high, and so I started dancing quite unashamedly with one of the columns in the office as my partner. Everybody clapped their hands and the rhythm got wilder and wilder. After that dance, I was generally called 'Tarantella' at the office.

A few days later there was another party – for the office. It was a warm, light northern summer night, we had a blazing fire up on the roof terrace, and everyone wore unconventional clothes. We danced to gramophone music, Alvar and Aino flirted with a charming couple called Wiklund who were some kind of relations of Aino's. I wound up causing another little scandal. There was and still is a small, rectangular pool less than two feet deep in Aalto's garden. I got so warm dancing that I jumped into the pool – and was rescued by the gallant host.

Lisbeth Sachs's description of the origin of the Villa Mairea and the New York pavilion should be supplemented

181. *Aalto's sketch for the rejected version of the Mairea hall.*

182. *Aino Aalto's competition entry for the New York pavilion.*

with a few points that illustrate the inner affinity between the two plans and particularly the miraculous completion of the exhibition pavilion within three days from the basic conception to the finished competition entry.

We have already mentioned the raised hall with a serpentine wall front combined with an open staircase occurring in the preliminary sketches, but left out of the 'Proto-Mairea' drawings dated April 14, 1938. The idea seems to have gone on smouldering in Aalto's creative imagination.

The last date of entry for the New York competition was May 9, but on May 6 Aalto still had not decided to take part, since the assignment involved merely an interior in a large unit building. Then there was a sudden spark that transformed the hall intended for the Mairea into the extraordinary exhibition room through a theatrical dramatization of the basic idea. The fading echoes from the resulting explosion can still be detected in two less ambitious plans from 1938: a house designed for photographer Mäkinen and the Inkeroinen elementary school.

TO THE GREAT LAND OF THE FUTURE

To the reader who has gained some idea of Aalto's values, ambitions and temperament, it will probably appear inevitable that America exerted a strong attraction on him. We can pinpoint several factors that predestined him to be drawn to what was considered the great land of the future in those days. The foundations of his admiration of technical inventions and his belief in 'progress' and the blessings it is supposed to bring had been laid in childhood. He was enthusiastic about motoring and flying, and was attracted to unconventional modern forms of life in general, to sports and the open air, to equality on an individualistic basis — in short, to the optimistic ideas of free, natural man, liberated from the tyranny of conventions according to Rousseau's recipe.

In the years between the wars, the United States and the Soviet Union were the two great poles of attraction for the social utopians to whom Aalto openly adhered from 1927 on. Hopes were projected in both directions, since the two societies were not thought of as opposites but as variations on the same theme. Those who believed that social upheaval would bring welfare to all were attracted to the Soviet Union, while those who thought welfare brought by technology would solve all social problems were more interested in the United States. It was easy enough to be drawn in both directions: Le Corbusier is a case in point. He tackled the assignment of designing the great Centrosoyuz building in Moscow with genuine enthusiasm, and a little later concentrated all his efforts on the competition for the central building of the Communist state, the Palace of the Soviets. When he arrived in the United States for the first time in 1935, he exclaimed:

America, which is in a permanent state of development, has unlimited material resources, and is powered by an energy potential unique in the world, is truly the land which will define the order of our times first and most completely.

The skyscrapers of Manhattan and its logical street system with numbered traffic arteries in a grid arrangement appealed to him, but as in the USSR, there were unsolved problems in the U.S.A. Le Corbusier criticized the chaotic traffic and the shocking slums of New York, but had no doubt that they were temporary defects. America appeared to him as "the optimistic promise of machine civilization" and "the land of all opportunities" (from *Quand les cathédrales étaient blanches*).

We find something of the same dualism in the young Aalto, though he was far less inclined than Le Corbusier to be carried away by the seductive promise of either model of society. This was because he "had the gift of doubt" (as he himself expressed it); in other words, he had more confidence

in empirical tests and concrete applications than in tenuous theories. His enthusiasm for the Russian model started to cool in 1933, when the consequences of Stalin's dictatorship began to be known. America came into his life later, as it did into Le Corbusier's, but again Aalto's original admiration was tempered by closer acquaintance with the great industrial country.

In any case, there is not the slightest doubt about the favourableness of Aalto's initial attitude to the United States or about his early wish to adopt the American lifestyle and technical achievements. Back in the early '20s he had appeared as a kind of expert on America when he lectured at the Architects' Association together with his older colleague Gustaf Strengell on the

183. Arrival in New York, photo Aino Aalto 1938.

architecture of Manhattan. In 1930 he wrote (in an article for *Domus*) with such expert knowledge about transatlantic passenger ships, American millionaires, and the philosophy of the Pullman Co. that the readers must have taken him for a seasoned transatlantic traveller. In fact, he did not have the opportunity to make the crossing until 1938.

Aalto's contact with American colleagues increased gradually during the '30s. When architectural critic Robert W. Slott of New York wrote to him in 1929 to ask for a few photographs of his latest buildings, Aalto immediately sent him no less than thirty-one photos. The first American architect to make personal contact with Aalto was Philip Johnson, who alertly sought out Aalto in Stockholm in 1930 and in Berlin the following year (he was preparing his epoch-making book *The International Style* together with H.R. Hitchcock). The two men got on well together thanks to Johnson's excellent German; as we know, Aalto spoke no English at the time.

In 1933 Aalto made three new American acquaintances. That summer in Zurich he met the New York critic Albert Frey, who asked for permission to publish the Paimio Sanatorium plans in *Architectural Record.* In London he met architect William Lescaze, who visited him in Finland the following year and bought a large quantity of Aalto furniture. Finally, Aalto received a visit from another colleague, Leonard Cox, who sent him a letter from Honolulu a few months later, thanking him for "the unique Finnish hospitality" and frankly declaring that "the Paimio Sanatorium is the best modern architecture I have seen". In summer 1936, Harmon H. Goldstone, a young architect who was in Stockholm at the time, wrote to ask if he could visit Aalto in Helsinki. The acquaintance proved very useful to Aalto when he went to America for the first time.

In 1937 Aalto made an acquaintance which proved even more important in the long run. One August eve-

ning, architect William W. Wurster, equipped with a letter of recommendation from a Swedish-American common acquaintance and accompanied by his Californian friends Tommy and Betty Church, rang Aalto's doorbell in Munkkiniemi. Wurster remained a close friend of Aalto's long into both men's old age. In the 1940s, when he was Dean of the Department of Architecture at MIT in Boston, Wurster carried through the decision that Aalto should design the new student dormitory; this was Aalto's biggest commission in the United States. Another Boston architect, Lawrence B. Anderson, also visited Aalto in 1937.

The personal ties between Aalto and the Americans thus strengthened gradually during the 1930s, while American interest in his work grew as increasing amounts of Aalto furniture were exported. It was only with the much-praised Paris pavilion, however, that Aalto appeared in his full stature before an international public, and became a leading figure in the new architecture. The invitation extended to him by the New York Museum of Modern Art in autumn 1937 to arrange an exhibition of his architecture and furniture the following spring was a direct consequence of his success in Paris. The substantial catalogue produced by the museum for this occasion was actually the first book to be published on Aalto. Its co-authors were Simon Breines, who described Aalto's Rationalist production up to that time with great insight, and Lawrence Kocher, who wrote about furniture design from a general point of view rather than with direct reference to Aalto's work.

The Aalto exhibition at the Museum of Modern Art opened on March 15, 1938, and went on in the summer to several schools of architecture in various American cities. Aalto did not go to New York: the organizers thought he had too much work, but the real reason was that a trip to America was financially impossible for him at the time. The practical arrangements were made by Harmon Goldstone and the museum officials with the help of the

184. From the Aalto exhibition at the Museum of Modern Art in 1938.

Finnish consulate general. Photographs, plan drawings, building models and several wood reliefs were sent from Finland, while most of the furniture was borrowed from private American owners, including H.R. Hitchcock and William Lescaze. We find probably the most accurate description of the exhibition in a confidential report sent by the consulate to the Finnish Foreign Ministry shortly after the opening. In it we read that a large display window was placed in the hall to catch the public's attention. The exhibition comprised three rooms: the first displayed furniture, the other two architecture. Among approximately sixty pieces of furniture, there were only a handful of soft easy chairs: all the other chairs were plywood. A few Paimio armchairs were hung from the wall. There were also stackable serial chairs, children's furniture and tea trolleys, and several plywood sculptures hung on the walls. Photographs showed individual pieces of furniture, interiors and buildings, the latter including the Paimio Sanatorium, the Turun Sanomat building, the Viipuri Library and the Turku Theatre. There

were models of the Paris pavilion, the Tallinn museum entry and Sunila. Plan drawings illustrated the projects for Tampere railway station, a high-rise block in Munkkiniemi, weekend cottages, etc. Finally, some glass vases from Karhula were on show. A panel with biographical information hung on the wall. The entrance fee was 25 cents. There were not very many visitors; the exhibition did not seem to interest the lay public. It did, however, attract professionals, who could be seen copying models onto their drawing pads. The consulate therefore pointed out that there was considerable risk of plagiarism. The general assessment was that the exhibition provided an attractive image of modern Finnish architecture to the Americans.

There is no doubt that this report was studied carefully by the authorities in the summer of 1938 when Aalto submitted an application for a grant of 60,000 marks to cover the expenses of the New York exhibition together with the London exhibition of 1933 and two exhibitions in 1938 in Oslo and Copenhagen. He needed the money in order to travel to the United States, but it was not forthcoming, and it was only after he had collected a total of 38,000 marks for first, second and third prizes in the competition for the Finnish pavilion at the World's Fair in New York that he could start thinking of buying a ticket to America.

On October 13, 1938, Alvar and Aino boarded the *Gripsholm,* a passenger ship of the Svenska Amerika Linjen, in the port of Gothenburg. Before they sailed, Alvar sent a few lines to Maire Gullichsen: *Forgive me for deserting your building site like this, but I'll be back before anything awful happens.* Construction of the Mairea was proceeding apace, but since only the frame was being built at the time, the Aaltos' six-week absence was not too serious. Unfortunately, I have been able to obtain very little information about this voyage, which was, after all, an auspicious event in Aalto's life. He landed in the midst of the set that represented the most influential and significant trends in American society at the time, people who would later have a strong influence on him or, to put it more precisely, whose influence would

accentuate existing features of his personality. This seems a suitable occasion to touch upon the intellectual set among whom Aalto very quickly found himself at home.

We may say with a touch of exaggeration that the severe economic depression set off by the crash of 1929 was a shock of the same magnitude for the Americans as the First World War had been for the Europeans. Their carefree confidence in the old order was shattered, and they felt themselves abandoned amid dangerous, chaotic forces. In this situation, Americans and Europeans alike instinctively sought salvation in the historical and ideological foundations of modern civilization, in the rational philosophy of the Age of Enlightenment, which they hoped would reveal mistaken judgements and point out remedies. In Europe, with its well-established workers' movement, these aspirations took more or less Marxist forms. In America, the demand for reform was channelled into Roosevelt's New Deal.

It may seem odd that Marxism did not gain more ground in the United States in the '30s in spite of ten million unemployed, flagrant social inequality and an influx from Europe of émigré intellectuals with Marxist leanings, but this can be explained by the loyalty of the nation to its heritage: freedom of the individual, not of supra-individual organizations, was the cornerstone America was built on. When in 1933 Roosevelt faced the necessity of leading the nation out of chaos, he had no political or social theory to rely on, only an optimistic determination to feel his way forward pragmatically with the help of experienced, intelligent advisors. His 'brain trust' consisted of university professors, experts and businessmen rather than professional politicians. 'Intelligent leadership', brilliant problem analysis, interdisciplinary synthesis, and bold 'social inventions' were the forces that would redress the economy and society. America had never been closer to a social revolution; however, the aim was not a

185. *Aalto with his colleague Fredrik Kiesler in a horse-drawn cab in front of Grand Central Station, New York 1938.*

Marxist society with collectivization of the means of production and party dictatorship, but an 'expert society' with unselfish individuals – scientists, technologists and organizers – wielding power.

All of this tallied exactly with Aalto's ideas. The cultural heritage of his childhood home was based on the positivism, individualism and spontaneous community spirit of the Age of Reason. These were also American ideals, but less common in Europe at the time. Aalto's boyhood interest in American Indian books was another channel of 'American influence'. In fact he never lost this interest: as it amused him in his old age to relive his old, naive faith in progress by reading the books of Jules Verne, so he enjoyed reading about the real-life models of the heroes and outlaws of the Wild West. He secretly sympathized with their anarchistic life beyond the pale of the law and social conventions. It is easy enough to moralize about the dangerous and ludicrous aspects of the cowboy myth, which is still strong enough to be an ingredient of the present American president's image. Like other myths, however, the cowboy myth also has positive aspects. Aalto's weakness for cowboys was not due merely to their eternal boyish adventurousness, their superhuman accuracy with a revolver, and their chivalry towards helpless women. They were also loyal friends, unselfish, incorruptible, puritanically industrious, and sometimes even poor. Above all, they were fiercely independent men. Much of what is positive about American society, but less typical of Europe – the obsession with individual freedom, spontaneous charity, unconventional behaviour, and natural equality – can be traced back to the Wild West tradition. Aalto was too complex and protean a man to settle definitively into any set role, but an important *persona* in his register was surely released when he first set foot on American soil on October 23, 1938.

In New York Aalto played his part magnificently, and was favoured by

186. Aalto pretending to be a cowboy near Fort Williams, Arizona in 1939.

exceptional circumstances. From the beginning, he was surrounded by the nimbus of genius emanating from the exhibition arranged nine months before at the Museum of Modern Art. The newly-opened museum played a key role as the assembly point for the country's progressive élite; it was a playground for both radicals and millionaires. Even if the young Harmon Goldstone had not stood on the quay, prepared to act as Alvar and Aino's energetic public relations man and to introduce them to all the right people, they would have made useful contacts among the New York intellectuals through the museum. As it was, their trip turned almost into a State visit. Goldstone was employed by Wallace K. Harrison's famous architects' office at the time. Together with Harrison and Lawrence Rockefeller he had started a small company called New Furniture Inc. for importing and selling Aalto furniture, and had connections with both the university set and the world of finance. His efforts soon filled Aalto's calendar with cocktail invitations, dinners, interviews and lectures, all among the very highest social and artistic circles.

Aalto's English was still fairly rudimentary in spite of Linguaphone lessons and the practice he had had in London, but with his usual audacity he was perfectly prepared to appear as a lecturer. Only four days after his arrival he went to New Haven with his old friend Fernand Léger, who also happened to be on a visit to America, and the two gentlemen spellbound the architecture students of Yale University with their near-incomprehensible gibberish. At the Museum of Modern Art he lectured on "The humanization of architecture" and at New York University on "How to solve a problem", showing slides of his buildings accompanied by brief but humorous comments. His success was immediate. However halting his English might have been, his personality fitted into the American pattern perfectly.

Léger was not his only European friend to be in the United States at the time. Giedion was also in New York, launching a long career as visiting professor and arbiter of taste in the West. When Alexander Calder, another friend from the days of the Paris World's Fair, opened a large exhibition of mobiles in Springfield, Massachusetts, the friends gathered for a festive meeting. Aalto had arranged a tandem exhibition of Léger's and Calder's work at Artek in Helsinki the year before, but only Léger had made it to Finland in person. Alvar and Aino made another excursion from New York to visit Eliel Saarinen in Cranbrook. Relations between the two

architects had been rather chilly in the '20s, but had improved on the older man's initiative during his visit to Finland in 1936, and now Aalto wished to pay his respects to his famous countryman.

The most important result of Aalto's first trip to America, however, was the connections he formed with the people involved with the Museum of Modern Art. Besides Alfred H. Barr Jr, then head of the museum, John McAndrew, head of the architectural department, and James J. Sweeney, who became Aalto's perhaps closest personal friend in the United States, his contacts included members of the Rockefeller family — old Mrs. John Rockefeller was treasurer of the museum, and Nelson

187. Aalto at Eliel Saarinen's home in Cranbrook.

Rockefeller became its president the following year. There was also Edgar Kaufmann Jr., who became head of the industrial design department after the war. The members of this set were not professed supporters of the New Deal, but their ambitions and attitudes were largely the same, since like Roosevelt's supporters they felt that they had been called to steer America out of the crisis. In a way, the exhibitions of the museum reflected this attitude, not least its architectural exhibitions, which had an openly reformative programme.

Aalto was thus automatically incorporated into the team of physicians ministering to the sick American society. He was not slow to adopt the role, though he only learned it properly during his following visit to the States. His many appearances as an oracle and social expert in post-war Finland — rivalling Frank Lloyd Wright in propagating the humanization of technology, or trying to outdo Lewis Mumford as a theoretician of environmental conservation and regional planning — bear witness to how completely he came to identify himself with this role. Finland was not used to private social philosophers who did not represent any political doctrine or organization, and he was listened to with a certain distrust. Only in his later days, when he could speak as President of the Academy of Finland, did his opinions on environmental problems start to carry the authority he had enjoyed from the beginning in the United States.

SECOND JOURNEY TO AMERICA

When Alvar and Aino returned to Finland in late autumn 1938, they already knew they would be going back to New York the following spring to supervise the installation of the Finnish pavilion at the World's Fair. They had negotiated with the constructor of the long, narrow 'unit building' the Americans were making for a number of small countries, in which Finland was to have one of the end-modules. They had also made an agreement with the Fuller Company, the contractor handling Aalto's project. American law required that an American architect should be responsible for construction. An ideal solution to this problem was found: Wallace Harrison's office took the job and delegated Harmon Goldstone to represent it on the construction site.

Thus everything had been taken care of by the time Aalto arrived in New York for his second visit in early March 1939 on board the *Queen Mary*. Aino followed at the end of the month together with Aalto's assistant Jarl Jaatinen and photographer Eino Mäkinen. All that remained to be done was to complete the pavilion and get the exhibition material in place. In this work Aalto received invaluable practical assistance and moral support from

188. Aino and Alvar in the Finnish Pavilion at the World's Fair in 1939.

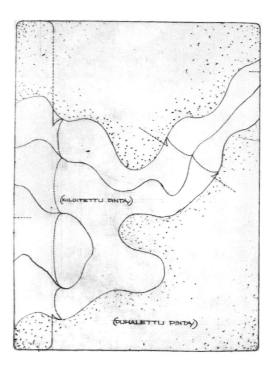

189. Sketch for a granite relief for the New York pavilion.

(KILOITETTU PINTA)

(PUHALETTU PINTA)

William Lehtinen, the Finnish consul in New York, who later became managing director of the big wood-processing company Enso-Gutzeit and provided Aalto with several major commissions. This time Aalto had secured himself against conflicts of the kind that had embittered him in Paris. The participating commissioners and representatives of various industries had pledged themselves to follow Aalto's overall conception, according to which *exhibition objects as such cannot project a living image of a country. This can be done convincingly only by the atmosphere they evoke together, through a wholeness which is grasped instinctively.* (Aalto's programme as quoted in *Arkkitehti,* 1939, p. 113).

The following example illustrates what sacrifices were actually required. Painter Anton Lindfors had done a large glass painting representing a Finnish landscape for the only window in the pavilion. The painting was installed, but Aalto covered it on the inside with a wall surface of sawed-off log ends, completely masking Lindfors's ambitious contribution. It is not known how Aalto felt about engaging in this

brutality towards another artist; we only know that he thought every artist must have an uncompromising faith in his own vision if he wishes to create genuine works of art.

Aalto himself characterized his New York pavilion as "a building with the facade inside", an apt description of the basic architectural idea. If we include the exhibition material, however, 'assemblage' is a more fitting description. What Aalto produced was something in the style of the contemporary 'Merz' constructions of Schwitters, a spatial entity with varied, mutually contrasting elements. In this composition of concrete objects, Lindfors's figurative window would undeniably have been out of place. Aalto even wanted to present the products of the granite industry by displaying several stone slabs engraved with soft, wavy forms, but it turned out that this was not technically feasible on the site. Instead, Alexander Calder made abstract sculptures from some copper plates from Outokumpu.

The result was both original and magnificent. As the summer went on, it turned out that Aalto's message about a vital, nature-loving, export-minded country far away on the northern confines of Europe went home even better than in Paris. Finland's modest but elegant pavilion was one of the most widely discussed exhibitions — at least in artistic circles.

As usual, Aalto found the energy for other activities, too, in New York. Between April 14 and May 9, he gave a series of seven lectures on the social problems of architecture to the students of Yale University. His social life was also intense. Many of his European friends arrived in American well before the Fair opening, among them Hélène de Mandrot, Walter Gropius and Marcel Breuer. On April 15 they all took part in an architectural congress in Phoenixville, Pennsylvania. American participants who became friends of Aalto's included Richard Neutra, Wallace Harrison, Oscar Storonoff, Fritz Gutheim, Joseph Hudnut and Edward Stone.

The World's Fair was opened in style by President Roosevelt on May 1. The official opening of the Finnish pavilion was three days later. The most prominent guest on the occasion was New York's Mayor La Guardia, but a young couple from Finland who had disembarked that same morning were also present, namely Maire and Harry Gullichsen. Here is what Maire Gullichsen remembered of that remote spring in an interview taped on a winter's day in 1978:

When we left Finland, the Mairea was still draped in scaffolding, so we didn't really know what it looked like. The room in which we are sitting now was empty and we had only tested the open fireplace once. But just on the basis of that fire I had the feeling it was going to be a good room. So off we went — by ship from Italy to New York. The voyage took two weeks in those days, so we had a bit of a seesaw feeling when we got back onto dry land. But since Alvar's pavilion was being opened that day, there was nothing for it but to go there directly. Fine speeches were made and we felt very patriotic. When the ceremony was over, the Rockefeller boys asked us whether we could come over to their yachting club for a light lunch with the Aaltos. We went and discovered to our astonishment that the whole club was furnished with Aalto furniture. That evening the new building of the Museum of Modern Arts was inaugurated, and blessed if there weren't Aalto chairs in all the rooms there, too! We got the impression that the whole of New York was nothing but Aalto.

There was an architectural exhibition at the museum showing plans and photographs of one of Le Corbusier's villas and of another by Frank Lloyd Wright. And then, to our amazement, of the Mairea. The boys at the office had grouped a few pieces of Aalto furniture around this fireplace and the scaffolding in front of the facade had been dismantled so that a few photos could be taken and sent to New York by air mail to complement the drawings. That's how we saw our future home for the first time in New York.

Later, in the small hours, we were sitting in our hotel, Alvar, Prucke [Hjalmar Procopé, the Finnish ambassador to the United States], Harry and myself — yes, Aino must have gone to bed — and Alvar said: "Maire, now I'm going to show you 'the great white way'," New York by night, that is. We went off and left Harry and Prucke with their grogs. Alvar was in tails, I had a really chic lined jacket from Ateljé ICA in Helsinki and enormous Calder jewellery. In those days 'all the right people' wore Calder jewellery. Alvar kept saying this was 'the great white way,' but we must have been in the dingiest dance joints in Harlem, all the possible and impossible places. I can't even tell you about all the places we went to and all the things we did that night, but we certainly had fun. When we came crawling back to the hotel at around five o'clock in the morning, Harry and Prucke were still sitting quietly downing their grogs just like we'd left them, as if they'd never noticed we were gone.

190. Excursion to Phoenixville. Aino Aalto and Hélène de Mandrot in the foreground, Alvar Aalto at the left.

174

There were more parties in the days that followed. We met Calder and many other friends of Alvar's. After a week, we went together to Chicago, where Moholy had his New Bauhaus at the time. The premises were in an old pighouse, or maybe it was a former slaughterhouse – anyway it was right in the city. Moholy wanted the school to honour Alvar, so he had all the pupils gathered in the assembly hall when we arrived. Moholy made a speech, and they applauded Alvar and Aino, but then there was applause for Harry and me as well. First we had no idea why, but then we realized that it was because Harry had been involved in creating Sunila. In fact the pupils knew everything about Sunila, which made us awfully glad. Not just to be the master's shadow, but to have a value of our own.

192. At Sandy Calder's in Roxbury, 1939, photo Aino Aalto.

193. In California, June 1939.

*194. Aalto in Chicago in 1939,
photo Maire Gullichsen.*

In Chicago their ways parted: the Gullichsens went back home to Finland, whereas Alvar and Aino went on to California more as tourists than on a professional visit. In Los Angeles they looked up Aalto's CIAM colleague Richard Neutra, who had settled down in the United States before the other immigrant architects, and had succeeded in building up a flourishing practice for himself there. They went on to San Francisco, where the Golden Gate Exposition had been set up as a rival to the great World's Fair on the east coast. Through William Wurster, who lived there, Aalto had been invited to send a smaller collection of his furniture to San Francisco, so he started his visit with a look at his own exhibition stand. Wurster and his travel companions during his trip to Finland, Tommy and Betty Church, had followed the example of Goldstone and Lawrence Rockefeller in starting up a small company for importing and selling Aalto furniture, which no doubt added a few degrees of warmth to their friendship. Aalto was invited to give a talk at the San Francisco Museum of Art, and he was drawn into a lively round of social events with dinners, parties and excursions to the countryside.

We should bear Aalto's success in America in mind and think of the relaxed, optimistic west-coast way of life in order to understand the surprising initiative he took during his stay in San Francisco. He asked Wurster to call a meeting of the élite among local architects and planners in order to convince them of the need to reform American architecture. The fact that after just a few months in the New World he thought he understood its problems better than the Americans themselves can of course be put down largely to his usual self-confidence, but it was also because he recognized his own inmost dilemma in the way things were going in the States. The cleft between the technological and the humanist attitude to life had haunted him since childhood, gradually giving rise to the personal solution he now hoped to pass on to the country in which the conflict seemed most acute.

Aalto was in some ways just as technology-minded as the Americans. The empirical criterion, the principle that all inventions should be tested in practice and improved gradually by experiment, was a basic rule of architecture for him. He rejected the artist's principle according to which every work of art is final, the definitive result of the creative impulses to hand. For him all buildings were temporary, in a certain sense; they could always be improved or varied until they approached the ideal. But the goal must not be purely technical or economic. What should be sought was not the constructively most advantageous and economically most profitable solution, but what is nowadays called 'quality of life', though Aalto called it "the little man's best".

Aalto detected two unfortunate trends in America. The first was exploitation of the environment determined by short-sighted technical and economic considerations, the second the belief that the demands of humanism could be satisfied within a separate sector of art. The idea he put to his colleagues in San Francisco was that an Institute for Architectural Research, a body that would investigate various planning models from the point of view of their influence on people, should be set up in the United States.

It is research in architectural synthesis that we need today – research in how to bind materials together, how to make a living totality from technical details – a HUMAN RESEARCH, how the human being reacts to this totality.

These words come from a summary of his appeal, sent to Wurster by Aalto from New York on June 13.

The idea that architects should have access to experimental laboratories in which they would be able to test various ideas to full scale was not a casual notion of Aalto's during his 'missionary expedition' to San Francisco; it recurred in various forms throughout his life, and led to tangible though fairly modest results during his professorship

195. *Aalto panning for gold, California 1939.*

in Boston in the 1940s, cropping up again as late as 1966 in his plan for Gammelbacka in Finland.

In principle, Aalto's idea that architects, sociologists, psychologists, physiologists and economists should form a brain trust could have met with a response in the America of the New Deal, but for some reason it was received with incomprehension by his San Francisco audience. They took his criticism of technical and economic goals as "an excessive devotion to aesthetics" (see Pearson, p. 191). Perhaps they were not used to thinking about social and psychological questions of principle, or perhaps they were less alert than their colleagues on the east coast, where Aalto's ideas met with a much more sympathetic response from other critics of narrow technology. In particular Lewis Mumford, whom Aalto met during his stay, took a similar attitude to environmental problems in his book *The Culture of Cities.*

Aino and Alvar left San Francisco in early June to visit Arizona and New

Mexico, then returned to New York. On the way they sent a letter to Maire Gullichsen, in which we read:

Just left the Mississippi behind. A wonderful trip in a way. Relaxed from civilization in California and went to the mountains to the east – washed gold in Sutter Creek to help make your house cheaper – you remember our agreement – found 5 cents' worth of gold and just as well – in Arizona we found a ranch in the desert where friendly cowboys taught us to throw a lasso. Wished you and Harry had been there, you would have understood it. Only oxen in the corral – Aino asked who milked them – the cowboys were left thinking the city lady was risqué.

The travellers were back in Finland shortly before midsummer 1939, after nearly four months abroad. Aalto had never been gone so long from home before. His impressions of America were unmixedly favourable at the time, and he was especially delighted with the west coast, as a welcome interview published in the Helsinki paper *Nya Pressen* on June 23 shows:

With the exception of San Francisco and Los Angeles, we mainly travelled through the countryside and studied its architecture. The primitive architecture of the Gold Rush period was a real sensation; it seems to have had a strong influence on modern American architecture. In general the West made a civilized impression on us. A propitious mixture of races and cultural impulses and a favourable climate have resulted in something they call a 'happy disposition'. San Francisco could be compared with Marseilles, but it is more civilized. California and New Mexico remind one of European countries, particularly Greece, and this goes for profane architecture, too.

These impressions were still fresh in his mind in 1945 when he wrote an introduction to the catalogue for a major exhibition of American architecture in Helsinki immediately after the war ended. In it he wrote:

In a paradoxical twist, one might say that the inheritance of Palladio was recreated in America in the form of architectural democracy. A remarkable freedom appears in the buildings just as in the plans of garden towns and in interior design right up to technical details in furniture. We meet housing design of extraordinary refinement, allowing the buildings to adapt to the greatest variety of human needs, to terrain and other conditions, and also making it possible to enlarge the buildings stage by stage. The shift from the East to the former wilds of the West kept American architecture in a perpetual state of mobilization, and gave it a flexibility and lightness that cannot be found in other countries to the same extent. In the foothills of the Sierra Nevada, one can still see the abandoned ghost towns of the days of the Gold Rush. Their spontaneous lightness and elegance and the temporary character which always goes with construction of this kind provide an excellent illustration of the most recent trends in American architecture.

196. Aalto dressed up as an American Indian, Arizona 1939.

197. *Aalto among the ghost houses in Yosemite Valley, California 1939.*

obliged to leave Europe, like so many of his Continental colleagues. Perhaps America's future would also be his? If this was the case, he might as well believe in it.

THE HUMAN SIDE

The reader may have wondered why in my presentation of Aalto's life I have all but ignored the trend which overshadows everything else from our present-day perspective: the darkening political climate, the storm of violence and mass destruction that was just about to begin in the summer of 1939, when Aalto returned from America. Did Aalto live in a closed world of private ambitions? Was Finland an oasis beyond the reach of these storms?

Of course not. But compared to his continental colleagues, such as Moholy-Nagy, Gropius and Breuer, who had had personal experience of Hitler's methods since the early '30s, Aalto lived a sheltered life in an apparently safe country. His reaction against oppressive régimes was therefore less pronounced; it was an attitude of instinctive aversion rather than committed action. Since the world has always been filled with injustice and suffering, man has an instinctive tendency to accept the prevailing conditions for as long as possible, and to adapt his life as best he can. True, many of the world's newspapers wrote about the terror in Stalin's Russia and the persecution of Jews in Germany, but these were endured with remarkable equanimity by the people of other countries. Hitler grabbed Austria, and the world chose to look the other way. Hitler started chipping off pieces of Czechoslovakia at the corners, but Chamberlain flew to Munich and thought he could save peace by making concessions. Finland, too, counted on continued peace. The country prepared to hold the Olympic Games in Helsinki in 1940. Defence was neglected and the country's youth trained for peacetime professions,

On the other hand, Aalto was sharply critical about the American idea of 'industrial design' at the time. *This brash surface formalism, 'superficial streamlining', not at all unknown to us, is not in my opinion particularly American in character. It will probably disappear quickly, perhaps sooner than we think.* (*Hufvudstadsbladet,* June 23, 1939.)

As we see, Aalto's interpretation of America had a highly personal point of departure. His unwillingness to attach any real importance to the negative aspects which were undoubtedly there may have been connected with a thought that cannot have been entirely unfamiliar to him: he might soon be homes were built and children brought into the world for the same reasons as today. War is quite simply something that peaceful-minded people never wish to reckon with, which is why it always comes as a surprise.

Aalto's unwillingness to commit himself politically both before and after the war had an obvious connection with his scepticism about all ideologies, but also with Finland's special geopolitical position. The country's very existence depended on a balance between an eastern and a western great power. A large proportion of the country's middle classes sympathized with Hitler, because they saw Germany as their only protection against the Russians. Aalto was never carried away on these right-wing winds: his liberal family background induced him to repudiate Fascism and Nazism categorically. Since the mid '30s, he had also lost all faith in Soviet society. Thus he settled for living with open eyes in a bad world, fought within his profession for the humane values he believed in, and refrained from meddling with situations beyond his control. His attitude is clearly expressed by his response to an invitation from Fascist Italy to give a big one-man exhibition at the 1936 Milan Triennale. Artek was to make the practical arrangements, and Nils-Gustav Hahl, the head of the company, wrote to Maire Gullichsen on April 11, 1936:

Of course it is not particularly pleasant to be in contact with Mussolini's country, but I firmly maintain that it is better to offer our hand to the young architects of Italy, who complain with one voice that their situation is difficult in spite of Mussolini's supposed 'interest in Functionalism', than to take a purely political line. Aalto agrees.

The balance between two threatening powers and two aggressive ideologies on which Finland had based its existence during the '30s, and which had given Aalto a deep-seated distrust in politics, was heading for collapse in the summer of 1939. The stormclouds were gathering above the horizon in Finland and elsewhere, and Finland hastily proceeded to fortify her unprotected borders. When the pact between Germany and Russia became known towards the end of August, the protection offered to the fringe states by the tension between the great powers fell away. The full extent of the danger became evident somewhat later, when Stalin and Hitler started appropriating their respective shares of the spoils, first in Poland, then in the Baltic countries. They had cynically divided up the whole series of countries between Germany and Russia. Finland had been allotted to Stalin, and he did not expect the Red Army to meet any more resistance there than it had to the south of the Gulf of Finland.

It was thus to a deeply troubled land in crisis that Aalto returned after four bright months in peaceful America. Many assignments had piled up on his drawing-board meanwhile. The finishing touches had to be put to the Mairea, and the major housing projects in Sunila, Varkaus, Kauttua and Inkeroinen had to be completed. But above all there was a great housing exhibition scheduled to open in the autumn at the Helsinki Fair Hall. The initiative was Aalto's own, and he was chairman of the exhibition committee. The theme to be illustrated was 'socially oriented housing construction on the basis of type plans'. This theme had been introduced in Helsinki back in 1917, in a small exhibition held at the House of Estates, had reappeared at the minimum apartment exhibition at the Art Hall in 1930 and again at the Nordic housing congress in 1932. Now it was time to summarize the results achieved and to point out "the social, physiological and psychological prerequisites for good housing", to quote the exhibition catalogue. Gregor Paulsson had been invited from Sweden as expert advisor, and Sweden had a very extensive section of the exhibition, while Estonia, Norway and Denmark had smaller stands. The Fair Hall was thus filled with model apartments. There were designs for agglomerations and for rural areas, terrace houses, lamellar houses and single-family homes for civil servants, workers and small farmers. There were Aalto's EKA types, Hilding Ekelund's HAKA types, and the results of experiments by many other architects.

The exhibition opened on October 7 and was visited by 11,000 people on the very first day. After only four days, however, the doors had to be closed as Finland called general mobilization in response to an ultimatum from the Russians. Thus the exhibition ironically had the effect of a peaceful reply to the Russians' demand for 'liberation' of the oppressed Finnish working classes. The efforts during the previous decade by Aalto and those who shared his views to improve housing standards and to build a more just society had not been in vain. They had done much to heal the wounds of the civil war, and the people of Finland faced the ordeal forced upon it in an unexpectedly united front.

For Aalto the exhibition was the first sign of a political awakening. It arose partly from the pact between Communists and Nazis, which made it easier to lump them together. But even more important were Aalto's growing connections with the West, his old friendship with the radical circles of Stockholm, which had led to similar contacts in Britain and finally provided him with influential American friends who thought the same way. All this now crystallized to form a clear political pattern. Aalto came to the conclusion that the real opposition was not between Communism and Capitalism, as had generally been thought until then, but between political structures which oppress the little man and menace the surrounding world on the one hand, and states which foster the liberal tradition and seek to strike an honourable balance between social responsibility and individual freedom on the other.

As we already know, Aalto was not a man to keep his beliefs to himself. In the United States, he had unhesitatingly told the Americans how they should tend their architectural environ-ment. Now he thought he should enlighten not only his countrymen but all Scandinavians and, in the long run, the whole English-speaking world on the subject of the great issue of the age. In the summer of 1939, he discussed how this should be done with his old friend Gregor Paulsson when the latter came to Finland to prepare the exhibition of model housing. Aalto formulated such a grand proposition on this occasion that it took all of his winged imagination and all of Paulsson's methodical idealism to take it seriously. Together they were going to start a cultural journal called *The Human Side – Den Mänskliga Sidan* to carry their humanist message around the world.

The oldest preserved outline for this publication dates back to just before the war, and defines the journal's guidelines as follows:

Purpose and contents: *To inform the general public in straightforward, non-technical language about new, sociobiologically valid phenomena appearing today in culture, social life, industry and politics, in various parts of the world, and which together indicate that structures in these spheres are going through a complete metamorphosis. Furthermore, to direct attention to the necessity of forming a new system of values associated with the new structures to replace the value nihilism which is at the root of the present chaotic situation. The ultimate purpose is thus a synthesis of culture, social life, industry and politics.*

Along with this, to investigate 'declined' cultural functions in order to distinguish them from others. This work shall be carried out quite independently of present political ideologies.

Format: *A weekly issue of 6–10 pages, as a rule devoted to a single question. Compiled as necessary by a single author or in the form of an inquiry. Keeping strictly to the point, the presentation should be as non-technical and as universally comprehensible as possible. Presentation to be aimed at influencing the reader without degenerating into agitation.*

Authors: *Leading, independent persons from the élite of the 'democratic' countries, people with first-hand knowledge of the problems the journal discusses.*

Finances: *According to calculations, costs per issue should amount to 2,500 Swedish kronor. An edition of 20,000 of the first ten issues will be distributed as a test (according to address lists to be drawn up). Subscription fee at present assumed to be no more than 25 öre per issue. Estimated starting costs 25,000 kronor. At the above price of 25 öre per issue, the publication will pay if it gets 10,000 subscribers, whereupon another 10, 000 free copies can be distributed.*

Editors: *Various suggestions being discussed. The preparatory work has been done by Gregor Paulsson and Alvar Aalto.*

Distribution: *Centres to be set up in the Nordic countries, Britain and USA.*

Place of publication: *Being discussed. Preferably Sweden or centres in Sweden and Finland. Editorial office in Uppsala/Stockholm, possibly printed in Finland.*

The outbreak of war with Hitler's invasion of Poland on September 1, 1939, did not deter the plans for the new periodical. On the contrary, the two initiators thought it was all the more necessary. In a new declaration, they wrote:

There can be nothing more distinctive of the culture for which we have worked in the countries of northern Europe than our striving for a state of equilibrium between individual and group phenomena, for harmony between the personal activity of individuals and collective creation. This view of life is in glaring contrast to social systems which do not seek this equilibrium. In this time of war and conflict, the publication THE HUMAN SIDE is therefore considered even more important, if possible, than it would have been in a time of peace. It is of the utmost importance at this very moment that the voice of northern Europe be heard and that what we have to offer the world in the form of desire for harmony and constructive thinking be noticed. Preparatory work has been done both in America and in Europe. A very considerable number of authors among the international élite have enlisted, and the project can be launched as soon as the financial side is in order.

A rather vague general outline of contents was drawn up in October. The basic theme was given as the relationship between the individual and social superstructures. The objective of this relationship should be "a life with value". Anything that makes individual existence meaningful and satisfying is to the good. There is a polarity between "joint efforts versus power", "group or mass", "freedom of thought or dictation". These and other antitheses should be studied empirically in various contexts, beginning with the state, which can be either a "welfare state" or a "power state". "Cultural and moral superstructures" are also important. The journal proposes to study the social functions of science and art, and the problem of religion. Other points of interest are "social superstructures", i.e., work environment, family, communities, welfare, leisure, security and school, and "economic superstructures, economic ways of life".

As we see, the summary is rather diffuse, but the list of planned and promised articles has more substance. Gregor Paulsson was to write about "A life with value" in "a discussion of values by way of prologue" and about "Goods", presumably from a Marxist perspective. Aalto's subjects were "Concrete and abstract ways of life", "The ideal society (concrete)" and "Industrial differentiation versus uniformity in standardization". Other promised articles included "The large society" by Lewis Mumford, "The environment of production" by Walter Gropius, "The problem of leisure – a discussion of values" by Morton Shand, "Psychological wholeness, psychosynthesis" by Alexis Carrel, "The invisible popularity of art" by James Sweeney, "Rule by thought or rule by power" by Francis Hackett (a

British-American author and sociologist who was living in Denmark at the time and was a candidate for the post of managing editor for the English edition of *The Human Side*). Moholy-Nagy promised to write about "The Bauhaus heritage", while Frank Lloyd Wright wished to expound on the thesis "It is better to build society by raising the individual to a higher power than by reducing him to the lowest common denominator". Nordic collaborators were to include The Svedberg, who was to write on "Man and biological life", Gunnar Myrdal on "Cultural race and blood race", Elin Wägner on "Lifestyles", Alf Ahlberg on "What is right", Gotthard Johansson on "Housing", Torgny Segerstedt Jr. on "Group or mass", and A.I. Virtanen on "Nutritional physiology as an aid in transforming the geographical environment".

This programme is dated November 4, 1939. Not even the first issue had been published when the Russian attack on Finland on November 30 forced the editors to revise their plans. In a preserved memorandum, we read:

Since war broke out in Finland, the character of The Human Side *has been revised and linked up as closely as possible with the war in Finland, but still within the ideological bounds of the original programme. The contents of the first issues have been laid down as follows:*

No. 1 will contain short statements by the American, British and northern European contributors about the ideological battle being waged in the world today, with special reference to the opposition between the social systems of Finland and Russia. This issue will also present a cultural picture gallery with as many photos as possible from Finland, partly of people fighting at the front. The purpose is to illustrate with human types the biological impossibility of collectivizing man into a pure productive force. The photos will be supplemented with quotations from literature on the balance between individuals and group phenomena. Furthermore, the issue will present some

psychologically unsuccessful Russian attempts at organization in which the fundamental errors were dilettante treatment of 'the masses' and unwise terror against individual ambition. Strictly scientific discussion.

No. 2 will contain an article by Gunnar Beskow on the crisis of culture and its transformation into open conflict in Finland. Francis Hackett and Theodore Dreiser will present their views on the social content of this conflict.

No. 3 will comprise two sections. In the first, J.J. Sweeney and Lewis Mumford will answer the question "Is collectivization of the social organism the only alternative to bourgeois liberalism and to the forms of organization and culture inherited from it?" Then an article on forms of mutual understanding and cooperation between workers and employers in Finland, followed by four authentic examples of mistaken collectivization, three from Russia, one from the West.

198. Aalto mobilized during the war, 1942.

No. 4 will feature statements by Frederick Gutheim and Richard Buckminster Fuller on the worker-employer relationship. After this, views on the intrinsic solidarity within Finnish working life will be presented by 10 workers and organizers, engineers, etc.

No. 5 will discuss "Technical humanism", with a presentation by Alvar Aalto of the problem of and new trends in rationalization. Should people be treated as individuals or as a mass? In this issue, P. Morton Shand will also write about "The ideology of world strife from the point of view of organization of technology and production".

No. 6 will be written completely by Gregor Paulsson, and will deal with people and the environment, tomorrow's urbanism and existing Nordic solutions. A number of Russian efforts at organization will be presented: the provincial side of Russian construction, propaganda as the basis of Russian settlement and formation of communities, resulting in inhuman, pompous formalism and neglect of the biological foundation of life.

No. 7 will contain twenty lines by Sibelius, together with articles in which Francis Hackett, Lewis Mumford and Morton Shand discuss the theme "Rule by thought or rule by power".

No. 8 will be a women's issue, in which Elin Wägner will write about the status of women and the failure of an amateurish attempt to align their tasks with the social machinery, illustrated by Russian examples of misguided women's emancipation. Bernard Shaw will contribute "More guidance in socialism and capitalism for the wise woman", and the issue will be finished off with the article "The family, an inquiry among maidservants".

Other sources in the Aalto archives tell us about the channels through which the editors had access to some of the intended contributors. One of Aalto's British friends, H. de C. Hastings, had contacts with Shaw; Hackett knew Theodore Dreiser, Eugene O'Neill, Ernest Hemingway, and Sinclair Lewis. Certainly *The Human Side* would have had a team of contributors

few other journals could have equalled – if only it could ever have been published. As it is, we must be content to read the names of the authors and the titles of the articles as we might recite poetry.

Various approaches can be taken to the Finnish defensive struggle. It can be considered as an unfortunate conflict between a great power's very understandable need for security in face of the impending World War and a small nation's need to defend its existence. From the perspective of the shadow government set up by the Russians in Terijoki, it was a question of liberating the workers of Finland from the shackles of capitalism. As far as Aalto was concerned, he saw the struggle from his own, rather special ideological point of view. We read in a preserved declaration related to the journal project:

The war in Finland is not a struggle between socialist and capitalist rule, but a war in which the aggressor represents an imperialism which has completely betrayed socialism and dragged its name in the mud, besides which it has proved to lack all organizational capacity. In contrast, the defender is a small state, but strong and well-organized in relation to its size, with a more democratic social system and with a population consisting mostly of small farmers. In constructing the country's industrial and production machinery, a remarkably high proportion of socialist principles has been applied in conjunction with capitalist ones, resulting in generally accepted social ideas. Thus the struggle is between a bad system masquerading behind 'the socialist view of the world' and a deep, genuine social mentality.

We should naturally remember that these lines were written under the enormous pressure of the Winter War which had just broken out, and contain a great deal of propagandistic simplification. Not a single issue of *The Human Side* was ever published, and the whole project was buried as being out of touch with reality in a world where arms spoke so much more eloquently than ideas.

In spite of everything, the journal that never got off the ground beautifully summarizes Aalto's experiences and aspirations during the eventful '30s. In this project Gregor Paulsson, his old fellow idealist from the days of the Stockholm exhibition, stood by his side; Gropius and Moholy, his friends from the CIAM years, were with him; so were the Englishman Morton Shand and the whole horde of new American friends. The anarchistic individualism of his youth had been liberated in America from the collectivist straitjacket of the early '30s, and the reconcilement of apparent opposites in a harmonious synthesis made its appearance as his central endeavour.

It was an endeavour of great value in times of peace, but alien to the wartime spirit of confrontation. Aalto was unusually poorly equipped to function during wartime conditions, but his shortcomings in this respect fall outside the time scheme of the present book. If this biography is continued, I hope to be able to show how Aalto, after his comparative failure during the war years, managed to find his way through the trials into a post-war world in which his ability to balance off opposites and to create harmony between the disparate elements of life could come into its own again.

AALTO AND THE RATIONALIST IDEOLOGY

I. An aesthetic dilemma

THE ARTIST'S ROLE
IN SOCIETY

When we visit one of the world's great art museums – the Metropolitan Museum of Art, the British Museum or the Louvre – we are confirmed in our belief that art is one of mankind's eternal companions, that there have always been individuals with the calling to satisfy the needs of their fellow men by making special kinds of objects called works of art. We find further confirmation for this belief when we plunge into books with titles like *World Art History* or selected chapters such as "The Art of Ancient Egypt", "Pre-Columbian Art" or "Paleolithic Art". The fact that the concepts *art* and *art-*

ist appeared at a relatively late stage in the history of western civilization and were unknown during both Antiquity and the Middle Ages rarely gives rise to doubts about the existence of a special art sector in our intellectual life. Did not the circulation of the blood, the pituitary gland, and even the Oedipus complex exist long before man became aware of them?

The problem is that while man's physiological functions are largely constant and specific, his social and psychological reality are determined to a large extent by the changing conceptual apparatus he builds up in order to interpret and organize his existence. There are good grounds for saying that 'art' is an idea that was not fully formulated until the 19th century, and that the 'artist' is an amalgam of ingredients from a whole series of older social roles such as the craftsman, magician, blacksmith, priest, prophet, fool, rebel, and village idiot. In Leonardo da Vinci these elements had not yet wholly merged. Michelangelo was one of the first to assert his role as an independent artist with full authority. Much later, the advent of museums strengthened the idea of art as a separate sector of human existence.

If this assumption is correct, the following question arises: why have we endeavoured with increasing consistency to build up the myths of Art and the Artist during the last 400 years? A conceivable explanation is that religion and the social order previously had sufficient authority to permeate man's whole existence and thus to guide his thoughts in a direction acceptable to the powers that be. Those who shaped the ideas of their fellow men by producing pictures, melodies, songs, stories, monuments, and works of architecture were fully integrated into society and performed a service, though they might be in as great demand and as highly admired as any other specialist. The reason was that individualism was so undeveloped that people did not even try to think independently. The self-sufficient, free Artist appeared as a product of individualization: he embodied the independence of the man in the street. This did not mean that Art or the Artists programmatically turned away from religion or opposed the authorities. The fact is that people still rely on authority and depend on groups today. What is new is that they wish to do so as individual beings, with the free Artist as their mediator. They wish to feel that they are following the current of their own free will, and that they are free to make an alternative choice, even to rebel, if they feel like it. In this system, the uncommitted Artist is an important figure, an indispensable warrant of freedom.

The myth of the independence of

Art has other advantages besides reinforcing individuality. By defining a separate art sector, 'aesthetic life' in contrast to 'practical life' or 'everyday life', we permit a kind of laboratory experiment with sets of values and interpretations that are not directly relevant to reality. Art can also function as therapy in rather the same way as we rid ourselves of latent tensions and needs in our dreams at night. The consciously 'disinterested' character of our experience of art (to apply Kant's well-known definition) permits us to cross all boundaries of taboo with impunity, to enlarge our sphere of experience and in general to obtain a broader view of the alternatives of life than that offered by 'reality'.

Like other inventions, the new conception of Art brought drawbacks as well as advantages, and the former have become increasingly obvious as the conception has been perfected. The most serious consequence may be that the liberated artist has left 'real life' so far behind that the link has been broken. The rift appeared in the 19th century, when architects devoted their efforts to planning elegantly 'artistic' monumental buildings, while inhuman slums and brutal industrialization were allowed to spread uncontrolledly. Even today Art tills its field with high ambition, but lets the rest of the world get on as best it can.

Just as fatal is the cleft that has appeared within Art itself, all too free as it is. On the one hand a 'high culture' sector has emerged, turning into an increasingly hermetic concern of specialists, while on the other a 'popular' sector concentrates with growing cynicism on the economic exploitation of the frustrated needs and undeveloped taste of the great masses. Art, which at its best can generate values, liberate and point the way, thereby loses all its influence − if it does not actually serve the forces of destruction by acting as decorative camouflage, a diverting alibi or a medium of mass suggestion leading to frightening dehumanization.

This threat, which is evident to most

people today, was much more difficult to detect back in the 1920s, but Alvar Aalto was sensitive enough to do so. It is both exciting and instructive to see how an apparently innocent competition for a monument design in 1927 became a catalyst of ideas which forced him to reassess his whole approach to the problem of aesthetics. For him it was the door to a new world and a new architectural vocation.

INDEPENDENCE MONUMENT FOR HELSINKI

The background: after Finland's declaration of independence in 1917, a well-meaning citizen founded an association called *Itsenäisyyden Liitto* (Independence Union), which took upon itself the guarding of patriotic values in various ways. In 1927, this association decided on the occasion of the tenth anniversary of independence

to build an imposing monument in the Finnish capital.

The intended site was Helsinki's Tähtitorninmäki (Observatory Hill), but there was some doubt as to whether a sculpture or a monumental building would be more appropriate. There were examples of both kinds of memorials around the world — the Statue of Liberty in New York and the Victor Emmanuel Monument in Rome, to name one well-known example of each. The jury was to consist of citizens of good repute, but it was to include one sculptor and one architect to assure the necessary expertise. This was why the matter was taken up at the annual meeting of the Architects' Association on November 11, 1927.

This was the first occasion on which the young Turku architect Alvar Aalto assumed a leading role within his profession and as a moulder of public opinion. With the authority conferred by his recent victory in an important

199. Helsinki Stadium on Tähtitorninmäki hill as Aalto envisaged it in his entry in the 1928 competition.

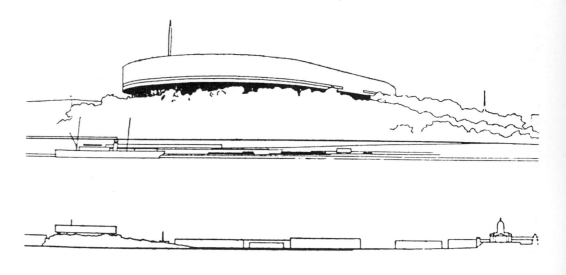

200. Stadium elevation facing Kaivopuisto park.

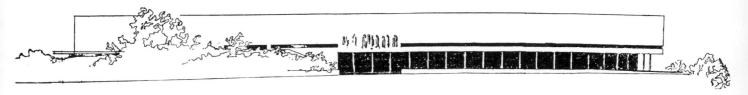

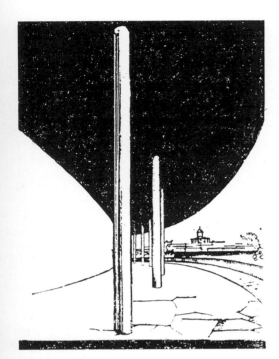

*201. View towards the
Cathedral from the colonnade
below Aalto's stadium.*

architectural competition and the firm
conviction that he was representing
the ideas of radical European architecture, he delivered a well-turned speech
criticizing the whole idea of a traditional monument as a tribute to independence. Instead he offered a completely
different solution, which was intended
as no more than a contribution to the
debate, but had a decisive influence on
the final outcome. Aalto summarized
his argument in a newspaper article
published in *Uusi Suomi* on November
25 and followed up with inquiries
among prominent Finnish 'personalities'.

He started by explaining the real
social significance monuments such as
the equestrian statues of Colleoni and
Gattamelata had in Renaissance Italy.
He then went on to point out that these
monuments had the right scale for their
urban environment, and that images
held special interest in those days
owing to their relative scarcity. Against
this background, he considered it obvi-

ous that an allegorical figure could
have at most a loose, sentimental connection with Finland's independence,
further weakened by the lack of unity in
the scale of the modern urban environment and by the surfeit of images with
which modern man is confronted.

He was equally against the idea of a
building without a real purpose. *It can
never be beautiful, for the beauty of a
building does not depend on a set of
proportions that happens to be in
fashion and is considered monumental, but on a correspondence between
form and purpose. A building must
serve God or man; it cannot be the
shell of an idea, least of all an allegory.*

The conclusion is that the 'artistic'
monument should be rejected. *It will be
inartistic in a deeper sense: it will not
mirror our time, the time when we
achieved independence, and it can
never fulfil the social function of uniting
the people which is required of a
monument.*

Instead he suggested that the Independence Monument should take the
form of a utility building with a real connection with independence; e.g., a
sports stadium, monumental in itself,
that would promote physical fitness
among the young – a particularly important factor for independence. A
stadium would also provide a suitable
setting for the great patriotic events,
song and music festivals, etc., arranged in the nation's capital. He
wound up with a challenge: *The Finnish
Independence Stadium – in the heart
of the city: if space and resources suffice, preferably on Tähtitorninmäki hill.*

The final solution to the problem of
the Independence Monument was influenced to an unexpected extent by
Aalto's suggestion, but it brought him
a long series of personal disappoint-
ments. When the controversial competition was announced in spring
1928, the programme was altered:
besides sculptures and memorial buildings, utility buildings such as a stadium
would also be accepted, while the
question of placing was left open. The
results were published at the end of the
year, and signified a severe setback for

the traditionalists. Just as Aalto had predicted, no one succeeded in creating an acceptable monumental sculpture or symbolic building, though architect Haakon Lindén shared third prize for a columned hall housing a perpetual flame, while one of the first prizes went to sculptor Gunnar Finne, who had imagined a gilded bronze figure, forty metres high, on the Market Square. Aalto, who sent in a brilliant though ultimately unrealistic entry for a stadium building on Tähtitorninmäki, did not get even a mention. The jury merely awarded another third prize to architects E. Aminoff and J. Wahlroos for a very ordinary stadium building in the district of Töölö.

Since none of these entries were really feasible, the Independence Union found itself in a blind alley. The only way out was a complete about-turn: the Union purchased Aalto's imaginative entry and recommended, with the support of the newspaper *Uusi Suomi,* that it should be carried out. The people of Helsinki, however, were unwilling to sacrifice most of the hillside park to the new installation. A new competition was announced in 1933 for the correct placing of the stadium, and another competition followed two years later for the final form of the building on the designated site in Töölö. Aalto faithfully took part in all of these competitions, but his entries were consistently passed over by the juries.

THE ARCHITECT AS SOCIAL ADMINISTRATOR

Let us take a look at Aalto's 1928 entry for a stadium on Tähtitorninmäki. It is a utility building without the slightest trace of 'artistry', an elegant engineer's construction, and Aalto discusses only the practical advantages in the building description. Visibility from the stands, extensive parking space on account of the terrain formation, a spacious restaurant and sauna facilities beneath the stands, a delightful view over the harbour — these were the principal attractions of the entry according to the architect.

We find the same approach in the description of the Paimio Sanatorium written by Aalto for the brochure distributed at the inauguration. He did not say a word about aesthetic effect, the quality which still makes the building complex one of the most enchanting artistic achievements of Rationalist architecture, a sculpture of white components balanced carefully against the green, wooded surroundings. Instead, Aalto obstinately reiterated his efforts to adapt the institution to the patients' subtlest physical and mental needs. The ventilation of the wards was designed to avoid draught. The washbasins were specially designed to damp the sound of splashing water when the tap was opened. The water, waste, and electricity systems could be serviced from the corridors so as not to disturb the patients. The ward ceilings, which would be constantly before the eyes of bedridden patients, were painted in restful colours. With the same subtlety, the architect protected the patients from the pressures of collectivity, yet gave them opportunities for various degrees of contact depending on their strength. The window pane under the sill permitted those who were most seriously ill to enjoy the sight of the wooded skyline from their beds. The somewhat healthier patients had direct visual contact through the corridor windows straight across the courtyard to the canteen, where their fellow patients gathered. The convalescent shared wards, which provided them with diversion, while at the last stage before signing out the patients had free access to the lounges and the park-like surroundings.

Everything in this vast building was dictated by functional considerations, from the 'filters' in the kitchen ceiling absorbing the smell of cooking to the pitch of the back of the plywood armchairs designed to facilitate the patients' breathing. This is the kind of architecture intended to influence the life of people directly, without taking the detour via their conscious

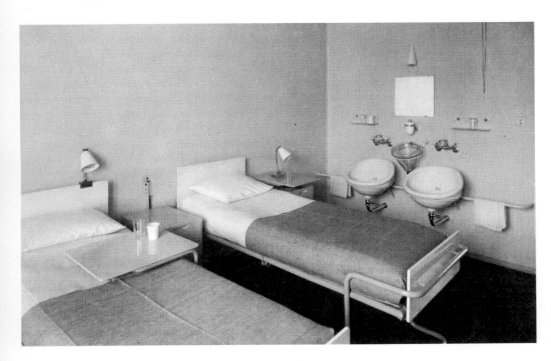

202. Patients' ward in Paimio Sanatorium with a specially-designed spittoon between two 'splash-free' washstands. The beds are also specially designed.

thoughts. The patient who sat in the Paimio chair (F 79) was not supposed to think, "This is a healthy chair"; he should automatically breathe more deeply than in an ordinary chair. What Aalto was aiming at was a kind of architecture that was as practical and 'conditioned by nature' as a bird's nest or a spider's web.

This ambition was complicated by the fact that man is not purely a creature of instinct; he accumulates conscious experience and acts on the basis of changeable notions. Our interpretation of reality, the conceptual message of a situation or an object, cannot be ignored, least of all with objects that are called works of art, whether correctly or not. It is therefore important to differentiate between the 'mute' influence the design of the Paimio Sanatorium may have exerted on patients, staff and visitors on the one hand, and the associations the building evoked on the other.

Aalto once told me that he had placed the lift in the patients' wing right at the end of the building in front of the nurses' room so that the noise of the lift would not disturb the patients. Ar-

riving at the sanatorium, the newcomer sees this lift through the glass wall (F 95) and perceives it as an element given a positive emphasis, a homage to technology. In the same way, the whole building evokes the idea of rational efficacy and the resources of science placed at the patients' disposition. This graphic demonstration of the will and ability of society to fight the insidious disease is part of the cure. After all, the hope of recovery is likely to contribute more to a favourable outcome than any medication, discreet lift, or 'splash-free' washbasin. As for the plywood armchair, it never gave any demonstrable therapeutic results; in fact it turned out to be rather uncomfortable for both healthy and sick people. On the other hand, it is aesthetically so pleasing that culturally minded people buy it as a sittable sculpture and an attractive symbol of Aalto's 'biological' philosophy of life.

The obvious discrepancy between Aalto's express intentions and ultimate results may seem puzzling, but it is easy to explain on the basis of the attitude of distrust in 'artistic values' he adopted during the Independence

Monument controversy. Since art had become estranged from 'practical life' through catastrophic neglect, Aalto chose to reject the artistic aspect and to concentrate entirely on the practical side of architecture. This was an effort to reconquer neglected territory, to reintegrate everyday reality with culture.

Aalto was not the only architect to take this attitude; it was shared by his continental precursors and colleagues. They all had anti-artistic tendencies inasmuch as they rejected the old 'decorative' or 'aestheticist' criteria of art and devoted themselves to what, in a letter to Gropius, Aalto called 'real architecture'. This meant that the design of a building should be dictated solely by real needs (as in Aalto's description of the Paimio complex) in conjunction with technical and economic considerations. Naturally they were aware that 'real architecture' could also make a secondary aesthetic impression, as it were, but they tackled this problem in other ways.

Le Corbusier's solution was undoubtedly the most conventional, for in his work extrinsic beauty reappeared in a new guise. In Le Corbusier's opinion the completely functional house, designed as a skilled engineer might plan it with purpose as his main criterion, was just a *house,* pure and simple. If, however, the sensitive architect gave the wall surfaces, door and window openings, etc., harmonious proportions, or *modénature,* preferably based on the golden section and other abstract constructs of the theory of form, the house became a *palace,* however small and unpretentious it might be. *The engineer satisfies the mind, the architect touches the heart,* exclaimed Le Corbusier. *A beautiful building is like a beautiful face,* he also said, evidently thinking of Classical statues with their pure features and well-proportioned foreheads, noses and lips rather than of Rembrandt's character portraits.

To the empirically minded, sceptical Aalto, this kind of a priori beauty was a completely alien notion, as were all geometrical systems forced upon living reality. This incompatibility soon effaced the strong initial influence of Le Corbusier's theses. There was something unreal and schematic about the latter's social visions of giant skyscrapers in which people would live like ants, subject to rigid organization. The Bauhaus architects stood on much more solid ground with their *Siedlungen,* which were actually built, and with their contacts with the workers' movement.

The most radical of the Bauhaus architects was Hannes Meyer, who denied that architecture had anything at all to do with any such irrational element as art, and who thought architects, like engineers, were pure technicians. *"Building is nothing but organization: social, technical, economic and psychological organization,"* he said. We find echoes of this proclamation in Aalto the newly converted Functionalist. In an interview with the journal *Tulenkantajat* in 1929 he explained that the architect should start out with functional component plans, or 'bits', resolved in the most rational and formally elegant way. *He then goes on to create a whole, a system of complete 'bits'. This calls for more reflection than drawing pretty gold ornaments. It is an* organizational problem [the emphasis is the author's] .

By the following year, when Aalto expounded the principles of the new architecture at a congress in Trondheim, this idea had grown into an ideology. *I do not believe that it is sensible to concentrate on* synthesis *in tackling an architectural assignment.* (In another context, Aalto used the expression *individual syntheses* to describe monumental buildings of an older type.*) *It is easier to build up a Functionalist system once one has acquired the right ingredients for the whole. In some fields the formulation of 'part solutions' is fairly advanced. Thus in town planning the problem of traffic has been worked out quite thoroughly. A*

*Stockholm Exhibition II in *Sketches*, p. 23.

clear formulation has also been found for a number of hygienic details. It is in this direction, the working through of individual elements, that the architect should proceed . . . The synthesis will follow by itself . . . The Functionalist architect is an entirely different professional type from the old-style architect. In fact he is not an architect at all; he is a social administrator. *

As I mentioned in the biographical section (page 64), Aalto gave a lecture in Sweden and Finland in the early '30s on 'non-synthetic architecture' and even planned to write a book on the subject. Now we know where the idea came from and have a point of comparison enabling us to judge the changes in Aalto's views that led him to correct his idea of 'non-synthetic' architecture in the mid '30s and to start speaking of synthesis as the true goal of architecture.

Aalto freed himself gradually from Hannes Meyer's rigid idea of the architect as an organizer or a social administrator. His adoption of Gropius's attitude to art marked an important stage in this change. Gropius did not believe that all architectural problems could be solved in a strictly rational way. In a letter to Markelius dated September 14, 1927, he wrote about the planning of Siedlung Törten: *Es bleiben eben ausser der sachlichsten Sachlichkeit immer noch Punkte im Bauen, denen unsere ganze Liebe und unser Gefühl anhängt.* (There are always aspects of architecture beyond the best common sense that require all our love and sensitivity.) This does not mean that the architect should set out to create works of art. *Only the brightest glimpses of heaven's mercy, which cannot be commanded, allow art to emerge unconsciously from work well done. The artist is a glorified professional, but without professional ability there can be no art. Practical skill is the source of creativity.* **

This attitude was endorsed wholeheartedly by Aalto. He never claimed that he created art; he merely sought to bring all his expertise to bear on his assignments. If others saw art in what he did, so much the better. There was no posing or sophisticated self-deception about his attitude, as is shown by the alacrity with which he accepted quite prosaic architectural assignments – standard housing, factories, garages and laundries – as well as regional and town planning work. These assuredly 'non-artistic' assignments actually dominated his output in the '30s, as a glance at the list of works at the end of this book shows, and they remained important throughout his life.

His willingness to work for big Finnish industrial enterprises (Toppila Oy, A. Ahlström, Tampella, Enso-Gutzeit, Strömberg, and later Typpi Oy) was not prompted by mercenary considerations. On the contrary, he had it very much at heart to contribute to 'civilizing' and 'harmonizing' a neglected sector of community planning. The fact that his industrial installations, simple one-family homes, and small flats in terraced houses soon seemed obsolete and unattractive did not worry him in the least. From the beginning, he considered them as stages in a long process, experimental designs which would be surpassed by new ones.

ART TAKES
ITS REVENGE

Naturally Aalto was aware that the more challenging assignments of the period, such as the Paimio Sanatorium and the Viipuri Library, were charged with a symbolic content which could be expressed in artistic terms. They afforded scope for his irrepressible artistic urge and gave the buildings a more permanent 'artistic' quality which greatly surpassed their functionality.

It was important to Aalto never to let himself be lured into the domain of pure artistry, never to use forms without practical significance or to fall into

Nidaros, June 28, 1930.

**W. Gropius: 'Programm des staatlichen Bauhauses in Weimar', 1919.

196

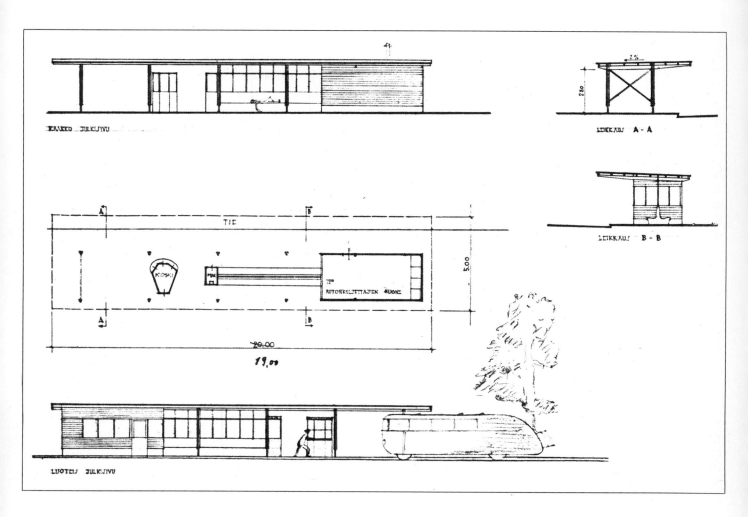

KAAKKO JULKISIVU

LEIKKAUS A - A

LEIKKAUS B - B

TIE

KIOSKI

AUTONKULJETTAJIEN HUONE

5.00

19,00

LUOTEIS JULKISIVU

203. Bus station for Sunila housing area, 1937.

aesthetic formalism. His genuine artistic imagination and his spontaneous love of the expressive line and the eloquent motif, however, exerted a continuous pressure against the demands of practicality and moral authenticity. More than once this led to makeshift solutions in which the practical function only seemed to furnish a pretext for the artistic form. It also gave the work the 'natural' and unaffected quality Aalto always strove for.

The ideal, of course, is complete equilibrium between practical purpose and artistic expressiveness. Take the bell tower, a very old invention and one of Aalto's favourite motifs. The practical *raison d'être* of the bell tower is to raise the church bells high enough to be heard far and wide, but it is also an eloquent artistic symbol of the heaven-

ward aspiration of religion and the domination of the church over everyday life and temporal abodes. It is easy to find examples of less well balanced blends of the practical and the aesthetic in Aalto's architecture. One of these is the great glass window in the lower left-hand corner of the Turun Sanomat building facade (see F 11). Its stated purpose was to provide a surface on which blow-ups of newsspreads could be projected after dark. The client, obsessed as he was with modernity, could hardly have hoped for a more exciting idea for a publicity stunt, and it must have been one of his reasons for accepting Aalto's plan. When the offices were built, however, producing the required projections turned out to be impossible, or at least too difficult, with the technology avail-

204. The Aalto office in Munkkiniemi, with a garden in the form of a theatre cavea.

able at the time, and in the end the window served no practical purpose. So much the more important was its position in the elegant, almost Mondrianesque composition of the facade, an abstract work of art on an elementarist ground.

Aalto's exhibition pavilion in New York was another example of the complete domination of artistic expression over a fairly simple practical purpose (see F 191). It is true that the magnificent undulating wall leaning forward towards the spectator provided a fine background for photographs of Finnish scenery and Finnish products, but its real purpose was to give artistic expression to the simultaneously open and closed 'forest space' that was such an important symbol of Aalto's conception of reality.

Aalto's office in Munkkiniemi provides an example of an even stronger domination of form, the function being all but a fiction. The principal motif is the inner yard in the form of a Classical theatre, with the convex wall of Aalto's private studio curving around the far end. For Aalto, however, it was important to see the design as based on a purely practical discovery. He explained that the 'theatre' with a 'stage' ending in a smooth whitewashed wall was to function as an auditorium when he lectured to students. The audience and he himself would stand inside the heated studio behind the convex glass wall, while pedagogic images would be projected right across the cold yard against the screen at the back. Thus he had saved the cost of both a roof and heating for his auditorium. Undoubtedly the idea was brilliant, but it had the slight drawback that he never gave any lectures to students there and thus never had the opportunity to project images out into the winter night. What he gained was a delightful studio home, a terraced yard verdant in the summer, and an exciting feeling of the theatre, which was charged with psychological and historical significance for him.

There was yet another case of conflict between practical and aesthetic motifs to which the original solution looked very promising, but the result turned out something of a tragedy for the aging master: the Finlandia Hall in Helsinki. Back in the '30s, Aalto had pondered the possibility of designing an auditorium with variable acoustics, that is, acoustics that could be altered for different purposes: orchestral music, chamber music, choral music, speeches, etc. The basic idea of the Finlandia Hall was to have an auditorium as high as a church, but with movable screens to vary reverberation from full cathedral effect to that of an intimate lecture room. Since the auditorium itself was to have an architecturally satisfactory permanent form, Aalto decided to divide the space into two sections. He gave the seating area – i.e., the concert hall proper – a louvred false ceiling forming an optically closed ceiling surface, but acoustically permitting the passage of sound waves to the screen structure above. This 'upper auditorium' furnished the pretext for the tower-like form and pitched roof that make the Finlandia Hall so prominent in the townscape. Unfortunately, Aalto's idea never worked out in practice. The sound

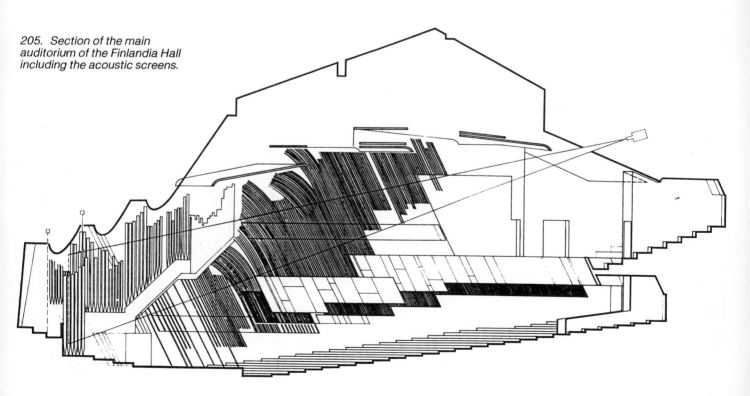

205. Section of the main auditorium of the Finlandia Hall including the acoustic screens.

waves simply disappeared through the louvres never to return. In order to save the concert hall, the ceiling had to be sealed off completely. Now the building is like one of those Gothic churches with a high ceiling concealing a vast, empty garret with no practical purpose. Aalto took the criticism of the Finlandia Hall's acoustics very hard. He had thought that he had worked in harmony with nature's laws, and that his intuition would lead him to find the way.

But was Aalto's idea so unrealistic after all? Construction of his Essen Opera House has finally got under way. In it the false ceiling will be made of a considerably lighter material more permeable to sound waves. Aalto will have the last laugh in his architects' heaven if the two-part concert hall with adjustable acoustics turns out to be successful after all.

Of course, we should remember that Aalto's greatness as an architect was not based on his practical innovations, however seriously he himself took them. The truth is that hardly a single idea of the many he brought out with such pride and sometimes even sought patents for has interested the practical men. He produced an endless succession of inventions, including a rounded brick for universal use, a variable standard staircase, splash-free washbasins, various ways to bend laminated wood, 'growing' summer cottages, organically formed door-handles, connectable double windows, a house without foundations, stackable glasses, and motorboats that can reach the shore in shallow waters. His inventions were rarely praised for technical brilliance, but they were admired and even imitated for their aesthetic merit.

This gives us an indication of what Aalto gained from his adherence to practical objectives. The very fact that he had such an unreserved belief in the designer's duty to approach concrete reality as closely as possible and never to give in to the temptation of creating 'free', purely artistic forms allowed him to achieve the 'natural' style and the

206. Relief of laminated wood slats, 1965.

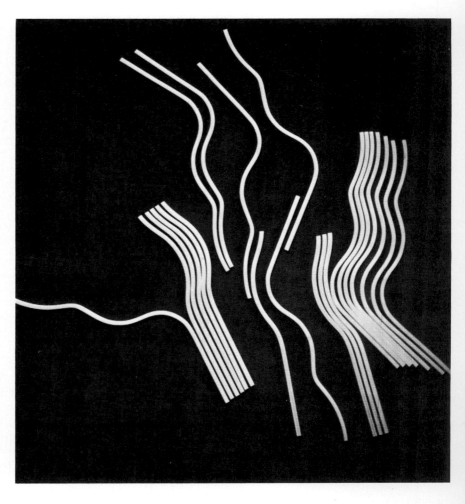

207. *Oil painting from the 1950s, gift from Aalto to Göran Schildt.*

demonstration of harmony between man and his environment which constituted his special message.

AALTO'S
AESTHETIC GAMES

We have seen above how the influence of Aalto's instinct for aesthetic formulation frequently raised his practical work into the realm of artistic symbolism. An inverse transformation can be observed in the 'aesthetic games' he started playing in 1931 with

abstract wood reliefs (F 77, 80 and 206) and non-figurative painting. The impetus for these games probably came from Bauhaus through Moholy-Nagy, and like the exercises with materials on the preliminary course at the Bauhaus school, they were intended to activate the designer's creativity through close contact with material and forms. It is easy enough to find the reason why he never wished to consider these works as art in their own right; the attitude of 'anti-artistry' learned from Gropius forbade this. The thought that his aesthetic games ultimately aimed at inventions with a practical application permitted him to devote himself without inhibitions to free artistic creation, for which he had a strong penchant in spite of his practical ambitions. Few of his wood reliefs ever led to practical furniture designs, whereas he produced free artistic variations on the structures of many of his furniture models.

LIFE'S TOTAL HARMONY

Aalto's distrust of the idea of 'art' appeared in his words as well as his works. A typical comment was published in a newspaper interview after he returned home from the Stockholm exhibition. He praised the exhibition for the following reasons:

. . . it aims at levelling the idea of art. Motor boats, buses, railway carriages, refrigerators and gramophones are placed side by side with objects which were once thought to be on a higher level and were called the fine art of interior decoration. All these new objects make the same claim to be treated as culturally valuable . . . I think it most encouraging that the artist, as it were, denies himself by venturing outside his traditional sphere. He goes among the people to help bring harmony into life with his intuitive ideas instead of stubbornly asserting an opposition between art and non-art which can only lead to acute tragedies and life without hope. *

An illustration of the kind of tragedies he means is provided by an interview published in *Uusi Aura* on January 1, 1928:

. . . one might compare the mass people of our age with the poor girl standing outside on a cold winter night and staring in through the gentlefolks' window at the ball inside, convinced that nothing else can be beautiful except the dance she sees in the lighted ballroom, quite unaware that in her own life there is beauty of at least as great value as in the festivities she witnesses.

The few times that Aalto used the word 'art', he did so to underline integration with the totality of life, and to emphasize that fragmentation of existence must not be permitted. *Artistry is the spontaneous ability to combine different elements in the environment and in human life,* he declared to the readers of *Uusi Aura* in autumn 1928. He preferred the word 'culture' because of its broader application. *A cultivated taste expresses itself in social equality,* he said in the same interview. For him, culture was a totality in which each component had its proper place and significance, a frame of reference to which all details, however trivial, should be assigned.

The error in distinguishing between art and non-art does not appear merely in judging the cultural achievements of the past. Using the classical orders of columns merely as decoration is not the only way to create pseudo-art. The Rationalist idiom can also be applied in a superficial, aestheticizing way. Aalto reacted strongly (cf. page 44) against the tendency towards quasi-Functionalism and a formalistic use of the vocabulary of the new style in designing utility ware which was already setting in during the Stockholm Exhibition in 1930. In his old age he still deeply despised all the supposedly artistic furniture, lamps, cutlery, etc., that is pawned off on people under the label 'industrial design'. To quote the conclusion of the interview in *Uusi Aura:*

After all, the most positive culture is that which aspires to universal harmony in every detail of both private and public life instead of surrounding itself with decorative objects and forms without resolving the problems of everyday life.

He expressed similar ideas eight years later in an interview with the Stockholm daily *Dagens Nyheter:*

The structures which were means to create a new architecture have been wrested from us and turned into com-

*Åbo Underrättelser, May 22, 1930.

202

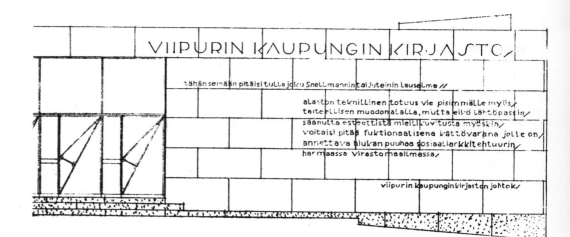

208. Aalto's joking inscription on one of the Viipuri Library elevation drawings.

mercialized decorative ends in themselves with no inner value. There was a time when a misconstrued, lifeless traditionalism was the chief enemy of good architecture. Today its worst enemy is the superficial decorative misuse of the means acquired during the breakthrough . . . The contrast between deep social responsibility and decorative 'surface effects' is perhaps the oldest and certainly the most topical issue in the debate on architecture. Please do not think that I wish to disparage beauty in rejecting decorativeness. Architecture must have charm; it is a factor of beauty in society. But real beauty is not a conception of form which can be taught, it is the result of harmony between several intrinsic factors, not least the social. *

These ideas really were fundamental to Aalto's philosophy of life, as we see from the fact that he returned to them as late as 1958 when speaking at the centenary celebration of his old school in Jyväskylä:

The word 'culture' should not be misunderstood or misused. It is not an isolated phenomenon, separable from life, there must be no so-called cultural circles among people or special decorative elements in the environment, because culture is the warp which runs through all phenomena. Even the smallest daily chore can be humanized and invested with the harmony of culture.

The Catholic cathedral, in its flowering in the late Middle Ages, invariably towered above a cluster of insignificant houses, a symbol of the incomprehensible unity of life. Later the surroundings of these cathedrals have been cleared of the clusters of houses, with the unexpected result that the idiom of the cathedrals has lost its power.

This reference to conditions as they were before the Renaissance introduced 'art' as an independent concept brings us back to our initial observation concerning the artist's role. Aalto was no opponent of modern individualism − in fact it was one of his key values − but he wanted individuals to take responsibility for the whole of society in seeking life's elusive harmony.

Now that we have defined Aalto's basic attitude to the aesthetic sector of life, it should be pointed out how undogmatic he was in this, as in all other questions. He rejected art, but did not object if the best of his buildings were experienced by others as works of art. Perhaps he sometimes even consciously smuggled a drop of artistic ambition into his more spectacular works? He half playfully admitted as much in a drawing from 1935 for the Viipuri Library. In this sketch, the entrance section of the facade displays

*Dagens Nyheter, October 28, 1936.

the monumental text VIIPURIN KAU-PUNGINKIRJASTO (Viipuri City Library), beneath which he initially wrote: "there should be some saying by Snellman or Juteini on the wall". For a variant drawing he produced the following wisdom from his own head, naturally without the slightest intention of actually placing the text on the wall:

THE NAKED TECHNICAL TRUTH ALSO TAKES US FURTHEST IN ARTISTIC FORM; BUT PERHAPS THE REJECTED AESTHETIC IMAGINATION SHOULD BE KEPT AS A USEFUL RESERVE WHICH CAN BE GIVEN A LITTLE WORK NOW AND THEN IN THE GREY OFFICE WORLD OF SOCIAL ARCHITECTURE.

II. Rationalism and the problem of form

FUNCTIONALISM
À LA MARKELIUS

The thesis that gave Functionalism its name and which the Rationalist architects never tired of repeating was: *form is dictated by the combined effect of function, material, and technical construction.* The problem with this definition is that the word 'function' can be given virtually any meaning, from random viability for some practical purpose to the subtlest cluster of ideas. A grenade shell can function excellently as a flower pot, while if you load a cannon with a flower pot, the result is a highly functional pacifist demonstration. If we wish to find out what the Functionalists of the '20s really meant, we would do well to ignore abstract theory and to concentrate on the cases in which they thought Functionalism had actually been achieved.

At the beginning of this book I mentioned a lecture Sven Markelius gave to his Turku colleagues in 1928, sparking off many conversions among the Finnish congregation. Since Aalto and Markelius were ideologically close in those days, it is worth studying the preserved manuscript of this lecture. The audience evidently considered the arguments relevant to the issues that were in the air. Some extracts from Markelius's lecture:

We travel by aeroplane and by ex-

209. Aino and Alvar Aalto in 1928, surrounded by the other participants at the inaugural ceremony of the Turku Finnish Theatre.

press train, perfect symbols of modern comfort clothed in matter-of-fact form, and we think with pity of the stagecoach and horse and cart of times past. We demand strict utility and comfort from everything related to our clothing, luggage and personal effects. But as soon as it comes to our homes, we live under the illusion that the principal function of a great number of things which serve a no less useful purpose – furniture, light fittings – is decorative. Not only does this illusion relegate utility in the broadest sense of the word into second place, it also has the result that these objects do not clearly express the significance we, people living in this day and age, connect with these objects. In other words, we wind up with a sort of camouflage instead of creating genuine culture.

Markelius goes on to furnish examples of spurious industrial art products and unsatisfactory architecture, from a prize-winning American radio set camouflaged as a miniature model of Columbus's flagship, the *Santa Maria*, to theatres, concert halls and auditoria of recent years, whether inspired by a Classical atrium, the court of an Italian palace or an Arabian chieftain's tent. He was treading on dangerous ground here, not only considering Asplund's brand-new Skandia cinema and Tengbom's concert hall in Stockholm, inaugurated two years before; both his own concert hall in Helsingborg and Aalto's Turku theatre had been designed just a little before in the most refined Neo-Classical masquerade style, though Markelius and Aalto had expiated their sins by leaving out the entire decorative apparatus at the last minute. It was thus with a good conscience that Markelius could praise Gropius's recently published plan for Piscator's total theatre as a specimen of exemplary theatre design: *The more precisely the purely objective principles can be defined – I am thinking of the practical and theoretical experience that has been gained in the last few years in the field of acoustics – the more meaningless it seems to base the design of, say, a concert hall on a decorative idea. Congeniality between form and content has been the hallmark of great architecture throughout the ages. When a manifest conflict arises between function and architectural form, we begin to lose sight of our goal.*

Aalto saw the relation between function and form in the same way as Markelius at the time, as can be seen from an interview published by *Uusi Aura* on October 21, 1928:

The time is over when furnishing homes was considered a separate task based on sentimental preferences for form . . . Instead of form-based interior design, which starts exclusively from forms and then attempts to serve the practical purpose to the extent permitted by this constraint, the Functionalist method starts out from the real demands of life and then creates forms to suit needs. An example: what is the living room carpet? Its purpose is not decorative, it is there to provide a soft surface for children's play and perhaps also for their parents. The most difficult problem with the carpet is to make it hygienic; colour should also be considered from the point of view of hygiene. And what is a piece of furniture? A light, inexpensive object, available to all social classes, easy to clean and durable. It must combine maximum comfort with maximum facility of technical production.

Speaking of the new architecture in a more general way, he says (*Uusi Aura*, January 1, 1928): *It strives to assess the content of the work (on which its form depends) correctly and to make it the only point of departure in creating form.*

Seeking a more exact definition of the Functionalist principles on the basis of these quotations, we find that the Functionalists' most imperative ob-

jective was to suppress many of the psychological needs to which earlier architecture had catered. These included the affinity with the historical past implied by adherence to traditional styles, the social prestige involved in imitating upper-class architecture, and the assertion of independent identity by means of unusual forms and exotic ornaments and souvenirs. Their ideas reveal a puritanical demand for simplicity and humility, a demand that was bound to find response in the countries where Protestant sects once triumphed.

We also find that the doctrine of form dictated directly by practical need raised the Functionalists out of the world of symbols and ideas into an ahistoric timelessness. They considered that Functionalism is basically a trend that has existed as long as man himself; it is not a style but an attitude expressed in all good architecture since the dawn of time, though sometimes masked by a decorative or fashionable shell. One of the consequences was that the Functionalists rejected all formal loans, whether from the masters of the past or from contemporary designers. In their view, every building should be an adequate and anonymous expression of the purpose for which it was built and nothing else. The only thinkable variations in form were those determined by the various practical considerations of climate and historical period. In all other respects, they expected a totally objective, uniform architecture to spread throughout the world.

SOURCES OF FUNCTIONALIST FORM

The Functionalists' claim that their inspiration derived directly from underlying practical needs and their unwillingness to admit that they operated to a considerable extent with clichés borrowed from the repertoire of ancient and modern art provide a striking illustration of man's propensity to close his eyes to the most obvious facts. In fact,

Rationalism had a family tree with many ramifications as far as the forms it used went. Its history is too complex for me to attempt even a summary description, so I will restrict myself to pointing out a few of the most obvious sources of Aalto's Rationalism.

Justice demands that I start by naming Le Corbusier, not so much for his own discoveries in form but for his role as mediator in assembling the idiom of Modern architecture from older sources. In *Vers une architecture,* Le Corbusier admitted that *painting was the model for the other arts.* He particularly mentioned Cézanne, who wrote in his famous letter to Emile Bernard (1904) that the cylinder, the sphere and the cube were the basic elements of composition in painting. According to Le Corbusier, these 'Philebic bodies' (named after Plato's dialogue *Philebon*) should also be the basic forms of the new architecture. *Architecture is the refined equilibrium between plastic forms in changing light conditions,* was one of Le Corbusier's most frequently quoted statements.

Le Corbusier also drew from a more modern source, the works of the Cubist painters. From them he learned about interpenetrating geometric forms as well as about juxtaposing surfaces of different materials in the manner of collage. Since he did not, however, accept the Cubists' disregard for the rules of geometrical space, he founded a new movement, Purism, together with the painter Ozenfant. Unlike Cubism, this school of painting respected the sculptural physicality of the object depicted, but made use of the same banally typical subjects, such as bottles, jugs, glasses, pipes, guitars, fiddles, and schematic human figures. Léger's Cubism developed in the same direction, and in time he came to associate very closely with the Rationalist architects, not least with Aalto. The abstract organic forms introduced by Le Corbusier in his architecture in the mid '20s, including the famous free-form entrance canopy in the Palace of the League of Nations plan, were clearly borrowed from the jugs and guitars of the Cubists and Purists.

The impulses Le Corbusier received from the world of technology were, however, more important than his loans from the sister art of painting. His obsession with the machine as a model for architecture went even further than his famous metaphor of the house as a machine for living in. He also borrowed formal ideas from machines, considering the pure functionality of their construction as exemplary. The only problem was that machines have no distinctive style; they can have almost any appearance. In terms of form, a Stone Age axe, a locomotive and an electronic computer have little in common. Le Corbusier's technical precedents were actually a small but select number of machines that he raised to the status of art because of their symbolic associations. The transatlantic passenger ship, the biplane of the period and the elegant automobile were charged with positive associations for him. They brought new dimensions to man's dream of freedom, and a new way of life along with them. This is why he reproduced a ship's strip windows, round portholes, skylight openings, cabin corridors, spiral staircases, tubular steel railings, and deck levels forming horizontal roofs in his 'Rationalist' houses. This is also why he converted the wings and fins of the biplane into his Dom-ino system and started making chairs on the same principles that are applied to the body of an automobile.

Le Corbusier's influence on Aalto during the latter's early Rationalist years was undeniable, and can be confirmed by no more than a hasty glance at works like the Turun Sanomat building and the Paimio Sanatorium. It was also evident in some projects that were never carried out, such as the entrance canopy and garden roof terrace in the second version of the Viipuri Library plan. To what extent Aalto was influenced by Le Corbusier's plan for the Palace of the League of Nations in designing the main entrance to the Paimio Sanatorium remains an open question. It should, however, be emphasized that whereas Le Corbusier used free form to provide a contrast to the lucid geometry that dominated his work and as an emotive ornament which also appeared in his Constructivist painting, organic form and structure were the very cornerstones of Aalto's architecture. The profound disparity between the views of the two architects had the result that Aalto soon sought new sources of influence after his first dazzling encounter with Le Corbusier's genius in Paris in 1928.

Apart from Le Corbusier, Aalto sought inspiration for form in the late '20s from the Dutch De Stijl school, Russian Constructivism and the Bauhaus masters. The Dutch and Russian features we detect in the Turun Sanomat building must have come via architectural journals, since Aalto designed it before his first journey to the Continent. Any influence Duiker might have had on the Paimio Sanatorium design was in fact both superficial and short-lived, while the German influence was much more significant. The problem of Rationalist form is not merely or even principally a question of external stylistic features (flat roof, white walls, intersecting geometric volumes); even more important is the overall planning of the environment on the basis of an unquestioning belief in the absolute value of rationalization. This leads to maximum exploitation of natural resources and turns man into a machine that works as hard, consumes as much, and performs as effectively as possible. The new world the Rationalists hoped to build was intimately connected with two portentous changes in the social pattern: industrialization and urbanization. Neither of them had struck provincial Finland with full force yet, whereas the Weimar Republic had made considerable progress in mastering the resulting architectural problems. It was natural that the solutions worked out by the Bauhaus architects should make a deep impression on the young Aalto.

His promptness in adopting the principles of the German *Siedlung* designers appears from an article he wrote towards the end of 1927 for the newspaper *Sosialisti.* The title was "The minimum apartment – a social and economic stumbling-block". The article was illustrated by two photos from the recent Weissenhof Exhibition in Stuttgart, one of a single-family house by Gropius and the other of a terrace house by Oud. Aalto wrote: *Creative young Continental architects gifted with intuition . . . are following the path of pure Constructivism with fresh enthusiasm.* He hoped that Finland would also start placing housing construction *on a sound socialist basis* (this is what the article says; it seems likely, however, that Aalto had written "on a sound social basis", but that the typesetter had put in the signature phrase of the party publication out of pure habit), since this required *that a quite decisive step should be taken in the process of social recovery, implying a threat of catastrophe to irresponsible speculation,* that is, to profit-minded private housing construction.

From his first visit to Germany in connection with the CIAM congress in 1929, Aalto brought back the idea of the Minimum Apartment Exhibition that he arranged the following year in Helsinki as well as the ideas on the rationalization of family life set forth by Gropius in a lecture at the congress. Aalto repeated Gropius's propositions almost word for word in an article he wrote in 1932 for the Turku periodical *Granskaren.* The idea was that the needs formerly fulfilled by the private home should be taken over by collective services. Aalto wrote:

During our education we 'live' at school. *When we are born we 'live' at the* maternity clinic. *During the hours when our mother sits in the office we 'live' perhaps in* kindergarten. *When we are ill we 'live' in* hospital. *In our leisure hours we 'live' in the* cinema, *on the* sports fields *or at a* nightclub. *And a similar change has taken place inside the home. We buy our food semi-processed. Water, electricity and heating . . . link up homes, so does the public traffic network . . . Although this is only a sketchy summary of the housing* question, one fact should be obvious: *the modern home is a system of institutions and places where we spend time, with the home proper as its centre.* The good home *consequently arises from planning which encompasses the entire system, all circumstances and functions connected with it, together with a scientific solution to the relevant problems.*

As we see, the total rationalization of everyday life was a positive goal for Aalto at the time. His tone was slightly more human in an article with the title "Our home as a problem", published in 1930 in the Finnish journal *Domus*. He pointed out that *the emancipation of women and their subsequent rise from subjection to a status of equality both at work and at home places completely new demands on the home. In modern society it is at least theoretically possible for the father to be a mason, the mother a university professor, the daughter a film star and the son something even worse. Obviously these people have their special demands to be allowed to think and work undisturbed. The modern home must be built to meet these demands.*

When Aalto presented these basic points, he could hardly have anticipated that only a few years later he would be in a better position to apply and develop them in practice than most of his Finnish colleagues could ever hope to be. The work he began with Finnish big industry in 1936 led to plans for a great variety of dwellings, from simple one-family homes to terrace houses, point blocks and multi-storey lamellar buildings. He remained faithful to the rational principles of Bauhaus in housing design, though he added a measure of comfort and psychological finesse. Aalto's housing planning was well within the mainstream of Rationalist architecture, and differed relatively little from what many of his Scandinavian colleagues designed according to the cold principles of minimum requirements and technical exploitation. On the other hand, he took greater liberties with buildings for 'collective living' – i.e., schools, hospitals, libraries, theatres, sports installations, and clubhouses. In them we meet Aalto the artist instead of the follower of the rigid Bauhaus line. In them he abandoned the idea of rationalizing human life and attempted to humanize Rationalist technology.

The strength of Gropius's influence on Aalto during the early '30s can be seen also in his ideas about form. Aalto's early house plans, such as the physicians' homes in Paimio, the Villa Tammekann and his own home in Munkkiniemi, bore an obvious family resemblance to the masters' halls in Dessau. Even more important, however, were a number of basic theoretical ideas for which Aalto fought throughout his life and which obviously went back to Gropius. The latter had spoken as early as 1910 about the correct proportion between industrial rationalization and consideration for individual needs. Gropius thought that maximum standardization permitted maximum variability. In his book *Die Architektur und das Bauhaus* we read:

Standardization of replaceable parts, including windows, doors, wall units and stairs, in no way excludes the

210. Gropius's 'masters' houses' in Dessau were a source of inspiration for Aalto's private house designs.

211. Staff housing, Paimio Sanatorium.

212. Aalto's Munkkiniemi home seen from the street.

individual design we all hope for . . . Through variation in combining these parts, individuality is given all the scope it could desire, while the building retains the same kind of beneficial unity as there is in the way we dress — individually, but in keeping with the times.

The question of the size of the standardized units remained open. Gropius and Adolf Meyer tried in 1923 to introduce a 'Baukastensystem' (building block system) that would make it possible to produce a variety of combinations of relatively large standardized building components comprising whole rooms, rather like children's toy blocks. The idea worked better in theory than in practice, however, and in our days it has given way to construction with smaller prefabricated units. Aalto devoted a great deal of effort in the late '30s and during post-war reconstruction to designing standard prefabricated wooden housing permitting unlimited variation according to site, family size, individual wishes and financial resources. The results, however, were meagre, as the time was not ripe for the rise of prefabricated house construction.

Aalto was also one of the initiators of the Finnish Standardization Institute, which has had a considerable influence on Finnish building practice, though not exactly with the results Aalto hoped for. The following statement reveals his expectations from standardization:

It is obvious that standardization in architecture should not aim at complete buildings or large, rigid units, but should concentrate on the inner system of elements and components, the main emphasis being placed on a formulation of these elements which makes it possible to combine them in endless different ways . . . This would result in a flexibility which could ideally be compared with nature's unlimited variability. ("The reconstruction of Europe", *Arkkitehti,* no. 5, 1941).

Aalto's idea of *'the growing house'* is a variation on this theme, basically intended as a way to build new housing gradually in rural areas during the barren post-war years. First the family was to move into a primitive housing cell designed to meet its most urgent needs. The house would then be gradually enlarged in all directions, allowing for more differentiation. Aalto also designed summer cottages on the principle of the growing house. It is interesting that back in 1926 in Törten near Dessau the Bauhaus architects Muche and Paulick had built a prefabricated steel unit building which could either grow or shrink, depending on the residents' needs. In 1931 Ludwig Hilbersheimer launched another experiment with the revealing name "Das wachsende Haus im Siedlungsgelände" (The growing house in suburban areas). However attractive this idea was in theory, it never led to results of any practical significance either in Dessau or in Aalto's Finland, no doubt because the way man lives and builds is not as rational as the Bauhaus idealists imagined.

THE THEORY
OF TYPES

One of the cornerstones of Rationalist morphology was the theory of types. Aalto referred to this theory as early as January 1928 as something generally known and accepted. In his book *Theory and Design in the Machine Age,* Reyner Banham discussed the early history of the theory of types and examined its dissemination among Rationalist circles in the '20s. The idea seems to have stemmed from the German *Werkbund* group, particularly from Hermann Muthesius, but it first really became established when, after finishing his studies in Germany, Le Corbusier introduced it in Paris and gave it a key position in the Purist vocabulary.

The idea of types was perhaps most clearly expressed by Paul Valéry in his Socratic dialogue *Eupalinos,* written in 1921. Phaedros, one of the characters, says: *There are wonderful tools as well-formed as bones,* to which Socra-

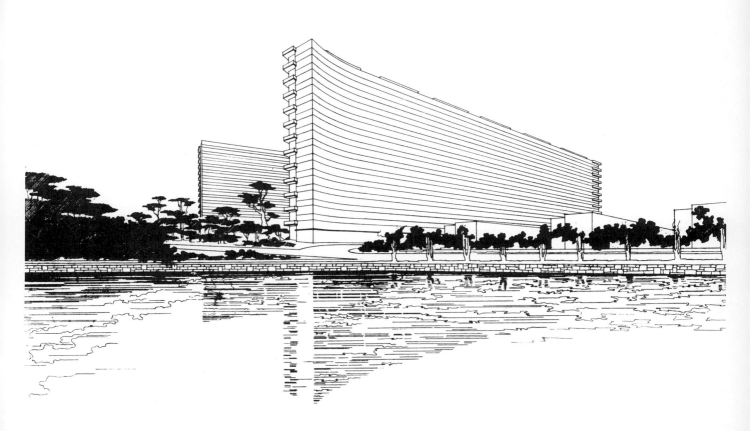

213. Aalto's most monumental model housing plan in the '30s was the lamellar block for the Stenius company, unsurpassed until his tower blocks in Bremen and Lucerne in the '60s.

tes replies: *They have, at least to a certain extent, come into being by themselves. The use of centuries has resulted of necessity in the best form imaginable; unceasing activity leads to the ideal, and that is where change comes to an end. The efforts of thousands of men to attain the best gradually lead to the most economical and surest form.* Philosophically the idea is related to Platonism and the *Urgestalten* (archetypes) as defined by Goethe. In practice the types include such anonymous and perfect utility articles as the hammer, the sickle, the scissors, the wine bottle, the drinking glass and the various musical instruments. The last of these were favourite subjects of the Cubists and Purists in their efforts to capture the essence of reality on canvas. Le Corbusier took it for granted that this process also applied to the new technical inventions, particularly to those which incarnated the promise of the future by virtue of their emotional appeal. He was convinced that the motor car, the aeroplane and the transatlantic passenger

liner were on the way to reaching their definitive typological form, thanks to the efforts of gifted designers. In this respect, architects were far behind, but might catch up if they truly decided to work in the same spirit as engineers. His book *Vers une architecture* pointed out the direction to be followed – that is, type design. The last picture in the book was of an almost archetypal type, the classic English pipe, which he set up as an ideal for architects to emulate.

It is easy enough for us, the children of a later age, to dismiss the theory of types as naive: we have seen how little inclination the automobile and aviation industry have shown for adhering to definitive type designs, and we have generally lost all faith in the spontaneous capacity of technological progress to lead to the 'best possible result'. The historical importance of the theory cannot be denied, however, and in Aalto's case it was crucial.

The theory of types influenced two different aspects of Aalto's work. The first was housing design. The weekend

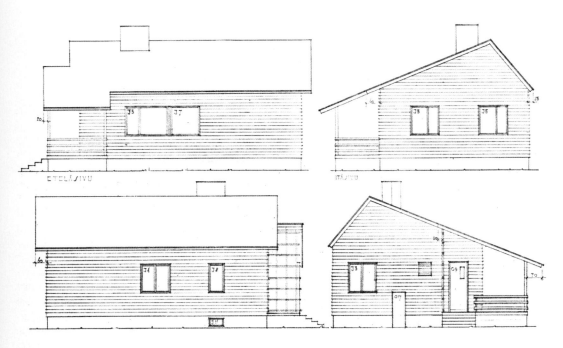

214. In the '30s Aalto began to develop small house types which were produced serially in the '40s under the 'AA system'. This type house for Varkaus is dated November 11, 1937.

215. Housing for workers of the Inkeroinen pulp mill, 1937. The houses have a common heating unit and accommodate four families each. For a photo of the house, see F 293.

cottages he designed for the *Aitta* competition in 1928 were already intended as 'type houses', as were the one-family house he designed for the Insulite Company in 1932 and the weekend cottage for Enso-Gutzeit from the same year. These were standard plans intended to be carried out in identical form throughout the country, but in practice no more than a handful of samples were built, sometimes not even one. The 1928 standard block of flats in Turku was also based on type design, as its name indicated. Aalto made his next effort to create a universally applicable type in 1935 with a high-rise block for the Stenius company in Munkkiniemi, but this project never got off the drawing board (the plan was, however, much admired at the 1939 exhibition 'Art in our time' at the Museum of Modern Art in New York*).

Aalto's ambition to design type housing became more realistic in 1937 when he received commissions to plan new housing areas in Sunila, Varkaus and Inkeroinen for the workers and officials of local factories. In the following years he designed a great variety of large and small residential buildings, which he always presented as 'types' with alphabetical and numerical symbols on the plans, as if they made up a complete system for the production of innumerable individually variable standard products. These designations seem a bit pathetic now that we know that in fact only a few samples of his 'standardized' inventions were ever built.

Types also had a wider significance for Aalto than their role in serializing housing production. They should be set in the context of his purely aesthetic goals. To the Rationalists of the '20s and '30s, the Greek temple, the Gothic cathedral and the park-surrounded Baroque castle – to cite a few well-known examples – represented generally accepted types. It was Aalto's ambition to extend the existing typology with new types characteristic of his own age. The Paimio Sanatorium was not intended merely as a unique work of art, but as an attempt to define the standard modern sanatorium. He therefore unhesitatingly made use of contributions other architects such as Duiker had made to solving the general problem. Aalto's many variants on the library building were all based on the standard idea of a sunken floor in the lending room, and his theatres also tended towards a type plan with a fan-shaped auditorium and an asymmetrical distribution of tiers.

Did Aalto succeed in his efforts to create architectural types? In housing design, we may conclude that the stars were unfavourable, as they were for Le Corbusier before him. Only one exhibition sample was built of the latter's Maison Citrohan, although the name implied that it was intended to become as widespread as the Citroën motor car, and his renowned 'standard' block of flats in Marseilles also remained unique. Similarly, only one of Aalto's standard terrace houses was ever built (in Kauttua); nor did his libraries and theatres ever become generally established types.

There is all the more reason to rejoice that Aalto's typological dream came true in another sector in which he attempted to apply it; that is, in furniture design. Many of the prototypes he designed in the early '30s have been produced by the hundreds of thousands, and they are still sold throughout the world as true – i.e., final – type products. Imitations and variations of his bentwood chairs can be found in every shop selling modern furniture. It is a fact that none of the Rationalist architects succeeded in creating a permanent type building or apartment, and precious few modern designers have produced lasting models for utility goods. Thus Aalto's feat in designing type furniture deserves all our admiration.

*See John McAndrew's article 'Housing' in the exhibition catalogue.

THE MACHINE
AS A MODEL

We have already discussed Le Corbusier's idea of the machine as a model for architecture. He implanted his belief in many followers, one of whom was Markelius. The rousing lecture the latter gave to Finnish architects in 1928 included the following passage:

Technical form implies rejection of the superfluous. It is, so to speak, the minimum form. The machine works impersonally, that is its nature ... There can hardly be any more doubt that the technical form will increasingly make its mark on the design of our time. In the construction of houses and in industrial art, too, it will make order out of chaos. In purely technical production methods, in construction, purpose and function, design has the fixed point of departure it has lacked up to now.

These words were bound to be received with sympathy by the listener who was intellectually closest to Markelius, namely Aalto. Knowing Aalto's attraction to the modern way of life, his enthusiasm for flying and car travel, his interest in the cinema, and most of all his inextinguishable desire to be a technical inventor, one is bound to expect a eulogy of machines and of the promise of technological progress from him, at least at the early stages of his 'conversion'. I discovered to my considerable surprise that in an article on the new architecture, published by Aalto in *Uusi Aura* a few months before Markelius's lecture, he did not even touch upon the subject of machines, and that in another article published a few months later he actually uttered an express warning against the dangers of technocracy:

Technology has placed at our disposal machines which are far more effective than anything that ever existed in the past. We must devote increasing attention to designing them carefully, also with a view to hygiene, since not only their usefulness but also their harmfulness increases at the same rate as their efficiency. *

This declaration from Aalto's earliest, most fiercely Rationalist period is remarkable in that it clearly denotes a far deeper insight into the problems of Rationalism than most of his contemporaries possessed. *"Functional is beautiful,"* Gregor Paulsson declared in the heat of the debate on Functionalism in 1930. But was this not a dangerous thought? Like an atom bomb, a building can be extremely functional for a specific purpose, but frighteningly un-functional in a wider context. For the unit builders and bureaucrat planners of our day, suburban construction with endless series of prefabricated concrete units is undoubtedly functional. But this is a functionality that Aalto aptly compared with 19th century Pullman cars. *They were said to be practical and economical, but the wise traveller soon realized that their practicality and economy was all for the Pullman Company, not for the passenger.* ** Efficiency for its own sake and profit hunger actually found a dangerous ally in extreme Functionalism.

NATURE
AS A MODEL

Now we begin to understand why Aalto's declarations about architecture never turned into an ode to machines even in the early '30s, and why he never stopped at the technical level but was always pondering the hygienic, social, and psychological needs he thought most important. In an article written for the book *Arkitektur och samhälle* (Architecture and Society), brought out by the Swedish publisher Spektrum in 1932, he introduced what was to become one of his favourite themes: *Nature, not the machine, is the most important model for architecture.* Aalto's article starts from the basic fact that the new technological

*Iltalehti, February 23, 1929.

**Sketches, p. 28.

216. Already in 1930 Aalto preferred organic forms to geometric ones. Three alternatives for the linkup of the conveyor and the cooker at the Toppila mill. The last of these was built.

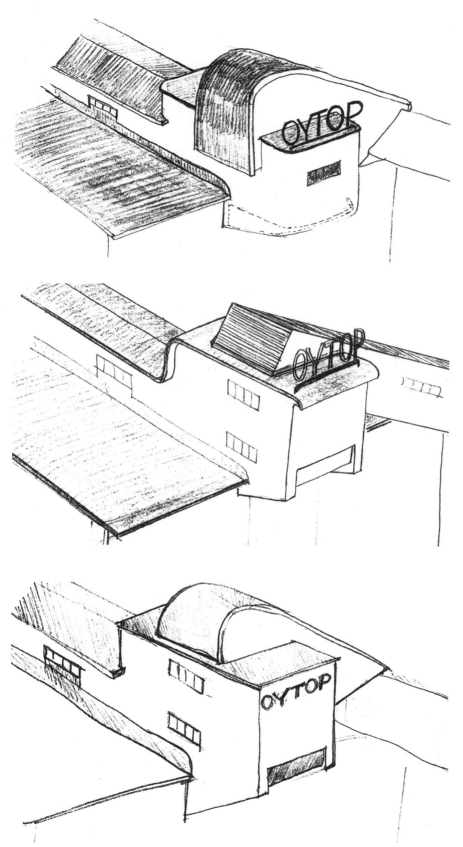

inventions (electricity, the motor car, the radio, etc.) have changed the way people live. He goes on to predict that the old contrast between city and countryside will be levelled out. For the first time, people will be able to avoid both the cultural isolation brought about by sparse rural settlement and the stifling collectivism and isolation from nature offered by the big city. He discusses the question of which type of housing organization is most conducive to psychological and social well-being. He compares the model provided by the new means of communication with the structure of higher organisms: just as the individual cells form tissues, which in turn are combined to constitute parts of the body controlled by the central organs, so society should be organized into small units combined progressively into more extensive entities. There is an optimum grouping of dwellings in which families have sufficient contacts and the most important services near at hand. These primary groups combine to form larger ones for which the more demanding services such as schools, health care and individual jobs are available. Finally, the most demanding social services, including institutes of higher education and administrative institutions, cater to whole regions with the help of effective modern communications.

The interest of this article lies in the basic principle of organization rather than in the rather trivial practical instructions for successful regional planning. Instead of seeking the most efficient solutions to various subsidiary problems such as fast traffic communications, maximum land use, optimization of industrial production conditions, and housing the greatest possible number of people in the smallest possible area, Aalto approached human life as a complex biological phenomenon. Instead of basing his ideas on the exploitative mentality that gave rise not only to real cities like New York but also to Le Corbusier's vision of *la ville radieuse,* Aalto attempted to adapt the life of the human community

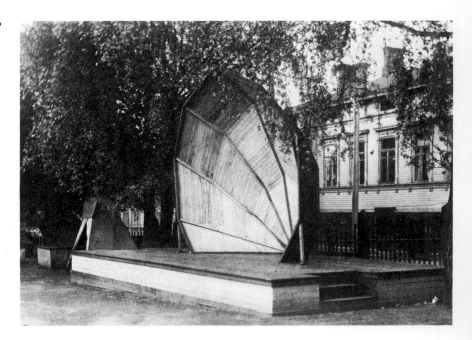

217. Bandstand at the Tampere exhibition in 1922.

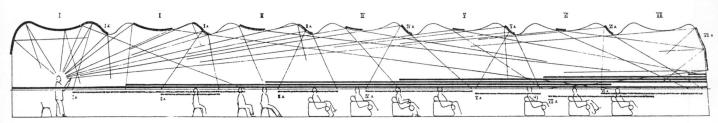

218. The acoustically designed ceiling of the Viipuri Library auditorium. Cf. F 87.

to nature's course, starting from psychological and physiological considerations beneficial to the individual.

As I attempted to show in the first part of this biography, the affinity with nature which was Aalto's distinguishing quality had its roots in his childhood home, in his communion with the lakeland scenery he learned to know on innumerable excursions, and in the idyllic small town in which he grew up. It was strengthened by the intellectual influence of his surveyor father and his forester grandfather. They both took a positivist view of the promise of technology and were in the vanguard of modernization in their time, but they did not take technology as an end in itself; it was a means to improve the quality of life. Their respect for nature appears touchingly in the ergonomic forms given by the grandfather to his

repeater rifle, the 'soft' shapes of which reappear in many of Aalto's inventions.

In fact the adaptation of technical inventions to the human body and sensory organs often leads spontaneously to organic forms. The first of these forms found in Aalto's architecture, the small music stand for the Tampere fair in 1922, was based on acoustic considerations. The same principles were applied to the more complicated music stand for the Turku exhibition in 1928 and to the design of the vaults in the Tehtaanpuisto and Vallila church entries. Aalto sought to justify the free form of the undulating wooden ceiling of the Viipuri Library auditorium by appealing again – not altogether convincingly – to acoustic considerations. The motif first took on an independent character as the ex-

218

pression of the quintessence of Aalto's architectural ideas in the small pond in front of the Paris pavilion, in the 'northern lights' wall of the New York pavilion, and in the Savoy vase.

THE PRECEPTS
OF MOHOLY-NAGY

It is clear that Aalto was spontaneously attracted to a biological model for architecture. What he needed in the early '30s was help and encouragement in finding an intellectual justification for architecture inspired by nature rather than machines. Moholy-Nagy gave him the help he needed. We have already discussed several important impulses passed on to Aalto by Moholy, who was well versed in the radical art trends of the time and was a creative artist himself. We also pointed out that the book Moholy sent Aalto after his visit to Finland, *von material zu architektur,* which contained a summary of his teaching programme at Bauhaus from 1923 to 1929, could also be assumed to provide an indication of what problems the two

219. *Moholy-Nagy's book* von material zu architektur *was published in 1929 as no. 14 in the* bauhausbücher *series.*

friends discussed together. There is thus every reason to take a look at this remarkable work.

As the title suggests, the book starts out from the special studies of materials and experiments with form which were intended to give the Bauhaus students *das erlebnishafte begreifen des materials* (an experiential understanding of material). The designer's first duty, according to Moholy, is to become familiar with the structure, texture, and 'facture' of the material (i.e., its interior organization, tactile qualities and marks left on it by the production process); his second duty – whether he is making an abstract sculptural work of art or simple utility goods – is always to keep nature's biological order as his goal.

Under the heading *'biotechnology as a method of creative activity'* Moholy exhorts his pupils to adhere as closely as possible to the principles manifested in nature's own creations, in plants and animals. *Of course it can happen that by immersing oneself deeply in the task, one comes to understand the interrelationships between the material (the medium), the tool (the machine) and the desired function so well that one finds the correct constructions even without studying a natural model, and these constructions are later confirmed as agreeing with nature's own creations.*

Moholy goes on to what he considers the core of artistic creation: attainment of a biologically satisfactory equilibrium between man and the world around him. He describes how Cézanne, and after him the Neo-Plasticists (Mondrian, Doesburg), the Suprematists (Malevich) and the Constructivists (Tatlin, Rodchenko, Lissitzky, Moholy-Nagy) created various models for 'the plastic experience'. He stresses the significance of intuition and spontaneity. *Harmony does not lie in an aesthetic formula, but in organic, undisruptedly flowing function. Conformity to the laws of nature then appears by itself, for man's biological construction is the true source of all organic expression.* Thus one must empirically

220. *Moholy-Nagy in Finland in 1931, photo Aino Aalto.*

seek the state of equilibrium that is *regulated from within, reflex-wise.*

The final section discusses the spatial experience, the correct perception of which is perhaps the most important way for Moholy to establish a harmonious relationship between man and his surroundings. *Architecture shall no longer be a complex of restricted spaces, a protection against the weather and dangers from outside, a rigid enclosure and an immutable disposition of rooms. It shall be a model of the organization of universal space, a mobile image which helps us control our existence, an organic component of life itself.*

The most important thing in architecture is *the indescribable equilibrium of fettered tensions, fluctuation between interpenetrating spatial energies. Spatial configuration is based on the overlapping of spatial elements, giving rise to invisible but clearly per-*ceptible relative movement in all dimensions and with varying strength. Spatial strata, not plastic configurations, are the building blocks of architecture.* If these strata are used, *the interior of the building finds its spatial articulation and at the same time is linked with the exterior.* For the time being, however, architecture has only achieved intimations of what is to come – an example being the way Gropius excised portions of the cosmic outdoor space in his theatre for Piscator. *The problem of totality is only beginning to emerge today, after careful preparation.* Important experiments with exhibition architecture, and Moholy's own stage designs and films reveal the particular aptness of free form for these art forms. The goal is *space open in all directions, space without boundaries.* The task lies with the new architecture, which will shortly *announce to man that he has taken the* *weightless, invisible and yet all-enveloping space into his possession.*

The attentive reader has no doubt been struck by how closely these quotations from a book written in 1929 describe Aalto's work of the '30s. Here we find the furniture in which the intrinsic, biologically determined laws of materials, mechanical manufacturing methods, and function are so closely observed that the result 'conforms with nature's own creations'. Here is the intuitive working method which rejects all rules of form and allows artistic vision to find the synthesis of rich content with balance that is proper to natural growth. And here is the space without boundaries, built from spatial strata according to the principles of experiential psychology (basically Gestalt psychology) instead of the geometrical spatial principles of Le Corbusier and Mies van der Rohe, or the abstract plastic solids used by the Russian Elementarists as building components.

As I pointed out in the first volume, we find these principles in embryo – as a spontaneous inclination – in the young Aalto. Their roots were in his childhood love of nature, in the 'backwoodsman' that always remained a part of him. His encounter with the engineer mentality, geometric Constructivism, and demand for efficiency of international Rationalism in 1927 might well have silenced the forest voice within him and turned him into a blind tool for the reductive exploitation of nature in the manner of other architects of the Functionalist awakening. We saw how far he had allowed himself to be tempted in this direction in his plea for 'non-synthetic architecture' in 1930, when like Hannes Meyer he denied the architect's artistic role and claimed that architecture is merely a question of combining analytically resolved component problems.

THE BIOLOGICAL SYNTHESIS

Biology as the architect's best source of inspiration is a theme which grows forth gradually in Aalto's pronouncements from these years. In 1935 he gave a lecture to the Swedish Society of Industrial Design in Stockholm:

Nature, biology, has rich and luxuriant forms; with the same construction, the same tissues and the same principles of cellular organization, it can create billions of combinations, each of which represents a definitive, highly-developed form. Man's life belongs to the same category. The things that surround him are hardly fetishes or allegories with mystical eternal value; more than anything else, they are cells and tissues, living beings like himself, building components which make up human life. They cannot be treated differently from other biological units, lest they run the risk of not fitting into the system and becoming dehumanized.

At the Nordic Building Congress in Oslo in 1938, he said:

Nature herself is the best standardization committee in the world. But in nature, standardization is almost exclusively applied to the smallest possible unit, the cell. This results in millions of different combinations which never become schematic. It also results in unlimited riches and perpetual variation in organically growing forms. The same path should be followed by standardization in architecture . . . The very essence of architecture consists of variety and development reminiscent of natural organic life. This is the only true style in architecture.

Aalto's argument can be connected with an author he first read in 1935 and frequently quoted in later speeches. Alexis Carrel, a French-American psychologist who had won the Nobel Prize, was working at the Rockefeller Institute in New York at the time, and his popular scientific pamphlet *Man the Unknown* created a sensation. The book, which was translated into Swedish in 1936, was intended (as the author said) as "a synthesis of what we know about ourselves", specifically about the biological foundations of the body and the psyche. Carrel was clearly influenced by Henri Bergson's idea of *l'évolution créatrice* (creative evolution), but he combined this with the expert up-to-date knowledge of the natural scientist. He was sharply critical of one-sidedly technocratic trends: *All those countries which have uncritically embraced the spirit and technology of industrialism, Russia no less than Britain, France and Germany, are menaced by the same danger as the United States. Humanity must turn its thoughts from machines and the inert material world to the human body and soul, and to the mental and physical processes which have created both the machines and the universes of Newton and Einstein . . . This book was written for those who are bold enough to realize that we must change not only spiritually, socially and politically, but we must also throw machine civilization overboard and embrace new ideas about human progress.*

In his architecture, Aalto had the same aims as Carrel, as can be deduced from a passage from his obituary for Gunnar Asplund, written in 1940:

A new architecture has sprung forth: it is based on the views of the social scientists, but it also encompasses the study of psychological problems, "man the unknown" in the full meaning of the phrase. This trend shows that architecture still has untapped resources which spring directly from nature and the inexplicable reactions of the human psyche. (*Arkkitehti*, no. 10, 1940)

The architecture that is created to meet a restricted, rationally defined need, for example to provide people with cheap minimum housing with a number of required amenities, can with good reason be compared with a machine. If we wish, however, to extend our functional demands to such complex needs as quality of life, mental well-being and social equilibrium, the machine model is no longer adequate; what is required is a dialogue with all the intermingled influences that combine in the same way as in living nature. The architect's problem is to assess the relative weight of the indefinable but most real needs that affect the relevant building assignment and to give them their due importance. In the early '30s, when Aalto still believed in straightforward Functionalism and spoke out for 'non-synthetic architecture', he thought that all that was needed was to analyse the various components of the assignment in a rational way and to add them up to make a functional whole. When he adopted his biologically oriented philosophy, he realized that his earlier views had been mistaken. In fact, he had never followed them in his architecture; he had created works like the Viipuri Library and Paimio Sanatorium on completely different principles. It took a long time before he was prepared to disavow his 'non-synthetic' thesis publicly. In 1940 he published an article in the *Technological Review*:

Architecture is a synthetic phenomenon which covers practically all human activity. An architectural detail can be Functionalist from one point of view and un-Functionalist from another . . . If a way could be found to develop architecture step by step, starting from economic and technical principles and going on to other, more complex forms of human activity, purely technical Functionalism might be acceptable. But there is no way to do this.

Does this imply a capitulation on Aalto's part, a return to the individual, irrational 'artistic syntheses' he repudiated in 1927? The answer is no. Aalto found a third way, a combination of lucid analysis and deep intuition. He described it in a famous article for the Italian journal *Domus* in 1947, 'The Trout and the Stream':

The architectural planner operates with countless mutually discordant elements. Social, humanitarian, economic and technical requirements are combined with psychological problems affecting the individual and the group, the movements and internal friction of both crowds of people and individuals. All this builds up into a tangled web, which cannot be straightened out rationally or mechanically. The sheer number of various demands and problems forms an obstacle which makes it hard for the basic architectural idea to make itself felt. This is what I do — sometimes quite instinctively — in such cases. I forget the whole maze of problems for a while, as soon as the feel of the assignment and the innumerable demands it involves are fully engraved on my subconscious. A reworking, a regrouping, a creative process takes place in the subconscious, making use of all the material fed into it plus the architect's accumulated human and professional wisdom. This path gradually takes me to the main idea, a kind of universal substance, which helps me to bring the numerous conflicting elements into harmony.

This was a beautiful and logical solution to the problem of Rationalist form, but it was not a formula likely to help other architects to achieve good results.

III. Harmony and the cultural heritage

One of the thinkers who has had the greatest influence – perhaps one should add, for better or worse – on the ideas and life patterns of our time is Jean-Jacques Rousseau. It was Rousseau who introduced the idea of the *original, naturally good man.* The innocent child we all once were, with all the right feelings and thoughts, which were stifled by a warped education and adverse social conditions; this thought had an explosive political and cultural impact which still seems unabated after two centuries. There is no other idea more apt to implant equality among men while raising their self-esteem, since it permits them to blame all their shortcomings on others, while they are themselves endowed with virtues that they need not trouble themselves to show.

Rousseau's thought had a particularly interesting influence on pedagogics. The problem is how to bring up people who are perfect by nature but who risk being corrupted by the conventional teaching methods. The Bauhaus school in Dessau produced a logical and later increasingly widespread solution to the problem. Instruction on the preliminary one-year basic course was aimed at setting the pupils free from all traditional forms and clichés about artistic creation. Instead of assimilating the cultural heritage and practising its idiom, the pupils were expected to recover the child's spontaneous relationship to the world, to create a

221. Moholy-Nagy's present to Aalto: a lithograph from his Kestner Mappe, No. 6, made in 1923.

für alte Herrlichkeit!   Moholy-Nagy
                                                                              1920

tabula rasa within themselves, a completely unprejudiced attitude that would liberate their genuinely creative powers.

We have seen that Moholy stressed the prime importance of sensory physiology and experiential psychology to creativity. The art to which he devoted himself together with the avant-garde painters and sculptors he reviewed was an elementary art, based on presumptions they thought valid for all men throughout history. The same denial of the significance of the cultural heritage, the same lack of a sense of history, characterized the architectural goals of the Bauhaus school. The Rationalists denied that Rationalism was a style, claiming that it merely perfected an architectural principle that had always existed and had been applied equally by the designers of Stone Age huts and the straightforward, uncorrupted engineers who erected the bold utility buildings of the 19th century. Their ahistorical approach resulted in a rewriting of architectural history, which now set out to describe how 'natural man' had always worked in the right spirit, though he had frequently been overshadowed by the consciously artistic designers of a corrupt civilization. Siegfried Giedion, the chief ideologue of the CIAM movement, wrote his famous history book *Time, Space and Architecture* in this vein, describing the progress of basically Rationalist architecture from the dawn of time to the apotheosis of the CIAM masters.

Aalto's reaction to this attitude was quite surprising. Just after his conversion to Rationalism, he wrote two newspaper articles in which he clearly expressed dissent with the rejection of history. The first was the previously quoted polemical piece on the Finnish Independence Monument in *Uusi Suomi* on November 25, 1927, in which he wrote:

Art is like a pair of scales at one end of which we find the so-called free arts (monumental architecture, sculpture, painting, poetry) and at the other those more restricted by practical demands (town planning, housing, technical inventions, utility art, journalism). The centre of gravity, the art form which reflects the truest image of its time, shifts from one end to the other, depending on which is favoured by prevailing conditions. In the days of Louis XIV, pomp and circumstance and the glorification of kingship were the principal social requirements. The key question was how to achieve all this, and it was enough of a challenge to enhance the skills of those who tackled the task and to give rise to free art of high quality. At other times, such as our own, the social requirements almost exclusively employ the utilitarian arts. This is why the most enduring, the most characteristic works of our time arise in connection with strict workaday utility, in most cases at least in assignments which involve giving form (construction) to a real content.

As we see, Aalto admits that we share in older art, and emphasizes the fact that different ages have given permanently valid expression to certain sectors of civilization, to which our own age must add its own contribution. These ideas were elaborated by Aalto in an article published barely a month later, on New Year's Day, 1928, in *Uusi Aura:*

We might compare a Classical statue of a god with a part of some modern machine: both have something of the same aspiration to provide the perfectly refined form for a content with real significance and a resonance of truth in their time ... We cannot create new form where there is no new content. We cannot make a church building as a whole the perfect representation of civilization in 1927; we cannot create modern church architecture in the true sense of the word, since the content (the divine service) for which the form was created is an old tradition with no connection with the pressing problems of our time. On the other hand, in this year 1927 the actual technical aspect of construction (even of a church) cannot be based on tradition, unless we choose to be childishly content with a mask instead of the truth. In these conditions, the construction itself, as well as its forms, may contain a creative artistic mission (creation of a new form, concept or type), and the forms required by the spiritual content and function of the building may be based on tradition; the assignment must then be considered reproductive art. This dual task calls for an artist with a Latin clarity of thought, who is able to keep the various requirements separate and yet create harmony. The reason why we have so rarely succeeded in doing this is that we have not fully appreciated the duality of the task ...

There are other assignments which do not directly involve the traditional art aspect; only these can give rise to 'modern art', a complete image of the age and a type-creating process ... This also implies a clear-sighted acknowledgment of the significance of tradition and a much more favourable attitude to it than has been the case.
(The emphasis is the present author's.)

This promise to continue to build upon tradition, given on the very threshold of Aalto's shift to Modernism, was not the last backward glance of a man hesitant about abandoning Neo-Classicism, but an almost prophetic anticipation of his own life's work. The undisputed domination of the CIAM architects during the following decades and the vigilance of the ideologues of Rationalism prevented the wily Aalto from engaging in theoretical argument, but what he actually built expressed his faith in the heritage he defined in the article quoted above. When pestered with questions about architectural theory in later years, Aalto's standard reply was: "I answer with my buildings". Since he did not go out of his way to point out the traditional motifs he cherished, he was accepted as a genuine Modernist. It is actually astonishing to discover that in the heyday of Rationalism everyone remained blind to the deep historical roots of Aalto's architecture. This may be partly explained by the fact that he clothed the traditional motifs in modern garb with 'a Latin clarity of thought' (to borrow a

phrase from his article in *Uusi Aura*). This is why the columns, mediaeval towers, cloisters, theatre *caveae, cortili, campanili,* Italian *piazze,* Venetian staircases, fortress walls, and other historical elements that abound in his buildings were not recognized, though observers derived pleasure from the expressiveness of these elements and from their viability for the practical purpose they were designed for.

Where did Aalto get the strength to withstand the general rejection of culture, and what were the psychological roots of his attitude, highly controversial as it was for most of his life? This question brings us to an interesting theme. In the first volume I described an extraordinary work, the "Book of Inventions", which Aalto first read as a boy and which continued to amuse him in later life. The evolutionary thesis of the book was that man has made incessant progress through the ages with the help of new inventions. The word 'invention' is here used in its broadest sense, encompassing everything from the making of fire and the first tools to the shaping of language as a means of communication, from the substitution of money for barter to the preparation of various raw materials and the making of compound products, including the various types of buildings. The column, architrave, and various entablatures were all inventions, as were the larger entities of which they are a part, such as the gabled temple, the amphitheatre, the stoa and the block of flats, all of them representing what Aalto called 'types'. For him the architect's task was to apply the existing stock of architectural inventions in a fresh way, adding to them whenever possible. The idea that the architect should reject this laboriously accumulated stock-in-trade and start from nothing on every new assignment was as alien to him as it would have been to trade the existing languages for a primitive Dada.

The only problem was that new architecture had to be adapted to today's — and, if possible, tomorrow's — needs in a world that is constantly changing, with the appearance of new inventions covering everything from new models of social and political organization to technological innovations and a deeper knowledge of man's psyche and the biological makeup of life. To solve the new problems correctly, it was essential to be familiar with the stages of development that brought about most of the available inventions. In short, Aalto thought history important, and books about life in bygone days were his favourite reading.

His sense of the world's inevitable forward march made Aalto sensitive to man's perennial problems. He had learned from Nietzsche that Ancient Greece had been no noble, harmonious idyll, for it had rested on a tragic, divided foundation. The great gift of the Greeks to the afterworld was not the illusion that they had led godlike, harmonious lives, but their unerring diagnosis: life is always fragmented and tragic, but by striving with all one's might to overcome chaos, hubris, and other disharmony and to adjust to the laws of the cosmos, one may survive after all and share in divinity.

A word that recurred constantly in Aalto's pronouncements on his own efforts and on those of other architects of generally well disposed people was *harmony*. He believed that to seek equilibrium, interaction, well-being and health had always been man's most important task, if not the one most frequently crowned with success. In fact it had always been so difficult that it had only come true in exceptional, isolated cases. Man has, however, always had the need to envisage life's harmony as a real possibility, and has therefore created historical myths, fantasies of places and times of perfect happiness. The Greeks spoke of a lost Golden Age, the Renaissance created the image of Classical Antiquity as a world in which man had lived in perfect harmony with nature and himself, and the 19th century idealized the Renaissance as an era lost to real life.

As I attempted to show in the first part of this biography, Aalto received

his due share of the myths of both Antiquity and the Renaissance through Goethe and Burckhardt. The sunny Mediterranean and picturesque Italy in particular were mirrors of harmony for him. It is interesting to find that besides his obsession with the South, he had another ideal image of harmony. This image was deeply rooted in his childhood experiences of the Finnish forest, but also contained elements of the then widespread 'Kalevala syndrome', the myth of Karelia, the setting of the Finnish folk epic, as a land where man lived in harmony with himself and his surroundings. On November 2, 1941, *Uusi Suomi* ran an article signed by

222. *Niemelä farm, moved from Konginkangas to the Seurasaari open-air museum in Helsinki, an architectural model of the highest quality for Aalto.*

223. 'Naturally grown' furniture in a Karelian cottage, Seurasaari open-air museum, Helsinki.

Alvar Aalto and including the following passage:

East Karelia, with its vast isolated zones, is an architectural reserve most unusual in Europe; external influences have played an exceptionally small role there. By this I mean that the region has largely been left to fend for itself and has therefore grown directly from natural conditions . . . It is forest architecture pure and simple, with wood dominating almost one hundred per cent both as a building material and in jointing . . . generally left naked, without the effect of immateriality given by colouring. A tumbledown Karelian village is externally somehow related to Greek ruins, where the unity of material is also a salient feature, though in them wood is replaced by marble up to the entablature.

In a way the Karelian house is a building which begins with a single small cell or dispersed, embryonic shacks – shelters for people and animals – and grows, figuratively speaking, year by year. 'The great Karelian house' is comparable with a biological cluster of cells; the possibility of a larger and more complete structure always remains open.

This curious property of growth and flexibility is best reflected in the basic principle of the Karelian house: the lack of a constant roof angle. This very fact, the apparently arbitrary use of roof pitch, gives rise to the crystal-like jumble of buildings. In itself, the principle of free roof pitch is uncommon enough: in stereotyped architecture, which usually stems from foreign literary influence or even the needs of imperialist propaganda, the roof pitch rigidifies without exception, and generally winds up as a typical artificially unifying factor. In the refined free roof formations of Karelia, which nevertheless have a certain organization, we see a contact with nature which has remained fresh, a kind of struggle for survival which has led to the creation of the straightforward, living, flexible forms necessary for victory.

This architectural freedom holds a special interest for our day and age.

The architectural reform of our time, the Renaissance which we see throughout the world, has consistently sought to liberate architectural form and to achieve a flexible unity in town planning and architecture thereby. In this it has reached practically the same conclusions as the architecture of the Karelian backwoods. The first requirement in the last Renaissance of architecture is to replace stereotyped roof structure with a more elastic kind, all the way from the flat roof to a variety of pitches and angles.

. . . Karelian furniture design, just as the Karelian building, is based on the growing tree. While a standard material − tree trunks − is used for the building, smaller parts of trees − the pliant branches and the sometimes quite astonishing knots and other formations − are used to make furniture.

It would be hard to find a naturalness more logical in its beauty: the sturdy pine stands for the building, while its curving branches and pliant parts represent furniture and movables.

The striking point in this conception of a harmonious architecture mirroring a harmonious relationship with nature is Aalto's comparison of the Karelian house with a Classical ruin (which he thought of as consisting entirely of marble). The strong appeal of ruins to modern, alienated man does not arise merely from their representation of a supposedly harmonious Antiquity, but also from the atonement implicit in the way nature reclaims what man has borrowed, as ivy and grazing sheep invade his buildings. Romanticization of ruins expresses a pessimistic view of man's earthly toil: complete reconcilement with nature is perhaps only possible after life has ebbed out. This streak of pessimism can be detected in many of Aalto's buildings, beginning with the clinging ivy of the Viipuri Library and culminating in the ruin forms of Aalto's own summer home in Muuratsalo and his office home in Munkkiniemi.

In a world obsessed with technology, Aalto's ambition was to attain the same kind of harmony with the cosmos as he imagined that the Karelian village once had. The yardstick he applied to his own house in Munkkiniemi shows how literally he took the idea of continuity: it was to be "the Niemelä farm of our time" (see page 130). Aalto was deeply conscious that harmonization of life had become much more difficult in his time than it was for the Karelian villagers. As he put it in a newspaper interview in 1929 (see page 216), technology has placed aids at our disposal, but their utility may be outweighed by their harmfulness, and thus the utmost caution is necessary in planning their use. In older days, Aalto was far from being an evolutionary optimist; his insight into the dangers that beset our earth made resistance so much the more necessary.

The darker the world around him became, the more pressing was the task of creating buildings for technocratic society that would contribute to harmony and provide an artistic example of the equilibrium between technology and biology, civilization, and nature that is so often lacking. He knew that the odds were against a successful outcome. In 1928, he could still write: *A conscious regard in artistic creation for the problems of our time implies a tremendous goal, the step by step transition of industrialism into what it is in any case destined to be some day − a harmonious factor of civilization.* (*Uusi Aura*, January 1, 1928). In his old age, he merely said (in a conversation with the present author): *"You can't save the world, you can only set it an example."*

This hint helps us understand what Aalto ultimately aspired to in his life's work: to bequeath models of a kind, made up of concrete artistic examples, works bringing the deepest conflicts of our age into an exemplary harmony. This was basically the same goal as the Classical Greek artists had. We know how little they were able to save the world, but we also know how much guidance and encouragement individual men have derived from their 'examples' over the centuries. The suggestive power of Classical sculpture and architecture does not depend on whether they seek to illustrate some explanation of the world or to prove a theory, but on their direct revelation of the existence of harmony. In this biography, I have laboriously sought to trace the ways by which Aalto arrived at his credo, but it is more important that he was able to bring it to life so directly and dazzlingly in his work. I stand before Säynätsalo Town Hall, Rovaniemi Library and many other Aalto works with the same inexpressible feeling of joy as before the Parthenon in Athens.

LIST OF WORKS FROM 1928 TO 1939

The following list of Aalto's works from 1928 to 1939 is a continuation of the list in the first volume *(Alvar Aalto: The Early Years)* of this biography. I have left a space between the last entry for 1927, which bears the number 109, and the first for 1928, numbered 120, as I think it likely that works unknown to me from Aalto's early career will be discovered, in which case the remaining numbers can be used. My descriptions are tentative, and will certainly be supplemented and corrected by more persevering researchers. The numbering is not entirely consistent: variants of certain important works have been given a number of their own, while in some cases works of dissimilar character have been grouped under the same heading. In the biographical and critical section of the book, the number of the works mentioned is preceded by the letter W. The list of works contains references to the pages (= P) on which the work in question is cited and to the figures (= F) which illustrate it.

120. Furnishing of various interiors in the Agricultural Cooperative Building in Turku. Aalto was wholly responsible for the interiors of the Turku Finnish Theatre, the Itämeri Restaurant, the Western Finland Cooperative Bank, the Cooperative Butchers' shop, and a sports shop, while he acted as consultant for furnishing the Maakunta Hotel, the Autohalli car dealers', the Maanmiesten Kauppa shop and a hardware store. He mainly used Poul Henningsen's lamps for lighting, and furnished the gallery level of the restaurant with Marcel Breuer's tubular steel furniture. His own furniture marked a transition from 'style design' to Rationalism. P 33–34, 38, 55. F 25, 224.

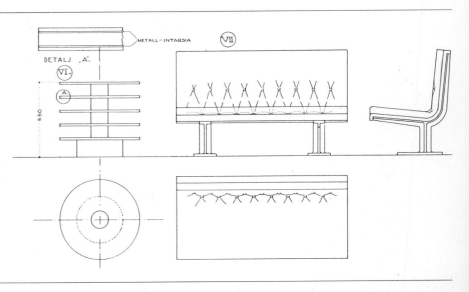

224. Sofa and newspaper table for Länsi-Suomen Pankki (Bank of Western Finland), Turku, March 1928.

225. Second version of Viipuri Library, with espaliers, ivy and Le Corbusier strip windows.

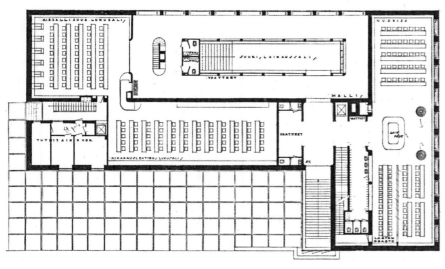

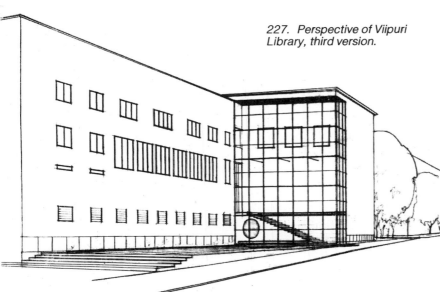

227. Perspective of Viipuri Library, third version.

121. Viipuri City Library, second version. Aalto reworked his own winning competition entry, probably in the summer of 1928, retaining the plan solution, but eliminating all Neo-Classical elements, giving the plan a distinct touch of Le Corbusier. The entire left-hand side of the projecting stair hall is glazed, strip windows both in front and at the back light the lending room (the competition jury had criticized the glazed roof of the lending room in Aalto's original entry), and the building is crowned by a Le Corbusier roof garden with four 'reading terraces'. The entrance to one of the gable ends has a volute-formed concrete baldachin – another Le Corbusier loan. A new, original note is struck by the espalier for climbing ivy which covers a large part of the rear wall and one of the ends. P 29, 208. F 18, 225.

226. Plan of Viipuri Library, third version, with the lending office in the middle and the children's section on the right.

122. Viipuri City Library, third version. In January 1929 Aalto started work on the third plan for the library. It was still to be placed on the same plot on Aleksanterinkatu (later Karjalankatu), but was now combined with a cultural centre on the other side of the street, giving rise to a monumental square dominated by an equestrian statue. The stair hall, glazed on one side, is now connected with an L-shaped projecting wing containing a children's library. The entire wall of the stair hall is decorated by a gigantic relief or fresco representing Classical temples, gods and warriors. The lending room of the main library with its sunken centre part and the adjoining reading room resemble those in the second version, but in drawings dated January 21, 1929 the strip windows have been replaced by rows of separate windows, while in another version dated July 22, 1929, a strip window runs the entire 27-metre length of the rear wall. The rooftop garden with reading terraces, the baldachin over the end entrance and the climbing ivy correspond to the second version. F 226, 227.

235

123. Viipuri City Library, fourth and final version. After the City Council decided on the new placing of the library in the Torkkeli park in autumn 1933, Aalto drafted the final version and signed the drawings in December 1933. Construction got under way in 1934, and the library was inaugurated on October 13, 1935. Besides the new disposition of rooms dictated by the change of location, the plans featured some brand-new 'inventions'. The rooftop garden was deleted, and Aalto returned to his original idea of skylights for the lending and reading rooms, though this time he solved the problems of winter snow and direct sunlight by having rows of round lighting shafts rising from the roof surface (previously used by Aalto for some basement storerooms in the Turun Sanomat building). To make up for the acoustically unfavourable elongated shape of the auditorium, Aalto developed the acoustic ceiling design of his competition entry for Tehtaanpuisto Church (W 148), using an apparently free — but in fact quite uniform — undulating form for the library. The convincing overall grasp, the density of ideas and the care taken in every detail guarantee the Viipuri Library a prime position in Aalto's pre-war output. P 29, 83, 84, 88, 106, 114, 117, 121, 129, 168, 203–204, 218, 230. F 87, 94, 111, 126, 170, 208, 218, 228.

228. The Viipuri Library reading room was separated from the lending office by an apse-shaped terrace and fringed by a curtain on a bar partly in free form. Cf. F 170.

124. Turun Sanomat building in Turku. Aalto started work in January 1928 and signed a complete series of drawings in 1 : 100 scale on June 15 the same year. Reworking and detail drawing continued up to July 1929. This was a multipurpose building with a printing works and rotary presses in the basement, rented shop facilities on street level, a typesetting room and newspaper office one storey up, editorial offices on the second floor, nine flats on the third, a 29-room hotel on the fourth, and finally on the top floor a process engraving works on the courtyard side and a luxury flat with a roof terrace looking out on the street. Aalto thought his idea of displaying the pages of the newspaper in giant format on the large facade window could be carried out by placing a projector on a post at the verge of the pavement. Two important elements made their first appearance in January 1929: the round skylights at the back of the basement and the asymmetrical, 'organic' capitals of the columns in the printing works (the drawings for these are not among the 226 detail drawings in the Aalto archives). P 23–25, 35, 45–46, 55, 62, 102, 103, 197–198, 209. F 11–12, 30, 50, 229.

229. The Turun Sanomat newspaper offices photographed in spring 1930. Alvar Aalto's new Buick in front.

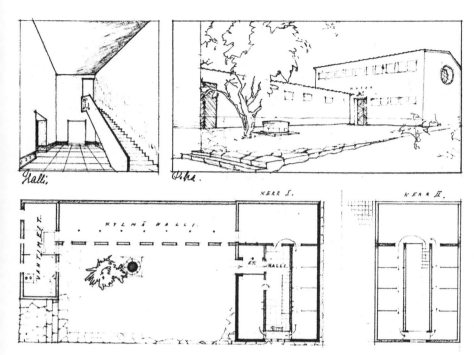

125. Perniö Museum. The Perniö museum society, founded in 1925, commissioned drawings for a local history museum from Alvar Aalto and A. Rancken in early 1928. For both aesthetic and economic reasons, the clients preferred the latter architect's proposal, which accommodated the museum's space requirements to the facades of a vicarage built in Sweden in 1731. Aalto's Neo-Classical plan contains three continuous building volumes surrounding a courtyard left open on the fourth side. One of the short wings contains the caretaker's minuscule flat, the long wing consists of a low hall for exhibiting sleighs, carts and large agricultural equipment, while the two-storey main building with a hip roof contains a central 'church hall' two storeys high with an open staircase. Alcoves for minor exhibits are grouped around this hall on both storeys in such a way that a tour of the museum leads past each. P 20. F 230.

230. Idea sketch for Perniö museum, March 1928.

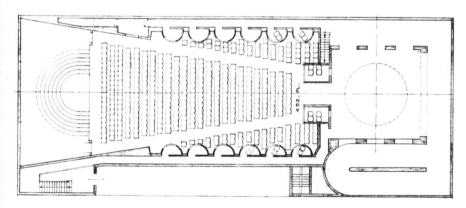

231. Plan of large cinema for Turku.

126. Suomen Biografi cinema in Turku. Suomi-Filmi decided to have a large cinema built at Aurakatu in Turku in early 1928 and commissioned the plans from Aalto. The spectator comes from the street through a corridor to a courtyard, and then turns to enter a low hall communicating through a large circular opening with an upper hall at the same level as the stalls and the boxes on both sides of the auditorium. An open stairway leads from the hall to the balconies. In the simplest plan, there is only one balcony, giving a total of 636 seats; an alternative design features two balconies and 746 seats and the most ambitious plan has three balconies and a total of 820 seats. The cinema was designed at the same time as the Turun Sanomat building, but is dominated by Neo-Classical motifs. The front part of the auditorium features the folded, sound-absorbing, black wall facing invented by Aalto for 'the universal cinema'. Because of the depression which began in 1929 the cinema was never built. P 20–21. F 1, 8, 231.

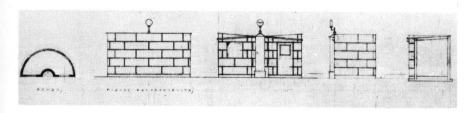

127. Petrol station kiosks in Jyväskylä. In March 1928 Aalto designed two petrol station stands for the Sisä-Suomen Rautakauppa (a hardware store) in Jyväskylä, one to be built obliquely in front of the church on Vapaudenkatu and the other on the corner of Puistokatu and Kauppakatu. The first of them was in exedra form, with the pump at the centre of a semicircle, and imitation ashlar slabs painted on the front. The latter stand has horizontal windows, a rectangular single-pitch roof leaning out asymmetrically over the pump and a round glass holder for measuring petrol, and approaches present-day petrol pumps in form. The kiosks were probably built, but were replaced some years later by more up-to-date constructions. F 332.

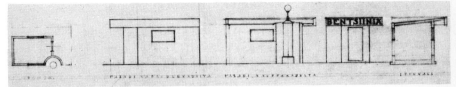

232. Petrol station kiosks for Jyväskylä, 1928.

128. Summer and weekend cottage plans for *Aitta* competition. In spring 1928, *Aitta* magazine announced a competition with April 12 as the closing date. Aalto sent in three plans, winning first prize in both categories with the emphatically Rationalist entries 'Merry-go-round' and 'Konsoli' and gaining a purchase for his more traditional weekend cottage 'Kumeli'. Some examples of 'Merry-go-round', at least, have been built, e.g. in Säynätsalo. P 25–26, 215. F 13–14, 233.

233. 'Merry-go-round' built in Säynätsalo.

129. Block of flats at Uudenmaankatu 6, Turku. Arvo Ketonen, the owner of *Turun Sanomat,* commissioned the drawings for a block of rented flats and shops from Aalto in May 1928. His plan comprised seven shops at street level and 42 flats (from one to four rooms) on the six upper storeys. The depression which paralysed the construction business in Finland in 1929 also prevented implementation of this project. P 24.

130. Modernization of lawyer Ilmari Kataja's home. Aalto was responsible for the relatively extensive renovation from June to September 1928 of this luxury flat at Tuureporinkatu 3 in Turku, the home of the manager of the Agricultural Cooperative Building. The main alterations were a new bathroom, a kitchen with specially designed cupboards and several new doors and windows for the eight rooms, some of them painted with Classical ornaments.

131. Tombstone for Usko Nyström. In late autumn 1928, Aalto designed the entry which won the competition for the grave monument of his former teacher Usko Nyström (1861–1925) in Helsinki's new graveyard, grave no. 468, section 6. The principal motif is an acanthus leaf on an upright stele. Aalto suggested the Finnish inscription "Do not ask the dead body, ask his living fame", but the family preferred "Bene latuit" (He lived unnoticed). See pp. 79–81 in Part I, *Alvar Aalto: The Early Years.*

132. Competition entry for an Independence Monument on Tähtitorninmäki hill in Helsinki. The Finnish Independence Union announced a competition in autumn 1928, with November 25 as the last date of entry, for a monument celebrating Finland's tenth anniversary of independence. Aalto suggested in his entry 'Helsingin horisontti' that instead of a traditional monument, a boldly Rationalist stadium should be built in the centre of the Finnish capital. Under the oval amphitheatre-shaped stands crowned by a high sheltering brim, he placed a restaurant and sauna with a view over the south harbour, and below these a large parking area. P 58, 191–193. F 199–200, 234.

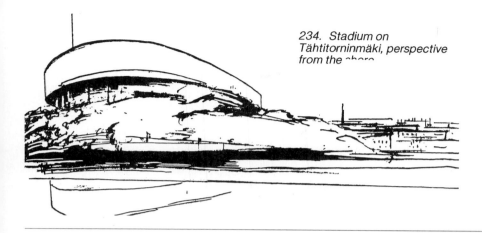

234. Stadium on Tähtitorninmäki, perspective from the shore.

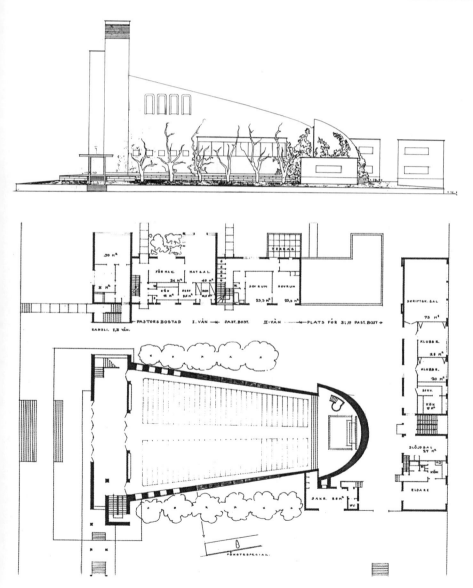

133. Competition entry for Vallila Church, Helsinki. The entry date was January 15, 1929, two weeks before the last date for the great Paimio competition. Aalto's entry 'Gloria' included features which recurred in his later work, such as the entry for Temppeliaukio Church (W 166) and the 1959 Wolfsburg Church. This applies particularly to the wedge-shaped floor plan and the vaulted area between the back wall of the chancel and the ceiling. The church interior appears like a tapering vaulted tunnel and Aalto imagined the exterior, which is also vaulted, as covered by climbing vine. The entrance hall and the bell tower set into it are ascetically Cubistic. The form of the interior was mainly dictated by acoustic considerations based on the principles applied to the Salle Pleyel in Paris. The jury criticized the entry on the grounds that the acoustics were directed one-sidedly outward from the chancel, and Aalto did not win a prize. P 58, 218. F 235.

235. Vallila Church, side elevation and plan.

134. Paimio tuberculosis sanatorium. The competition was announced in November 1928, with January 31, 1929 as the last date of entry. Aalto's winning entry 'Piirretty ikkuna', marked with a drawing of an L-shaped window, divides up the functions among a number of freely combined building volumes. A dominating patients' wing with a slightly angled open-air ward facing south communicates with a central entrance section containing the stairs and lifts. This part has access to a lower wing placed at an angle, containing the canteen, kitchen and social facilities, beyond which another obliquely placed service wing connects with the freely articulated whole. Aalto borrowed the L-shaped windows of the patients' rooms from André Lurçat, but at the construction stage these were replaced for practical reasons by conventional ones. Increased space requirements had the result that the building ultimately became three storeys higher than in the original plan, accentuating the monumental impression. The pantiled single-pitch roof of the competition entry was also replaced with a flat Rationalist roof both for the main building and the surrounding staff housing (designed and built in 1932–33), which comprised: 1) *The chief physician's house* in two storeys with eight rooms and kitchen, a loggia and a terrace; 2) Three-part *terrace house for the assistant physicians,* with four rooms and a kitchen on two levels for each family; 3) Four *flats for office staff,* on two levels and of flexible size, as a bedroom between two flats could be linked up with either, depending on the size of the family. Since tuberculosis sanatoria are no longer needed in Finland, Aalto's masterpiece has been converted into an ordinary hospital: extensive alterations have been made to the interiors, the open-air ward has been glazed in and minor annexes have been added. The building is thus no longer to be seen in its original form. P 41, 43, 56–58, 67, 83–86, 88–90, 102–103, 168, 193–194, 208–210, 215. F 53, 60, 86, 88, 92, 95, 202, 211, 236.

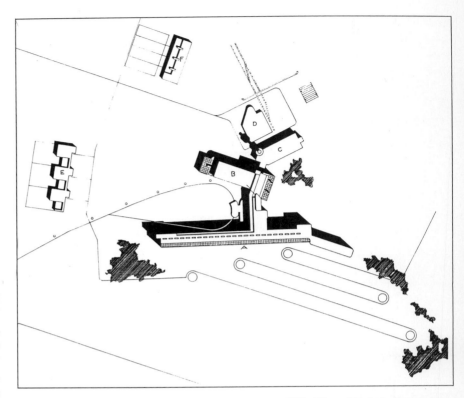

236. Plan of Paimio Sanatorium:
A wards and solarium wing,
B community facilities,
C kitchen, heating plant, etc.
D garage, E assistant physicians' housing, F office staff housing.

135. Furniture developed in collaboration with Otto Korhonen for the Paimio Sanatorium and other interiors between 1928 and 1931. See the description and illustrations in the chapters 'Aalto's first modern furniture' and 'The wooden chair perfected', P 33–39, 56, 70, 78–86, 168, 193–194. F 25–35, 110, 112, 114, 184.

136. Competition entry for a lighthouse in the Dominican Republic. The Pan American Union in Washington announced a competition for ideas for a giant lighthouse in San Domingo in 1928, intended to house the remains of Christopher Columbus, supposedly discovered in the city cathedral in 1877. The entries were to be sent by April 1, 1929 to a jury in Madrid including Eliel Saarinen and Frank Lloyd Wright as members. Aalto took part with an entry beautifully drawn and coloured on six rolls of cloth, which did not win a prize but was displayed in a touring exhibition of the competition project.

His idea was a cylindrical tower 17 storeys high, surrounded by a spiral ramp leading up to the lantern. The Columbus sarcophagus is placed in the middle of the basement, surrounded by a circular columned hall and flanked by a small museum. The lighthouse stands in the centre of an enormous circle divided into three sectors, one of which consists of a landing strip for aeroplanes, another of a stretch of water for hydroplanes and the third of a ships' harbour. Further inland is the Panamerican Park with the presidential palace and the coastal Caribbean Drive. P 44. F 237.

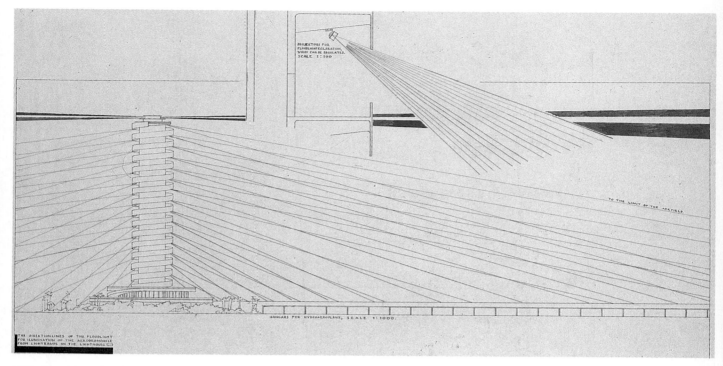

237. Elevation of Columbus
lighthouse for San Domingo.

238. Perspective of Kälviä
Sanatorium with a modern radio
aerial on the roof.

137. Competition entry for Kälviä tuberculosis sanatorium. In spring 1929 Aalto was invited to compete for designing the 200-bed Central Ostrobothnian Sanatorium in Kälviä with his colleagues Toivo and Jussi Paatela, who had defeated him in the competition for Kinkomaa Sanatorium. The floor plan of Aalto's entry differs from his two earlier sanatorium plans in that the various building volumes are not grouped around an open courtyard but embedded into one another in a way reminiscent of the Viipuri Library. Instead of designing a separate open-air ward, Aalto divided the solarium between the fourth floor above the sick wards and the short end of the same wing. The most interesting feature is the canteen, two storeys high, which can be linked up with a lower lounge. Above the latter is the library, part of which can be partitioned off to form a 'projector room' from which films can be projected against the back wall of the canteen. The library and the rooms adjacent to the canteen are lighted by a system of diagonal skylights. This design recurs in the 'Tsit tsit pum' entry to the Paris competition (W 184) and the art gallery of the 'Proto-Mairea' (W 218). Of the three members of the jury, two preferred the Paatela brothers' design and one voted for Aalto's. Owing to administrative changes, the sanatorium was finally never built. P 44. F 238.

138. Competition entry for the Nordic Union Bank head office in Helsinki. The competition was announced in April 1929, with June 22 as the last date of entry. Aalto ordered the programme and made a few sketches testing out ways to tackle the delicate task of adding a new corner to Helsinki's monumental Senate Square designed by C.L. Engel. True to his principles, he avoided pastiche and thought up a modern but perfectly plain and simple building with a giant window reaching right around the corner and a more businesslike wing at the other end of the block on the corner of Fabianinkatu. He also set back the top storey in order to adapt the building to the scale of the older buildings. The bank hall was something in the style of the inner court of the Rautatalo Building designed in 1951, but much larger. The strenuous effort of the Turku 700th anniversary exhibition hindered Aalto from completing the entry; his work was restricted to some summary sketches. F 239.

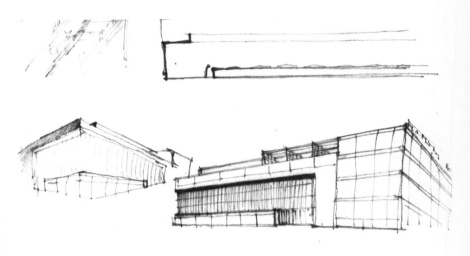

239. Sketch for Nordic Union Bank head office, Helsinki. The left-hand sketch shows the corner facing Senate Square.

139. City of Turku 700th anniversary exhibition. This event, which was also the 1929 Finnish Fair for industrial products, was planned by Alvar Aalto and Erik Bryggman. Their ideas were so close that they signed most of the pavilion drawings jointly. It was decided from the start, however, that Bryggman should be chiefly responsible for the largest building at the exhibition, a circular three-storey restaurant high up on Samppalinna hill, whereas Aalto should answer for the choir platform, designed 'organically' according to acoustic principles. A study of Aalto's archive, however, gives us the opportunity to determine the respective contributions of the two architects in greater detail. The architects' fee was 95,700 marks, of which Aalto's collaborators Wildhagen, Bjertnaes, Wiklund, Takala, Vetri, Rauta, Bäckström and Aino Aalto received 33,378 marks and Bryggman's collaborators Väänänen, Fürst, Elg and Vetri got 19,500 marks. The remaining 42,822 marks was shared equally between Aalto and Bryggman. For some reason, Aalto also made a note of his own contributions, which seem to have included the bazaars, the row pavilions, the main entrance, advertising stands and pillars, the stand on the railway station square, the furniture factory pavilion and the choir platform. In addition to these he was responsible for negotiations with the participating companies on their advertisements and for the typographical design of the advertising surfaces, and wrote a presentation of the event for *Arkkitehti* magazine. The machine hall, the bridge to the tivoli, the travel agent's stand, the main restaurant and the sharply contrasting barrel vaulting of the Karhula-Iittala pavilion, in which glass-blowing demonstrations were given, seem to have been principally Bryggman's work. The Turku

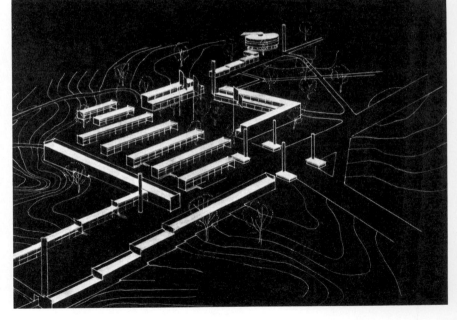

exhibition was the work in which Aalto most clearly showed what he meant by 'non-synthetic architecture'. Instead of creating an overriding total composition, he allowed individual but structurally standardized elements to combine spontaneously, forming a whole in the same way as articles on a newspaper page. Accordingly, the standardized advertising texts based on Bauhaus models were an essential architectural element. P 27, 31–32, 43–44, 218. F 15, 20–22, 26, 240.

240. Turku Exhibition 1929. View of pavilions on Samppalinna hill. The main entrance is in the lower left-hand corner, the round restaurant pavilion at the top.

140. Six entries to the Thonet Mundus furniture design competition. Aalto sent four chair designs and two table models to this international competition, the last date of entry for which was September 9, 1929. He sought to develop and perfect his furniture ideas for the Turku exhibition that summer. In spite of certain deficiencies due to Aalto's unfamiliarity with beech wood as a material, the designs undoubtedly had potential, but were overlooked in the mass of competing entries. See page 79 in the chapter "The wooden chair perfected". F 75–76.

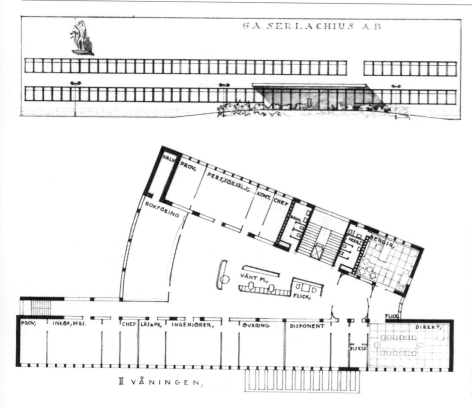

141. Competition entry for the G.A. Serlachius headquarters in Mänttä. Aalto, Bertel Jung, W.G. Palmqvist, Jarl Eklund and Väinö Vähäkallio were invited in December 1929 to compete for the design of the headquarters of this large wood-processing company. The architects had until February 15 the next year to complete their entries. Aalto's entry, 'G.A.S.', is based on the fan-shaped floor plan which later became so typical of his work. The main facade is a low rectangle with two rows of strip windows; the basement contains archives, a library and a small technical museum; the more public spaces, including the payroll office, are on ground floor; while the Board meeting room and the offices of the top management, notably the 'Counsellor's study', and the accounting office are one flight up. The staff canteen, a drawing office and a roof garden in Le Corbusier style are on top floor. The jury, headed by Gösta Serlachius, honorary 'Counsellor of Mining', considered that Aalto's entry had "an unmotivated, irregular contour", and gave precedence to "the dignified facade forms" of Jung's entry. P 68, 121, 142. F 151, 241.

241. Elevation and plan of second floor in office building designed for the Serlachius company.

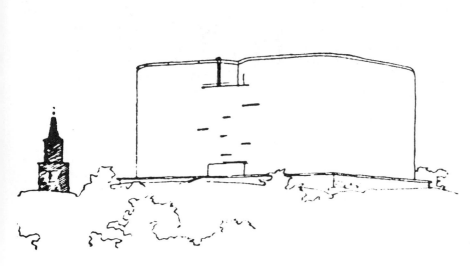

142. Competition entry for Turku water tower. The competition was announced in mid January 1930, and ended on February 28. Aalto sketched various ideas, including a cylindrical cistern resting on a forest of pillars, but finally settled for a softly rounded, dual block form, which foreshadows works like the main pavilion at the Paris World's Fair in 1937 (W 184). The entry 'Wolstead Act' won no prize, but was published in *Arkkitehti* no. 3, 1930. P 68. F 242.

242. Perspective of Turku water tower.

143. Toppila – Vaara pulp mill. In early 1930 Gösta Serlachius arranged an extensive assignment for Aalto. He was to give architectural form to the various buildings and technical installations which were needed for the pulp mill a British company was building in Oulu. Aalto took great care with the assignment, which gave him invaluable experience of the relationship between architecture and the idiom of modern technology. The tendency to seek his way from geometrically constructive to organically functional forms is evident in many details from the unschematic grouping of the buildings

to the free-span roof of the drying room, reminiscent of Maillart's bridge constructions, and from the cathedral ceiling of the chip container to the soft joints of the conveyor belt. The boldly modern colour contrasts of the wall surfaces and technical components were connected with contemporary painting and ideas Aalto later developed together with Fernand Léger. The Toppila mill, which was built between 1930 and 1933, remained relatively unchanged until 1985, but has been closed down as out-of-date and inefficient. P 68, 74, 103, 142. F 61, 68, 216, 243.

243. General view of Toppila pulp mill.

144. Office building for Toppila pulp mill. Besides the factory buildings, Aalto also drew up four different plans for an office building. One of the plans was for converting an old house nearby, while the other three were for new buildings of various sizes. Besides offices for the production manager, engineers and accountants and a payroll office, the plans included a varying number of rooms for accommodating visitors. The management opted for the renovation for reasons of economy, and Aalto's plans for new offices were never executed. F 244.

244. Perspective of Toppila mill office building.

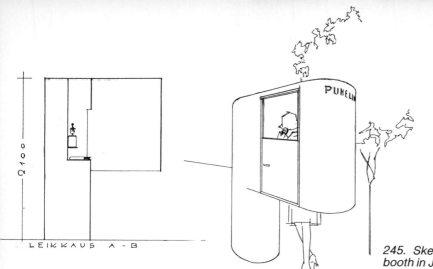

145. Telephone booth for Jyväskylä. It is appropriate to present this undated plan which was never implemented in connection with the Toppila project, since it is distinguished by the same desire to liberate the technical form from rigid geometry while seeking a boldly Functionalist idiom. F 245.

245. Sketch for telephone booth in Jyväskylä.

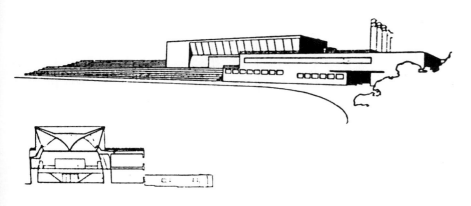

146. Competition entry for Vierumäki Sports Institute. Last date of entry: March 31, 1930. Aalto's entry 'Mens' presents five open-air 'arenas' grouped diagonally in front of the building itself, one side of which forms a spectators' stand for the largest of the arenas. The principal motif of the main building is a large indoor sports hall, spanned by parabolic arches and a hanging, concave vaulted ceiling broken off at the middle, forming a reflector for the indirect light let in by diagonal rows of windows. The whole plan is a typical example of Aalto's ambitions as an engineering inventor and of his feeling for expressive architecture. The functionally articulated main building also includes training rooms, classrooms, canteens, athletes' bedrooms and administrative facilities. The jury awarded first prize to Erik Bryggman's cautious but lucid Rationalist project, while Aalto won third prize. P 30, 68. F 246.

246. Perspective of Vierumäki sports institute with cross section of indoor sports courts.

247. 'Parking Park', stadium competition entry, 1930.

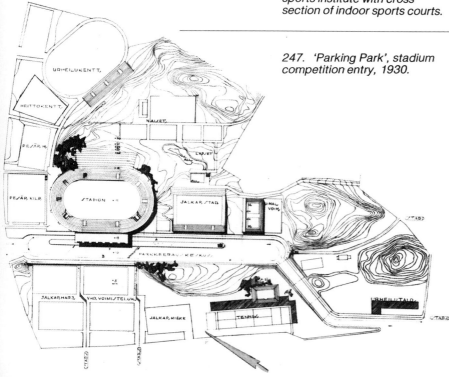

147. Competition entry for the placing of Helsinki Stadium. Aalto sent in two entries, 'Parking Park' and 'Petäjäkruunu', to the competition, which ended on April 30, 1930. He did not win a prize, but 'Parking Park' was purchased and has been preserved, whereas the other entry seems to have disappeared. The assignment involved placing the stadium building and other sports facilities in the hilly ground north of Töölö Bay, paying due attention to accessibility. Aalto gave a great deal of consideration to the natural contours of the site, which allowed him to increase the number of seats by placing benches on the slope above the stadium. Otherwise the building was a variant of his stadium entry for Tähtitorninmäki (W 132). P 68, 193. F 247.

148. Competition entry for Tehtaanpuisto Church, first competition. Aalto received the competition programme in mid September 1930 and submitted his entry 'Sekä että' on the last date of entry, November 15. He suggested a long hall church with a parish hall to the left of the chancel and a rectangular free-standing campanile with an open bell frame. The chancel merges through the acoustically rounded back wall into the ceiling, which is made up of parallel cylinder segments. Aalto seeks to illustrate the acoustic properties of these segments with a diagram showing the two-way passage of sound waves between the altar and the organ loft (cf. the jury's assessment of the Vallila Church entry, W 133). The interior side walls of the church are covered by slats similar to those in Aalto's 'standard cinema' (W 126), which here also serve to filter the light from the many side windows. Aalto's entry was passed over by the jury. P 68, 218. F 248–249.

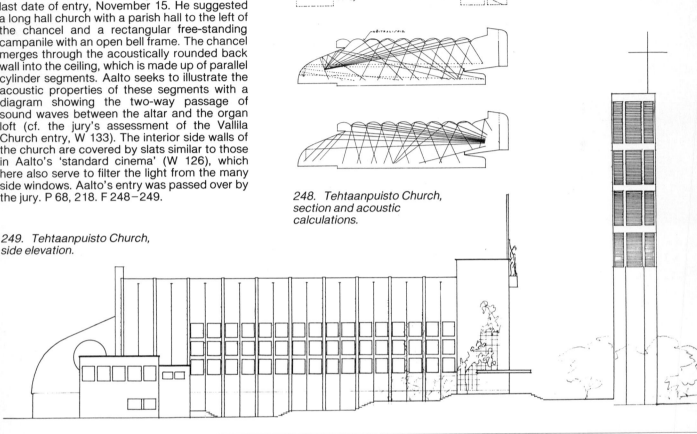

248. Tehtaanpuisto Church, section and acoustic calculations.

249. Tehtaanpuisto Church, side elevation.

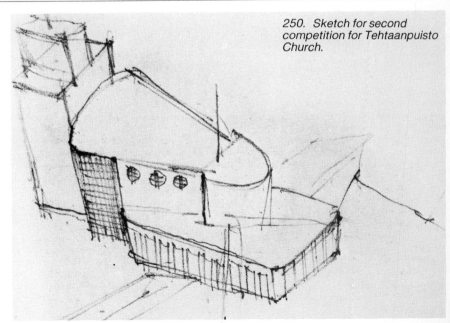

250. Sketch for second competition for Tehtaanpuisto Church.

149. Competition entry for Tehtaanpuisto Church, second competition. Four of the more conservative participants in the 1930 competition were invited to take part in a new competition two years later, with November 1, 1932 as the last date of entry. This competition was, however, also open to other architects. The Aalto archives contain some forty pencil sketches which prove that he took the competition seriously although he probably never sent in an entry. The main theme is now a wedge-shaped interior with the tip (i.e. the chancel) enclosed in a cube. The bell tower is still free-standing, but Aalto tried out various unusual forms for it and made it very high. F 250.

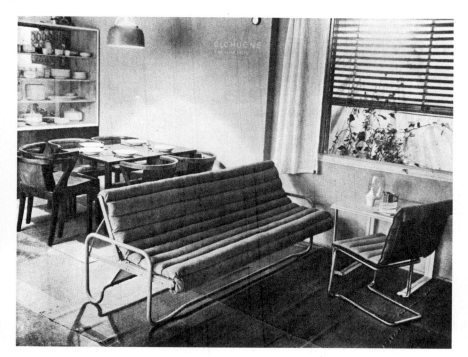

150. Minimum Apartment Exhibition in Helsinki Art Hall. Aalto was the initiator and chief arranger of this publicity event for social housing, opened on November 29, 1930. The idea of the exhibition was borrowed from the similar CIAM exhibition in Frankfurt the preceding winter. Aalto was responsible for the complete furnishing of a bedroom and a living room with a dining alcove, while Aino Aalto furnished a minimum kitchen with various Rationalist details including a rubbish bucket on wheels and extensible tables at which the housewife could work in a sitting position. The exhibition was important as an outlet for the new trends in home interior design and architecture, and it was also significant for Aalto's furniture design. P 43, 55, 66, 68–70, 209. F 62–63, 251.

251. Corner of Aalto's minimum apartment at the 1930 exhibition, with a stackable hybrid chair, a convertible sofa for which he had sought a patent and a dinner table surrounded by stackable chairs in Art Nouveau style.

151. Sets for Hagar Olsson's play SOS at Turku Finnish Theatre. In late autumn 1930, Hagar Olsson's pacifist play was performed in Aalto's newly-built theatre. Aalto was responsible for the stage design with boldly Modernist décor based on Constructivist elements and photographic projections. P 68, 71, 77. F 64.

152. Parish centre for Pöytyä. Through Aino Aalto's brother-in-law, Minister Waltari of Pöytyä parish, Aalto's office received a commission for a simple wooden parish building at the end of 1930. Besides a hall for church meetings, the building housed a conference room for the church authorities, a post office and a caretaker's flat. According to a letter written at the time by Bjertnaes, the building was designed entirely by Aino Aalto. It was still standing in 1984.

252. Perspective sketch of Zagreb hospital auditorium.

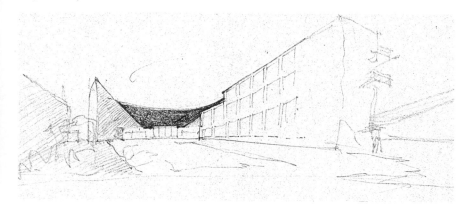

153. Competition entry for Zagreb central hospital. Aalto's entry ('SUD') for this international competition was one of his most extensive and inventive works from the breakthrough years. The last date of entry was January 15, 1931. Since the entry did not win a prize or a purchase, the carefully executed drawings were returned together with the plan description, the German original of which has been preserved in the Aalto archives. This vast institution was to include separate clinics for surgery, internal medicine, psychiatry, tuberculosis, eye diseases, etc. Aalto placed some twenty separate buildings on the extremely hilly site in a way that gave each both isolation and inner cohesion. He achieved this by an original system of bridges and underpasses, providing each building with a park of its own. The tuberculosis clinic is a right-angled variant of the Paimio Sanatorium, though the patients' ward is placed at an angle.

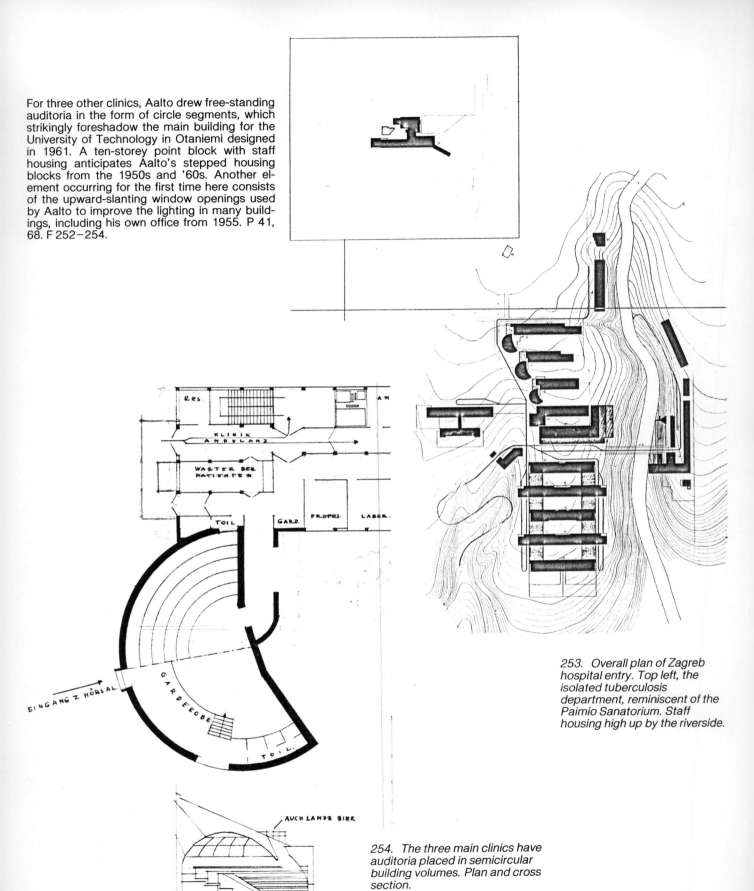

For three other clinics, Aalto drew free-standing auditoria in the form of circle segments, which strikingly foreshadow the main building for the University of Technology in Otaniemi designed in 1961. A ten-storey point block with staff housing anticipates Aalto's stepped housing blocks from the 1950s and '60s. Another element occurring for the first time here consists of the upward-slanting window openings used by Aalto to improve the lighting in many buildings, including his own office from 1955. P 41, 68. F 252–254.

253. Overall plan of Zagreb hospital entry. Top left, the isolated tuberculosis department, reminiscent of the Paimio Sanatorium. Staff housing high up by the riverside.

254. The three main clinics have auditoria placed in semicircular building volumes. Plan and cross section.

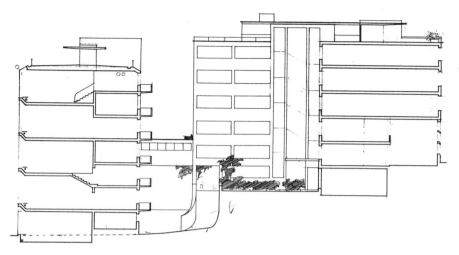

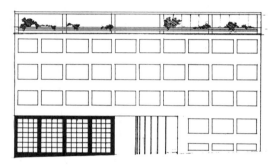

255. Competition entry for Lallukka artists' home in Helsinki, cross section and Apollonkatu elevation.

154. Competition entry for Lallukka artists' home in Helsinki. Aalto took part with two entries, 'Lucca' and 'The bees'. Entries had to be submitted by the end of March 1931. His main entry, 'Lucca', shows two building volumes, one with ordinary flats facing Apollonkatu, the other with studios facing Hesperiankatu, and linked by corridor bridges crossing an open planted courtyard, in addition to which the buildings have roof gardens. The studios are two storeys high and have a gallery loft in Le Corbusier style. The five storeys of the studio building are interwoven in a highly intricate way, making all of the apartments different, partly because they go either upward or downward from the eight separate entrance levels. Aalto's entry was rejected by the jury because he exceeded the stipulated four storeys on the Apollonkatu side and placed the studio windows in the short walls of the rooms. Hilding Ekelund, who was editor-in-chief of *Arkkitehti* at the time, protested sharply against the latter criticism referring to the size of the windows and their special upward angle (cf. W 153). P 70. F 255.

155. Plan for the Wiklund department store in Turku. Aalto designed a new department store for a Turku company which is still in operation today, but the plans were shelved during the economic depression. The drawings, for which he signed a receipt for 25,000 marks on December 4, 1931, have not been recovered.

156. Unknown assignment for the Crichton-Vulcan shipyard, for which Aalto received fees totalling 15,000 marks in 1931 and 1932.

157. Plan for a dock workers' housing block in Kotka. The Kotka stevedoring federation commissioned sketches from Aalto in 1931. The project was probably never completed, and the drawings have not been found.

158. Hunting lodge for an unknown client. Undated drawings in the Aalto archives which can be traced back to the early '30s show a semi-Functionalist single-storey wooden cottage with a verandah-type porch at both ends. At one end is a large living room in farmhouse style, at the other two bedrooms, between them a kitchen with two stoves (?) and a cubicle which can be curtained off.

159. Competition entry for The Insulite Co of Finland's type house. The assignment involved designing a house of 75–90 m² fit for winter habitation using insulite board as the main material. Entries had to be submitted by February 1, 1932. The Aalto archives contain a large number of sketches for several variant entries, including an extraordinary building with an overhanging loft inspired by Norwegian mountain huts. The single-storey plan which was sent in ('Bio') was a simple L-shaped box with strip windows and four identical cubicles in a row. Aalto did not win a prize, but his entry was purchased and published in *Arkkitehti*. P 85, 215. F 256.

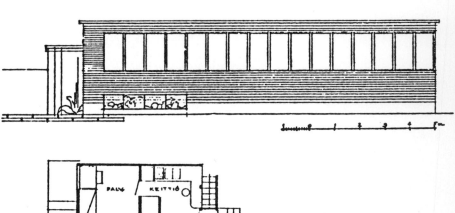

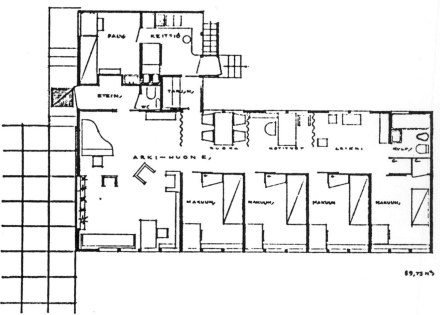

257. Weekend cottage made of ensonite, 1932.

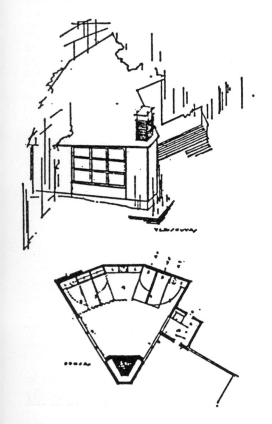

256. House made of insulite board, 1932.

160. Competition entry for Enso-Gutzeit weekend cottage. This wood-processing company, which like The Insulite Co. produced hardboard for building, arranged a competition in spring 1932 for a small holiday cottage of 25–35 m² and a larger one of 50–60 m², to be made of the company's 'ensonite' board. The last date of entry was May 9, 1932, and Aalto sent in a highly original entry ('Tuli') with a fan-shaped plan. Though it did not win a prize, it was purchased and praised by the jury for its clear, cosy and practical layout, but criticized for having "too many (10) corners". The drawings were published e.g. in the advertising brochure on the competition produced by the company. P 85–86, 168, 215. F 257.

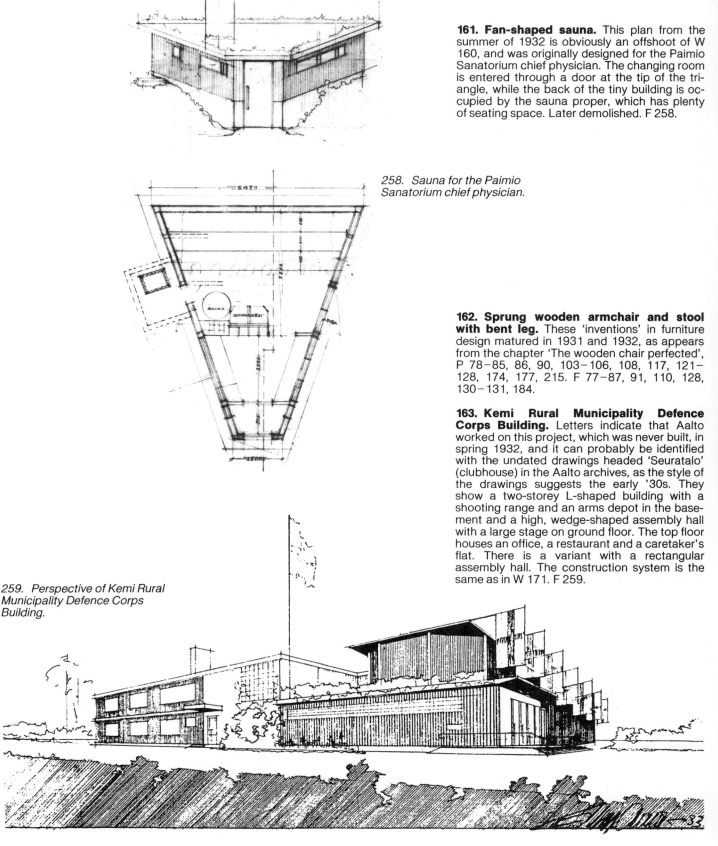

161. Fan-shaped sauna. This plan from the summer of 1932 is obviously an offshoot of W 160, and was originally designed for the Paimio Sanatorium chief physician. The changing room is entered through a door at the tip of the triangle, while the back of the tiny building is occupied by the sauna proper, which has plenty of seating space. Later demolished. F 258.

258. Sauna for the Paimio Sanatorium chief physician.

162. Sprung wooden armchair and stool with bent leg. These 'inventions' in furniture design matured in 1931 and 1932, as appears from the chapter 'The wooden chair perfected', P 78−85, 86, 90, 103−106, 108, 117, 121−128, 174, 177, 215. F 77−87, 91, 110, 128, 130−131, 184.

163. Kemi Rural Municipality Defence Corps Building. Letters indicate that Aalto worked on this project, which was never built, in spring 1932, and it can probably be identified with the undated drawings headed 'Seuratalo' (clubhouse) in the Aalto archives, as the style of the drawings suggests the early '30s. They show a two-storey L-shaped building with a shooting range and an arms depot in the basement and a high, wedge-shaped assembly hall with a large stage on ground floor. The top floor houses an office, a restaurant and a caretaker's flat. There is a variant with a rectangular assembly hall. The construction system is the same as in W 171. F 259.

259. Perspective of Kemi Rural Municipality Defence Corps Building.

164. Villa Tammekann in Tartu. In spring 1932 August Tammekann, an Estonian professor of geography, commissioned drawings from Aalto for a small private house. For technical and financial reasons it was finally built in a form which differed considerably from Aalto's design. For example, the Estonians did not know how to build a watertight horizontal roof, so they built a hip roof instead. Owing to primitive insulation techniques, the walls were made 25 cm thicker than planned, with the result that the rooms and corridors became at least 50 cm narrower than intended. Aalto's original plan is a strictly Rationalist forerunner of his later private-house designs; there is merely a touch of softening wood surface here and there to contrast with the white plaster walls and a fairly closed room disposition. The most original feature is the placing of the open fireplace inside the external wall under the strip window in the living room. P 85, 102, 210. F 260.

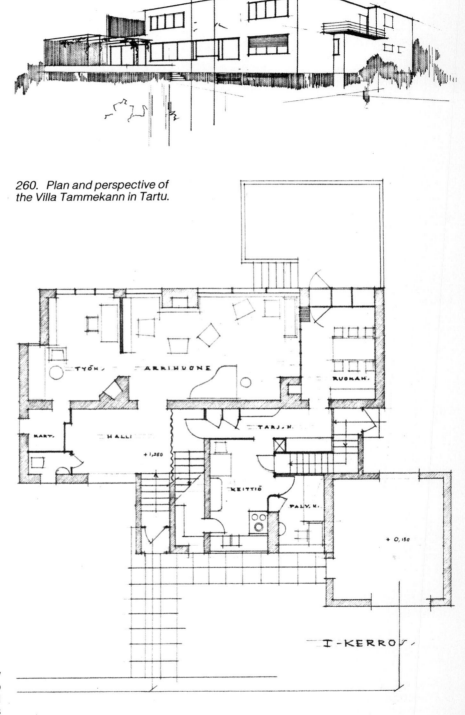

260. Plan and perspective of the Villa Tammekann in Tartu.

165. Competition entry for Karhula's utility glass competition in autumn 1932. Aino Aalto won second prize for a set of moulded utility glass entitled 'Bölgeblick', which was later manufactured serially. Aalto's entry 'karhiit' was purchased but never produced. P 113, 137. F 115, 147, 288.

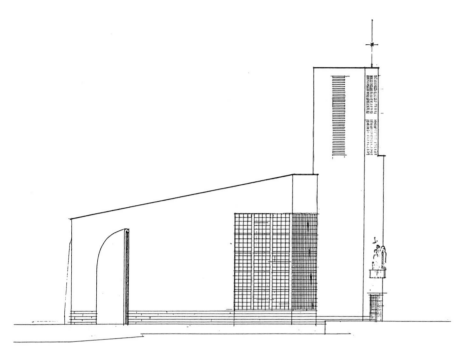

166. Competition entry for Temppeliaukio Church in Helsinki. The last date of entry in the first competition for a church in Temppeliaukio Square was January 16, 1933. The Aalto archives show that Aalto started with sketches of a rectangular hall church with the roof resting on 'organic' concrete pillars resembling those in the *Turun Sanomat* printing works, but later decided on a further development of an idea he had tested in W 133 (Vallila Church). His entry, bearing the figure '50' and a black triangle, shows an open bell tower rising asymmetrically from the entrance hall and a wedge-shaped floor plan with a vault-like rounded chancel lighted indirectly by a 'light channel' encircling the end wall. In this entry, too, the vestry (with a tiny wedding chapel) is in an annex next to the chancel. The elegant termination of Fredrikinkatu formed by the angle of the staircase rising to the church and the facade is a masterful stroke. The jury passed over Aalto's plan among the 57 entries submitted. No first prize was awarded, and a new competition was announced in 1936. This time Aalto did not take part, since he was a member of the jury. P 86. F 261.

261. Side elevation and plan for Temppeliaukio Church in Helsinki.

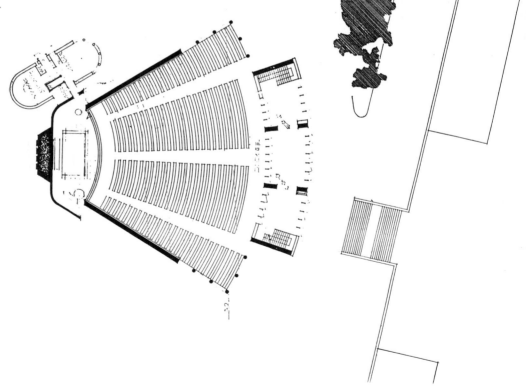

167. Entry for the Riihimäki glassworks competition. In this competition, which was held in February 1933, Aalto won second prize for his entry 'Riihimäen kukka' (Riihimäki flower). The idea was to have five simple glass objects – a platter, two bowls, a vase and a drinking glass – which could be stacked, producing a flower-like pattern. The series was produced in various sizes and shades of colour, and was displayed e.g. at the Aalto exhibition in London 1933. P 137–138. F 113.

168. Entry for the ideas competition for the renovation of the Nedre Norrmalm district in Stockholm. The City of Stockholm announced this international town planning competition in the winter of 1933, the last date of entry being March 1. Other participants notably included Le Corbusier, who recommended almost wholesale demolition of the city except for the most important old monumental buildings, with the idea of covering the vacated space with chains of blocks 50 metres high. Aalto's entry '7089' was relatively modest in comparison. He largely preserved the street network of the whole Norrmalm district, but not its old buildings. Instead he suggested that the 'commercial' city and traffic on ground level should form the low base for housing development consisting of high-rise blocks separated entirely from the street system and oriented for maximum sunlight, fresh air and an unobstructed view. The remaining roof surfaces of the 'base development' would form broad terraces suitable for promenades and greenery. Car traffic in the centre proper would only be permitted on the streets running from east to west, while the north–south streets and the shoreline in the vicinity of the City Hall and facing the castle would be reserved for pedestrian traffic. Aalto's plan attracted no attention among the 450 entries. P 86, 89, 102. F 262.

262. Town plan for Nedre Norrmalm, Stockholm, view towards the Royal Palace.

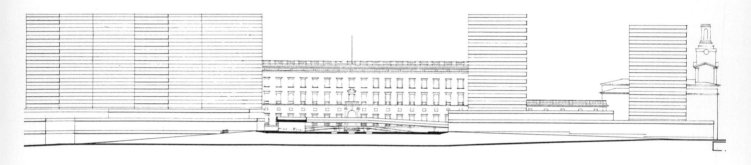

169. Entry for the first competition for Helsinki Stadium. After Aalto's controversial proposal for a stadium on Tähtitorninmäki (W 132) had led to a competition for a suitable

263. The suspended canopy in Aalto's stadium entry, 1933.

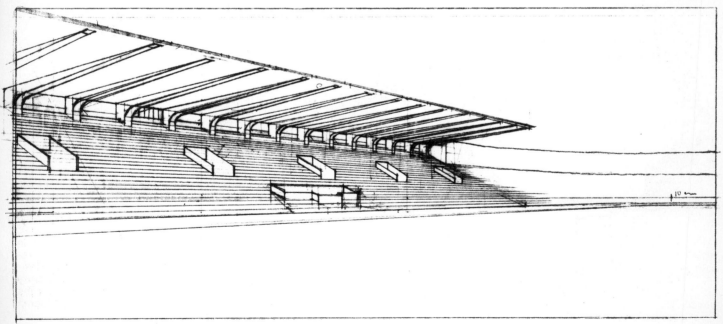

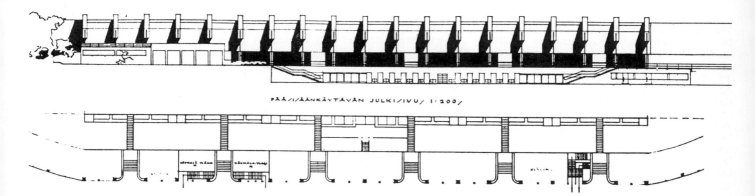

PÄÄ/I/ÄÄNKÄYTÄVÄN JULKI/IVU/ 1:200/

264. The counterweights to the canopy form a facade motif.

stadium location (W 147), the first competition for the actual building in what is known as the Eläintarha ('Zoo') district was announced in spring 1933, with April 1 as the last date of entry. Aalto submitted an entry ('456') which contained several improvements to his original shell-shaped sports building with a smooth brim running along the top to provide shelter from the wind. The most important addition was a gigantic suspended canopy of reinforced concrete protecting the stands of one long side from rain. Aalto produced a perhaps overly dar-

ing 'invention' to solve the technical difficulties: the freely hanging roof beams are counterweighed by heavy concrete ribs on the exterior forming a decorative element in the facade and anchored to the ground with thin steel wires. The main entrance leads to the space below the stands on this long side. Aalto did not win a prize, but the entry was purchased, which gave him the right to take part in the final competition as one of nine invited architects. P 89, 193. F 263–264.

265. Aalto's entry for the final stadium competition in 1933. Note the café terraces adapted to the terrain in the foreground.

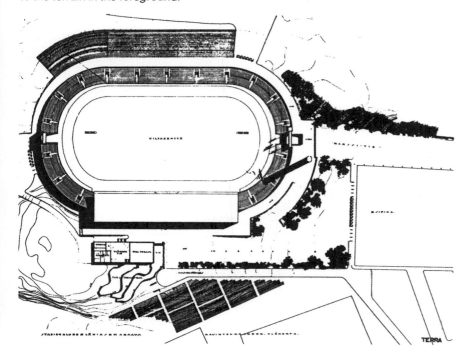

170. Entry for the final competition for Helsinki Stadium, the last date of entry being October 15, 1933. In his entry 'Terra', Aalto persisted in placing the stadium somewhat southeast of the spot the jury wanted, the reason being his unwillingness to make violent inroads into the terrain and his wish to provide for additional seats on an adjacent slope. He replaced the suspended canopy with a more conventional shelter supported by columns, allowing more space for the stands. He moved the main entrance to one of the short sides, adding a small tower for the Olympic flame in accordance with the new competition programme and a café with terraces freely following the contours of the terrain. Aalto's entry was neither purchased nor published, and the stadium was built by the winners Yrjö Lindegren and Toivo Jäntti. P 89, 193. F 265.

171. Physician's residence for Enso-Gutzeit in Enso. In connection with his exhibition in London in 1933, Aalto came into contact with the Enso-Gutzeit wood-processing company, which hoped to boost its exports to Britain with the help of an experimental house designed by Aalto for the Ideal Home Exhibition at the Olympia in London. His serious illness at the end of 1934 prevented this project from materializing. In spring 1934, however, he designed two type houses for the company to demonstrate how Le Corbusier's domino system could be combined with light interior and exterior walls of Enso board. The first of these pedagogic projects was a two-storey house called a 'physician's residence', which gives the impression of being a rather dull, square 'Functionalist box'. No houses of this type were ever built. P 142.

172. House for Enso-Gutzeit officials in Enso. The project had the same background as W 171. The roof slab of this bungalow is supported by eight concrete columns and all of the walls are free-standing. The house contains four rooms, a kitchen, a large terrace and a garage. In spite of the uncompromisingly Rationalist idiom, the flat roof and low horizontal lines make the house aesthetically pleasing; however, this type house also remained unbuilt.

173. Competition entry for Tampere railway station. Last date of entry: January 10, 1934. The competition attracted a record number of 67 entries, among which Aalto's had no success. His 'Loko' was the only entry without a tower, for which he substituted a round clock with a diameter of seven metres as a point of reference from the street perspective. With its adjacent platforms for long-distance coaches, its parking places, pedestrian ways and roundabouts, the entry had great practical merit, but the glazed two-storey facade, the lengthwise hall with shops at the bottom level and a mezzanine restaurant, and the Constructivist concrete roof covering the platforms, all breathe a chilly, Rationalist, anti-monumental matter-of-factness that must have alienated the jury. P 89, 106, 168. F 266.

266. Tampere Railway Station, perspective of facade and interior hall.

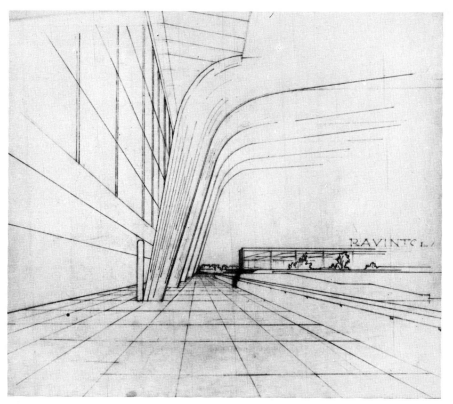

174. Competition entry for Helsinki Fair Hall. Last date of entry: February 20, 1934. Aalto won third prize for an entry ('MP') based on a roof construction to which his experiments with laminated wood furniture lent particular interest. Aalto envisaged the lower sections of the hall up to gallery height to be built from concrete and brick, while the higher parts were to be made of wood specially impregnated to minimize the fire risk. The roof is supported by *Hetzer arches* of laminated wood, soaring like boomerangs from the floor, passing the gallery and rising to the roof, which spans the entire square hall. Natural light enters through the strip windows running the length of the side walls just below the eaves and is reflected from the smooth sides of the wooden arches, while artificial lighting is provided by ceiling lamps forming rows of large, pale circles in the dark wooden ceiling. 'Venetian' stairs lead down to the sunken centre part of the hall and a separate restaurant building provides a markedly horizontal accent to one of the short ends. P 106. F 267.

267. Helsinki Fair Hall, interior.

175. Furnishing of the Corso Theatre restaurant, Zurich. In spring 1934 Aalto was commissioned to modernize this popular meeting place together with the painter Max Ernst. He placed a selection of his new laminated birchwood furniture in both the restaurant and the bar-café section. The place was opened in late summer and remained relatively unchanged until the end of the '40s. P 106. F 268.

268. Bar of the Corso Theatre, with painting by Max Ernst in the background (now in the Zurich Art Museum).

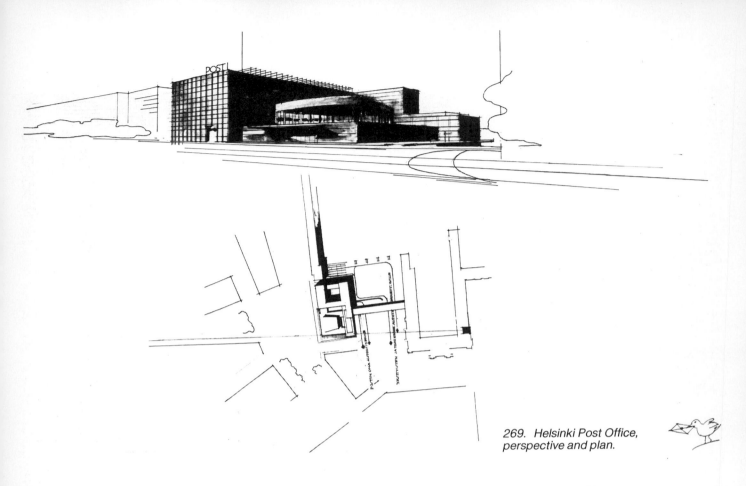

269. Helsinki Post Office, perspective and plan.

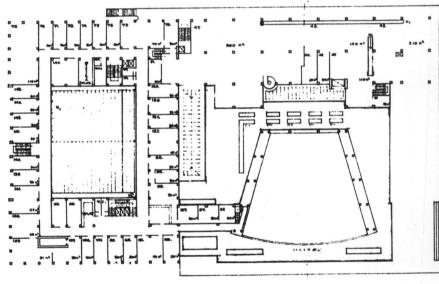

176. Competition entry for Helsinki's main post office, last date of entry: October 1, 1934. Aalto's code name for this entry was the picture of a carrier pigeon. The plan was based on an excellent idea, which in the jury's eyes involved such a grave error that it was rejected out of hand. To avoid an excessively massive effect, Aalto divided up the huge complex into more manageable components, placing the public services in a low hall on the corner of the plot, lighted by a wedge-shaped clerestory, while the offices and technical sections were placed in several higher lengths with a facade divided up into squares. Both the public interior and the well-balanced group of buildings were architecturally effective, but according to the jury access to the courtyard was unsatisfactorily arranged. In its built form (by Jorma Järvi and E. Lindroos), the post office has won few admirers. P 106. F 269.

177. Entry for the ideas competition for the planning of Helsinki's Malmi graveyard, last date of entry: December 15, 1934. Aalto submitted an outline plan in 1:1000 scale, showing a green belt separating several irregular burial areas and designating sites for three funeral chapels. He also made a sketch in 1:100 scale on the plan of one burial area. No building plans were required for the competition. Aalto's entry did not appeal to the jury, but when a new competition for the design of the three chapels was arranged in 1950, he took part again, winning the competition with an entry which, however, was never built. P 106.

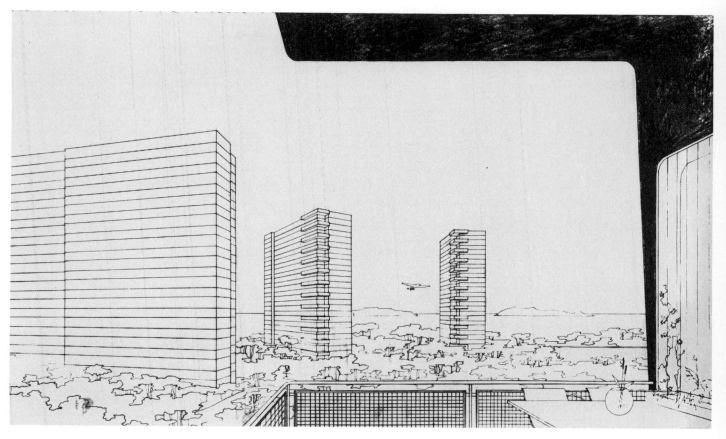

*270. Perspective of tower block
for Munkkiniemi, Helsinki.*

178. High-rise area for Stenius Oy in Munkkiniemi, Helsinki. At the end of 1934, Aalto was commissioned to design several residential blocks on the slope above the present site of the Kalastajatorppa restaurant. Striving to maximize the sea view, he placed four high blocks in free fan formation on the plot. The size of the buildings varied from a narrow tower block to a building 200 metres long and 14 storeys high, containing over 300 flats behind the monotonous strip windows of the vast facade. This exceptional colossal design, which marked the culmination of Aalto's orthodox Rationalism, attracted favourable notice at the 1939 exhibition, "Art in our time", at the Museum of Modern Art in New York. It was not built. P 117, 168, 215. F 213, 270.

179. Aalto's own home and office in Munkki-niemi, Helsinki. In connection with his planning assignment for Stenius Oy, Aalto acquired a plot at Riihitie 10 (today no. 20) in Munkkiniemi, and promptly started building a house there. Its departures from rigid Rationalism make this an important step in the series of private houses from the Villa Tammekann to the Villa Mairea. The intermingling of living and working facilities demonstrates Aalto's attitude to the integration of art and everyday life, and gives expression to his view of work as the meaning of life for the harmonious human being. The lower storey forms a spatial continuum of social and working rooms, while the bedrooms, children's rooms and sunlit terrace are in the upper storey. The interiors are elegantly furnished in every detail, but without the slightest trace of straining for effect. P 53, 117, 128–130, 210, 230. F 133, 212, 271.

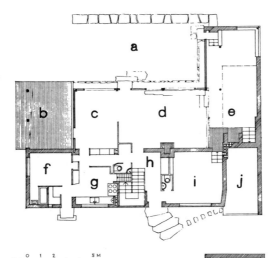

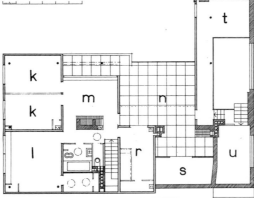

271. Floor plans of Aalto's own house. Ground floor: a garden, b loggia, c dining room, d living room, e architect's studio with balcony, f servant's room, g kitchen, i library, j garage. Upper floor: k and l bedrooms, m hall, n roof terrace, r guestroom, s storeroom, u architect's studio, t balcony over main studio.

180. Competition entry for Finnish embassy building in Moscow, last date of entry: July 27, 1935. Aalto's entry 'Ex occidente' shows a long, three-storey building, recessed from the street and housing the residence of the head of the embassy on the left, the banqueting suite in the middle (with a projecting room resting on *pilotti*), and the consulate and staff housing on the right. Aalto's penchant for softening climbing vines on the walls, already seen in the second version of the Viipuri Library plan and in the competition entry for Vallila Church (W 133), reappears here, combined with the tendency to divide up the building volume into manageable units. The jury did not care for Aalto's entry, and awarded first prize to Hilding Ekelund, but the outbreak of war in 1939 put an end to the project. P 30, 119. F 125, 272.

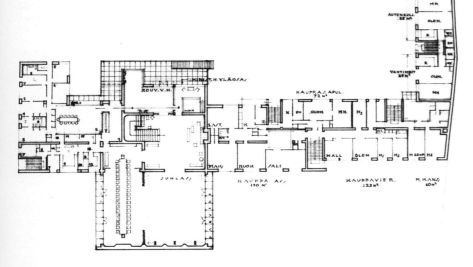

272. Plan of embassy building in Moscow, main floor.

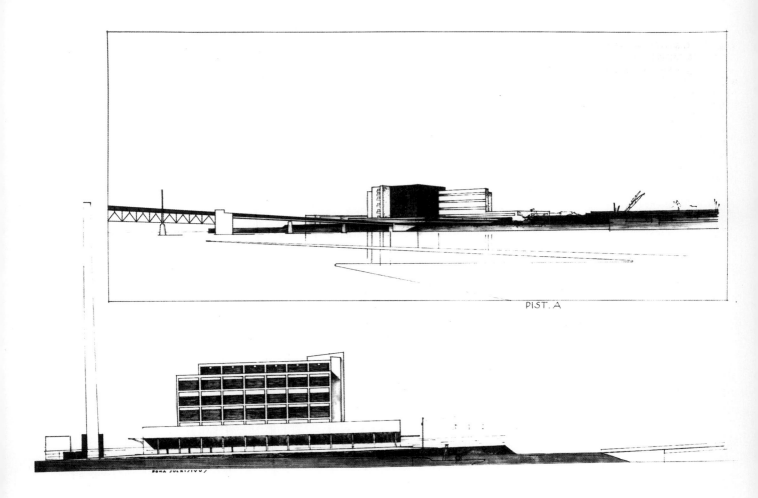

PIST. A

273. *Perspective and elevation of Alko central warehouse and factory.*

181. Competition entry for the central warehouse and factory of the State alcohol monopoly (Alko) in Helsinki. This competition, to which Aalto and three other architects were invited, was announced in September 1935 and continued until March 15, 1936. Aalto's entry 'In vino veritas' split up the large complex into parts which were intended "to give an idea of the various functions of the assignment". From a centrally placed dark brick cube containing the storage facilities, strictly Rationalist rough concrete wings radiate, some of the facades having a strongly horizontal, others a vertical emphasis. These are surrounded by low buildings from which a high factory chimney rises. There are loading platforms for sea, rail and lorry transport. Aalto's entry was purchased, while Väinö Vähäkallio won the competition and built the massive red brick complex which stands today next to the Lauttasaari bridge. P 119. F 273.

182. Ahto Virtanen's grave in Hietaniemi graveyard, Helsinki. To commemorate the death in 1926 of his brother-in-law and colleague, Aalto designed this monument which was erected on the grave in 1936. It consists of a pale marble stele placed against a rough-hewn granite boulder. The negative form of a Classical urn cut into the corner of the stele grippingly expresses the empty place behind by the dead. See F 148 in Part I, *The Early Years.*

183. Furnishing of Harry and Maire Gullichsen's home at Kaivopuisto 3 in Helsinki. This assignment, which was carried out between April and August 1936, marks the first professional contact between the parties, who had started up the Artek company together in December 1935. Two large flats in the building owned by the A. Ahlström company were combined to form a truly luxurious residence and reception suite for the company's managing director. In the course of the alterations, the kitchen and dining room were enlarged, a wintergarden and a bar complete with a bridge table being added to the latter. Among the specially designed furniture, a walnut dining table, easy chairs of beech and armchairs upholstered with ox leather are noteworthy. F 274.

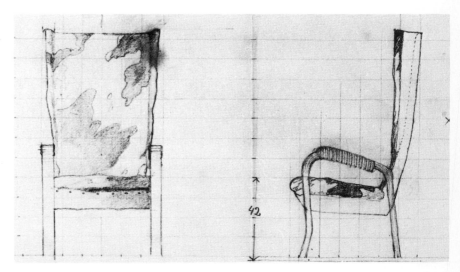

274. Cowhide easy chair for Harry and Maire Gullichsen.

184. Competition entry for the Finnish pavilion at the 1937 World's Fair in Paris. The competition was announced in April 1936 and ended on June 8. Aalto took part with two entries, 'Le bois est en marche' and 'Tsit tsit pum', which at last gave him his great triumph: both first and second prize. The plans are described in considerable detail in the main text. They were charged with new ideas, and took Aalto a decisive step forward towards a style of his own. P 118, 130—137, 167, 219. F 123, 134—142.

185. Association and club house for Toppila Oy, Oulu. In summer 1936, Aalto received a commission for a building with assembly facilities for the employees of the pulp mill designed by him (W 143). He produced three alternatives which met the cost ceiling of 750,000 marks, but the management postponed construction, which was finally abandoned at the outbreak of war. All three plans contain a large assembly room two storeys high, a café, several clubrooms and a separate caretaker's flat. The first alternative marks a return to Aalto's previous purely Rationalist period, with a square assembly room and the overall design consisting of cubes sunk into one another on the same principle as in the final version of Viipuri Library. The large roof terrace above the café has railings like those of a ship, and the facade has a vertical strip window running through two storeys. The second version features a wedge-shaped assembly room with rounded corners, while the café kitchen and service rooms form a separate round building volume in early Functionalist style, producing a somewhat disjointed effect. The third plan represents Aalto's new ideas, with the café in an amoeba-like freely formed wing to the left of the entrance, and the external walls of the clubrooms on the upper floor clad with wood panelling reminiscent of the Paris pavilion. The assembly hall tapers slightly and the overall design is well-integrated. F 275—276.

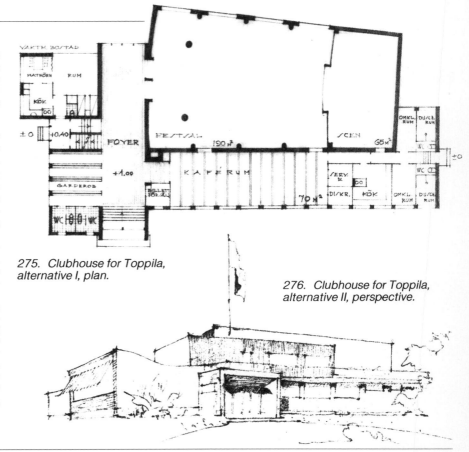

275. Clubhouse for Toppila, alternative I, plan.

276. Clubhouse for Toppila, alternative II, perspective.

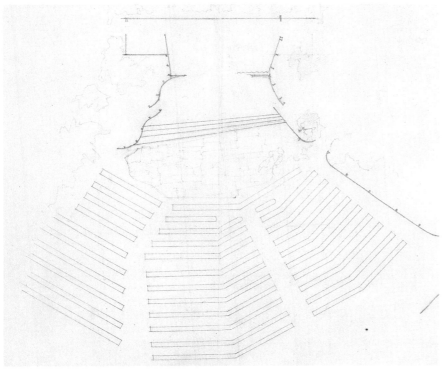

186. Alppiharju open-air theatre in Helsinki.
The Aalto archives contain undated sketches
for this modest theatre in the area of the present-day Lenin Park. It comprises twelve tiers in
three wedge-shaped sectors in front of a pro-
scenium placed slightly at an angle and a proper stage which can be curtained off. The pro-
scenium is flanked by four freely curving
screens. Aalto wrote on one of the drawings:
"The forms are not final, they merely indicate
the general character, which will be determined
freely by the topography and vegetation of the
site." The plan was not carried out. F 277.

*277. Alppiharju open-air
theatre, plan and perspective.*

**187. Block of flats for the Riviera housing
company in Kaivopuisto Park, Helsinki.** This
undated and unrealized project for a four-storey
block of flats on the plot now occupied by the
United States Embassy contains some twenty
luxury flats ranging in size from 45 to 150 m².

The plan features a sauna and an open-air terrace with a fountain on the roof. The plan solutions are neither original nor particularly successful: some of the living rooms, for example,
are poorly lit.

188. 'Sonnenblick' summer house for John M. Gylphe. This small house, designed by Aalto in September 1936, was intended to be erected on the island of Gloskär outside Hanko, but it was never built on account of the war. The plan contains a living room with an open fireplace and fixed sofas, a small bedroom and a miniature kitchen. The building is in the shape of an L, creating a sheltered, sunny spot at the corner. In spite of its modest appearance, simple pole construction and horizontal weatherboarding, the low, inventively designed house has great charm. F 278.

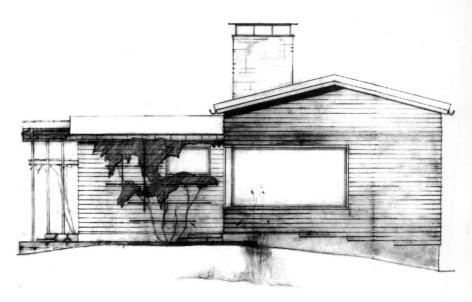

278. Summer house on Gloskär island.

189. Town plan of Varkaus. Aalto's long-standing association with the A. Ahlström company began in the summer of 1936 with the assignment of improving Carolus Lindberg's sketchy master plan for the industrial town of Varkaus. The plans for districts I–IV (Päiviönsaari, South Taulumäki and Kommila) were completed in 1939, while the plans for districts XIV–XV (Könönpelto and Veljeskylä) were approved only after the war. Major changes were later made to Aalto's plans, especially in Kommila. His ideas have essentially been worked into later revisions of the town plan. A sketch from December 1936 shows the general outline of how Aalto expected the industrial community to grow. P 142–143, 148. F 158, 279.

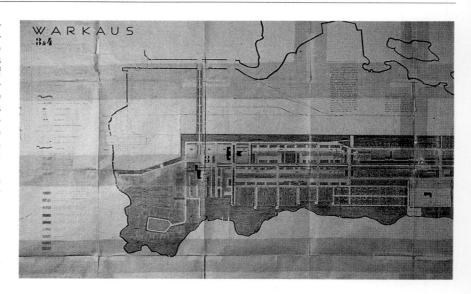

279. Part of 1939 master plan of Varkaus: Kommila district.

190. Standard housing for Varkaus. Between 1936 and 1939 Aalto designed the following housing for Ahlström in Varkaus: 1) *Koivikko House,* a chain house for factory officials on a plot next to the church. This three-storey building is faced with brick and has bearing transverse walls reaching through to the facade, horizontal weatherboarding between the windows producing a strip window effect, and a room disposition providing one three-room and one four-room flat on each landing for each of the three flights of stairs. At one end of the building is an indoor ball game court of 114 m². The outbreak of war prevented construction. 2) *House on Savontie* for lower officials. A two-storey chain house with four flights of stairs providing access to two two-room flats with kitch-

280. 'Savonmäen Alvari' – one of the few Aalto type houses built in the Savonmäki district of single-family homes in Varkaus.

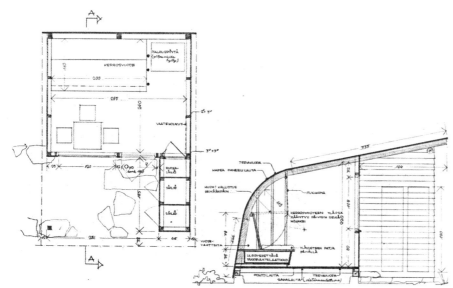

281. Plan and cross section of allotment hut for Varkaus factory workers, 1939.

enette and one studio flat with kitchenette per landing, making a total of 24 apartments. With its flat roof and balconies, the design makes a very modern impression, but the kitchens have wood stoves though the house is centrally heated. One of the units contains a photographer's studio on the upper floor. The house was not built. 3) *Wooden houses for Savonmäki housing area.* The drawings are dated August–November 1937 and marked as "type A1, A3, B2, C and G". They are evidently prototypes of the 'AA house' introduced in the 1940s by the Varkaus house factory. They have an asymmetrical hip roof and feature a food cellar, porch, large living room, kitchen, two bedrooms and wood heating and have neither toilet nor bathroom. Only four such houses seem to have been built in the area. The best-preserved among them is popularly called the "Alvari of Savonmäki". P 141, 144, 181, 215. F 152, 214, 280. 4) *Allotment huts* for workers wishing to cultivate a small garden patch. The huts consist of one room of a mere 7 m², containing a sofa which can be converted into a bunk bed, a tiny table, three chairs and a cooking recess. In front of this room is a relatively spacious roofed verandah and a tiny larder and shed. Aalto designed three variants in 1939, the most interesting having an arching back wall which merges with the slanted ceiling. Not built. F 281.

191. Service buildings in Varkaus. 1) Aalto designed a *sauna with laundry* for factory workers in 1937 in Luttila district. It features a high concrete basement containing a laundry and a wooden main storey with separate saunas and changing rooms for men and women. The build-

282. Sauna in Luttila, Varkaus.

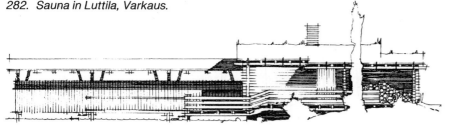

ing has an asymmetrical hip roof and low, roofed boat houses on both sides. The plan was changed considerably when the sauna was built in 1946. F 282. 2) In 1938 Aalto designed a *porter's house* containing a locker room for the workers' clothes and an open shed (for bicycles?). The building is a longish wooden bungalow with an asymmetrical hip roof. The flat consists of a bedroom with space for three beds and a living room with a cooking range, no toilet or bathroom. Not built. 3) In 1938 Aalto designed a *weekend cabin,* which was actually built, for factory officials on a lakeshore in Kinkamo. It is a fairly large wooden building with a horizontal emphasis and reminiscent of vernacular architecture. A roomy verandah and a cosy room with a fireplace provide the setting for conversation and meals, while two separate sleeping sections with four cubicles for men and three for women provide overnight accommodation. The cabin further includes a kitchen, a pantry and a room for the housekeeper. P 144. F 153.

192. Master plan of Sunila. In the summer of 1936 Aalto drew up a master plan for the future industrial estate. In it he separated the factory radically from the housing area by placing it on a rocky island with access from the mainland via a road embankment and with a steep cliff in front of which ocean-going ships could be

moored. He scattered the housing among the hills on the mainland, creating Finland's first 'forest town', that is, a combination of urban blocks of flats and a forest (or what remained of it). He continued this work in the 1940s and '50s. P 144 ff. F 154.

193. Sunila sulphate pulp mill and office building. Aalto started designing the pulp mill together with Aulis Kairamo, the engineer responsible for production technology, in the autumn of 1936. They divided up the manufacturing processes into several separate buildings with a concrete frame and red brick walls, while the warehouses and transport installations were built of white concrete. In the sulphate warehouse down by the wharf, Aalto found the opportunity to carry out the roof construction with the suspended parabolic arches of laminated wood on which he had based his competition entry for the Helsinki Fair Hall (W 174). The red brick office building stands next to a central 'piazza', which forms the heart of the estate. P 144–151. F 155–156, 283.

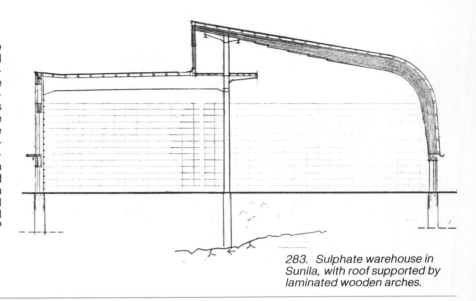

283. Sulphate warehouse in Sunila, with roof supported by laminated wooden arches.

194. Sunila mill housing area. The housing for mill employees was built in stages until the 1950s, giving Aalto the opportunity to develop new ideas in the meantime. The earliest stages (working drawings from 1936) include: 1) *The manager's residence,* also known as the A building, with its own beach and landing-stage. It contains some fifteen rooms, kitchen facilities, terraces and balconies. The exterior is characterized by rendered white walls, a flat roof and a cold Functionalist style, but certain accents such as wood panelling soften the overall impression. Aalto also designed a less pretentious variant more coherent than the version actually built. The manager's residence includes a separate sauna building made of logs jointed at the corners and a boathouse on the water resting on poles. 2) *Row house for the engineering staff,* known as the 'B building', consisting of five linked two-storey units with white rendering, which splays out slightly into the garden in front by virtue of the diagonal placing of the party walls. The slight indenting increases the effect of mutual isolation, which is further enhanced by screening vegetation. These houses are by far the most original and successful at Sunila. The engineers' area also included a series of storage sheds and a small sauna with a bathing platform by the shore. F 159–160. 3) *District heating plant, garage and fire station,* the 'C building', a partly underground two-storey structure, which includes a round water cistern on the roof, surrounded by a scaffold for drying fire hoses. Parts of the facades have vertical weatherboarding forming a contrast to the white rendered concrete surfaces. F 285. 4) *Chain house for foremen,* or 'D building', consisting of 14 white rendered two-storey units laid in a row on a slope, giving them a hint of a stair form. The flats contain a kitchen and living room on ground floor and two bedrooms and bathroom upstairs, but no balconies. Separate underground cellars and wooden sheds are included. 5) *Chain house for workers,*

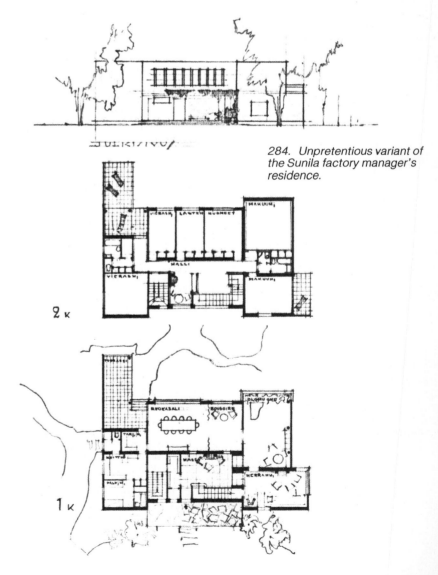

284. Unpretentious variant of the Sunila factory manager's residence.

285. Heating plant and fire station, Sunila housing area. Photo Kidder Smith.

286. Workers' chain house, first version 1936–37.

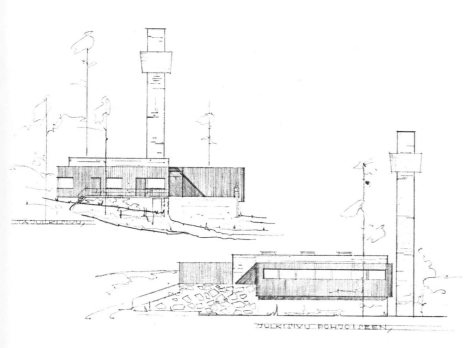

287. Elevation drawings for EKA heating plant, Sunila.

izontal weatherboarding. 7) Thirteen *standard wooden houses* designed by Aalto were built in the *Puistola* housing area. These resemble the earliest single-family houses in Varkaus. 8) The first stage of the housing area also includes a *bus station* with a flat canopy over the platform, benches, newspaper stand and a heated room for the drivers. The form of the bearing columns is reminiscent of Aalto's exhibition pavilion in Paris. F 203.

The next construction stage began in early 1938, and brought two new types of housing to Sunila: 9) *Three-storey house,* a variant of no. 5 above: it has the same room disposition, but Aalto fitted each flat with a balcony, which was so small, however, that the residents hardly used it. When he designed new housing for a third enlargement of the area in 1951, he corrected this error. 10) *Three-storey housing,* known as *type house ROT,* with two small flats (living room, tiny bedroom and kitchen, totalling 39 m²) on each floor. The sloping plot made it possible to give the flats on the two lower storeys their own ground-level entrances at the front and back, while the top storey is reached by a low stairway from the back. The ground floor flats have garden patches facing south in front of the entrance, while the upper levels have spacious stepped balconies also facing south. In 1938 and 1939, the EKA (South Kymi housing) company built 75 flats in Sunila, 63 in Karhula and another sixty-odd in the village of Halla to the plans for this type house and variants of no. 9. F 69, 161. 11) Aalto also designed a magnificent *heating plant* for EKA with high chimneys bearing water cisterns, and facades with vertical weatherboarding reminiscent of the studio section of the contemporary Villa Mairea, F 287. P 144–151, 168, 181.

consisting of two-storey rows similar to the preceding building, but with a strip window along the front and two two-room flats plus one studio flat for each flight of stairs, no balconies. F 286. 6) Aalto also designed a large *workers' sauna* which could be used both individually and by groups. The bottom storey, partly built into the slope, contains a large laundry with twelve enormous 'coppers' and a mangle. A separate transverse wing, connected with the sauna by a loggia, contained a post office faced with hor-

195. Renovation of old buildings in Sunila.
South of the housing area designed by Aalto
were two large wooden houses from the turn of
the century, which he was to convert into
assembly and club rooms for the mill employees. The house called *Pirtti* (F 157) contained a
large *salon*, which Aalto turned into a combined
assembly hall and theatre by having a new entrance with a staircase and a long, narrow
wardrobe room built on the right-hand side of
the main facade and by placing on the left-hand
side a stage, a changing room for the actors, a
washing room and a stage property room, with
a flight of stairs to the upper floor, which contains a room for the orchestra and two clubrooms. The building also contains a theatre foy-
er and smaller assembly rooms. In one alternative Aalto contrasted the lively old carpentry
style with the matter-of-factness of the new
sections, while in another he gave the whole
building a (rather dreary) modern appearance.
The other building, *Shanghai,* was intended to
function as a club for executive staff and as a
restaurant. The basement houses the kitchen,
storerooms, staff flats and a staircase leading
up to the main floor. The latter contains a
pantry, two dining rooms, coffee room, newspaper room, verandah and a large entrance hall
with a staircase leading up to the top storey,
which comprises a hall, four guestrooms and
the housekeeper's two-room flat. Both buildings still exist, but their use has changed. P 147.

**196. Presentation of the Karhula glass-
works' products at the Finnish exhibition in
Stockholm in spring 1936.** Aalto was
Karhula's exhibition architect for this event,
which attracted considerable interest in Sweden. He designed an L-shaped counter with a
glass top and a table with amoeboid contours.
A sketch, probably by Aino Aalto, contains an
interesting detail: there is a glass vase on the
table which strikingly foreshadows Aalto's later
'Savoy vase', although it has horizontal stripes
in the manner of Aino Aalto's 'Bölgeblick'
glasses. F 28.

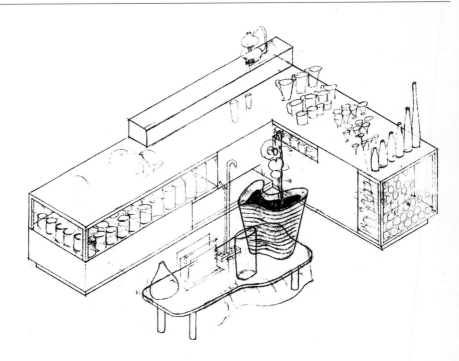

*288. Exhibition showcases for
Karhula.*

**197. Sketches for the Karhula glassworks
competition,** last date of entry: January 4,
1937. Aalto sent in five sketches to this competition for utility glass, for which he was awarded first prize; the design gave rise to the vase
later known as the 'Savoy vase'. See the chapter "Aalto as a glass designer", P 136—139,
168, 219. F 146, 148, 288.

198. Master plan for Karhula. Aalto visited
Karhula on June 23, 1936 in order to start on
the Ahlström company's assignment of working
out a master plan for this industrial community.
The plan was executed in stages and completed in 1942.

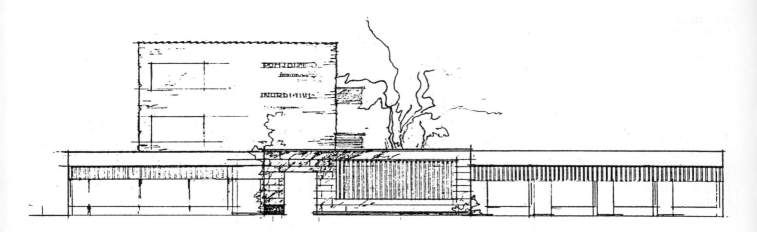

289. Local office of Union Bank in Karhula, elevation.

199. Nordic Union Bank branch office in Karhula. In early 1937 Aalto was commissioned to plan a building containing housing, shops and the local branch of a major bank (today the Union Bank of Finland). Built in 1938, the building consists of two building volumes on a street corner. One of these is three storeys high and contains six rented flats, the largest being the bank manager's flat with 124 m² and the smallest studio flats (for female employees) of 25 m². The other, single-storey wing is occupied chiefly by the bank office, the dignity of which is emphasized by hewn stone for part of the facade and a monumental door, the rest of the facade having merely a modest coat of plaster. Both wings have rented shop facilities on street level, including a creamery, a butcher's, a draper's and a shoe shop. P 144. F 289.

200. Staff housing for Karhula factory employees. Aalto designed the prefabricated housing built by the construction firm EKA in 1938 to his type drawings (see W 194, nos. 9 and 10) as well as wooden one-family houses variable in three ways, built in the Otsola housing area from 1938 on. Their floor area was 60 m², sufficient for an entrance hall, living room, kitchen, two bedrooms and verandah. The toilet was in the large cellar. The Aalto archives contain individual plans for named builders.

201. Industrialist Anders Kramer's waterside retreat in Karhula. This plan from 1939, which was shelved during the war, has not been found yet, but it is mentioned in several letters.

290. Anjala paper mill debarking plant, elevation.

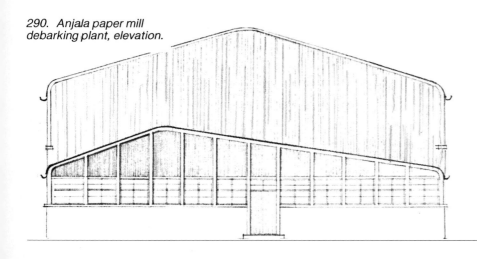

202. Anjala paper mill, Inkeroinen. Tampella was one of five joint owners of the Sunila mill, and the earlier project gave the management of this large industrial enterprise a favourable idea of Aalto's planning ability. The result was an important commission by Tampella for the industrial community of Inkeroinen, starting with a smaller paper mill than the one in Sunila. The drawings date from the summer of 1937, and consist of simplified variations on the form principles of the earlier plan. The main factory building is 300 metres long and contains offices, laboratories and storage facilities. The chimney is 105 metres high. The unusual roof construction of the debarking plant is the most interesting architectural feature in the plans. The mill was enlarged in 1953. P 151. F 290.

203. Staff housing for Tampella at Inkeroinen.

1) Aalto made extensive alterations to the *residence* of the local plant manager, Major Jörgen Schauman, which had been designed by B. Federley in the 1910s. The building is today used as the office of the wood-processing division. 2) *The chief engineer's house,* designed at the beginning of 1937, is the centremost of three similar two-storey houses with steep hip roofs of red tile and white rendered brick walls built for the mill engineers. Aalto designed two variants, the more interesting of which foreshadows the Villa Mairea in the way the vestibule, large hall with open fireplace, library, living room, dining room and verandah are run together, forming a spatial continuum on the lower floor. The kitchen, pantry and servants' rooms form a separate zone running through both storeys. The upper storey contains another large hall with an open fireplace, four bedrooms and a bathroom. F 163, 291–292. 3) *Two engineer's villas,* some 200 m³ smaller than no. 2, but with a similar room disposition. The three houses, overrun by climbing vines, spacious and reminiscent of English country houses, form a stately yet idyllic group on the forested ridge. 4) *Five houses for foremen,* each containing two mirror-image apartments with their own entrance, vestibule, living room, dining room and kitchen below and a hall with a sleeping alcove, bedroom and 'future bathroom' in the upper storey, reduced by the steep pitch of the hip roof. These houses, which were built, resemble the above described engineers' residences in style. 5) *The Jukkala housing area* for one-family homes was planned by Aalto in 1937, and a few of his type houses for Savonmäki in Varkaus (see W 190, no. 3) were built there, but an overwhelming majority of the houses were built to the residents' own plans. 6) *Four two-storey workers' housing units of wood,* designed in 1937 and built in slightly modified form, each intended for four families, with separate entrance porches to each flat. Half of the flats have two rooms and kitchen, the other half one room and kitchen, all of them have their own toilet and running water in the kitchen, but no bath or shower. The buildings have a common heating plant. P 151, 181. F 215, 293.

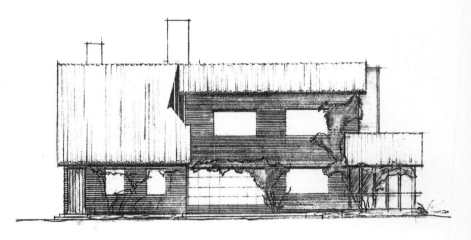

291. Elevation of chief engineer's house, Inkeroinen.

293. Photo of workers' housing described under item 6, W 203.

292. Chief engineer's house, discarded alternative with large all-purpose room on ground floor.

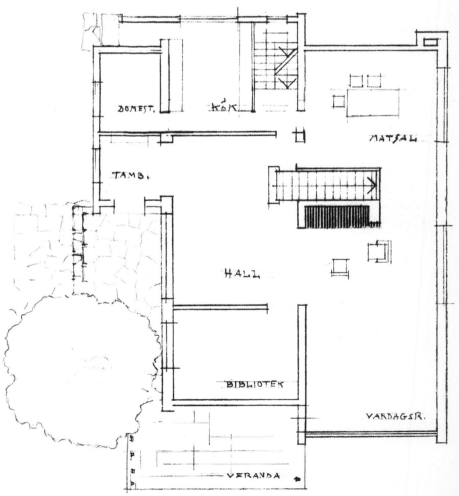

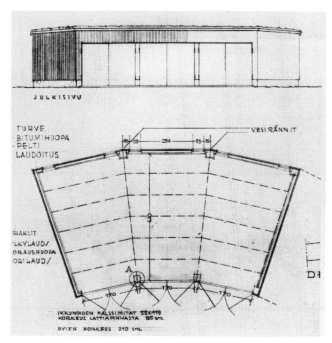

JULKISIVU

TURVE
BITUMIHUOPA
PELTI
LAUDOITUS

VESIRÄNNIT

RAKLIT
LKYLAUD/
ORAUSHUOPA
OBILAUD/

IKKUNOIDEN RALSSIMITAT 55×119
KORKEUS LATTIAPINNASTA 85 cm.
OVIEN KORKEUS 210 smL

*294. Fan-shaped garage,
Inkeroinen.*

*295. Elevation of WAC café,
Inkeroinen.*

*296. Overall plan for Inkeroinen
elementary school.*

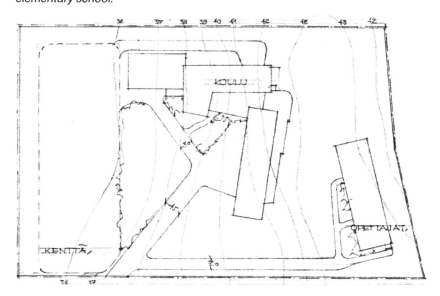

204. Renovation of Tampella's office building at Inkeroinen. In autumn 1938, Aalto converted this old, long wooden house with an attic room in the centre pediment into a modern, efficient office building by adding a porch in bold Le Corbusier style to the Classical facade and by dividing up the interiors so as to place the plant manager's and engineers' offices next to the main entrance, while the pay office, accounting office and cashier's office have a separate side entrance of their own. The plan was carried out.

205. Service buildings for Tampella at Inkeroinen. 1) *Separate garage building.* Towards the end of 1937, Aalto designed several variants of a fan-shaped garage for either three or four cars, with a flat sod roof and a small workshop. Built. F 294. 2) For Pasila Manor, which belonged to the factory, Aalto designed a soberly functional *storehouse* in June 1938, containing a seed bin 10 metres high and a shed for agricultural machines. Built in the 1950s and later demolished.

206. WAC café, Inkeroinen. This tiny stained wood cottage on the bank of the River Kymi was designed by Aalto in March 1939 and built before the Winter War broke out in November. Under the unusual 'beard' consisting of vertical boards hanging over the edge of the asymmetrical hip roof, the café contained an open verandah, a small serving room inside and a small kitchen. The house was demolished in 1980; it had been used as housing since the war. F 164, 295.

207. Inkeroinen elementary school. In autumn 1938, Aalto designed this school for about 200 pupils and an adjoining three-storey building for the teachers. The materials were white rendered brick and concrete beams, the latter being visible e.g. in the gymnasium and entrance hall. The school building, divided up into three blocks, stands on sloping ground, with a three-storey building highest up, then a two-storey unit and a single-storey block lowest down, dramatically accentuating the incline. The entrance hall, in two storeys with a staircase and a free-form gallery, shows that this building is contemporaneous with the New York pavilion and the Villa Mairea, while the overall effect of the strip windows, pilotis and spiral stairs harks back to Aalto's earlier Rationalist period. P 151. F 296.

208. Master plan for Inkeroinen. The minor district plans started by Aalto in 1937 were incorporated in 1939 in a master plan which he further developed during the 1940s in connection with his many assignments for Tampella in Inkeroinen.

271

209. Competition entry for Tallinn Art Museum. In January 1937, Aalto, Ragnar Östberg and several Estonian architects were invited to take part in the competition for a new art museum for the Estonian capital. Aalto achieved a most convincing result by combining ideas familiar from his earlier projects. The principal motif was an entrance hall reproducing the spatial scheme of the 'Tsit Tsit Pum' entry in the Paris pavilion competition (W 184), i.e. an unlimited space with a rising floor level, 'stage screen' wall surfaces, partial depth perspective and an opening outwards into free space. The staggered exhibition halls repeats the composite arrangement of the Zagreb hospital plan (W 153), and the lighting is provided by the now well-known round skylights of the Viipuri Library (W 123). The jury quite unjustifiably considered the skylights unsuitable for a snowy climate, the heating costs too high because there were some glass walls and the exterior 'unusual', i.e. disruptive to the Tallinn townscape. The assignment was awarded to two Estonian architects. P 128, 168. F 132, 297–298.

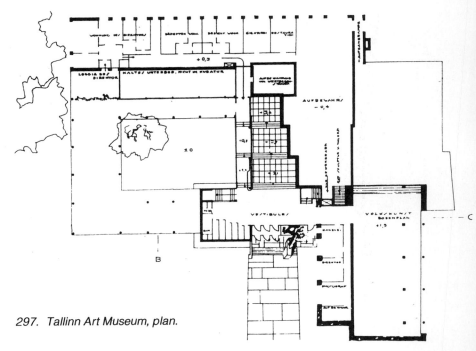

297. *Tallinn Art Museum, plan.*

298. *Tallinn Art Museum, perspective of entrance hall.*

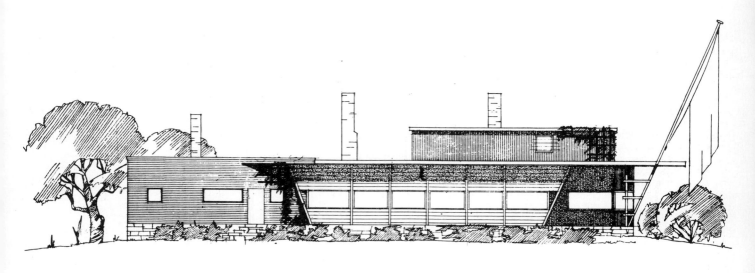

299. Richmond Temple's island house, northwest elevation.

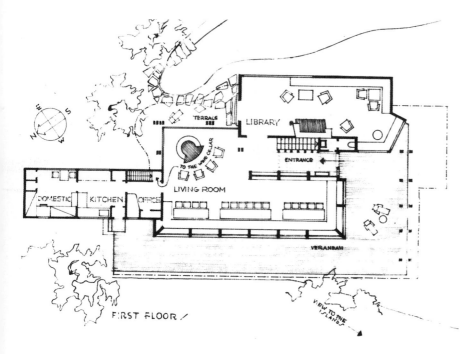

300. Richmond Temple's island house, plan of main floor.

210. Weekend house for Mr. Richmond Temple. This British hotel owner had fallen in love with the Turku archipelago, where he wished to rent the small island of Westerstyrskär and build a leisure house there. In 1937 Aalto designed an unusual wooden building adapted to Temple's personal tastes. The house was to stand on the smooth granite surface which constitutes most of the island, with a view out to the open sea on one side and to the islands on the other. A natural fissure in the rock below the house contains a spacious wine cellar with a staircase up to the pantry. The main floor consists of an intimate library and a large living room with walls inclined outward as in a ship, making space for 12 'berths' above the windows for overnight guests. The long benches under the windows along three long and narrow tables provide seating for 35 dinner guests and a perfect sea view through the strip windows. A round open fireplace is placed in front of the windows on the north side, with armchairs in a semicircle for admiring the sunset while enjoying an after-dinner drink. The kitchen and servant's room are also on the main floor, while the master of the house and the more fastidious guests have two bedrooms and a bathroom at their disposal on the smaller upper storey. The flat roof extends over a large verandah. Aalto assessed the total building costs as 343,000 marks, of which the architect's fee amounted to 32,000 (approximately £ 4,000 in present-day currency). All he ever got for the plans was an advance of ten pounds, as the growing threat of war made the client give up his plans. F 299–300.

211. Furnishing of the Savoy restaurant in Helsinki. The building at Etelä-Esplanadi 14 was designed by Bertel Jung as the head office of the Ahlström company. The two top storeys consist of a banqueting suite and a luxury restaurant with interiors designed by Aalto in 1937, which still preserve their original character. White rendered brick walls, a generous use of Oregon pine, mahogany and birch for various purposes – e.g. as partition screens and for the grilles of the ceiling lights – fitted carpeting, genuine Aalto furniture, Aalto's 'kultakello' (gold watch) lamps made of brass, diagonal beams forming a 'giraffe's crib' along the top of the wall – all these contribute to the intimate and soberly elegant effect. 100 guests can be seated at the tables, and another 150 can be served out on the roof terrace in the summer. The terrace was originally divided into a Japanese section (with Japanese plants), a Southern European section (with rhododendrons) and a Scandinavian rose garden. F 301.

301. The newly-opened Savoy restaurant in 1938.

212. Bathing beach for Mariehamn. In autumn 1937 Aalto designed a bathing establishment on a small island outside Mariehamn, the capital of the Åland Islands. It consisted of a relatively simple beach café with a bar and about fifty tables, a building with changing rooms and cabins for ladies, the same for men, a cashier's stand and privies. The cost was reckoned at 200,000 marks. The proposal found no response among the municipal council, which contented itself with a simple changing pavilion which was designed by a local master builder and cost 28,000 marks. F 302.

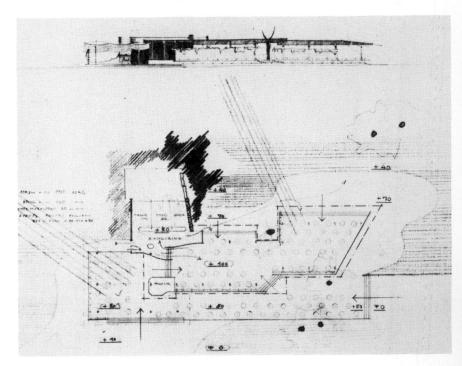

302. Bar for the public beach of Mariehamn.

274

303. Aalto's proposal for the renovation of the Helsinki University Library. Plan of alternative A with Engel's library in the foreground and a cross section with the reading room to the right (W 213). The perspective sketch shows the new reading room. Below, elevation of alternative B, showing the garden patch between the old and new building.

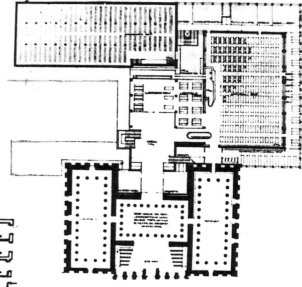

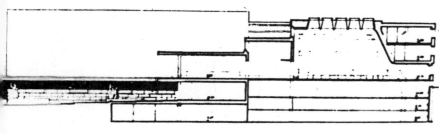

213 & 214. Competition entries for an extension to the Helsinki University Library. The assignment consisted of replacing the cast iron 'book tower', designed by Gustaf Nyström in 1903 and standing behind C.L. Engel's famous library, with a new wing housing a large reading room and book stores. The first competition took place in October 1937, and resulted in first prize for Aalto's former assistant Aarne Ervi, while Aalto himself won second prize with the entry 'ERI'. The organizers announced a new competition lasting until May 1, 1938 for the authors of the six best entries. Ervi won again, while Aalto's two alternative plans were considered less practical from the point of view of internal traffic. Alternative A (W 213), though a development of the 'ERI' entry, shows a new, highly dramatic reading room three storeys high, with a wooden ceiling pierced by 30 round light wells in the manner of the Viipuri Library and curving down for the whole length of the interior wall. There is no auditorium of this type in alternative B (W 214), in which the book stores and reading room changed place. Aalto solved the problem of harmonizing the exterior with Engel's Classical architecture by giving the street facade of alternative B an ashlar pattern to echo the base of the old library, and in both entries by separating the buildings with a small garden patch. F 303.

215. Master plan for Kauttua. In January 1938 Aalto drew a 1:500 sketch of the entire industrial estate, in which nearly all the streets and roads meander gently, following the contours of the terrain, with a new housing area including four 'terrace houses' for company officials. These are flanked by a school at one end and a sports centre at the other. The plan, which does honour to both the architect and the client (the Ahlström company through Harry Gullichsen) was abandoned on account of the war. F 304.

> *304. Part of the master plan of Kauttua, with four terrace houses grouped around the hill in the upper right-hand corner.*

---

216. Terrace house in Kauttua. The only fragment of the new Kauttua plan (W 215) to be carried out was the first of the terrace houses. Aalto started working on it in November 1937, and the final drawings were completed in May 1938. This was a logical development of the Sunila housing, cf. W 194 nos. 4 and 10. Aalto made use of the sloping ground to give each of four stepped single-storey blocks their own ground-level entrance. The three upper blocks have half of the lower block's roof for a terrace; in this way no-one has a view of his neighbour's terrace. The three lower dwellings have a cellar cut into the slope and contain three bedrooms, a kitchen, a servant's room and a large living room looking out onto the terrace. The top block comprises three small flats, two of which face out over the windowed back of the building. The terrace rails and pergolas for climbing plants consist of unstripped saplings, as in the Villa Mairea. P 151, 181, 215. F 162.

---

217. Villa Mairea, first version. In February-March 1938, Aalto drew a plan proposal on a 1:100 scale for Maire and Harry Gullichsen's private residence in Noormarkku, the site of the Ahlström family estate near Pori. The plan comprises an L-shaped building volume with three storeys on the entrance side and two facing the walled garden, which contains a sauna and a swimming pool in free form. An intricate system of mezzanines and stairs leads to a raised inner hall partly encompassing a free-form studio placed on a higher level. The external wall of the basement level is also in free form and drawn in under the strongly emphasized balcony front of the main storey. P 154, 165. F 167–169, 181, 305–306.

> *305. Plan of the main floor, first version of the Villa Mairea. See the sketches (F 169 and 181) of the raised hall with free-form wall section.*

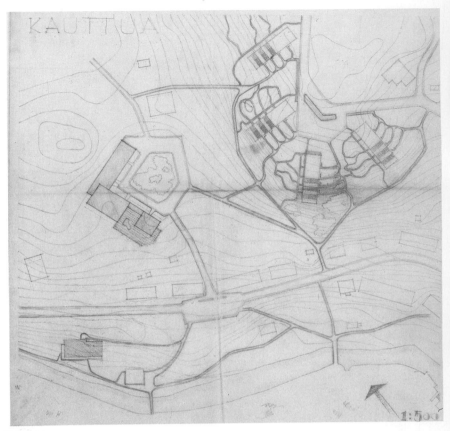

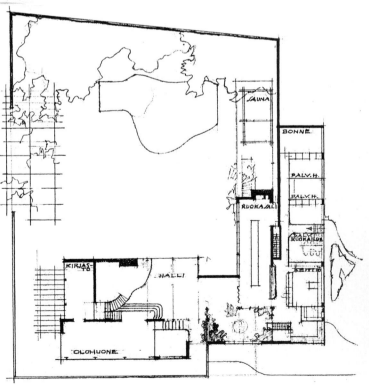

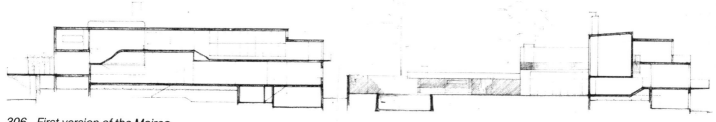

306. First version of the Mairea,
sections showing the complex
plan with several levels.

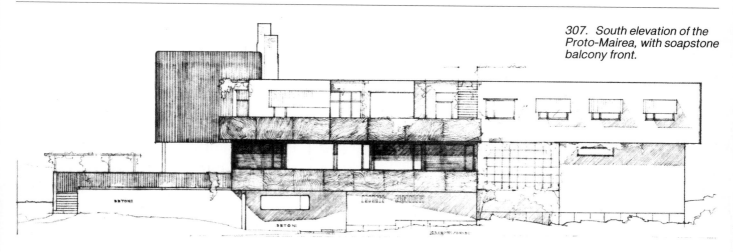

307. South elevation of the
Proto-Mairea, with soapstone
balcony front.

218. 'Proto–Mairea'. On April 14, 1938 Aalto
signed a modified proposal omitting the raised
hall, and with the studio rising from the flat third

floor. The basement and the main storey still
show variation on the floor level, with various
landings and a whole series of various drawing
rooms. A separate art gallery frames the open
coutyard beyond the swimming pool. The entrance facade has collage-like sections of slate
facing, especially along the projecting balcony
of the bedroom storey. P 154–158. F 171–
173, 307.

219. Villa Mairea, final version from May 1938.
The basement storey has disappeared, while
the drawing rooms as well as the art gallery
have been combined into one large 'all-purpose
room'. The sauna now stands at one end of the
open courtyard beyond the kidney-shaped
swimming pool. The last of the 422 final working drawings for the building are dated January
30, 1939. The contract sum for the house, ex-
cluding furniture, rose to 2,162,000 marks. The
Aalto office received a fee of 200,000 marks
(approximately the equivalent of 30,000 dollars) and travel expenses. P 158–161, 169,
174, 181. F 70, 174–175, 177, 308.

308. The 'all-purpose room' of
the Mairea, with an open
fireplace, Moroccan carpets and
a painting by Juan Gris. Photo
Kidder Smith.

220. Two competition entries for the New York exhibition pavilion. Alvar Aalto submitted two entries ('Maa Kansa Työ Tulos' and 'Kas kuusen latvassa korkealla'), and Aino Aalto a third ('USA 39') for the competition for the Finnish pavilion at the New York World's Fair in 1939. The last date of entry was May 9, 1938, and the result was that Alvar won first and second prize, while Aino took third place. The two first entries have already been discussed on pages 161–165. Aino's entry (F 182) had a straight balcony running the length of one side, an area planted with trees and creepers in the middle and some free-form galleries with a 'Venetian' staircase on the other side, leaving the entire ceiling area of the box-shaped standard exhibition hall open. Aalto's winning entry provided two alternatives for the slanting, undulating surface of the dominating 'Northern Lights' wall, which was later reworked and finally built in a third way. The final drawings, completed just before and after Aalto's first trip to America, are dated between August 1938 and April 1939. P 161–165, 172–174, 198, 219. F 178–180, 182, 188–189, 191, 309.

309. Section of the New York pavilion, with back wall covered by logs. Right, screen for projecting two images simultaneously; left, section of three free-form batten screens.

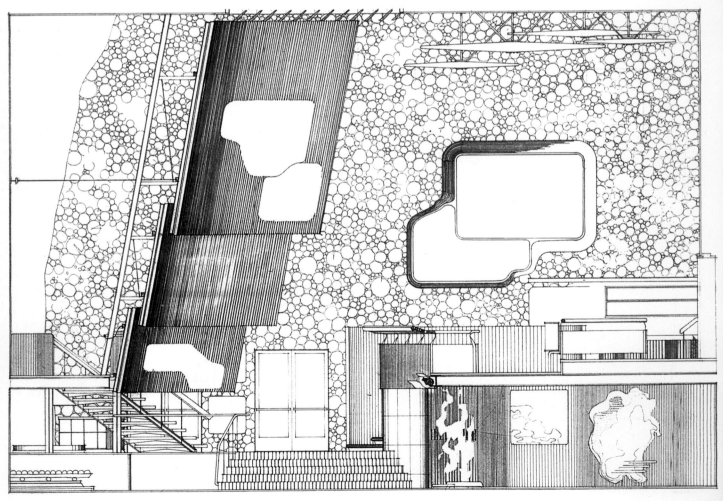

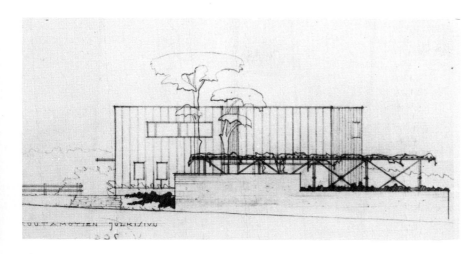

310. Photographer Mäkinen's house. Elevation and ground floor plan of the smaller version.

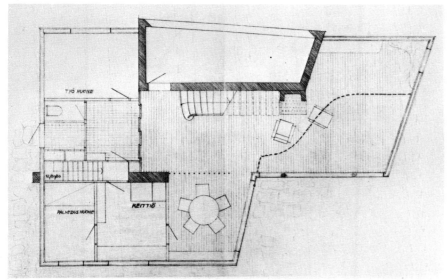

221. Drawings for photographer Eino Mäkinen's residence. In spring 1939 Aalto designed a wooden house for his photographer friend at Kuutamotie 27 in Käpylä, a Helsinki suburb. The first, more elaborate proposal contains a large double-storey living room, with a curving, free-form gallery from which slides can be projected onto the end wall, while the upper storey otherwise comprises three bedrooms, a bathroom, a photographer's studio and a dark room. The cost estimate, 247,000 marks, frightened the client, so Aalto reduced the size of the house without altering its basic character. This plan, however, was also abandoned owing to confusion about the building plot. F 310.

222. Engineer H. Rydgren's summer cottage was designed in April 1938 and built the same year in Espoo's Suvisaaristo ('Summer Islands'). It originally consisted of a concrete basement block containing a sauna and a guestroom, and a main storey comprising a living room, a small kitchen and a servant's room, a bedroom, three small sleeping alcoves and a large verandah. After the war, the cottage was partially rebuilt for year-round use. F 311.

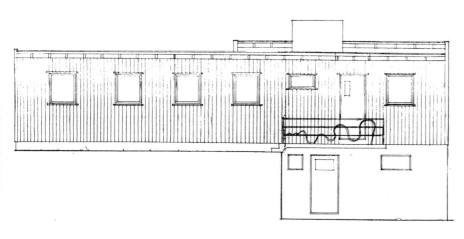

311. Engineer Rydgren's house, elevation.

279

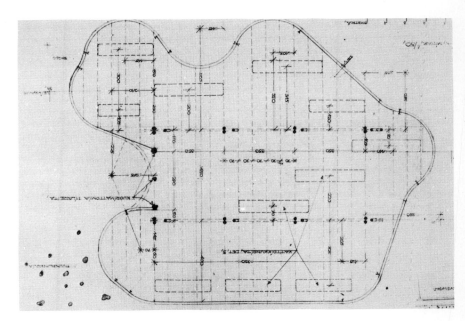

312. Forest pavilion in Lapua, plan and elevation.

223. 'Forest pavilion' for the agricultural exhibition at Lapua. The event took place in late summer 1938, and Aalto designed his highly original pavilion in June. Its external dimensions were 18 x 14.5 metres, with the height falling from 4.75 to 2.75 metres. Softly curving, with no corners, its form appeared to be free, but the drawings reveal that the walls consisted of straight surfaces alternating with circle segments having a standard radius of 200 cm (the famous 'free-form' ceiling of the Viipuri Library auditorium was also based on perfectly regular repetition). The vertical panelling of overlapping poles is a variant of the Paris pavilion and the Villa Mairea. The flat roof leaning backwards is supported by eight clusters of pillars, each consisting of three unstripped pine saplings. The light enters through eleven 250 x 50 cm skylights. Various wood-processing companies had their stands and information desks in the pavilion. The building was designed quite independently according to Aalto's instructions by Jarl Jaatinen, the most talented assistant at the office at the time, who was killed in the war shortly afterwards. F 312.

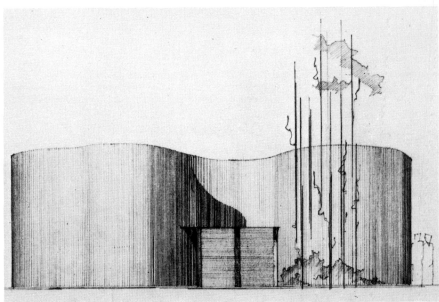

224. Master plan for Munkkiniemi. In the summer of 1938, Aalto continued his town planning work for the Stenius company, which owned large areas of the suburbs of Munkkiniemi, Haaga and the island of Kuusisaari near Helsinki. This involved "building for dense settlement" in the area above the Kalastajatorppa (Fisherman's Cottage) restaurant, for which he had drawn up a plan in 1935, and which he now completed with a series of low-rise buildings: on ordinary streetside plots he designed free-standing houses of one, two or three storeys, elsewhere he placed point blocks and chain houses in free formation. The plans were all shelved shortly after when the company sold its land holdings to the City of Helsinki.

313. Erik Blomberg's film
studio, ground plan. The arrows
indicate the developing process.

225. Film studio for Erik Blomberg in West-end near Helsinki. In summer 1938, the well-known film director and photographer commissioned drawings from Aalto for a studio complete with a workshop for constructing settings, a large property store, actors' changing rooms, a director's room, a developing laboratory, an editing room, a projector room and a room for viewing rushes, an office, a staff café and a two-room flat with bathroom. Located on a seashore site, the complex consists of low building volumes partly clad with vertical weatherboarding and grouped around the studio block. The studio is designed as a separate windowless three-storey building block, faced with white plaster, and furnished with an interesting roof construction. The whole complex links up with many of Aalto's contemporary projects, including the Paris pavilion, the Villa Mairea and the Lapua pavilion with its serpentine external wall. Financing difficulties and the intervention of war prevented implementation. F 313–314.

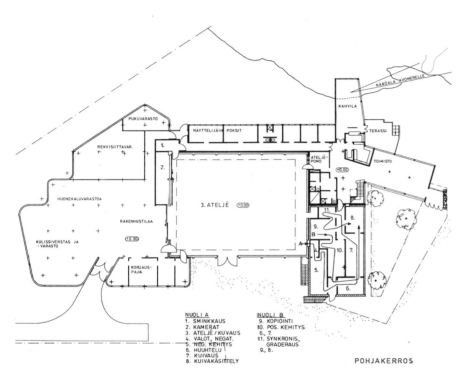

NUOLI A
1. SMINKKAUS
2. KAMERAT
3. ATELJÉ / KUVAUS
4. VALOT, NEGAT.
5. NEG. KEHITYS
6. HUUHTELU
7. KUIVAUS
8. KUIVAKÄSITTELY

NUOLI B
9. KOPIOINTI
10. POS. KEHITYS
6., 7.
11. SYNKRONIS.,
    GRADERAUS
9., 8.

POHJAKERROS

314. Erik Blomberg's film
studio, south elevation. In the
middle, the acoustically isolated
studio, on the right, a staff café
supported by piles driven into
the ground at the edge of the
beach.

ETELÄJULKISIVU, 1/100,

226. Jalasjärvi Defence Corps Building. The drawings for this building complex, in 1:200 scale, are dated December 13, 1938. It is a stately building adorned with high flagstaffs, and in a style of Cubist Rationalism softened by the weatherboarding covering part of the external walls. The basement comprises a boiler room, storeroom, sauna and large 'gas shelter'. The ground floor contains the office, two lecture rooms, a caretaker's flat and a dominating assembly hall and theatre two storeys high, with a stage which can be opened out towards an outdoor auditorium behind the building. The top floor contains living quarters for 194 men and the district commander's residence with a separate entrance. On the roof above the assembly hall are spectators' stands overlooking a sports field in front of the building. The project was interrupted by the war and abandoned when the Defence Corps were dissolved in 1945. F 315.

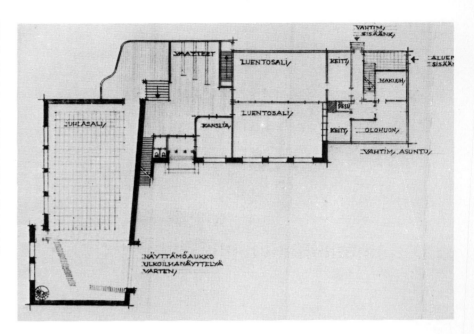

315. Jalasjärvi Defence Corps Building, plan and elevation.

227. Material for the Housing Exhibition in Helsinki in 1939. Aalto's archives contain the following material assembled by the office for the exhibition described on pages 181–182: 1) A screen in free form reminiscent of the Savoy vase, with pictures of the various home radiators made by Ahlström. 2) A screen with pictures from the Kauttua terrace house. 3) A screen with pictures of the Mairea. 4) A screen showing regional plans for EKA. 5) A screen showing EKA type houses. 6) EKA minimum apartment (= in the ROT house, W 194, no. 10). 7) A large kitchen and a small one with EKA fittings. 8) Drawings and pictures of "prefabricated single-family houses with 60 m² living area" made by Ahlström, a test sample of which was built in the Pirkko residential area in the Helsinki district of Oulunkylä, block 228, plot C. 9) Pencil sketches of Aalto's ROT type house, W 194 no. 9. P 181–182.